Musical Box

By the same author

COLLECTING MUSICAL BOXES
PLAYER PIANO
CLOCKWORK MUSIC
MECHANICAL MUSIC
PERPETUAL MOTION
BARREL ORGAN
RESTORING MUSICAL BOXES

Musical Box

A HISTORY AND COLLECTOR'S GUIDE

ARTHUR W. J. G. ORD-HUME

Illustrated by the author

London
GEORGE ALLEN & UNWIN
Boston   Sydney

GEORGE ALLEN & UNWIN LTD
40 Museum Street, London WC1A 1LU

© Arthur W. J. G. Ord-Hume, 1980

British Library Cataloguing in Publication Data

Ord-Hume, Arthur Wolfgang Julius Gerald
   Musical box.
   1. Music box – Collectors and collecting
   I. Title
   789.8   ML1055   79-40178

   ISBN 0-04-789007-X

Typeset in 11 on 12 point Plantin by Western Printing Services Ltd, Bristol
Printed and bound in Great Britain by
Fakenham Press Limited, Fakenham, Norfolk

Author's Note

The entire contents of this book serves as a memorial to those craftsmen of the past who devoted their lives to the creation of a means of making music mechanically. Even so, the sum total of the worth of such art would have been naught were it not for the music which provided their motivation. And so this book is first and foremost offered as an appreciation of music.
Its mechanisation is thus secondary and but coincidental.
Never overlook the music *part of mechanical music.*
To do this is to be insensitive to a whole realm of history.

Acknowledgements

I gratefully acknowledge the help and assistance which I have received from very many people in the compilation of this book. Almost without exception, these have been my fellow members in the Musical Box Society of Great Britain and the Musical Box Society International, the two principal world-wide organisations which are, through the activities of their members, dedicated to the investigation, research and recording of instruments of mechanical music and their music itself. Essentially organisations for the collector, restorer and historian, nobody seriously interested in mechanical music should fail to be a member of one or both societies. Other and smaller societies include the French-speaking Association des Amis des Instruments et de la Musique Mécanique, and the German-speaking Gesellschaft der Freunde Mechanischer Musikinstrumente EV, and the Musikhistorische Gesellschaft.

To my fellow members of these organisations, I acknowledge my thanks and appreciation for their allowing me to broaden my knowledge through their unselfishness, friendship and help. Particular thanks are due to the founder, first secretary and former president of the MBSOGB, Dr Cyril de Vere Green, FDS, RCS(Eng), DDS(Tor), for his sustained help and encouragement over the many years of our close friendship.

Special thanks go to Dr Jan-Jaap Haspels, conservator/director of Holland's Nationaal Museum van Speelklok tot Pierement in Utrecht, and to the museum's senior technician and restorer, Dick van Minnen. This fine museum, which now contains the de Vere Green collection, is the only State-sponsored museum of mechanical music in the world and it is to the credit of the Dutch that so fine an exhibit has been created. Dr Haspels, who has assiduously applied himself to the task of building up the musical box section from almost nothing to its present extensive size, has allowed me full and free access to the instruments in the collection for examination and documentation. By his enthusiasm, help and hospitality, this book is the richer.

Those who have contributed much in the field of historical research include Pierre Germain and his daughter Suzanne Maurer in Geneva, Hendrik Strengers in Holland, and Q. David Bowers, Howard and Helen Fitch, and Hughes M. Ryder in the United States of America. Specific thanks to others who have provided help or have been quoted is given in appropriate places. For his help with establishing key sizes, my thanks to Charles Allix, author of *Carriage Clocks*.

For their generous agreement to allow me to use photographs which remain their copyright, I thank Messrs Sotheby's Belgravia and Christie's South Kensington and in

9

particular Mr Jon Baddeley and Ms Hilary Kay of the former, and Mr Christopher Proudfoot of the latter, who have so often allowed me to examine unusual and rare items which pass through their famous auction rooms.

Mr Keith Harding deserves a special word of thanks for the careful manner in which he has photographed many of the musical boxes which pass through his workshop. Mr Jack MacLean has once again taken a number of pictures for this book, a task shared with Dick van Minnen and myself. Picture credits are listed at the end of the index.

Foreword

There is an irony about life and the arts today. Somewhere along the line, a sense of purpose seems to have been lost and the end seems to claim justification from the means. In ages past when Man had no social services or benefits, and before the spatial contractions which modern improvements in travel and communications have brought about today, art, including music, flourished. Bad plumbing, the risk of death from countless minor causes, primitive living and an ignorance of hygiene bridged the ever-present dichotomy of the classes. The sharply defined masses, amongst the poorer regions of which a majority of the finest artists flourished, fought a continual struggle for succour – indeed, for life itself. It was this environment which vivified the finest in Man's latent creativity.

For proof of the validity of this observation, one has only to note how many of these creators still have their works revered today.

The twentieth century, with its increasing revelations of Man's greed, avarice and powers of lethal intervention, has on the one hand brought about the rise of living standards, comforts, convenience and health for the fortunate ones, while on the other it has bred an unrest and disquiet on a greater scale than ever before. Our prowess in good is more than matched with our capabilities in evil, the awful truth being that often it seems that it is the evil which triumphs in our midst. The finer points of Man have been lost: the so-called primitive man is known to have possessed powers and abilities which we have carefully bred out of ourselves through the years. Put modern man in a raw environment and he probably would not have the first notion how to survive!

In the way that disease affects growth in nature and a blight can cause a tender plant to convert into a distorted, grotesque mass, so has this age in which we live affected art and given birth to deformed, jarring abstracts in all art forms. True, good survives but, unlike a Hollywood film, good does not always triumph over evil and the bacillus has thrown up art mutations everywhere, and in some cases killed off art and artistry in the interests of functionalism. How much good architecture has been swept away for concrete and glass boxes! And the tuneless cacophony of modern music along with so-called mixed-media contemporary art make one wonder just who is mad – us or them.

Fortunately for us, the much maligned Victorian era and its contemporary equivalents throughout Europe and America brought about a strange mixture of equally false values, the consummation of the Industrial Revolution, and the inventiveness and artistry to capitalise on earlier teachings. Mechanical music, nowhere near a new thing, was ever fascinating and

11

the spectacle of creativity which the era fostered, culminating early on with the Great Exhibition of 1851 and continuing to a lesser extent with the subsequent industrial and artistic exhibitions right up to the late 1920s, induced the right environment for the perfection of mechanical music for the masses.

This musical medium was provided by two principal instruments – the clockwork musical box and the ordinary piano. The organ was in a class of its own and few people had a pipe organ.* Many, though, had pianos and musical boxes.

Invention and technique unfolded gradually, starting with the orchestrion and its ability to offer flamboyance in appearance and musical virtuosity, and continuing well into the present century with the sophisticated reproducing piano.

But if the old wooden upright piano was the paradigm of the Victorian drawing-room, then the musical box was both its precursor and companion as a means of producing music, this time without human intervention or skill.

In the 1920s, there were still those who prophesied the return of the cylinder phonograph record, seeing the Berliner-style flat disc as still a fad, albeit a slow-passing one. Although events proved these pontificators to have been barking down the wrong horn, so to speak, the gramophone had much to offer, particularly in more recent years with the advent of long-playing recordings and the various trappings of the modern hi-fi enthusiast.

Having ascended to the realms of perfection, the automatic musical instruments ceased to be needed as musical interpreters. Player organs reverted to being just organs, player pianos became just pianos. Only the musical box has really survived to command our interest today for, unlike all the many other instruments of mechanical music, it was, from first to last, an instrument with no manually played counterpart. It had a sound all of its own. If the gramophone was a cuckoo in the nest, having no voice of its own but being able to impersonate everything, the musical box had a voice so clearly identifiable, so unique, that it was instantly recognisable anywhere and could hardly hope to be replaced.

There are those who believe that to cherish objects from the past is to reveal some character weakness – even an inability to face up to the present day. This may even be right, I am not equipped to comment. What I would say, however, is that more and more people seem to be turning to the artefacts of our forefathers, who lived in times which were cruder but demonstrably more gentle than those in which we live today.

The musical box, particularly the early ones, must have been a labour of love indeed for its maker. It was the product of a cottage industry whose workers were poorly paid, lived humbly and who were destined to suffer the early consequences of eye-strain as they worked in oil-lit surroundings. They were built by dedicated men who literally gave their eyes and ultimately their lives that we might have musical boxes today.

The collector collects for various reasons. Sometimes it is plain, undisguised avarice. Other times it is stony-hearted investment, or just for the love of the items he collects. It doesn't matter why you collect or how you collect. What does matter is that you appreciate just how important the musical box was in its time and how that value has not changed all that much today. You owe it to future generations of collectors to look after and preserve your musical boxes. If you break you arm it will heal. Damage a musical box and it is for all time.

ARTHUR W. J. G. ORD-HUME

* The growth and popularity of the domestic reed organ is another story.

Contents

List of Plates

The Plates are arranged in four sections. Plates 1 to 40 are between pages 77 and 88; Plates 41 to 83 between pages 143 and 154; Plates 84 to 118 between pages 209 and 220; Plates 119 to 161 between pages 277 and 288. To aid the student of styles, the Plates are further divided according to the following synopsis:

The birth of the comb-playing mechanism = Plates 1 to 26
The evolution of the cylinder musical box = Plates 27 to 57
The development of the cylinder mechanism = Plates 58 to 78
The overture and grand format styles = Plates 79 to 86
Evolution of the changeable-cylinder box = Plates 87 to 106
Evolution of the orchestral accompaniment = Plates 107 to 121
The long-play cylinder musical box = Plates 122 to 128
The disc-playing musical box = Plates 129 to 161

14

List of Figures

Musical Box

A History and Collector's Guide

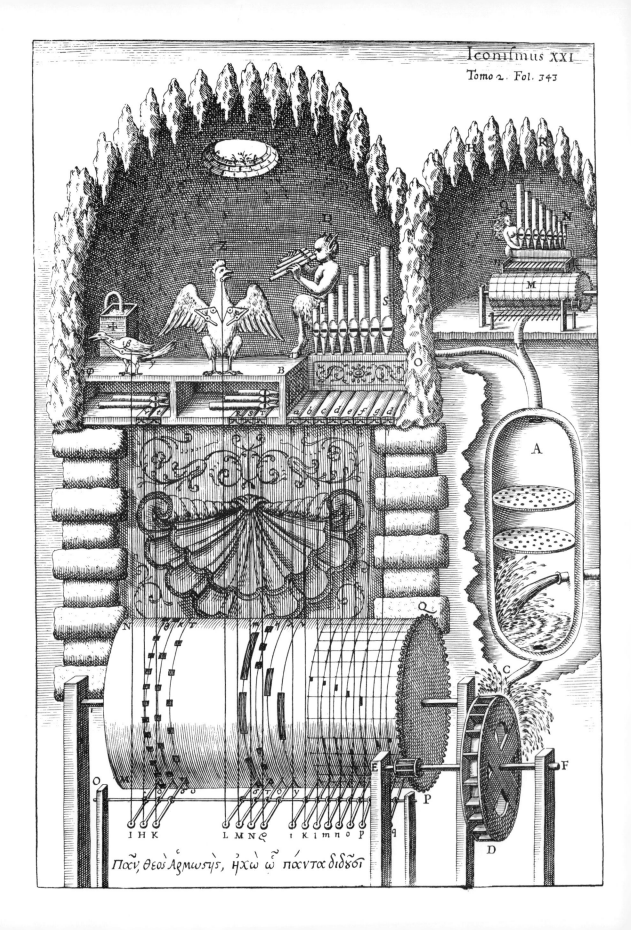

Πᾶν, θεὸς Ἁρμωσὶς, Ἠχὼ ὦ πάντα διδῦσι

Introduction

The history of the mechanical production of music is almost as old as that of music itself. The earliest attempts at fulfilling this objective appear to predate the birth of Christ for it can be established that primitive systems for playing either stringed instruments or organs go back more than 2,000 years. Significantly, the organ itself is an instrument of great antiquity and in its primeval form it was considered almost as a matter of course that there were two equally important methods of playing – either by hand or by mechanical means. As the centuries advanced, we find that by the second half of the first millennium writers describing how to make an organ included a method of automatic performance in their words. In order of importance, then, it was the organ which achieved supremacy at the earliest date and which, no doubt because of its relative simplicity of manufacture (in terms of available materials such as wood, leather, bone and animal sinew), reached a technical perfection long before any other musical instrument. The bell came next and, as the carillon, was the second instrument to be automated successfully. Again, eleventh-century manuscripts dealing with bell founding describe also how to play the bells automatically. A discussion on these primitive mechanical instruments is contained in my book *Barrel Organ* and further information is to be found in *Clockwork Music*.

The earliest mechanical stringed instruments were plucked and these formed not just the earliest stringed instruments but also the earliest use of the production of sound by the action of plucking. It was this group which unconsciously was the primogenitor of the instrument which forms the subject of this book, the musical box.

Here it must be admitted that the term 'musical box' serves as a collective term for a number of different forms of musical automaton. In the terminology of the lay person, it encompasses almost everything from organette to player piano, from mechanical organ to carillon. In the considered eyes of the more knowledgeable, it is frequently used to define the comb-playing mechanism as well as the complete unit, and may apply whether or not the musical movement has a box in the truest sense of the word.

While discussing terminology, it is also necessary to explain what the words 'musical box' really mean. The verbal form of the noun *music* is *musical* and this informs us that the second noun *box* is capable of producing musical sound. *The Shorter Oxford English Dictionary* tells us that the subject of this book should be the *musical box* and not the *music box*, this latter serving merely as a mute receptacle for music, presumably sheet music. It might be worth mentioning in passing that it was this subtlety of etymology which caused the Journal of the Musical Box Society of Great Britain to be called *The Music Box*, for it is a form of receptacle for musical box information, rather than a *musical box*, which it is patently incapable of being.

It is now more than ten years since my first book on mechanical musical instruments, *Collecting Musical Boxes and How to Repair Them*, was written. At that time, serious musical box collectors could be counted in minority terms, musical boxes were still very cheap and easy to buy, and there was no up-to-date book in print on the subject. The need which then presented itself was for a general-interest book which would provide sufficient information for the average collector to enable him to buy knowledgeably and to look after his musical boxes and carry out simple repairs. This book was based on the fruits of my years of collecting experience suitably tempered to attempt to reach the widest cross-section of readership.

What followed has been nothing short of remarkable. Musical boxes suddenly became big-time business; prices soared; the number of serious collectors doubled, multiplied, then doubled again and still grows at a rapid rate. My book, intended as little more than an introduction to the subject aimed at a slightly higher level than anything hitherto published, became a sort of vade-mecum, my every word was elevated to a didacticism, and I found myself being carried along on a rip-tide of my own literary consequence. One effect of the widening interest in the subject was that the burgeoning Musical Box Society of Great Britain and its American sister, the Musical Box Society International, have undergone a great expansion in terms of membership, while the whole quality of the interest has risen appreciably as people delve deeper into history and restoration.

As editor of the journal of the MBSOGB, an office which I have held, with the exception of a two-year break, since its inception, I was delighted to see how many other members were galvanised into conducting their own research into history and musical-box development. I also continued my own researches for, as a self-confessed perpetual student, I have never laid claim to knowing all or anything approaching all on my subject, which is mechanical music and its instruments.

Perhaps not surprisingly, much new information has been uncovered in the intervening years, some of it regarding the clarification of detail, but also some which has eroded the very roots of the accepted history of the musical box. A great deal of this revision work comes from the location and identification of specimens of musical boxes throughout the world (in itself a previously impossible task had not the bond of society membership united many of those with like interests), and from the development of many inquiring minds amongst the ever increasing number of dedicated enthusiasts.

What has materialised is a whole vast new technology on the one hand and a storehouse of newly discovered historical information on the other. The new technology has been a product of the mushrooming interest in mechanical musical instruments today. With good-quality cylinder musical boxes back in production in Switzerland and disc-playing musical boxes being produced in Germany as well as newly produced musical-box discs being made both here in the UK and in America, it may be said that the wheel has come the full circle. As for history, collectors throughout the world have played – and still are playing – their part in unearthing history both of musical boxes themselves and of their makers. In my first book, I wrote that individually we all know something; together we may know everything. That this is a truism is now clearly proved.

What of the musical box itself? From its simple beginnings as a replacement for the tuned steel bell in musical clocks, it reached its zenith at two different definable periods in time. The cylinder musical box achieved its peak in the years from the Great Exhibition of 1851 through to the 1880s. The significance of Great Britain's Crystal Palace display of 1851 on the Swiss musical-box industry will be explained in Chapter 2. The second peak concerned the disc-playing musical box and this centred on the years from 1895 to around 1905.

As for the birth of the comb-playing musical box, veneration can often bestow a sometimes undeserved degree of respectability upon stories that have come down to us from earlier times. Indeed, some of these stories even acquire the status of legends if they are repeated with sufficient regularity. And, like the 'laws' which tend to limit the vision of the traditional scientist, these legends can restrict the retrospection of the historian. The musical box has its share of such tales and, while until recently it was accepted that the instrument was the invention of a Swiss watchmaker called Antoine Favre in 1796, there is now mounting evidence that Favre was not the inventor of the tuned steel tooth in musical-box work, but that the application had been in use for perhaps half a century.

Certainly, however, Favre's perfection of the miniature musical movement for use in watches and jewellery was a catalyst in the development of the musical box. The musical snuff-box with its wafer-thin musical movement, the musical seal with compact little musicwork within, all combined to establish the comb-playing musical box on the path to becoming ultimately a whole vast industry. By around 1820, when serious production of musical boxes began, the instrument came into its own. Hitherto it had been manufactured as part of something else in the manner of a novelty. Now, however, the musical mechanism was being placed in a plain wooden box solely and simply as an interpreter of music. The skills of setting music as a forest of minute steel pins in the surface of the brass cylinder achieved such perfection that pieces of music could be set practically note-perfect. Largely chromatically tuned combs, aided by extended-play methods later perfected, made the unabbreviated performance of long pieces of music a reality.

Gradually, the cylinder musical box became an orchestra, the plucked tuned steel comb being supplemented by miniature beating drums, bells, a reed organ, castanets and, in some instances, a miniature pipe organ, all driven by clockwork.

The major disadvantage of the cylinder musical box was the inherent limitations on its repertoire. Initially, cylinders played only a few tunes, usually four, but by diligent crafting it became possible to pin six or even eight tunes on one cylinder. By altering the shape of the comb, so allowing the teeth to be spaced wider apart (and having fewer teeth), it was possible to play ten or twelve tunes from the one cylinder. With very large-diameter cylinders, it was possible to play two turns per revolution as a further adjunct to programme variety. The fact remained, however, that the quality cylinder musical box was a costly item and played a limited repertoire.

The first breakthrough came with the perfection of interchangeable cylinders, so that one cylinder could be removed and another, with a fresh programme of music, inserted into the mechanism in its place. This type of box was produced with six or eight spare cylinders; some even had twenty-four or, in special cases, thirty-six cylinders. Even so, these were extremely expensive instruments.

It was in an attempt to remove this objection to the cylinder musical box that the disc-playing musical box was invented. Not only were the instruments better suited to being made as articles of furniture, but the discs, each of which played one tune (with one or two exceptions detailed further on), were available very cheaply. Here at last was a musical box which could play a thousand tunes, or at least as many as the number of discs you chose to buy for it.

The disc musical box was manufactured by a great number of makers in sizes which played discs only a few inches across to giants which not only played discs 36 inches across, but could change their own tunes as well from a clutch of spares stored in the base.

These were handsome articles of furniture, intended to blend with the home of the period rather like the television receiver of today.

To some, the musical box is a quaint toy to be eyed with the same fond expression as the mangle, the candle-snuffer and the copper kettle. However, at a time when music in the home was either the outcome of hard practice and manual dexterity – or nothing, the musical box fulfilled a clearly defined requirement in home life. Its task as an interpreter of music brought music to all who could afford it. Undoubtedly the first instruments were outside the pockets of other than the wealthy. It is related* that Beethoven listened to a musical box at the time he was afflicted by increasing deafness. In 1822, with the hearing of his right ear almost completely gone, he listened with his left ear to a musical box playing the trio in *Fidelio* and Cherubini's overture to *Medea*.

If the musical box brought a moment of peace to the torture of the ailing Beethoven, it brought inspiration to Puccini in the composition of the music for his last opera, *Turandot*. Puccini had struggled for some years to find a libretto which would enable him to launch out on something fresh to break away from the era of *La Bohème*. Having at last managed to find a subject (a task which in itself took some years), and inspired librettists Adami and Simoni to work, Puccini realised that his opera, set in China, needed music that had an Oriental flavour. Since Chinese music is based on the pentatonic scale it is not unnatural that we find that Turandot's main theme in Act II falls entirely on the black notes as Calaf's subsequent aria. But still the principal theme eluded Puccini, who had once instructed his librettist to 'try unknown paths'. He spent in all four and a half years writing the music for *Turandot*. Exhausted and ailing, he allowed himself to be entertained by one Baron Fassani who had worked in China and consequently had decorated his Italian villa in totally Chinese style. As he entered the Baron's home he was greeted by the strains of the authentic Imperial hymn played by a valuable musical box. At once, it is said, Puccini knew he had found what he wanted and as a result the Princess Turandot's theme is directly copied from the sounds heard that day from the Baron's musical box. Apart from some subtle harmonisation, the music is identical. The actual musical box exists today for comparison and plays in all three Chinese tunes which Puccini employed in *Turandot*. Sadly the composer did not live to hear the first performance at La Scala, Milan, in April 1926 – he died two years earlier and left final completion of his masterpiece to another. From this story comes a gentle reminder that it always pays to know a little about the music your musical box plays, and the date when operas or musical shows were premiered. How easy it would have been for some unsuspecting person to lay claim to having a nineteenth-century musical box playing the music from *Turandot*! A case of chickens before the egg!

When newspaper proprietor A. C. Harmsworth, later Viscount Northcliffe, financed the search for the North-West passage by explorer and polar expert F. G. Jackson in 1894, the ship *Windward* was provided with a Symphonion for the entertainment of the 33-man party.

---

* Grove's *Dictionary of Music & Musicians* (London, 1921), p. 229.

He bought the 'largest one made' for £15 and prudently ordered a couple of spare main-springs in case the polar cold should break the original. However, his order for 500 tunes could not be met by Henry Klein, agent for the Leipzig distributors H. Peters & Co. In the end he had to settle for between three and four hundred. The ship, complete with musical box and food for seven years, left the Thames on 12 July, spent the winter frozen in at Franz-Josef Land, presumably seeking a relief from boredom by means of the Symphonion. Whether the Symphonion was left there, or whether it did, in fact, come back to Gravesend the following year (Jackson stayed behind) is not known.

The characteristic arrangement of popular music for the cylinder musical box, rich in arpeggio, appoggiatura and embellishment in melody and accompaniment (the florid, running bass line of some of the disc musical-box tunes epitomised this wherein accompaniment and melody stemmed from what Percy A. Scholes* called a 'luxuriant jungle-growth of ornament'), encouraged parody. Liadov (1855–1914) composed his Opus 32, 'Musical Snuff-Box', in imitation of the playing of a musical box which gradually slowed down to a stop. This piece was to become a popular piano piece in the repertoire of the British entertainers and broadcasters, the two pianists Rawitz and Landauer.

Even contemporary composers saw the musical box as a style to emulate in keyboard music and the anonymous composer of the once celebrated 'Snuff-Box Waltz', identified only by the initials M. S., earned royalties in abundance for himself (presumably) and rewards for his publishers, Monro & May, during the mid-1830s.

Musical boxes are also to be heard occasionally in films, their use being restricted usually to the setting of a period scene. Significantly, although invariably the instrument appears as a cylinder machine, it is either a modern musical movement which is heard or a disc-playing instrument, the latter no doubt chosen for its more strident tones which are thought better suited to cinematographic recording techniques.

The references to the musical box in literature are legion and, generally, are of little consequence other than to prove the popularity of the instrument as a disseminator of music.

An interesting feature of the musical box, in particular the disc-playing musical box, is that somehow the right to produce music mechanically was thought to be covered *in toto* and in perpetuity by the first man to take out a patent. This same controversy surrounded the invention of the player piano in that McTammany, who had thought of a way of playing a reed organ by means of a perforated tune sheet, reckoned that when the player piano was invented it was a direct copy of his discovery. The division between establishing principles and the problems of practical engineering was obviously understood but little. The same controversy played havoc with the early days of the disc musical box. Ellis Parr, who had thought of a manner whereby reed-playing spinning tops and the like could be played by a punched sheet, immediately threatened legal action against the inventor of the Symphonion, although the two systems were little related. And later on Ehrlich tried to prevent anyone from using starwheels in musical boxes – although they weren't even his invention in the first place!

Even earlier, the Court of Orleans effectively prevented the manufacturing of musical boxes in France – until common sense prevailed. A Parisian manufacturer of automatic pianos, Alexandre Debain, instituted legal proceedings against Auguste L'Épée claiming infringement of the music editions in the making of musical boxes in 1861. On 16 April 1863

* *Oxford Companion to Music*, article 'Ornaments'.

the Court upheld Debain's fatuous claims. Not until 1866 did the government intervene and restore the right to produce musical boxes to L'Épée. This long and costly nonsense almost put paid to L'Épée's business.

And of course the musical box lived through the period which saw the establishment of the copyright laws and the performing rights laws. The first major case, indeed the test case, concerned perforated music rolls for the Orchestrelle Company's Aeoline player reed organ, forerunner of the Aeolian Grand and Orchestrelle, and sister of the Pianola. The argument was put forward in defence of the mechanical instruments that the music took the form of an unreadable type of notation only capable of being 'read' by the instrument. The legal big-wigs debated, and finally found in favour of the plaintiff, in this case the music publishers Boosey & Co., against the defendants, George Whight & Co. This one large and lengthy case completely reshaped the whole question of the right of a musical-box or music-roll maker to produce a copy of music without paying for the privilege. The first musical-box maker to fall foul of the new law was the Polyphon Company, which had inadvisedly issued a disc of the French song 'Marche Lorraine'. In another history-making legal wrangle, the courts found for the plaintiff, although under the then ruling French law there was nothing to prevent anybody pirating a composer's music outside his country of origin. 'Marche Lorraine' was banned and all the discs and masters for their production were confiscated.

All this marked not just the reversal but the supersession of the old Berne Convention decision of 1886 when, at the insistence of Switzerland (where most of the piracy was then centred), it was expressly laid down that the mechanical reproduction of musical airs should not constitute an infringement of copyright.

I feel bound to express some measure of amazement at how few collectors of musical boxes really understand what musical boxes are all about. A man will describe in infinite detail the technicalities of the mechanism of his prize item, but when you ask what music it plays he will probably be unable to offer a satisfactory answer.

Musical boxes are mechanisms for producing music. They serve now as they served when first made, as an intermediary between composer and listener, and so, when explained in these terms, it must be apparent that without the music the box would be but a mechanical curiosity. The music is at least as important as the mechanism by which it is produced. The music will tell you the final quality of the musical box. The choice of music on the cylinder will tell you at least some of the history of the box.

It is the immature, almost banal collector who will prize a musical box purely for its mechanism. Even more decadent is the collector who likes a box for its 'pretty tunes' and can't tell Handel from Sullivan.

These collectors do, however, serve the basic requirement that they preserve and, one hopes, cherish their boxes, which will survive them and perhaps pass into more appreciative, inquisitive ownership in years to come.

To own a box and to take only a passing interest in what it plays is rather like having an expensive car and never driving it in third or top gear.

The musical programme will at least help you in some cases to date your musical box – a knowledge of popular music in the sixty or so years from 1850 could prevent your falling for suggestions as to the age of a box made by the vendor which may amount to offering you a box 130 years old which plays music from *The Gondoliers*!

For the student of music, the early musical box has much to offer. At the time when the art

28

and craft of pinning cylinders was at the peak of its perfection, eclectic tastes, fortunately, demanded that much in the way of music from the opera and the classical repertoire should be set on the musical box. In a number of instances, music which has subsequently been lost, has fallen out of favour or is for other reasons now forgotten can be brought to life once more by the movement of a lever. It is only comparatively recently that the vast storehouse of this special kind of music has become of interest to the musicologist and student. As an instance of the extreme importance of mechanical instruments, some outstanding performances of rare music have recently come to light, probably the most important being the discovery of an otherwise unknown composition by Mozart on the cylinder of a small-chamber barrel-organ today preserved in Holland's Nationaal Museum van Speelklok tot Pierement in Utrecht.

The discovery of overtures and arias from the minor works of Handel, Mozart, Donizetti, Auber and others is a thrill many collectors have experienced and the overture to Mozart's opera *Belisario*, played on an early musical box and broadcast by Bruce Angrave, was largely responsible for a recent revival in the popularity of this piece.

Besides preserving these lost and forgotten items, the early musical box, as with the barrel organ which it superseded, can teach us much about accepted styles of interpretation, embellishment and counterpoint. The sheer skill of the musical arrangers of the period often reveals that they must have ranked equally as musical-box mechanicians and musicians. Not for them the quaint simplicity of single-note melody, Alberti bass and rigid tempi.

Of course, it is not just the classics which we find preserved on musical box cylinders. One-time popular melodies and hymns also abound – songs which once meant so much, poignant melodies from a distant age. As the musical box advanced through the nineteenth century and its quality diminished, it became less able to serve as a musical educator, yet it still dutifully preserved the light music of its age.

An examination of the sort of music which can be found on the musical box shows a fair cross-section of the field from the popular, folk tune, light, classical, operatic and oratorio right through to the music-hall and its comic ballad. During the first quarter of the nineteenth century, the music was almost exclusively of the eclectic Viennese popular music, a great deal of which is now forgotten. In the second quarter one starts to find the introduction of better music including pieces from the operas. The music of Rossini appears here for the first time – a significant feature, for his compositions were to remain popular from that time right through to the end of the musical box era. Another composer who appears at this time is Flotow, once equally popular with Rossini and another whose popularity was sustained. In the third quarter, we find the greatest expansion of the repertoire with a great deal of opera and oratorio, hymns, national melodies and the better quality popular ballad. We also find names such as Meyerbeer, Auber and a host of similar composers who were then riding the crest of a wave of musical expression for the more privileged classes. It is in the fourth quarter, though, that we find the most diversification. To begin with, the quality of the preceding quarter is sustained, but then, after about 1890, quality starts to decline on an increasing scale. New composers such as Sullivan still produced good music – many of Sullivan's more serious works went cheek by jowl with Handel – but they were served less and less adequately by the musical box. As the quarter came to an end and with it the nineteenth century, musical boxes had progressed from the gentle, subtle and refined sounds of the early days through to the brash, noisy and cheap product which heralded the end of the era. An analysis of tune sheets, however, reveals one interesting fact and that is that the music of Bach was seldom to be found on a musical box – a strange and surprising omission?

Although, throughout the entire era of mechanical music, almost every musical instrument has at some time been mechanised, from piano to violin, harp to banjo, all these played with a sound which had a non-mechanical, manually-induced equal. The musical box, however, spoke with a voice of its own – a distinctive one which had no non-mechanical counterpart. In later years, several experimenters tried to alter this but without success. This uniqueness of the musical box and its sound presented the musical arrangers with some limitations on the one hand but some hefty advantages on the other, inasmuch as orchestral music could be interpreted only in one tonality, yet treated harmonically to create an orchestral illusion. This goal was achieved remarkably well by most top-quality makers.

Two events put paid to the musical box industry of the time. The first was the phonograph, and the second was the outbreak of the 1914–18 war. In spite of its success, the capabilities of the musical box stopped short of one goal – the reproduction of the human voice. In the face of the enormous competition of an instrument which could reproduce any sound including the human voice in all its inimitable nuances, the days of the musical box were numbered. A number of musical-box manufacturers read the writing on the wall and first devised dual-purpose instruments which could play like a musical box or play a gramophone record. Later, the musical box lines were closed and phonograph production was instituted in its place. The coming of war in 1914 wrote 'finis' to a great era, for the Swiss had already lost out on world markets to the successful German industry of disc musical box production and now Germany was at war, and the industry closed.

The interest in collecting musical boxes today is world-wide. From tiny beginnings in 1961, the Musical Box Society of Great Britain now has members all over the world – more than a third are in the United States – and its quarterly journal, *The Music Box*, which began as a four-sheet hand-duplicated newsletter, is now a professionally printed A4-sized fully illustrated magazine which goes to collectors, restorers, dealers, museums and libraries throughout the world. The quest for information, far from becoming less, is escalating and it is an undeniable fact that something 'new' turns up regularly just as if to remind us not to sink into the frame of mind which might induce us to think that we already know it all.

From the standpoint of the collector, there is much to be learned and many points to look for. Much has to be learned by experience, such as the fact that most musical boxes found today were produced after 1880. It is these very late instruments, in fact, which comprise the bulk of those that find their way on the market and, since they are the product of a period when quality was becoming secondary to production quantity, their value to the serious collector is not as great as that of an earlier specimen. The top-quality boxes were, generally speaking, the earlier ones and the comparison at once becomes obvious if you listen to a late-1890s box playing an abbreviated Gilbert and Sullivan air, and then hear a specimen from the 1840s playing a Mozart overture.

Since my earlier book, there have been at least four other books published on musical boxes, three of which were in English. All are now out of print. So once again there is a paucity of authoritative reading matter on musical boxes. It is in an attempt both to bridge this gap and also to present the latest and thus most up-to-date information on the musical box that this present work has been written. It is in no way a pure revision of *Collecting Musical Boxes* but is a fresh work in entirety.

The enthusiast in any field can easily be misled into making an unwise purchase unless he knows a little about his subject. Many would-be collectors have been put off by the acquisition of an unsuitable box or one in bad order which they could not rectify, and their inexperience has encouraged them to adopt the line of least resistance and abandon their fleeting interest. Antique dealers, on the other hand, who are normally shrewd and often knowledgeable people, even today appear quite lost when confronted by a musical box and many honestly cannot tell a good musical box from a bad one. Admittedly there are expert dealers in the field, but there are, as in every profession, the opposite kind.

And so this book is written with the view to setting out in simple and, I hope, readable form a history of the musical box and sufficient details of the various common types to enable both the collector and the dealer to know better just what they are handling. To this end, there is an extensive list of makers and patentees of musical boxes, an illustrated list of some fifty-two different identification marks found on boxes, and an appendix devoted to reproductions of a large number of tune-sheets with their makers identified. This is followed by a list of British patents relating to musical boxes.

Many beliefs, deductions and prior teachings contained in my earlier book have been modified with subsequent investigation and research not only by myself but by other researchers within both the Musical Box Society of Great Britain and the Musical Box Society International. It is for this reason that the earlier book, *Collecting Musical Boxes*, which took one week to write more than a decade ago and was based on fifteen years of musical box collecting and repairing, is now totally replaced by the present work.

My earlier book contained a small section on repair and overhaul since musical boxes are frequently found which are in need of restoration. It has been decided that rather than produce one very large and expensive volume containing restoration information – which may only be of interest to a limited number of my readers – it would be better to have this as the subject of a separate book.

To this end, this book has a companion volume called *Restoring Musical Boxes*. This work, which is in matching format, is no simple restatement of what I wrote before, but is again a wholly new and copiously detailed treatise on the repair, restoration and conservation of all types of musical box and concludes with details of case repair and an appendix of technical terms in three languages. The text is fully revised in the light of the abilities which collectors now demonstrate. As an example of what I mean, let me instance cylinder repinning. This was at one time considered well beyond the abilities of the amateur but there are now many collectors who are undertaking most successfully this highly skilled and exacting work and this one aspect of repair has been the subject of more letters from readers of my previous book than any other. As the reader may deduce from this statement, I have benefited from helpful criticism, suggestions and correspondence with readers of the earlier book inasmuch as they have highlighted the shortcomings for me, and have told me what they think others may need to know. Many techniques which I considered beyond the enthusiastic amateur and so excluded from the earlier book will be found within the companion volume to this. Marcus Aurelius (AD 120–80) wrote: 'A man does not sin by commission alone, but also by omission'!

The wealth of new or redefined information has dictated that the scope of this book should be more discriminating and circumspect in dealing with musical boxes and therefore much of the general approach to mechanical music has been dropped. Since this is covered in my other books and by other sources I hope that this will be seen as no decrement to the work as a whole.

There is something humbling about owning an example of the craftsmanship and art of some man who has long since turned to dust. Something, some part of his soul, must lie imprisoned betwixt brass cylinder, comb and mainspring. And no matter how much you may have paid for your musical box this intangible something you may never own: it can only be entrusted to you for safe keeping until it may pass to yet another who will continue to love and cherish it. Even if for this reason alone, it is incumbent upon you, the collector, restorer or dealer, to do everything in your power to preserve and not to destroy, even if this means accepting your own limitations and leaving well alone.

For those who would wish to see contemporary advertisements, to see copies of catalogues of musical boxes and to read in depth about the dealer and distribution set-up in London, I would of necessity recommend their perusing my book *Clockwork Music*, which also covers automata, player pianos and fair organs. For those with specific need of information on automatic pianos, my book *Player Piano* describes the history and overhaul. A similar coverage relating to mechanical organs is in *Barrel Organ*, and for those who would wish to explore the possibilities of pinning cylinders for organs or making piano rolls, *Mechanical Music* gives practical instruction as to how this was done and how to do it today. A complete bibliography, listing also many other works, is to be found at the end of this book.

Tune sheets form an important aid to the dating and identification of a musical box. First they provide a list of the music played – an invaluable asset if you cannot recognise any of the melodies – which at once provides the ability to assess the *earliest* date at which the box was manufactured, i.e. a box pinned with Indy's overture 'Piccolomini' cannot have been made prior to the first performance of that opera in 1874. The second feature is that the tune sheet can indicate very clearly who made the box. In Appendix II are reproductions of some of the very many styles of sheet used. Many of these either bore the name of the musical-box maker (not to be confused with the lithographer's name in tiny print right at the bottom on some) or were particular to that maker. However, some early styles of tune sheet appear to have been used by several different makers. On these boxes, the tune sheet should be considered only in the light of other indications as to the true identity of the maker. A few unidentified tune sheets are included in the hope that somebody might recognise them.

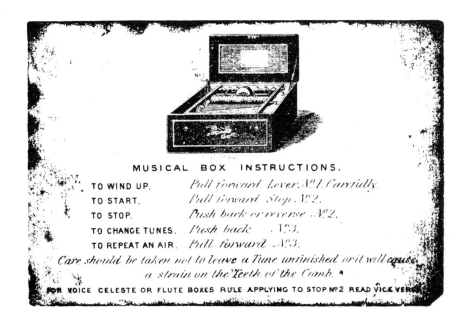

MUSICAL BOX INSTRUCTIONS.

TO WIND UP.   *Pull forward Lever N° 1. Carefully.*
TO START.   *Pull forward Stop N° 2.*
TO STOP.   *Push back or reverse N° 2.*
TO CHANGE TUNES. *Push back N° 3.*
TO REPEAT AN AIR. *Pull forward N° 3.*

Care should be taken not to leave a Tune unfinished or it will cause a strain on the Teeth of the Comb.

FOR VOICE CELESTE OR FLUTE BOXES RULE APPLYING TO STOP N° 2 READ VICE VERSA

CHAPTER 1

Mechanical Musical Instruments

The term 'mechanical musical instrument' has come to mean any type of musical instrument which has a self-playing capability, whether that capability is achieved by strictly mechanical means or by some other means, such as pneumatic or electromagnetic. As outlined in Chapter 9, there are very many types of instrument which have been either specially built or otherwise adapted for self-playing, but the number which are truly mechanical is small. Significantly, the musical box is one of them wherein a tuned steel tooth is made to vibrate via a mechanically arranged programme.

The earliest mechanical musical instruments date from prehistory. It may seem strange to relate, but all available evidence points to the fact that the primitive instruments of music were conceived of not solely for playing by a human, but also for automatic operation. That this approach was slow to die is demonstrated by the discovery of horological manuscripts dating from the thirteenth century which describe how to make an automaton player for a carillon and an even earlier one describing how to use a series of pinned discs to play a tune on a pipe organ automatically. These rare indications of the arts of former times are set out in my book *Barrel Organ*.

If we consider the developments of the mechanical musical instrument we find that for at least six centuries it has been closely allied to the history of the bell.

Bells have their origin far, far back in prehistory. Two prime types were to be found – cast (meaning those formed in a mould from molten metal) and uncast (meaning those folded up or bent from sheet metal). Cast bells offered advantages in that they could be made larger and produce louder sounds. By the year 2000 BC they were in use in China and the Romans invented a means of advising the time of day by sounding a bell. Their introduction into the Christian church took place either about the year 400 through Paulinus, Bishop of Nola, Campania, or in about 600 by Pope Sabinianus, and the Venerable Bede brought to England a large bell from Italy in the year 608 which he installed in the Abbey of Wearmouth. By the ninth century, bells cast in musical intervals were installed in a tower of Sancta Sophia, subsequently destroyed by the Turks. Clocks with bells, a much later union, came to England from the Low Countries and gave us the word 'clock' from the Flemish word for bell.

As industry assumed a greater importance and working hours became regularised, the demand for defining the hours of the day arose. Originally, a man had ascended the church tower and blown a horn; later he was employed to strike the bell with a hammer. In the year

1354 it is recorded that a man was assigned to this task and styled *campanaris* or *klokkenist*. Known as the 'town Johnnie', he would ascend the tower at regular intervals and sound the hours. For the rest of his time, he would sweep the streets and was classed as nothing but a menial servant.

By the latter half of the fourteenth century, though, developments in the design and realisation of the weight-driven clock had reached the stage where it became feasible to use them in towers. The time was then visibly indicated by the use of automaton figures. Dials with hands had yet to appear on this form of public clock, so the sounding of the hours on bells struck by puppets or jacks was resorted to.

It was usual for jacks to operate in pairs striking upon two bells. The number of bells was increased to four until in France the term *carillon* was derived. According to Larousse, the word is derived from the low Latin *quatrinio* meaning a group of four. Tyack, however, derives it from the Italian *quadriglio*, a dance measure from which comes the English word 'quadrille'. Whatever the derivation, from those early times forward, any assemblage of tuned bells, chromatic or semi-chromatic, has been termed a carillon regardless of their number. However, it is generally implicit that the bells be fixed stationary and produce their sound by means of a hammer or as an adjunct to a clock.

In time the number of bells had increased to six or eight and the Flemish created a word for such a set-up – *beiaard*. This term, according to Price,* has since been applied to the larger carillon which developed in the country north-east of France and which the French more specifically designate as a *carillon de Flandres*.

Meanwhile, *beiaard* with its specific meaning has been used in a limited area. In Holland the instrument is called *klokkenspel*. *Beiaard* is from the Netherland-German word *beieren* which means to play on two or more bells. In more Frenchified form, the *bayard* was an old Flemish dance.

As more and more bells were employed to sound the hours, the use of jacks was discontinued and in its place came the mechanically played tune called a chime. This was at first only played before the hour, its purpose being to call the listener's attention and to warn him to count all of the following single-bell hour strokes, not missing the first. This stems from the earlier practice of sounding the bell once to draw attention to the clock, and then to strike the hours. This was called the *voorslag* or fore-stroke. So eminently practical was the method that it was also incorporated in the half-hour, followed eventually by the tolling on a bell of higher pitch than the hour bell a thirty-minute warning of the oncoming hour. Soon the terminology was not precise enough: the word *voorslag* came to be applied to the complete set of bells, so the word *voorspel* was introduced to indicate the foreplay, and the word *klokkenspel* for the bell-play.

The bell-play was achieved by the use of a rotating iron drum† into the surface of which could be set at intervals different types of steel pegs which could engage, as the drum rotated, with levers which in turn would cause the bells to be struck by their hammers. Today we call this a carillon mechanism, yet the carillon proper did not really materialise until about 1480 when a manual was added so that the bells could be played by hand as well.

In truth, then, the mechanical operation of bells by means of a rotating pinned cylinder should be called by the only name which it at first had – the *voorslag*, pronounced 'fore-

---

* Frank Percival Price, *The Carillon* (Oxford University Press, 1933), p. 13.
† By the middle of the seventeenth century the drum was usually made of bell-metal.

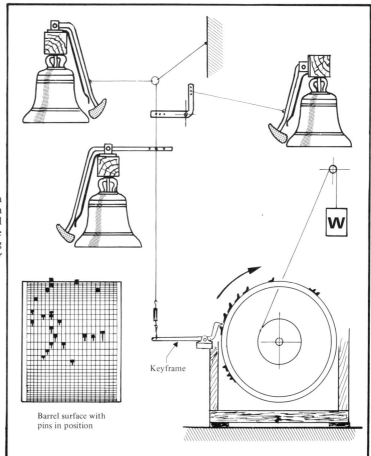

Figure 1 The different ways in which a bell may be struck by linkages from a carillon barrel. The spring of flat steel between hammer and bell keeps the hammer clear of the bell except during the actual striking. (*Illustration after Andre Lehr.*)

slagh'. However, by common acceptance, this is now called by the name given to the later and improved mechanism – *carillon*. And the person who plays a set of bells manually is properly termed *klokkenist* in Holland, *beiaardier* in Flanders, and *carillonneur* in France. In English, we have adopted the last-mentioned term.

To be able to produce melodious music on a set of bells demanded the utmost attention to design, manufacture and tuning of the bells. The mid-seventeenth-century Dutch bell makers Francois and Pieter Hemony gained wide acclaim for their ability to wring superlative overtones from a carefully tuned bell and, although other carillon makers have come close to the Hemonys' art, very few have equalled it. The Dutch poet Vondel was inspired, upon hearing a Hemony carillon, to write: 'Hemony makes the most heavenly bell music.'*

The first tower bells to be equipped with an automatic device appear to have been those in the Sint Nicolaas-kerk in Brussels installed by the year 1381. Within half a century, many other churches had similar mechanisms.

* 'Hemoni speelt een hemels klokmuzijk.'

One of the earliest carillon-playing mechanisms is on view today in the Nederlands Goud-Zilver-en Klokkenmuseum in Utrecht. This was made in 1541 and, along with other, later, mechanisms on show at the Beiaardmuseum in Asten, shows clearly how the music was transferred from engraved score into pegs with a spanner. The drum of the famous Mechlin Cathedral carillon, made in 1736, has a diameter of 15 ft and a length in excess of 6 ft. It operates on 90 levers and plays eight times during the hour, each tune calling for only a small amount of revolution, one full turn of the drum representing all eight tunes. The Mechlin

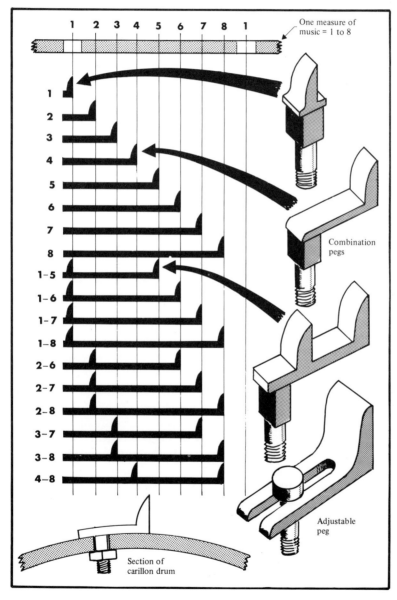

One measure of music = 1 to 8

Combination pegs

Adjustable peg

Section of carillon drum

Figure 2 The various pegs which are used when pinning music on the barrel of a carillon. The distance between the rows of holes across the width of the barrel is divided into eight parts and in addition to normal pegs, cranked ones are made so that any note position within that measure may be pinned. Fast repetition within a measure can be achieved using special double pegs. (*Illustration after Andre Lehr.*)

cylinder can play a total of 108 bars of music and has 180 radial rows of holes around its periphery. With 90 holes in each row, this means that there are 16,200 holes for tune-setting. With eight different types of peg plus three combination pegs, as shown in Fig. 2, this produces a possible combination of 176,000. The largest automatic playing drum is at Châlons-sur-Marne with about 34,000 holes. The drum with the largest diameter is in Salzburg.

Automatic carillons are still made today, only they have succumbed to modern technology. In place of the drum with its pegs is an endless band of perforated plastic rather like a player-piano music-roll. Metal fingers running over the plastic as it is unwound make electric contact through the perforations and energise a solenoid-striking apparatus. Let it be said, though, that the revival of the Dutch carillon since 1950 has produced many fine new instruments, that at Eindhoven built by Eijsbouts for Philips being the largest in the country.

Most carillons are playable by both mechanical means and by hand. However, it is significant that the number played by mechanical means only is almost as great as those played only from a keyboard. Small carillons, namely those with from $1\frac{1}{2}$ octaves to perhaps $2\frac{1}{2}$, are played only by mechanical means.

The mechanical organ can be traced back to pre-Christian times although the first definitive reference was not written down until the ninth century, in the works of the Banu Musa. This is quoted at length and described in full in my book *Barrel Organ*.

The earliest surviving mechanical organ which is still in playing condition is that which is built into the wall of Salzburg Castle. This instrument was built in the year 1502 and still performs regularly, having had several careful restorations over the years.

From this it will be observed that means of making mechanical music have been known to Man for some considerable length of time – more than 2,000 years in fact. The perfection of the rotating musical programme came with the carillon in about the fourteenth century.

The great era of mechanical music began in the closing years of the sixteenth century with the start of an era during which increasingly complex and beautiful musical automata were made in Augsburg in Germany. The organ was generally the most popular instrument to feature in these, but there were also miniature carillons, dulcimer or harp mechanisms and regals. The great centre of European automata building shifted to London and by the first half of the eighteenth century craftsmen such as Charles Clay, James Cox, John Joseph Merlin and Thomas Weeks were at work. They gathered around them a group of talented artisans which included painters, sculptors, carvers and musicians to further their collective talent. As the nineteenth century began, so London's reputation as the centre of European clock- and watchmaking attracted great horological workers such as Jaquet-Droz, Maillardet, Leschot and others from the Swiss industry.

From the end of the seventeenth century onwards, mechanical musical instruments became fashionable and soon specific areas became associated with their manufacture and cottage industries sprang up. A small area of the Black Forest close to the Swiss border, for example, became the cradle of the flute-playing clock – the so-called Black Forest clock with its ebullient, rich carving and its bucolic figures and decoration. Mirecourt in France became the cradle of the French barrel-organ industry and the English barrel organ largely became the chief product of a remarkably small area of London – part of Soho.

The musical box relies for its production of musical sound on the plucking of tuned steel elements. The musical pitch of the sound produced by such an element is dependent upon the relationship between the length, thickness and breadth. The shorter and more slender

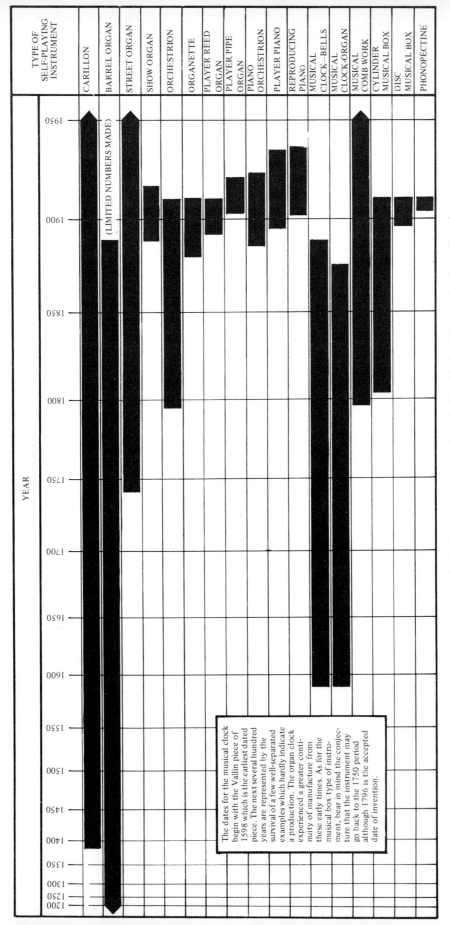

Figure 3   The periods of various mechanical instrument types are shown in this table. It will be seen that the carillon, the street organ and musical comb work of various types are aspects still being made today.

the element, the higher the pitch and the quieter the sound it will emit when plucked. The longer and thicker the element, then the lower and louder it will sound.

Every schoolboy knows that if he inserts the end of his wooden school ruler under the flap of his desk and twangs it, it will produce a sound which will vary in pitch according to how much of the ruler is protruding. It was this very elementary principle which resulted in the invention of a primitive African instrument which, by all accounts, is of great antiquity. This is the *sanza* or *zanza* which is made in various forms throughout Africa, though its basic details remain constant throughout its geographical and individual styles. It comprises a resonant base usually of hollowed out hardwood or a hollow gourd upon which are mounted a number of bamboo or, in later examples, metal strips of differing lengths and thicknesses. These are securely laced with a thong of leather so that they protrude across a bridge similar to that on a piano or guitar. When the ends of the reeds so formed are plucked with the fingers, sounds are produced which are separated by various musical intervals. Just how this principle was adapted to the familiar cylinder musical box is established in the next chapter.

The comb-playing mechanism, as related later, was extant as the eighteenth century came to a close. The next big invention came with the perfection of pneumatic action, first tried experimentally in the 1860s and finally to emerge in the shape of the player reed organ and player piano in the 1880–90 period. This unleashed a fresh torrent of mechano-musical inventiveness which demonstrated itself in the superb concert orchestrion organs made in Germany. This climaxed with the so-called reproducing player mechanism for the piano which, although resembling the simple player piano, enabled fully automatic recordings in perforated paper of artists to be played back on a suitably equipped piano.

By the early 1930s even this was wearing thin as a general market decay took place. Wireless and the cinema – which now had talking pictures – meant fewer and fewer people wanted to make their own music at home.

Mechanical music really should have closed its era in those years immediately preceding the Second World War. But it was not to be. Simple musical movements for use in toys and novelties continued to find a demand and so even to this day Switzerland has a thriving, albeit small, musical-box industry making these small mass-produced items. They are also made by the Japanese, who in the space of a generation altered the term 'made in Japan' from being indicative of cheap tat to meaning comparable and competitive quality.

There are some interesting toy mechanical instruments to be found; one can be programmed with a tune rather like a carillon, and another will play a musical box from a punched strip of plastic. Other than these, though, mechanical musical instruments are now the province solely of collectors and enthusiasts who make new piano rolls, books for fair organs, or the occasional often Heath Robinson player instrument. One or two, though, have re-created the musical box of old: their names, aptly, are included in Chapter 11.

CHAPTER 2

The Musical Box – Its Definition, Birth and Evolution

In this chapter, I intend to set out first of all just what a musical box is, and then to define those areas of the world where it was born, developed and manufactured.

First, though, when we talk of a musical box, just what do we mean? A glance at some early writings and even sale-room catalogues today will suffice to show that these two words cover a multitude of appliances, not all of which can truly be described as musical boxes. Just what is this thing to which we refer, and how does it work?

A musical box is a device for the mechanical production of music and belongs to that class of instruments called idiophones. Although the term 'musical box' is often applied loosely to other types of self-acting musical instrument such as the organette, serinette and singing bird, the real musical box relies for its sound on the tone produced by plucking a tuned steel element which is capable of vibrating to a predetermined frequency.

In practice, the musical box comprises a series of such elements arranged in such a manner that a scale of musical sounds may be produced. Each steel element is plucked in a precise sequence.

The process of plucking is carried out in one of two ways and it is the determination of which system is used which defines the two major types of musical mechanism. The first is the cylinder movement wherein the teeth are plucked by being brought into direct contact with a programme of short steel pins arranged in the surface of a slowly-rotating metal cylinder or barrel. This cylinder is caused to rotate in such a manner that the tuned elements, by common usage referred to as 'teeth', are set in vibration. Whereas the earliest musical box featured single teeth individually made and attached to the mechanism, later musical boxes had teeth cut in groups, or sections, of two or more teeth and finally these teeth were machined from one piece of special steel to comb-like format. Hence this is usually referred to as the comb, although some early writers erroneously dubbed it 'the keyboard'.

In the second and later form, the musical box featured, in place of a pinned cylinder as a means of providing the musical programme, an exchangeable flat disc punched with projections or, in some cases, slots. This was caused to turn slowly in such a manner that the musical comb teeth were plucked through the intermediary of small, multi-pointed star-wheels.

Initially, the Swiss musical movement was probably a very small piece of craftsmanship intended to augment the attractions of the pocket watch and, prior to the invention of the plucked steel tooth system, the only means of providing such music was by the use of hammers and small bells, nested one inside the other. Even so, this made for a bulky watch with a scale of only a few notes.

In the early part of 1796, a watchmaker named Antoine Favre (1767–1828) reported to the Geneva Society of Arts that he had 'succeeded in establishing carillons without bells or hammers'. Favre's invention was to use a tuned steel tooth plucked, in the earliest examples, either by pins set in a flat wheel or by projections set in the outer surface of the spring barrel.

Because these tiny movements often formed part of some other work, such as a watch, gold vinaigrette or even a seal, they are not only extremely rare but also valuable. Musically their performance is poor yet in them can be recognised the very beginnings of what was to become a major industry for almost a century.

Whereas the earliest pieces were built exclusively by watchmakers in the Swiss Jura, the next twenty years saw the steady development of the technique of the musical movement and a handful of craftsmen began to concentrate on this offshoot of horology. The art spread north-east from the Jura right up to the Bavarian hinterland of Baden, and south-west along the Vallée de Joux as far as Le Brassus. Although Geneva soon became the centre of trade, manufacture in that city was unknown before about 1840.

From its early beginnings as a novelty addition to a timepiece, the musical mechanism gradually became an instrument in its own right and by 1820 or so, instead of the musical movement being hidden in the base of a clock to play on the hour, it became elevated to the status of being a solo instrument within its own case. The musical box proper was born.

At a time when music in the home was dependent on the manual dexterity of a member of the family (and almost every home in the land possessed a piano), the musical box became the disseminator of music for the well-to-do. Boxes were expensive and it was not until Paillard established the first factory and went in for mass-production techniques in 1875 that boxes became cheap enough to tempt the pockets of the lower classes.

The music played on the earlier boxes was of three distinct types: operatic, hymns and psalms, and popular airs. Examples built in this early epoch were almost without exception of high quality with superbly arranged music. Manufacturers such as Ducommun Girod, Lecoultre, Falconnet et Reymond, Capt, Alibert, Nicole Frères and, a little later, Bremond and Greiner produced work which today demonstrates not just beauty but sheer musical mastery.

Sadly, the majority of surviving boxes found on the market today are those built between the years of about 1870 and the outbreak of the First World War, by which time quality and aesthetics had been overtaken by commercialism.

Much of the reason for this was the competition provided by the disc-playing musical box which offered definite advantages over the cylinder box. Whereas the cylinder played from four to twelve tunes (some costly musical boxes were built with interchangeable cylinders which could play a considerably wider choice), the disc box could play an endless variety of tunes. And all but the very simplest cylinder boxes were expensive and offered no more musical variety than was to be found on their cylinders.

The disc-playing musical box was invented jointly by a Londoner, Ellis Parr, and a Leipzig industrialist, Paul Lochmann, in the year 1885. It at once made possible the

41

ownership of an enormous repertoire of music as, gramophone-like, the instrument could play whatever discs its owner chose.

The first disc musical box, called the Symphonion, came on the market in 1885 but serious production did not start until three years later. Meanwhile, two senior employees of Lochmann's factory, Gustav Brachhausen and Paul Riessner, left and established a rival factory close by to produce the Polyphon which, as an instrument, not only surpassed the subsequent successes of Symphonion but for many, was to become the name representing the genus 'disc-playing musical box'.

Disc boxes were an immediate success. With both Polyphon and Symphonion in Leipzig, the Swiss tried to meet the competition head on by introducing their own brands such as the Britannia and, later, the technically superior Stella with its smooth, projectionless discs.

Disc instruments were produced with names such as Monopol, Orphenion, Euphonia, Helvetia (Swiss), Sirion and Fortuna. Models ranged from tiny hand-cranked *manivelles* playing discs about four inches in diameter up to giants such as the Komet whose huge clockwork motor turned a disc almost three feet across.

Meanwhile, Brachhausen crossed the Atlantic to America and in the New Jersey town of Rahway established the Regina Music Box Company. Using Polyphon technology he produced some of the most acoustically advanced disc musical boxes which were sold not just in America but in England and even Germany.

Aimed not only at the domestic market, the disc box was also available with coin-feed operation for use in public places. In this form it was popular as a music provider in public houses, tea-rooms and waiting-rooms.

If the disc-playing musical box spelled the end of the quality cylinder musical box, then the combined events of the second decade of the present century marked the end of the disc machine. The burgeoning phonograph could do the one thing which the musical box was incapable of – it could reproduce that most elusive of all sounds, the human voice. And war in Europe put paid to musical boxes in the face of other forms of music in the home – player pianos, player organs and, ultimately, wireless.

In the intervening sixty years, the musical box industry of Switzerland has continued to mass-produce small, cheap musical movements for use in novelties. As interpreters of music, these cannot rank with the pieces produced a hundred and more years ago. Very recently, however, a line of hand-built quality cylinder musical boxes has emerged and one maker, Reuge, is currently making a small number of expensive and tonally pleasing pieces.

In the United States, there are two craftsmen each producing a replica of the Regina disc musical box in an endeavour to meet a growing demand for these machines which the second-hand original market cannot sate. In Germany, a Cologne manufacturer has also begun production of a facsimile of a disc-playing musical box, this time the Kalliope, which sounds indistinguishable from the original. And in London a replica of the 19⅝ in. (50 cm) Polyphon is being hand-built to order. While these demonstrations of a resurgence in the art are encouraging and serve to prevent our writing 'finis' to the story of the musical box, the importance of the instrument as a means of preserving music and bringing music to the masses has passed and only the early ones still give us the sounds of long-lost, forgotten music by once-venerated composers.

Generally, the expression 'musical box' is used to refer to both the mechanism and its case and to the mechanism on its own. In this latter instance the term is something of a misnomer and for this reason I have chosen to use the word 'musicwork' to refer to the earliest movements which so often did not feature what might, with the full cognisance of the English language, pass for a musical box. As explained in my book *Clockwork Music* (p. 17), the German word for mechanical musical instruments is *musikwerk(e)* which is easy to anglicise to musicwork. The German word for musical box, incidentally, is *spieldosen*, which is hardly suitable for any similar such treatment.

It is perhaps worth mentioning that much of the publicised history of the musical box has come from Switzerland and, while there is no doubt that Switzerland contributed an immense amount to the birth of the mechanism and its subsequent development and production, there is a growing suspicion in the minds of serious historians that the comb-playing musical box did not emanate from Switzerland.

In order to assess the probability of this, it is necessary to examine the writings of one of the leading figures in the Swiss industry, who spent his closing years in the United States, where he died in 1938. Louis Gustave Jaccard was born in L'Auberson near Ste-Croix in the Jura Mountains of Switzerland on 25 June 1861. He was thus born seventy-five years after Antoine Favre's claimed invention of the plucked steel tooth. Jaccard lived to be a respected craftsman who worked in Switzerland until about 1883, then went to New York City to work for M. J. Paillard. In 1886 he transferred to the Jacot Music Box Co., with whom he worked until that business was dissolved in 1911. Jacccard was thus in a good position to be privy to the immediate history of the musical box and so his words must carry considerable weight. Fortunately, he prepared for the Edison Institute a history of the musical box which was later printed in *Hobbies* magazine.*

Jaccard's testimony is thus of especial interest and value, particularly as he wrote it in the United States more than forty years after he had taken out US citizenship and therefore when in a better position to assess the knowledge which he had acquired. Allow me to quote, admittedly fairly extensively, from his writings:

Switzerland is the cradle of the music box; it is there it came to birth and developed in a remarkable manner. The original instrument was composed of a few individual steel prongs tuned to a scale, and the one tune it produced was scarcely discernible. However, its development was such that it rivaled and even surpassed all that which had been accomplished in automatic music up to the time of the phonograph.

The 'lieu d'origine' of the music box is 'La Vallée de Joux,' near the border of France. The villages of this section also manufactured watches of the most skilled workmanship, in fact, the best in the world even to this day. Among these expert watchmakers there was one who conceived the idea of an instrument consisting of a few separate vibrating steel prongs set in motion by a revolving disc or platform inset with small steel pins. These pins were about one or two millimeters in length and after raising the prongs would permit them to escape, thus producing a pleasing sound. It remained now but to set these pins in their correct position on the disc to obtain the desired melody. This was accomplished and the first music box was created.

The growth of the music box was not spontaneous but gradually developed, beginning about 1750. These first undertakings were accomplished more or less secretly, thus making the early period of growth of the music box indefinite and unknown. Regardless of

* L. G. Jaccard, 'Origin & Development of the Music Box', *Hobbies Magazine*, August, September, October and November 1938, Chicago, Illinois.

difficulties, it is known that a man named Philippe Meylan, of 'le Brassus,' in the Vallée de Joux, set up musical combs in watches. Philippe Meylan was born in 1770. He arranged the musical combs in such a manner that the 'lames d'acier' [steel prongs] vibrated, thus producing the musical tune. La Vallée de Joux, although an industrial center, lacked facilities of export of these works, and Geneva consequently soon became the new manufacturing locality.

In 1815 a number of expert workers with Pierrot, nicknamed Pierroton, as their leader migrated from their villages and settled in Geneva, where they began the manufacturing of music works. Soon after, rivals and imitators, Henri Capt, les frères Longchamps, Moise Aubert, all of 'Le Lieu', Vallée de Joux, and Pierre Rochat, with his son from 'Chez Meylan,' also of the Vallée de Joux, left their villages and began manufacturing in the city.

The above-mentioned workers now began placing music works in 'objets d'art,' such as watches, seals, cane tops, small bottles, bonbonnières, jewelry boxes and 'tabatières' [snuff boxes]. The latter became so popular that this type of music box was and still is called the Tabatière. By this time Henri and François Lecoultre became established in Geneva and were directors of a factory whose products were well known. These transactions took place in about 1815. Nevertheless, it may be assumed that music boxes were already known in Geneva, as an inventory taken in 1780 indicates musical watches and small musical bottles were already made that could play two airs. In about 1806 it was also known that delicate and complicated mechanisms were made, such as the spring motor which set in motion some figurines; these were artistic and delicate figures wrought in gold or silver and accompanied by a music box tune. This seeming discrepancy in dates strengthens the supposition that the early artisans had worked secretly and independently introduced their products in Geneva before the migration took place. It was also found in an old report of the Exposition of 1828 that Salomon Favre was the first Genevan who introduced music boxes in watches, and in 1802 Isac Piguet [sic] replaced in a ring watch works with those of a music box. These rings were scarce and greatly treasured by their owners.

The music box industry has always been closely associated with watchmaking. For instance, in Sainte Croix, a large village in the Jura, repeater watches had been made since 1752. The watchmakers working on these articles were *en rapport* with the leaders of the Geneva industry. This relationship was the means by which Abram Louis Cuendet implanted a similar industry in Sainte Croix. In about 1811 A. L. Cuendet came secretly in contact with the frères Lecoultre 'au Bas du Chenit, Vallée de Joux' and with the Justice of Peace of 'Le Lieu' and shortly after Henri Jaccard of 'Cuillairy', Sainte Croix, and Henri Jaccard, nicknamed 'a chez Baptiste', put themselves at his service and began manufacturing instruments similar to those of La Vallée.

The La Vallée instruments were called 'carillons à musique' and were usually set in watches. As already mentioned, they were of simple construction, i.e., a platform of brass inset with pins acting as levers in contact with a few steel prongs or teeth tuned to a scale. The motor of the watch also set in motion the music. This extremely simple construction was sufficient to complete the first attempt at making music boxes. Instruments placed in articles other than watches, such as cane tops, bottles, jewelry boxes, etc., had, of necessity, a special spring motor and spring barrel. This is the first instance of modifying the construction of the music box. The little steel pins were now set on the surface of the revolving spring barrel.

These later changes induced David Lecoultre to replace the platform with a special cylinder placed parallel to the 'lames d'acier' [comb]. A new relationship of the different parts now permitted the magnifying of the mechanism and in consequence transformed the primitive 'montre à carillon' into an instrument of great exactitude. It was now possible to reproduce the most complicated tunes. The 'lames d'acier' [steel prongs of the comb] are no longer single but made in groups of four or five, and screwed on a brass block. This latter improvement was the precursor of the modern 'Tabatière' music box. The ingenuity of this article may be credited to David Lecoultre, of Geneva. From 1820 the combs were now made of a single piece of steel and this new conception of the comb brought to an end the more expensive and detailed work of the former type.

Remembering that this was written by Jaccard when he was in his seventies and that he was writing about things which were history long before he was born, we are struck by several things. First is the amazing detail contained here which belies the fact that he was an old man. Next is his reference to the musical box having been evolved in conditions of secrecy before Favre's claimed invention of what we have hitherto assumed to be the musical box. His reference to an inventory of 1780 listing numbers of musical watches and bottles being produced might best be treated with reserve since it may be that the watches mentioned were repeaters or alarm watches.

Let us examine Favre's claim. The most definitive evidence of this is set out in Chapuis's *Histoire de la Boîte à Musique*. In this interesting and, unfortunately, now rare book, the author gives a brief list of early writers from 1828 who have written on the subject and goes on to claim that, contrary to the opinion of other writers and, indeed, contrary to what he himself had earlier written, he now has evidence which enables him to date the invention precisely. His claim is based on an extract from the records of the Society of Arts in Geneva for the 15 February, 1796 of which a photograph is given in his book and which I now quote (in translation) in full:

Mr Decombas reports that Mr Favre has found the means of establishing carillons without bells or hammers. He presents a tin box containing one on this principle: as this discovery could be useful in watch and clock-making: the same commissioners named to examine Mr Quosig's instrument are asked to examine it and report.

Chapuis adds that unfortunately the commissioners reported on Quosig's instrument* but not on Favre's. As Chapuis points out, this is easily understood because the Republic of Geneva was in political turmoil at the time. She was encircled by the French Republic and was defending her independence desperately. Widespread unemployment was prevalent and in 1798 French troops entered Geneva, thereby annexing the oldest republic in Europe. Only on 15 May 1799 is there a further reference to Favre's invention. Again Chapuis reproduces a photograph of the extract of which a translation is as follows:

The secretary reports that he was visited by Citizen Favre, who two years ago presented some carillons invented by himself and to whom the Society made an award by way of encouragement. His position has become even more unhappy, owing to the deterioration

* The only Quosig I have traced is listed in Baillie as being a Mannheim watchmaker of the early nineteenth century.

of his sight: he has some pieces of the same kind to send abroad, he has not the funds to do so: he requests the Society to lend him 36 louis for two months. The Society learns all these details with much distress; it would like to be able to assist Citizen Favre but the rules forbid it and the position of the Sociey makes infringement of the rules now more than ever impossible.

This is the essential evidence on which Chapuis attributes the invention of the musical box to Favre and indeed it is difficult to know what Favre's invention for producing 'carillons without bells or hammers' can have been if it was not the comb mechanism later so widely used in musical boxes. An interesting confusion arises in another book by Chapuis called *The Technique & History of the Swiss Watch** which says:

Isaac-Daniel Piguet was born at Le Chenit . . . in 1775. He specialized in costly and complicated pieces: watches with carillons, and clock-watches . . . He settled at Geneva . . . [in 1811] after he had gone into partnership with Philippe-Samuel Meylan (1772–1845) . . . born at Le Brassus. It was he who conceived the idea of adapting 'tongues' of sonorous metal for use in musical watches and in other small objects, introducing this innovation into striking watches, which played a tune after having struck the hours.

However, I have become increasingly aware of certain doubts in my mind over the years as to the justification for accepting that Favre was the inventor of the musical box as we know it. I spent some while analysing the situation as a result of which I delivered a lecture which aroused considerable interest and which was subsequently published in *The Music Box.†*

I knew, for example, that I had seen musical movements with combs and cylinders which somehow did not fit into the accepted story of Switzerland being the birthplace of the musical box. They certainly cast doubts about the date of invention being the closing years of the eighteenth century. The outcome was that I was forced to draw certain conclusions which contradict everything that we already know (or think we know) about the tuned steel tooth in musicwork.

Certainly the comb-playing movement had a date and place of invention or first use and the point I make is the somewhat controversial one that we know neither the date nor the place where the first movement made its appearance. And, as a corollary, we don't know the name of the inventor either.

Now this is not to suggest that the history of the musical box is entirely wrong, or that its salient characters from the end of the eighteenth century forward are suspect. The argument I make is that the tuned steel tooth in musicwork existed at a much earlier date.

During the eighteenth century, there was a growing interest – and associated market – for musical novelties such as clocks and watches. One of the principal problems facing the watchmaker was that of manufacturing a watch small enough to fit in the pocket yet large enough to contain a sufficient number of bells and each of ample size in order to allow music to be played. There was obviously much need for something which would combine the ability to produce a musical sound with that of compactness. At least one man was working

* Eugene Jaquet and Alfred Chapuis (Spring Books, London/New York, 1970), p. 149.

† 'Who Invented the Musical Box?', *The Music Box*, vol. 7 p. 50, based on author's lecture at the Summer Meeting of the Musical Box Society of Great Britain, London, 1975.

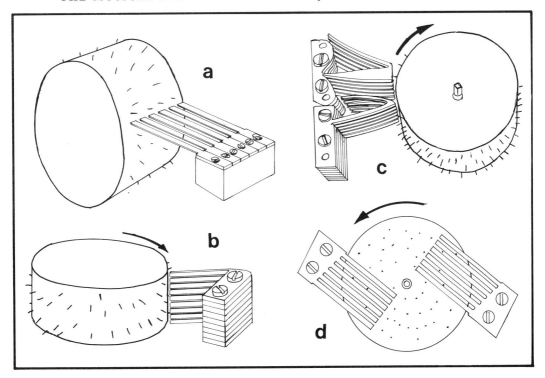

Figure 4 Different types of miniature musicwork. (a) comb of single teeth with pinned cylinder; (b) stacked comb of individual teeth and pinned spring barrel (the barillet style); (c) variation on (b) using two stacks of teeth plucked by different pins and shaped to produce a deeper sound; (d) variation on the *sur plateau* style using two short combs.

along these lines and this was undoubtedly Antoine Favre, who was born in Geneva in the year 1767. The original documentation surrounding this event is preserved in the Register of the Society of Arts of Geneva for 15 February 1798.

Although Antoine Favre indisputably achieved this goal in the year 1796, there are several writers who claim that the tuned steel comb had been used prior to this. Indeed there is some meagre evidence to suggest that Antide Janvier used the tooth principle in his musical clock of 1776 and even this may not have been the first use. Some attribute the invention to Piguet in 1802. While Piguet was certainly an early pioneer and was undoubtedly the maker of the thinnest musical movements ever produced, the incontrovertible evidence of Favre predates this claim by eight years. Other suggestions are that the celebrated clockmaker, Abraham-Louis Breguet (1747-1823), was the inventor.

Let me repeat that all the claims for Favre as the first to use the tuned steel tooth (i.e. the inventor) emanate from Swiss writers, namely Alfred Chapuis, Elie Wartmann and J. D. Blavignac, and the Swiss archives. Antide Janvier, on the other hand, was a Parisian, and, although he later worked at Neuchatel, so was Breguet.

One should also comment that, while Favre's may have been the only recorded use of the tuned steel tooth, it does not automatically follow that it was the first.

The arrival of the tuned steel tooth in the watchmaking circles of Switzerland made possible the production of musical items of extreme smallness and neatness. It was now possible to place the movement within, say, the tiny confines of a seal. According to Chapuis (*ibid.*), Favre used a musical movement of the type having the pins for the music arranged around the barrel of the spring so that, as the barrel rotated, the pins plucked steel vibrators or teeth. This was known as the *barillet* type of musical movement, and would suggest that in miniature work it was the cylinder format which came first, but it is not conclusive evidence.

The *sur plateau* or disc movement appears to have been in use for an astonishingly long period of time. The man who perfected the *sur plateau* was almost certainly Isaac Daniel Piguet, who was born in Le Brassus near Geneva in 1775 and died in 1841. In the Chaux-de-Fonds museum of watches there is a specimen of I. D. Piguet's work dating from the very early years of the nineteenth century.

A grandson of his, Louis Elisée Piguet, was born in 1836 and lived right up until 1924. From the same Chaux-de-Fonds museum collection we find a fine *sur plateau* musical watch, employing the identical 1802 technology, but not made until well into the second half of the nineteenth century (see Fig. 5).

So from this we make the first deduction. Do not be misled into thinking that all *sur plateau* musical movements are very early: they may not be.

Because musicwork was such a cottage industry, developments and improvements in one quarter might not be taken up in another for perhaps several generations. A master craftsman who excelled in the making of one style of musicwork would probably see no reason or justification for changing to a fresh method. As a businessman, he would probably consider that the necessary 'learning curve' to be spent getting used to the revised technology was not worth the effort if his present style of work was satisfactory. The Piguet story is a typical instance of this. The family (for a time the business was known as Piguet et Meylan) was famed for its extremely thin pocket watches and snuff-boxes which played music. Some of their musical movements are no more than one quarter of an inch thick! It stands to reason that, having established this capability, the technology would remain even as time went by and fashions changed, if only for occasional use.

We can now show that both the cylinder and the disc movement operated concurrently for very many years. As distinct from the pinned spring barrel of Favre's apparent early use, the definable cylinder as a separate entity was also used in music work for playing tuned steel teeth from a surprisingly early epoch.

In Utrecht's clock and watch museum there is on display a pocket watch with cylinder and sectional comb. The watch is perfectly original and bears the maker's name, Chevalier et Cochet of Paris, and if we examine clockmakers' records we find this to date from between 1790 and 1805 – apparently encompassing the earliest epoch of the tuned steel tooth in miniature musicwork.

We now arrive at a most unusual 'missing link' musical box which survives in the Reuge collection at Ste-Croix. Illustrated as Figure 142 in Chapuis's *Histoire de la Boîte à Musique* (p. 162), it is at first familiar in appearance, but if we look closely we find an altogether unfamiliar movement: eighteen pairs of teeth, each individual pair of different and apparently unrelated length, and each pair screwed down individually, a brass cylinder playing one air only, a motor inside the barrel and a gear train ending in a large paddlewheel air brake. This piece remains unlike anything else to have been produced in Switzerland, yet in spite of this it bears an apparent relationship to early musicwork in Paris and Vienna.

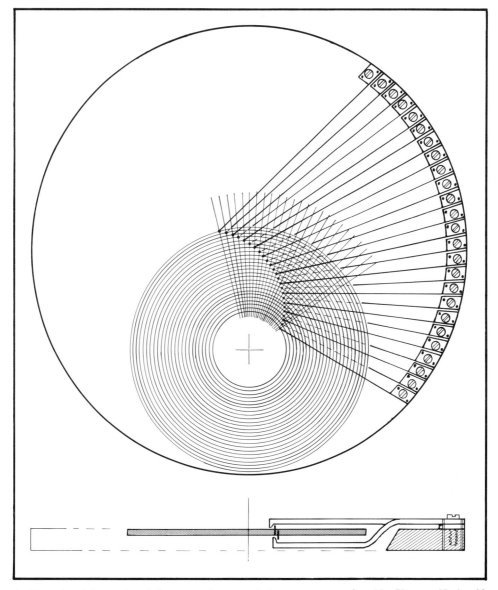

Figure 5   The early miniature pinned disc or *sur plateau* musical movement as perfected by Piguet et Meylan. Note how alternate teeth are cranked under the disc.

Now to the question of the sectional comb, made up in its earliest form of single, separate teeth, and in its apparently final form in groups of up to six teeth. It is generally supposed that after the introduction of the one-piece comb, attributed to Francois Lecoultre in 1814, the changeover to one-piece combs was effected within fifteen years or so. In spite of this, sectional-comb miniature movements which are capable of being dated by their musical programmes are to be found which date from as late as 1840 and possibly considerably later.

49

In Plates 30 to 40 three very different types of musical movement for use in clock-bases are illustrated. The first depicted a fusee-wound mechanism with single comb teeth. Although the base is at the left and treble right, the governor is at the left and the motor at the right, this being supported in accepted musical-box fashion by trunnions. The second (Plates 37–8) is similar in almost every respect except that here the treble teeth are in the centre, bass being at both ends.

The third, Plate 31, is still in reversed layout (governor left, motor right) and with the comb bass at the left. This time, though, the comb is in groups of four and the fusee-wound motor is mounted clock-fashion between plates. From the considerations of clockwork, it is my contention that only one of these is likely to be Swiss in origin, and that is the first. The third one I consider to be either French or Viennese, and the second one remains uncertain.

The argument here is the solution to the question: how did the musical box get invented in so many different styles and formats – all, apparently, around the same time?

The obvious answer is that, as with a burgeoning technology, everyone was trying to reach the end result by his own design path. I grant that that is one explanation, but it assumes that the starting-point in time and place was common to all and this I contest. Consider the facts: Favre invents a miniature musical movement for fitting inside a watch-case or seal. What is the connection between that achievement and something the size of a large sized musical movement for fitting in a clock-base? Why should one automatically progress to the other? Accepting that this may have been the case, then it is equally probable that the process may have taken place the other way about, and that Favre adopted an existing technique to make a miniature movement. This is a clearer line of argument than to assume the scaling-up to relatively large proportions of a miniature musical mechanism intended for a watch or seal.

An alternative is to explore the contemporary skills and level of craft to try to see if it was technically possible at the time we are considering – around the middle of the eighteenth century – for the technology of the tuned steel tooth to have been in use by clockmakers.

We find a clockwork-driven carillon playing a musically-pinned barrel in the Harbrecht clock in the British Museum. This is not the earliest such use, but it is an easy one to select. It was built by Isaac Harbrecht in 1589 – 207 years before Favre's invention.

The pinned brass cylinder which is shifted laterally to play alternative tunes by means of a snail and cam is also of early origin. Another example was built by Le Roy in 1759 and plays bells – thirty-seven years before Favre's invention.

If we look at ruling styles of clockwork we find that all the salient parts of the musical box were known, understood and in use at least fifty years before the date of Favre's invention. Manufacturing techniques, assembly and finish, all predate Favre by at least a century. And cylinder programming for music in clocks predated Favre by about a quarter of a millennium!*

Based on this alone, I find it illogical to assume that the tuned steel tooth was not discovered until 1796, for how can its presence have been felt in places so far afield as Paris

---

* It is interesting to relate in this context that within the craft of watch and clockmaking there has been for centuries the practice of making and tempering both curved and flat steel springs. When accurately tempered, these springs will produce a 'musical' sound when plucked – an indication that the process has been correctly carried out. An awareness that springs of differing lengths and masses could produce sounds of differing pitches must have existed since the early part of the eighteenth century. Significantly, many of the early written works, in referring to the musical movement teeth, and no doubt specifically concerning the sectional comb comprising, in its primigenial form, single teeth, always call these 'springs' rather than teeth.

and Switzerland at a time when the watchmaking industry was operating largely as a cottage industry situated in a remote area without adequate means of communication?

So was the cylinder musical box beyond the capabilities of the ruling technology of the eighteenth century? We find the answer to be an emphatic 'no'.

Cylinder-programmed music in clocks was well advanced a long time before Favre's invention of 1796. And the possibility of its use in conjunction with music played on tuned steel teeth before Favre's time cannot be ruled out. But if this is the case – and in a moment I shall discuss evidence – then what did Favre really invent, for we have proof that he invented something?

Did Favre invent the tuned steel tooth? There appear to be too many anomalies for us to be able to say with any certainty that he did. What he probably did do, though, was to miniaturise an existing technology to enable the musical movement to be fitted into objects smaller than clocks. Probably it was he who substituted the cylinder of the musical clock for the *barillet* or pinned spring barrel. This complies with the information which Chapuis provides.

So was Antoine Favre the first to use the tuned steel tooth? I think not and I believe that we do not have to look too far in order to turn up some evidence to show its earlier use.

Assuming that Favre's invention concerned the modification by miniaturisation of an existing practice, then our evidence should be in the annals of clockmaking. Unfortunately, though, while many clockmakers made musical clocks and there are plenty of references to them, writers on clockwork are notoriously imprecise in their definition of the means of providing music which features in a particular clock.* In so many cases, the scant reference 'musical' in a clock's description conceals whether the clock features a comb-playing movement, a harp or dulcimer, a carillon or even an organ, or in some cases, a combination.

For this reason, searching through clock descriptions can be a daunting and frustrating task. Even where the clock is pictured it is not always possible to determine that it is musical. Two exceptions to this immediately concern us. Both refer to clocks illustrated in the second volume of the three-volume work *La Pendule Française* by Tardy, published in Paris in several editions at various dates from 1961 to 1973.

The first illustration appears on page 320 and is of a glass-cased timepiece from the period of Louis XVI (1750–90). Described as a 'Régulateur à musique, quantième', this has a large cylinder musical movement as a visible feature of the case front. The lay-out of the movement is conventional as regards the juxtaposition of cylinder, motor, governor and comb, and the teeth are arranged in what appear to be segments of about ten teeth.

The second illustration appears on page 402 and features a small glass-cased clock by Breguet and clearly of the Empire period, an epoch which made itself noticeable in clock-making about 1804–5. Although this is subsequent to Favre, the comb-playing musical movement in this item is so clearly a development of the clock type of carillon as to justify the supposition that it is an interdependent conception.

The movement, which Tardy illustrates in close-up on page 403, has twenty-five separate pairs of teeth, each pair located with one screw. The comb and cylinder are directly derived from the carillon clock in style of embodiment within the clock. The cylinder is driven from behind by a spring barrel placed centrally and at right angles to the cylinder axis. The

* The author delivered a lecture on the classification of musical clocks to the Antiquarian Horological Society at the Science Museum, South Kensington, in May of 1978.

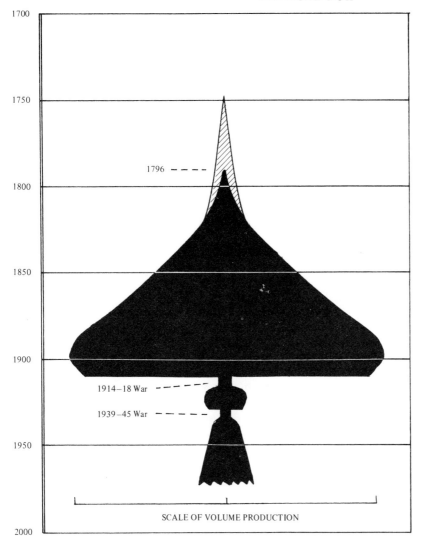

Figure 6 The period of musical-box production showing an indication of the volume of instruments turned out which peaked just before the turn of the century. War served to curtail production, but with the recent resurgence in musical boxes, there is a new and developing industry, albeit small, today. The shaded area indicates a period during which evidence suggests that a few comb-playing musical movements were produced outside Switzerland.

governor assembly is also arranged behind the clock plate; a layshaft axially parallel to the cylinder operates a conventional endless and air brake. Built as part of the clock, it is hard to consider this piece as dating much later than 1810.

There are other items which exist and pose this selfsame question of date and place of origin. See Plate 27.

So once again, did Favre make use of the pinned cylinder – for this we have seen was a ruling technology. If we reappraise the wording of the original claim made by Favre, we find that it was that he had found a way of making an artificial carillon for watches. I read this as indicating that he succeeded in making the whole arrangement very much smaller and very much more compact, so probably he made use of the spring barrel, or perhaps he was the first to use the primitive disc or sur plateau system subsequently perfected by Piguet.

Of course, if all this is so, it is rather a serious matter for us, for it means that the whole history of the musical box as we know it must be rewritten. And, even if that is the case, we are still left with the question: where did the first musical movement come from?

Now the cradle of the musical box, so we have always been told, was the Vallée de Joux in Switzerland – quite a distance from Geneva where Favre was at work. Close to Geneva is Le Brassus, whence, we know, many fine early musical movements emanated. But what about the movements in Viennese Empire clocks which have clockmaking styles of engineering rather than watchmaking? Well, they could have come from Paris, but they might also with equal probability have emanated from Vienna or Prague. Both were strong centres in the making of cylinder musical boxes in later years and presumably the industry had to start some time.

If we now relate the Viennese and Czech* clockmaking styles to the picture, it becomes no wild guesswork to be able to see the musical-box styles which are comparable. And somewhere between Geneva and Prague stands that early haven of musical clocks and mechanical music in general – Augsburg, famed for its art, its automata and its craftsmen as early as the start of the sixteenth century.

Relating clockwork to musicwork, it becomes possible to identify items in terms of two styles. Let's call them Le Brassus and Vienna, for we know that both had associations with the very early perfection of clockwork and were later centres of making comb-playing musical movements for use in clocks.

To summarise, then, we can represent the production of the musical box as we have hitherto been told it by a diagram as seen in Figure 6. The resemblance to a modern jet aircraft is interesting but quite incidental. At the apex we have the date of Antoine Favre's invention and the outward curves show the manner in which the industry responded to the stimulus, expanding through to the turn of the century after which it began to decline until the sudden inroads of the First World War, which effectively stopped production. After that, modern movements have been produced in vast quantities and are still being produced to this day – hence the jagged edge to the 'tail'.

But notice the shaded outline ahead of the nose of our futuristic jet plane. I claim that this represents a truer picture of the comb-playing musical movement and believe that its use predates Favre's invention by around half a century. In this prehistory period, I also believe that the technology was employed by but a few clockmakers in musical clocks as an extension of the carillon technology.

In conclusion, may I emphasise one point and that is that I believe a far better understanding of the early musical box, particularly where it survives in conjunction with a clock, may emerge from an appraisal of the musical movement in terms of clockmaking than to consider it in the light of what may now be suspect parameters regarding the musical box.

And the fact still remains that the Swiss accounts of the birth of the musical box may ultimately prove to have been coloured with a measure of chauvinism. Certainly, I believe that we should consider them with an open mind.

The evolution of the musical box was a long and slow process. If we consider that the first experiments with tuned steel teeth were taking place in secret around 1750, then the first

---

* Czechoslovakia, of course, post-dated the era of the musical box since it did not come into being until 1918. Prior to that, it was Austro-Hungaria comprising Bohemia, Moravia and part of Silesia. Bohemian style is thus a better description, yet to present-day readers Czech must better indicate the area in question.

half-century saw virtually no serious development, all work presumably being experimental and therefore primitive in relative terms. From the end of the eighteenth century evolution was rapid, the first two decades of the nineteenth century seeing the definition of the musical box as a recognisable entity, and, musically speaking, achieving a most acceptable level of performance. From then to 1850 just about all the development of the cylinder musical box reached a definitive state. Changeable cylinders, orchestral boxes, and quantity production were within the Swiss capability.

As the then most important country in the world, Britain played a major rôle in the development of the musical box in a sort of passive sense. Although we had no musical-box industry as such, we represented an important market-place and an important clearing-house for technology. This manifested itself in two ways. First it meant that all musical-box makers actively sought the British market and London representation, and, second, it meant that the British Patent Office became at least as important as the Swiss and, later, German patent offices when it came to protecting musical-box inventions and developments. This makes the records of the British Patent Office such a valuable storehouse of musical-box history.

When the Great Exhibition of 1851 was first mooted, not unnaturally the major musical-box makers on the Continent responded by manufacturing special exhibition models which themselves pushed further the ruling technology. By 1870–80, cheapness and mass production were beginning to erode quality and the process was not helped by the arrival of the disc musical box. Because of its time of introduction and its relatively short period of life, the disc machine suffered far less of a character change during its era than did the cylinder box, which was well on the way to decline by the start of the present century. Certainly some makers continued making quality changeables for a while, but the ascendancy of the phonograph completed the task started by the disc box – and killed that off, too.

The First World War effectively marked the end of the musical box. By the end of the war, economic depression, a changed set of values, wireless and the phonograph left little room for the grandeur of either cylinder or disc musical box. Production continued, of course, of the smaller instruments for novelty use but an era was closed.

CHAPTER 3

Miniature Musical Movements

In the preceding chapter we concluded that the miniature musical movement was a Swiss invention and that it probably emanated from Antoine Favre in 1796. We have discussed the likely possibility that the comb-playing musical movement started out in a large and manageable form and then underwent miniaturisation in the hands of the Swiss before it once more became of large size.

The size of some of these miniature pieces and the variety of their styles called for the highest standards of workmanship and yet the finished product, as a musical instrument, was almost never satisfactory due to the sheer smallness of the mechanism. That they played as well as they did is a tribute to the considerable skill that went into their making; that their inferior musical interpretation was acceptable reflects an age when 'recorded' music was unknown and anything which sounded something like a familiar tune was accorded considerable novelty value.

Although hitherto it has been a sort of unwritten classification that these pieces were all of the early epoch, I believe it essential to consider the strong possibility that, although the style was first used at an early date, the technology was not abandoned and, as already indicated in the case of the fan-disc or sur plateau movement, the pieces could have been and probably were produced over a much broader timespan than previously considered.

If Favre invented anything, then he invented the means of making the tuned steel tooth-playing mechanism very tiny indeed and I suspect that, while the pinned cylinder and linear-aligned comb may already have been in existence, Favre was the progenitor of the stacked comb. An examination of very early pieces points to a marked change in design and capability around the end of the eighteenth century and this I attribute to Favre. The stacked comb consisted of separate tuned steel teeth mounted one on top of the other to form a pile or stack which was then secured with a screw and usually two dowel pins. The second significant change was to consider the rotating barrel of the mainspring (the *barillet*) as capable also of being the carrier of the musical programme – the pinned cylinder. Let us re-establish these points in detail.

Miniaturisation demanded compactness of components and this, with the early pieces, invariably meant that the spring barrel of the clockwork motor was also used as the music barrel, the pins for plucking the teeth being arranged in its surface. This system in itself did not constitute an invention coeval with the pinned spring barrel. In fact it is to be found in early miniature bell-playing musicwork and Chapuis* illustrates a musical snuff-box with this type of music made by J. J. Barriere and J. Alaterre in 1768–9. The same source illustrates a five-bell movement of the same type dating from 1780 and preserved in the Count Lamberti collection, Rome.

The arrangement of the tuned steel teeth was possible in three formats, each dictating the shape of the final object into which the musicwork was to be built. The stacked comb, sometimes called the laminated comb because the teeth are stacked one on top of the other rather like the layers in plywood, made possible compact but dimensionally thick installations. Slim, fairly large-diameter musicwork was only possible with the use of a flat, watch-type mainspring driving a disc whose surface was arranged with pins. This was styled the platform or disc movement, *sur plateau* in French, and the teeth could be arranged either as short combs of several united teeth, or as single tuned elements. In the latter case, again there were two types of arrangement possible, both of which arranged the elements in a fan shape. The first played only on one side of the disc, but the second – a veritable watchmaker's *tour de force* – involved playing from pins on both sides of the disc by arranging alternate teeth above and below the disc. The problems involved in making this possible are worth pausing to consider, and it is small wonder that these movements seldom had well-tuned teeth and the music, on the smaller, earlier ones, was often erratic.

Not until after about 1812–15 did the miniature musical movement adopt its stylised, rectangular format with vertical spring barrel at the top left, cylinder along the top edge, governor assembly bottom left and comb in front of the cylinder.

As for the music played, or, indeed, that capable of being played, it was closely related to the size and number of teeth. The musical seal with its stacked comb of maybe only five notes could at the most manage a simple melody such as a jig. One such mechanism has six teeth tuned b, c, d, e, f, g and plays a simple 21-bar tune in 3/4 time, taking just twenty-eight seconds (Fig. 7).

The musical snuff-box was introduced somewhere around the start of the nineteenth century and almost invariably united the work of the finest goldsmith or silversmith, and sometimes the enameller, with the craft of the musicmaker. The finest worked metal case housed the musical movement (which might be of the laminated or stacked-comb variety, the sur plateau or the miniature cylinder) and in the earliest examples this was always hidden out of sight and covered by a case-metal divider or false bottom. The winding-key for these pieces would be inserted through a hole in the underside and, in the finest work, this keyhole would follow the practices adopted by the high-quality watchmakers of the time and be provided with a sliding cover or shield to conceal it when not in use.

Miniature musical movements came to be fitted into many small artefacts such as seals, watches, scent bottles and *objets d'art*. For the wealthy, some extraordinarily fine pieces were produced, uniting the skills of the fine metalworker, enameller and finisher with precious stones ranging from pearls to diamonds. A gold musical vinaigrette is pictured in Plate 7 and equally precious movements were fitted into chatelaines, fans and *nécessaires*.

The changeover from concealed musical movements to the early small musical box began around 1810 as on the one hand the large musical movements fitted into clock bases and on the other the pocket-sized movements went their divergent ways. The small movement became visible when, instead of its being covered by a metal plate, a cover of clear horn was fitted over it allowing space for snuff in the top and permitting the musical movement to be watched.

* *Histoire de la boîte à musique*, figs 120–22.

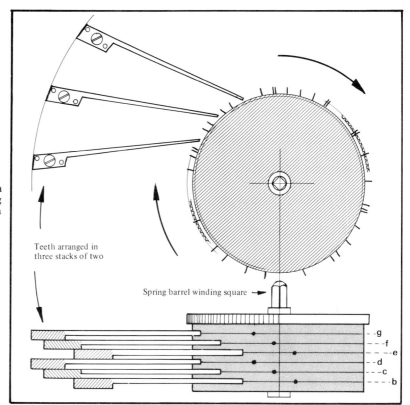

Figure 7 Arrangement of a barillet watch movement having three separate stacks of six teeth in total.

As the art of working tortoiseshell was developed in France and as the market indicated the need for a cheaper snuff-box, so the tortoiseshell snuff-box was introduced. It is not possible to say with certainty when this was, but it seems to have come along during the 1840–50 period. Shortly afterwards, the lids of boxes were decorated with miniature oil paintings in deeply recessed cut-outs rimmed with gold or silver. These paintings attained a high degree of artistry as they were reverse-painted on to glass. The detail on some is extraordinary.

The controls for the cylinder musical snuff-box were very simple. There were usually two small buttons on the front of the box. That on the left, when slid slightly to the right, would set the mechanism running. That on the right changed the tune, two tunes being pinned to the cylinder. The change button was slid a small distance from right to left or vice versa according to the starting position of the mechanism. Unlike the system used in the larger musical box, there was no provision made for preventing the change knob being moved during playing with consequent risk of damage to pins, comb tips and dampers.

At some extremely early point in the development of the miniature cylinder movement, the spring barrel was arranged at right angles to the cylinder arbor so that it could be wound from underneath. There is a possibility that this came about because both the laminated comb and pinned spring barrel type of movement and the sur plateau could be wound from the bottom of whatever type of box they were fitted into.

From the elemental tune change system wherein a forked lever engaged in a protruding rim on the opposite end of the cylinder to the spring, the next development was a simple snail type of change. Because no two-point cam can be made to turn adequately, the snail had a four-point cam and one complete rotation of the snail represented two complete cycles of the cylinder, i.e. 1 = left, 2 = right, 3 = left, 4 = right. Early movements of this type had the change button on the right-hand side of the box and all it did was move a change finger into engagement with the snail in the same manner as in the larger musical movements described in the next chapter. Later on, cheap movements were produced with a fixed change finger so that one tune followed the other with no facility for repeating. These boxes were fitted with only one control button – the stop/start.

Still later, an even simpler tune-changing system was invented. A rectangular steel cam was screwed to the top edge of one of the cylinder bearings so that as the cylinder rotated it could be pressed in contact with the cam by means of the usual cylinder arbor spring. The cam was freely pivoted. At a position corresponding with the end-of-tune position, there was a radial groove filed in the end of the cylinder. This automatically caught the edge of the rectangular cam and caused it to turn through 90°. In this manner, the tune barrel was moved from tune position 1 to 2 and back again without need for control or interference.

Three-air snuff-box movements, although fairly rare, were produced by several makers, among them Nicole, and one variety made by this maker used an unusual arrangement with the snail mounted on the bedplate and operating a cylinder shift lever (see Plate 55).

The governor assembly of the miniature musical movement was another feature to reach its finalised form at a very early stage. It traditionally occupied the space on the bedplate to the left of the comb, immediately in front of the spring barrel, and was driven by the cylinder great wheel which also accommodated the stop detent. Although virtually every early movement made through to those produced at the beginning of this century followed this component juxtaposition, there were a few variations and one movement in the Horngacher-Blyelle collection, while having the governor assembly in the usual place, carries the fan drive shaft horizontally under the comb to the right-hand end.

Much later, Mermod fitted these movements with a horizontally pivoted fan and early twentieth-century pieces dispensed with the governor of brass stock, replacing it with a bracket bent up out of sheet brass.

Early combs were often extremely finely pierced and the compass was considerable. Later on, combs became coarser and cylinder pins thicker as tunes played became thinner and shorter.

Returning to the subject of cases, the so-called Laurencekirk style of all-wood box, usually carved from yew or other hardwood and featuring a solid wooden hinge, was sometimes used. Again, fine florentine mosaic pictures were composed using minerals. The style known as Tonbridge, wherein a picture is formed from narrow slivers of end-grain woods, some dyed, others natural-coloured, was also used for case decoration.

When the French mastered the art of making mouldable plastics out of pieces of surplus horn ground up with lamp black and rubber, it became possible to mould the cases for miniature musical movements. Some of these were very beautifully decorated with titled scenes, allegorical themes or just geometric designs.

Soon, though, the market for pocket-sized musical boxes declined and these small movements came to be used in other objects. Musical chairs, plates, decanters, cigar dispensers and even toilet-roll holders were fitted with music, but perhaps the most popular

Figure 8   The manivelle.

line, and certainly the one which has survived in the greatest quantities today, is the musical photograph album first made about 1865* and still produced a century later. It was Christopher Proudfoot who stumbled quite by chance upon the fact that the firm of John G. Murdoch in London was virtually established on the musical snapshot album and it had many thousands of movements made and stamped with the initials J. G. M. Another line which was extremely popular in Germany at one time was the musical Christmas tree stand invented by J. C. Eckardt. This drove a miniature musical movement as well as a holder into which the tree was clamped, sans roots. No doubt the gyrations of trees produced nausea on top of over-indulgence in the festivities, but surely the end of Eckardt's enterprise must have come with the introduction of Christmas tree lights which demanded that the tree be stationary.

There was one other significant development in small musical movements and this was the invention, in 1857, of the toy instrument – the hand-cranked *manivelle*. This was invented in France by L'Épée who was soon forced to increase his production capacity so great was the

* Friederich Willhelm Bossert of Offenbach am Main, Germany, was granted British Patent number 1919 of 2 August 1864 for a musical movement mounted in the spine of a photograph or scrap album. This style is still occasionally seen today but is nowhere near as prolific as the usual recessed back-cover type, one variant of which is shown in Plate 40 of *Restoring Musical Boxes*.

demand for his new product. Strictly speaking, then, manivelle is a name which should only be applied to L'Épée products. However, today the term is applied to any hand-turned musical movement. Another maker who soon joined the manivelle production scene was Paillard. There were basically two forms of manivelle. The first was the *boîte ronde* or round model, and the other the *boîte carrée*, square or rectangular in shape. These were essentially children's nursery items and the survival of examples is, consequently, the exception to the rule.

The present-day musical-box industry centres fairly well on the making of tiny musical movements. Some manufacturers do this better than others and several make use of automatic comb-tuning techniques which ensure both mass-production volume and tonal quality. Although the modern Swiss musical movement is both well engineered and often extremely fine in quality, the quality and capabilities of the past may never again be equalled.

SQUARE MUSICAL BOXES, with Handle, Superior Quality.

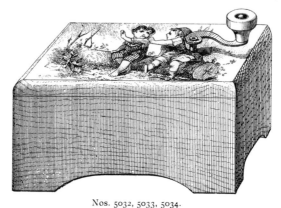

Nos. 5032, 5033, 5034.

Design showing actual size.

Our round and square musical boxes are unrivalled for quality. The prices vary according to the number of tongues.

Numbers.							£	s.	d.
	MUSICAL BOXES, with Handle, 1 Air.								
5030	Square Musical Box, varnished wood, with chromo, 1 air, 12 tongues, per doz.						1	2	0
5031	,,	,,	,,	,,	1 ,, 18	,,	,,	1	6	0
5032	,,	,,	,,	,,	1 ,, 28	,,	,,	1	17	0
5033	,,	,,	,,	,,	1 ,, 36	,,	,,	2	0	0
5034	,,	,,	,,	,,	1 ,, 48	,,	,,	2	16	0
	MUSICAL BOXES, with Handle, 2 Airs.								
5040	Square Musical Box, varnished wood, with chromo, 2 airs, 18 tongues, per doz.						1	15	0
5041	,,	,,	,,	,,	2 ,, 28	,,	,,	2	4	0
5042	,,	,,	,,	,,	2 ,, 40	,,	,,	3	10	0

CHAPTER 4

The Cylinder Musical Box

In Chapter 2 we saw that, according to Jaccard, Switzerland was the cradle of the musical box. This statement is supported by Alfred Chapuis, Edmond Droz, Fredy Baud – in fact all the Swiss chroniclers of the musical box. In the same chapter, I have stated my own belief that the existence of the musical box probably predates its introduction in Switzerland and suggested that prototype examples may go back to around the year 1750. However one chooses to consider this, it remains undeniable that the development and perfection of the cylinder musical box lay with the Swiss and that its formative years centred in an out-of-the-way corner of Alpine Switzerland – the Vallée de Joux close by the Jura Mountains and not too far from the French border. Precision engineering was nothing new to the Jura valley: its villages were already established as important centres of craftsmanship in the watch industry.

Because of the manner in which the industry started in an environment where, initially at any rate, product competition was almost unknown, there was little commercial incentive to vary a manufacturing technique or design style which had been proven mechanically successful. For this reason, the sectional comb remained in use with some makers long after it had ceased to be used by others, and Louis Élisée Piguet was still using radial teeth on sur plateau mechanisms more than half a century after the universal introduction of the pinned-cylinder systems (see page 48).

Not unnaturally, craftsmen jealously guarded their secrets and this had the result of making many musical-box makers consider the benefits of their own invention as a means of achieving a known end, or to 'industrial espionage'. The Swiss craftsmen being honourable workers already in the esteemed profession of watchmaking, until a formalised design became available for all workers to adopt, all early workers made truly unique pieces.

The first use of a one-piece comb is attributed to François Lecoultre, who claimed in a letter to have produced this in Geneva in 1814 although he said he did not produce them in quantity until 1818. Sectional combs were still in wide use until as late as 1830–40 while one small movement which I have examined appears to date from as late as about 1880 and still has this comb characteristic.

With the early miniature musical movements, spring power was let down via a naked pinion and this accounted for a considerable amount of noise during playing. Not until the early years of the nineteenth century was that pinion replaced by a large-diameter fan on the pinion shaft and, later, by an endless screw (worm drive) and proper air-brake.

With the larger pieces, the small clock-type fan or air-brake was discarded in favour of a miniature version of the large fan used on tower clocks and, at this time, on mechanical organs. One reason for this was no doubt the fact that a musical box required a considerably more powerful driving spring than the ordinary timepiece and therefore a more robust fan had to be provided.

According to Chapuis, it was David Lecoultre of Le Brassus who first applied the brass cylinder from the carillon musical clock to the musical box in about the year 1810. Whether or not this is true is hard to verify. Initial small musical movements used pinned spring barrels, playing stacked teeth or from the sur plateau style of system. The Lecoultres were well established as a family of quality watchmakers, so the improvement would not have been beyond the capability of David Lecoultre. The difficulty is in proving (a) that he was the first, and (b) that it had not already been in use elsewhere for some time. With the reservations between makers in the burgeoning years of the industry, nobody can say with certainty on this. David Lecoultre is also said to have been the first to arrange the teeth of his musical box parallel to each other and in one plane as distinct from the superimposed or stacked arrangement.

These dates appear to tie in with the accepted dates of the first musical-box movements of the new genre, which appear to have been produced at some time in the period 1809–12. This date is also corroborated by the style of the fusee-wound clockwork used. To begin with, the power-unit components were built clock-style, in other words they were mounted between rectangular plates with the cylinder pinion being driven by the great wheel of the fusee. Soon, though, the plates were replaced by individual brackets or bearing blocks attached to the bedplate of the mechanism. These styles are characteristic of the early clock-base musicwork and are illustrated in Plates 31 and 32. Another characteristic of the period was the supporting of the cylinder entirely above the bedplate on tall brackets. Only later was it lowered along with the comb, thereby necessitating a suitable cut-out in the bedplate. Earlier, the motor alone required a cut-out to accommodate the added diameter when the chain was fully on the spring barrel.

The arrangement of the musical teeth was also interesting. Possibly in some attempt to equalise the drag on the cylinder pins during playing, the treble notes were initially placed in the centre with the bass notes at each end. The appearance of the tooth arrangement was thus rather like a chevron or inverted letter V. Each single tooth was individually screwed to a brass bar which itself was then screwed to the bedplate. The hollow brass cylinder imparted a tinny tone to the music as some measure of the reaction of the cylinder pin plucking the tooth was fed back into the thin-walled tube in the form of reverberation.

Quite often, the comb of individual or grouped teeth would be supported as much as one inch (25 mm) above the bedplate on a thick brass bar. The bedplate itself was often under $\frac{3}{16}$ in. (4·75 mm) thick.

Another form of tooth arrangement was after the appearance of a zigzag, with the teeth forming three steps each ascending from bass to treble along the cylinder (see Fig. 9).

The carillon clocks from which the cylinder was borrowed were able to play more than one tune and this was achieved by moving the cylinder laterally along its axis a small amount between each tune. To do this, the snail changewheel or cam-starwheel system was used. The musical box used the same system and by moving the cylinder laterally another set of pins could be brought into alignment with the tuned steel comb teeth, allowing the previous set or sets to pass between the tips in silence. Four, six or eight sets of pins could be arranged to play

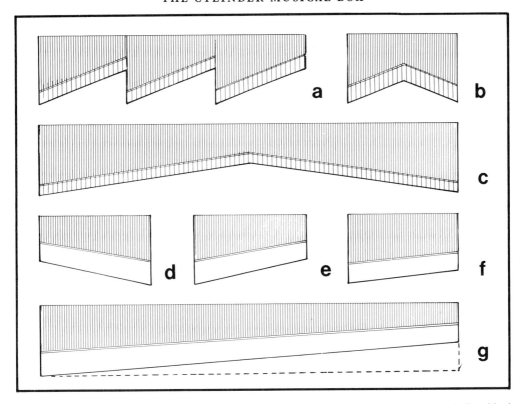

Figure 9 Development of the musical comb. (a) early type of single-tooth comb came in many styles including this zig-zag form; (b) chevron-style sectional comb movement for snuff boxes; (c) chevron-style used on larger musicwork sometimes forms of single teeth or groups of two or more teeth; (d) reversed one-piece comb with bass on right; (e) normal type one-piece comb with bass on left; (f) early one-piece comb with narrow, slender teeth having little difference in length along the comb; (g) normal type of one-piece comb. Dotted outline shows form sometimes used wherein the block of steel from which the comb is cut remains rectangular.

a like number of tunes. In a few early boxes, only three tunes would be played: this is a characteristic of some very early overture boxes by Lecoultre, who apparently experienced difficulty with the close tolerances involved, for he cut grooves in the left-hand end of the cylinder to engage with a small steel guide comb fixed at the back of the bedplate (see Fig. 10). This feature is also found on early three-air and four-air boxes made by François Nicole.

François Lecoultre was responsible, according to Swiss sources, for another important improvement in about 1814 when he found that the pitch of the musical sound produced by a tuned steel tooth could be lowered by attaching a lead weight to the underside of the tooth near the tip. Prior to this, it had for some time been understood that extra weight at the tip of a tooth lowered the musical pitch so, when the tooth was shaped from the solid, extra metal was left under the ends of bass ones. There was, though, a limit to how much metal could be left and this depended on the size of the piece of steel from which the tooth was cut.* Lecoultre's new technique not only made it easier to tune the finished tooth – all one had to

* Since all steels had to be specially made, this metal was both expensive and in short supply.

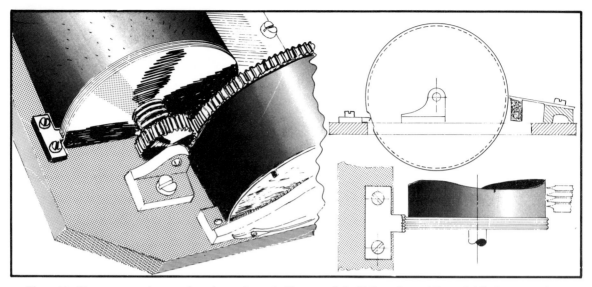

Figure 10   Engagement register comb used on early musical boxes made by F. Lecoultre and François Nicole among others. Comb engaged in grooves round the cylinder end, a suitable blank portion being provided so as to free the cylinder during the tune-changing sequence.

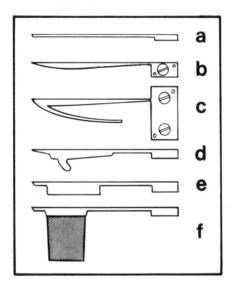

Figure 11   Development of the tuned steel tooth showing how its ability to produce lower and lower musical sounds was perfected. (a) shows a simple, plain tempered tooth; (b) the bellied tooth used by Piguet et Meylan in *sur plateau* movements and also seen in some early cylinder musicwork; (c) the knee-joint tooth cut from a single piece of steel; (d) the early weighted tooth, again all from one piece of steel; (e) one-piece combs in snuff-boxes often had teeth shaped like this in the bass – again machined from the solid; (f) developed form of one-piece comb tooth with lead tuning weight soldered to machined-out thicker portion of tooth.

do was to trim the lead – but it improved the speed of manufacture and also the tone of the finished tooth. The lead weights soon became a feature of all one-piece combs made from that point forward as well as being used on sectional combs (see Fig. 11).

Sustaining the resonance or vibratory period of a tooth was all very well, but it posed other, fresh problems. When the cylinder pin plucked the tooth and set it in vibration, if it was required to vibrate it again before it had naturally subdued its movement, the cylinder pin would contact a moving tooth and produce a disagreeable buzzing sound. While this would not show up in slow music, it was a serious drawback with faster melodies.

There had to be some method of stopping the vibration of a tooth just before it was time to pluck it again. The solution was to fit each tooth point with a tiny mute in the form of a piece of feather quill secured to it with shellac. The cylinder pin would make its first contact not with the vibrating tip but with the softer quill beneath it, push this against the tip and thus kill the vibration more or less silently the instant before it was lifted to be plucked a second time.

The quill mute had its disadvantages. While it was adequate for the treble teeth – in fact the extreme treble teeth vibrated for too short a period to need any form of muting at all – the heavier bass teeth with their extra weight soon took their toll of the quill which rapidly wore away, allowing the muteless tooth buzz to sound again.

The better-class Swiss makers were soon at work on this problem and in 1814 – quite a momentous year for improvements in the cylinder musical box – François Nicole of Geneva is said to have been the first to apply the hairspring damper made of flat-sectioned steel wire. This was a very fine curled piece of steel which fitted into a socket just under and behind the tooth point. The cylinder pin touched this first and gently pushed it against the tooth tip prior to plucking, so effectively silencing it from its previous plucking. The spring wire for dampers was made in a number of thicknesses so that heavy bass teeth could use thicker wire than the slender treble ones. Wire dampers were used from that time forward in almost unchanged form. Around 1840, experiments were made using brass wire dampers on overture boxes, but these tests were short-lived. Very occasionally today one of these is found and it can be seen that the brass has proven more embrittled with age than steel. Small snuff-box-type movements remained quill-damped, or sometimes strips of fine parchment were used. Rarely one finds a snuff-box with wire dampers – Lecoultre made these for a time in the early period. Styles of damper are shown in Figure 12.

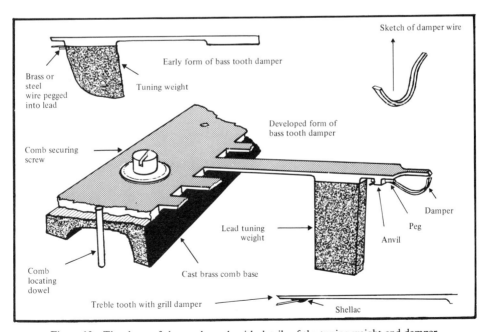

Figure 12 The shape of the comb tooth with details of the tuning weight and damper.

Musical snuff-boxes with brass cylinders, as distinct from movements with pinned spring barrels, were made from about 1810 or 1815 onwards and these were fitted into gold, silver or tortoise-shell boxes (see previous chapter).

The first proper musical box factory in Switzerland is said not to have been founded until as late as 1875 by the Paillard company at Ste-Croix.* Prior to this, the industry was carried out almost exclusively by workers in their own homes. One would be responsible for making pinions, another gears, and so on. The delicate and eye-taxing task of cylinder pinning was entrusted to women or even young children and the frightening thought of having to perform this task for a long working day is bad enough, but in the winter the short daylight period meant that oil-lamp light had to be used. No wonder old watchmakers and musical box makers are always portrayed wearing spectacles! The actual pins for cylinder pinning were prepared on a special pin lathe which took a length of wire and automatically notched it every $\frac{1}{4}$ in. (5 mm) or so, so that it could be readily snapped off after insertion. It also produced a tapered end to insert into the hole. In these early days, the pin wire used was very thin and quite brittle, so much so that it is today almost impossible to straighten a bent pin without breaking it off. Later on, somewhat thicker and softer wire was used. Whereas most Swiss boxes used pins which protruded about 1·5 mm from the cylinder, a few makers favoured ever shorter pins, while Austrian makers usually went for much longer pin protrusion – often more than 2 mm. This effectively increased the diameter of the cylinder and thus its playing time.

The next major improvement came about 1825 and was again attributed to François Nicole, who found that if the pinned cylinder was filled with a binding resin or cement it gave weight to the thin brass tube, held steady the cylinder pins and, most important of all, improved the tone appreciably.

There were many makers and all built boxes of quality, certainly in the early days. Programmes up to around 1850 tended to be centred on the classical repertoire with operatic music. However, some of the popular ballads of the early nineteenth century are also to be found, such as *She Wore a Wreath of Roses*, *Fly Not Yet*, and similar once-popular melodies. The box which played all hymn tunes was also popular at this time and it was not until after the middle of the century, with the growth and development of the music-hall and its music, that popular songs came to take the important part which they did in the 'middle-to-lower class' of musical boxes. The first real music-hall was the Canterbury, opened in London's Westminster Bridge Road in 1849. Within a dozen years this new means of mass entertain-

---

* Quoting from the publication on the history of the horological and musical box industries published by the Swiss Office for the Development of Trades:

The growing demands of foreign markets were met by the organisation for large-scale production of the industry which had previously been carried out in the home. The first factory was established in 1875 by E. Paillard & Co, one of the largest Sainte Croix firms. From that time on, the number of factories grew steadily and machinery replaced handwork in increasingly great proportions. The creation in 1878 of a model equipped with interchangeable cylinders opened a wide market for Jura district manufacturers.

It is interesting that the facts concerning the date of the interchangeable cylinder box are here confused, but what is particularly interesting is the wording of the second sentence, since the first factory for the making of production musical boxes must undoubtedly have been that begun in 1839 by Auguste L'Épée at Sainte-Suzanne, France. In 1845, this factory had thirty workers and the business expanded steadily up to its pillage in the Franco-Prussian war of 1870. Restarted after the end of the hostilites, by 1878 it had more than 350 employees.

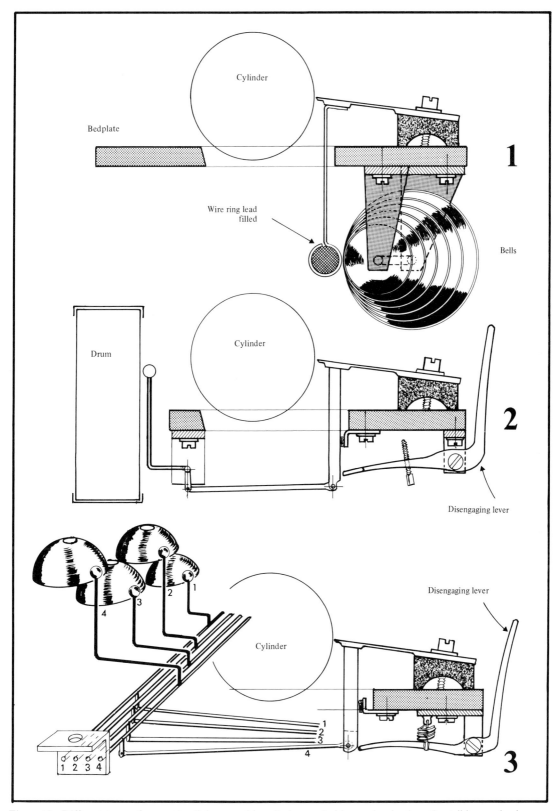

Figure 13 Different types of percussion linkage used in cylinder musical boxes showing how the striking mechanism was improved from the early form, which could not strike very hard, to the roller-bar style. Early styles of Type 1 also used clock-type bell hammers held to the wire rods with set-screws.

ment had caught on in a big way and soon afterwards the demand for popular music-hall tunes from London formed a major diet for instruments made for the British market.

Multiple-tune cylinders came in during the late 1840 period and some could play thirty or more tunes per single cylinder, a feature made possible by pinning three tunes per revolution so that each tune took up nominally one third of a revolution. Nicole Frères made a number of 'two-tunes-per-turn' boxes which usually played popular music, occasionally operatic in nature. Bremond and Lecoultre were others to make this type, along with three-tunes-per-turn boxes between 1850 and 1860. These were, however, not considered a great success.

In the beginning, all the early boxes had cast brass bedplates which were then polished smooth. Cast iron came into use as early as 1875 for boxes made by Paillard and Mermod. Others, such as Nicole Frères, Bremond and Lecoultre, continued to use polished brass for some while. The cast-iron bedplates invariably had a ribbed upper surface which was cast sufficiently accurately to require the minimum of finishing. One problem encountered with brass was the difficulty of avoiding blemishes in the casting such as inclusions and blow-holes. For miniature movements, particularly those of the type used in snuff-boxes, musical photograph albums and so on, cast brass was not superseded until comparatively modern times when a zinc alloy came into use.

Mermod Frères, Mojon Manger, and Paillard were among those who, at various times, adopted the nickel plating of all parts. Gilbert Alfred Cassagnes was granted a British Patent number 1282 of 25 March 1876 for the application by electro-deposition of nickel on musical-box parts. The plating did not detract from the mechanism and had the added merit of not tarnishing as quickly as brass. On cylinders, though, it tended eventually to peel off as a result of corrosion of the steel pins affecting the bond between plating and brass in the immediate vicinity. Nicole Frères actually experimented with silver plating at one time – but this was hardly a success for the silver tarnished quicker and more thoroughly than the brass beneath. Silver was used, however, for tune sheets on very special boxes and for this use it was usually lacquered.

By the mid-1840s, the cylinder musical box had been almost fully developed as a musical interpreter and there was hardly anything which could not be set upon its cylinder. Seeking to extend the market for the instrument, makers began experimenting with different tonal effects. One of the earliest was the mandoline style – these are detailed in the next chapter. Frederick William Ducommun Girod was making very good mandoline boxes in the 1850s, as were Nicole Frères, Lecoultre, Bremond and Paillard. The true mandoline box had upwards of ninety teeth although some had more than double that number.

One of the most effective of all styles was the forte-piano, which was introduced in 1840 by Nicole Frères and which, with its capability of playing soft and loud, was accorded many exhibition awards. The zenith of forte-piano mechanism was the mandoline forte-piano, another Nicole Frères invention. David Langdorff also produced a 4-air combination piano-forte mandoline movement with a 15 in. (381 mm) cylinder.

Next in line came the sublime harmonie with its tonal reinforcement of two combs being played simultaneously.

If Favre described his invention of the musical box as 'a carillon without bells', then the next step might well be seen as a retrograde one, for by 1845 musical boxes were being built which included drum and bell accompaniment. To begin with, these accessories were hidden out of sight underneath the bedplate but soon it was realised that they were an added sales aid, particularly if they could be seen. The hidden drum and bell accompaniment now

68

became a visible addition with the bells aligned at the back of the cylinder. Early striking linkages were made by attaching the hammers to simple rods soldered on to the underneath of special comb teeth which served only to operate the percussion effects. Later on, a much improved linkage was perfected which allowed the hammers to strike the bells much harder and thereby produce more sound. A simple roller or torsion bar of metal was provided for each bell horizontally under the bedplate and parallel to the cylinder. From one end a linkage went to the special bell tooth, by now forming part of its own special comb which could be raised off or lowered on at will and to which it was attached by a pin to a brass block soldered under the tooth. From the other end a hammer rod was fixed so that the bell could be struck. The hammers were thus properly poised and worked much better. Having such visible additions, the bell strikers were frequently embellished and decorated. Most popular was the making of them in the shape or form of butterflies or bees. Figure 13 refers.

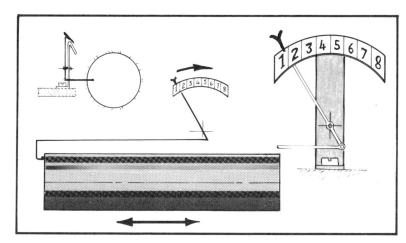

Figure 14   Tune indicators came in many styles: this one shows the principles of most and the detail of Bremond in particular. Bremond always used this shape of arrow. On one style, the tune-sheet is mounted inside the box behind the cylinder and the pointer moves up and down the side pointing to the air being played.

In another style used by makers such as Paillard and Nicole, the bells were struck by 'maces' held in the hands of seated mandarins at the back of the box. When disengaged, the mandarins would look down but when the bells were brought into play, they would look up, maces at the ready, and nod each time they struck a bell, one from each hand.

In the early mechanisms with hidden drum and bell effects, the drum usually had a thin brass skin and a semi-tubular metal appendage which served as a resonator – to allow for the fact that the hammers which served as drumsticks moved only a very small amount. The visible drum, on the other hand, had a thin parchment skin and a wire snare.

The percussion effects were completed by the provision of a castanet formed from a hollowed-out hardwood block struck, like the drum, by a series of hammers in rapid succession.

These additional effects were brought into play from special short combs mounted at each end of the musical comb and operated by special pins at the end of the cylinder. Often these pins were no different from ordinary cylinder pins, but on some mechanisms they are of a slightly thicker wire. The special combs outwardly resemble normal musical combs but in fact they are not tempered in the same way and are of slightly thinner, more springy and

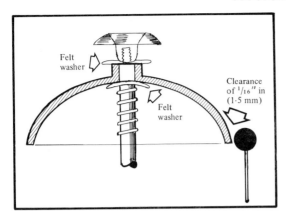

Figure 15   Setting up musical box bells so that they sound properly.

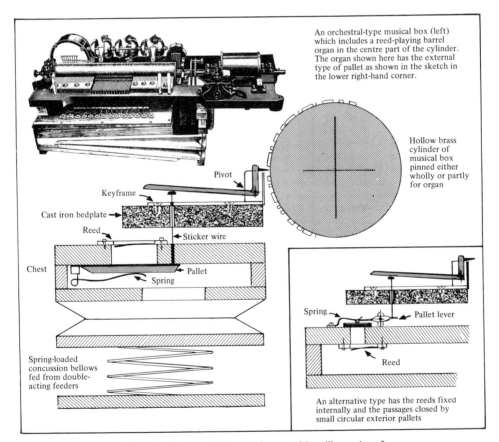

Figure 16   The musical box reed organ with an illustration of the Mermod Orchestral instrument, top left.

flexible material. Disengagement of the effect was achieved by the use of a lever which bends up the tooth tips clear of the cylinder pins.

The flutina or reed organ which was added to the comb-playing musical box was apparently the invention of Louis Ducommun in 1861, according to evidence found by Pierre Germain.* However, Louis Auguste Grosclaude, a maker of quality musical boxes in the late 1870s, attributes this invention to a collaboration between Ducommun and Kimmerling. Certainly I have the feeling that the specimen which I have seen bearing the name Ducommun predates 1861.

The number of reeds used was usually 14 in the smaller ones but up to 24 or even 36 in larger and more expensive models. Bremond was one maker who produced some very fine small organ-boxes, as indeed was Heller of Berne, Nicole Frères and Langdorff. George Baker made a fine series of very large boxes some of which featured a large lever for drawing the organ keys back from the cylinder, so leaving just the combs in play. This they styled 'Full Orchestra' and it was musically a fine instrument. In another variety, besides the eighteen reed notes would be provided a rank of fourteen small wooden organ pipes. The organ played the air while the musical combs and the percussion effects provided the accompaniment. John Clark relates that these were very fine pieces and were also very expensive. This type was exhibited widely at various exhibitions and world fairs as examples of top-quality Swiss workmanship and, although they did not apparently find much favour in England, they were sold in large numbers to customers from Persia, India and China. In one season, probably 1895–6, over 1,000 of these large organ-accompaniment boxes were ordered for Persia alone. The makers contrived to have music pinned which was indigenous to the country of sale and one complex box, supplied by Gueissaz Frères of La Sagne, a district of Chaux-de-Fonds, was made for the Shah of Persia and played Persian music. This piece was completed in April 1896, just one month before its recipient was murdered near Teheran. The man who produced the arrangements of foreign music for the Ste-Croix musical-box makers was a musician and cylinder pricker named Octave Felician Chaillet who later left Switzerland to work for the Regina Music Box Company in Rahway, New Jersey.

George Bendon produced full organ boxes with no comb at all, only organ reeds sounded by means of keys moved by pins and bridges in the brass cylinder. It is thought that Paillard made a similar series, and about 1880 Bremond produced a full organ box of this type which had interchangeable cylinders. The actual reed organ appeared in two distinct styles. In the early examples, the reeds were single, accordion-type ones mounted inside a pressure wind chest. The air passage linking the reed with the atmosphere was covered with a simple spring-loaded pallet like a clarinet key. The key tails were all arranged in a line and were pressed down by stickers from the organ keys. In the later style, the reeds were mounted externally on the pressure chest and the air passage closed by an internal pallet which was opened by stickers from the organ keys. This produced a louder, clearer sound. The so-called *voix célestes* used double reeds which were tuned to a rapid beat. Bremond, Langdorff and, later, Greiner, were most prolific makers of this type.

While the majority of voix céleste mechanisms used double reeds for each note which comprised a single brass frame with two cutouts for the two side-by-side vibrators, some preferred the complexity of having two separate reeds. Ami Rivenc used this to brilliant advantage on one style of large orchestral box produced about 1875–85. Whereas Baker fitted

* See *The Music Box*, vol. 7, p. 60.

a lever to draw the organ back away from the combs so effectively 'switching it off' (he was the only maker to provide this facility),* Rivenc provided a cartouche plate over the organ which had two levers connected to control rods beneath. The first was to silence the organ by the simple expedient of bleeding the contents of the air reservoir through a spill-valve. The second was marked 'Single flute' and 'Celestial voices' and blanked off the second reed air passage for each note to provide either the single, firm sound, or the double sound with the beat created by the slightly different tuning of the second reed.

These organ boxes all derived their wind power from bellows beneath the bedplate. With the early models, the bellows were of the so-called French feeder type in which there is a fixed upper board and a fixed lower board at an angle of about 30° between which is pivoted a feeder arranged to compress wind on both its upward and downward strokes. The reservoir was hinged to the lower board so that when fully open it was parallel with the top board. Later, see-saw bellows were used in which a spring-loaded central reservoir is fed from a centrally pivoted feeder which can compress wind in each half. The feeder was pumped by a brass rod or reciprocator attached eccentrically to a large brass wheel attached to an extension of the arbor of one of the wheels in the gear train or escapement. A parallel reservoir is centrally mounted on top with a coiled compression spring applying pressure.

The bellows needed so much power to drive them that very large clockwork motors had to be used to operate the mechanism and even so these movements only produced enough wind to play the music required. The slightest wear or maladjustment therefore drastically affected their performance. One large piece by Langdorff & Fils c. 1884, and which has a 41-note organ, has large double feeders worked from two eccentrics either side of the drive wheel.

Musical boxes were extremely expensive luxuries even for the well-to-do. And they suffered from the main drawback in that, apart from their high cost, they only played the tunes which they had been originally built to play. During the 1850s, experiments were being made by a number of makers in an endeavour to overcome this shortcoming. The goal was to make it possible to exchange the cylinder in the mechanism for another with different music. Interchangeable cylinders demanded a high standard of accuracy plus fine manufacturing tolerances in the making of the components. The location of the components became critical, for the slightest misplacement would spoil the music or cause the comb teeth to fall off the cylinder pins and probably pick up two tunes at once.

The first changeable cylinder boxes were indeed somewhat crude mechanisms (see p. 113). However, they were soon to attain the stature of the sublime combination of musical perfection and variety of repertoire, a position the type sustained until the invention of the disc musical box in the late 1880s. Amédée Paillard's invention of the Revolver musical box in 1870 (see next chapter) was an attempt to cream off some of the changeable-cylinder musical-box market, but failed because the mechanisms were costly to produce and infinitely more complex. Nevertheless, the revolver mechanism was also taken up by Nicole Frères, under whose name a few of these large, extremely heavy and very costly boxes were sold. In all, not very many were made and, although they are much sought after by collectors, they are not musically other than average.

---

* Since this was written, an unusual orchestral musical box has been seen which has two organs mounted side by side and both fitted with retracting levers. The first is provided with an abbreviated octave of bass reeds to double those on the main reed organ. This box has a tune sheet marked D. Allard & Co. (see item 3 in Appendix II) although it bears certain Baker characteristics.

72

Largest of all the musical boxes was the *Grand Format*, first introduced about 1882 and fitted with cylinders ranging from 18 to 33 in. long and from 4½ to 6 in. in diameter. Nicole Frères and Heller made a number of these, and some Lecoultre examples were even larger and had all the orchestral accompaniments as well. These last mentioned were up to six feet in length and looked not unlike ornate coffins.

At the International Exhibition of 1861–2, Paillard of Ste-Croix displayed an elaborate and ambitious changeable-cylinder musical box which had six cylinders which were 'telescopic' and expanded while the music was playing. The cylinders each revolved six times non-stop to play one tune. Fully expanded, the cylinders were 20 in. long. This was the *plerodiénique* box (see next chapter). The system was invented by Albert Jeanrenaud of Ste-Croix, although it was not patented until 1882.

George Baker of Geneva, formerly partner in Baker-Troll, was making some very high-quality overture boxes towards the mid-1880s and about this time introduced the *Duettino* movement which had a piccolo comb and so-called *tremolo* formed from the mandoline-like repetition of the musical theme. The piccolo comb had sixteen teeth and sounded the octave to the melody. This was one of the many endeavours to extend the capability of the musical-box comb and its tonality during this period. Many of these styles of movement are listed in the next chapter.

There were numerous attempts to produce musical boxes which could play for long periods without rewinding. The first, and most obvious, was to produce a longer and more powerful spring to drive the movement. This was not quite so easy as it at first may appear, so the next best solution was adopted – coupling spring motors together in series. Paillard produced such a box in the 1880s which they claimed was: 'Guaranteed to run for ninety minutes'. A fellow with the name of Timoleon Zoe Louis Maurel was granted a patent for an apparatus in 1858[*] for 'protracting indefinitely the working of a mechanism set in motion by springs such as . . . a musical box'. Smacking of perpetual motion, Maurel's motion seems not to have been sustained. John William Wignall was granted another patent[†] for a 'musical box automatically played by a descending weight rewound by a galvanic battery when descended'. Aubert & Son, through agent A. Browne, was granted a patent on 16 September 1879 for gearing a musical box so that it would go for a long time without rewinding when used in a clock. Four years or so earlier, Nicole Frères were making musical boxes having four spring barrels interconnected by a system of gearing. This mechanism would play for three hours on one winding. The main drive wheel was so large that it protruded through the bottom of the bedplate into the void beneath. This was the forerunner of the *Longue Marche* style patented by A. Karrer of Teufenthal in 1886.[‡]

The influence of the new science of electricity was demonstrated by the invention in 1881 by J. G. Dudley of a means of driving a musical box 'by means of an electromotor' and J. G. Lorrain went to great lengths to devise a method of storing energy to wind a musical box by an 'electromotor' in 1888. Fortunately, electrically powered cylinder musical boxes were more of a passing fad than a serious challenge to the clockwork motor and, although exhibition pieces were made with electric power, particularly some large and attractive mechanisms accompanied by dancing dolls which were at one time to be found on many of

[*] British Patent No. 3002, 31 December 1858.
[†] British Patent No. 1442, 25 April 1874.
[‡] British Patent No. 9024, 10 July 1886.

the Swiss railway stations for the entertainment of would-be travellers, they remain, happily, extremely rare. Not that the spring motor was threatened solely by electricity: besides Wignall's British patent referred to in the previous paragraph for a weight-driven musical box, the weight re-wound by 'galvanic battery', Henry A. Gautschi of Philadelphia was granted U.S. Patent number 476458 of 7 June 1892, for a musical box powered by a vacuum motor – a long U-shaped tube with a tight-fitting piston. No examples of any of these are known.

The first attempt at providing a positive means of indicating which tune on the tune sheet was actually being played was probably that of Henry Harburg who, in 1869, was granted a British patent number 593 for a tune indicator comprising a horizontal panel behind the cylinder containing a slot. Beneath this was mounted a small drum having the names of the tunes played printed in different type-faces on its surface. This drum was rotated to show a different title as the cylinder shifted by means of a hooked rod which was pushed by the end of the cylinder itself. When the programme was completed, a spring drew the rod and the tune-indicating drum back to the position of the first tune played. The following month, on 27 March, Abram and Jean Jaquillard were granted a patent (British number 932) for a combined tune indicator and selector. In the years which followed, both became features of musical boxes until the point when even cheap-quality boxes were so provided with one. Bremond at one time had a most attractive style wherein the actual tune-sheet was mounted behind the cylinder and, as the cylinder shifted, so a small finger pointer moved up and down the side of the sheet, pointing to the title being played.

Whereas many boxes had tune indicators, tune selectors were usually fitted only to the very best. By the mid-1880s, Mermod had combined the tune indicator and selector into one assembly which fitted on the end of the cylinder so that all the operator had to do was to turn a knob until the pointer of the indicator showed the tune of his choice. The mechanism was purely a means of rotating the change snail by hand. Tune indicators are illustrated in Figure 14.

One of the most controversial attachments provided for the musical box was the so-called timbre, also known by such erroneous soubriquets as zither, mandoline, celesta and sour-dine. In truth it is an addition which produces neither the sound of the zither nor of any of the other apparently similar instruments. However, a good zither on a box fitted with the right sort of percussive-toned comb (such as a *Fortissimo*) did prove that occasionally an interesting sound could be produced from the thing. It comprised a roll of thin tissue paper carried in a moveable rail which could be brought to press down on the vibrating comb teeth to produce a buzzing sound. Probably the invention of Amédée Paillard (his name and that of Alfred Sueur appear on the earliest traceable patent dated 1886), it was first supposed to operate on the underside of the comb – a system used on the small *Symphonion* disc machines produced later on. However, the obvious complication involved in trying to place the zither in a suitable position amidst the under-tooth lead weights and dampers, no doubt influenced by the psychology of selling a visible accessory, soon dictated that the device be mounted on top of the comb. Very soon, nearly every maker fitted these things. Some were cheap, nasty and detrimental to the music. The general opinion today is that they detract from the quality of the box and, indeed, repairers and dealers have long since become adept at discarding them. It is not suggested that this be done today, only that the zither be treated with reserve. Of course, some zithers can be pleasing, particularly those which can be lowered carefully and gradually by means of a thumb screw to vary the degree of contact with the teeth. If your

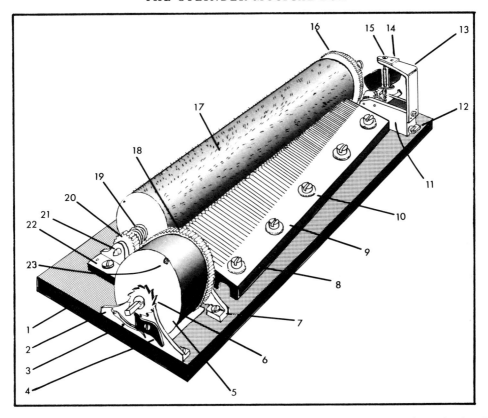

Figure 17   The parts of a simple, key-wound musical movement. 1. bedplate; 2. outer motor attachment bracket; 3. click spring to pawl; 4. ratchet pawl or click; 5. spring motor barrel; 6. ratchet wheel on spring arbor; 7. inner motor attachment bracket; 8. comb base; 9. comb; 10. comb attachment screw and washer; 11. governor assembly; 12. adjustable bottom bearing for air-brake; 13. cock (bracket) to support upper end of endless; 14. jewel or cock plate; 15. jewel, garnet or endstone; 16. great wheel fixed to cylinder arbor; 17. cylinder; 18. spring barrel wheel; 19. compression spring to hold cylinder against tune-change snail; 20. cylinder drive pinion; 21. cylinder arbor; 22. bracket supporting cylinder arbor; 23. oil slot in spring barrel lid.

musical box suffers from poor or non-existent dampers, then the constant use of the zither can prove highly beneficial for it will camouflage the defect admirably.

I should perhaps add that the cheap box used the zither as an added sales gimmick, the zither really doing nothing for the music itself. However, on the quality box, zither attachments could be used to pleasing advantage, enhancing the music. Whereas most zithers were either 'on' or 'off' via a simple lever, some were adjustable via a thumb-screw to allow the effect on the comb sound to be varied. The fully automatic zither, brought on and off according to the positioning of special zither-controlling bridges near the cylinder centre, was introduced in the 1880s but the obvious complexity of the system precluded general use. Automatic zithered musical boxes are thus rare, and, where found, generally indicate quality.

The Swiss musical-box industry had many pressures upon it to reduce costs in order to combat competition from France and elsewhere. The coming of the German disc machine increased the sense of urgency with which makers sought acceptable production short cuts.

Manufacturers such as Paillard and Mermod spearheaded a design campaign to eliminate many of the costly and lengthy processes in production and the first major step came in the early 1880s with the perfection of cylinder reproduction for the cheaper boxes, this dispensing with the lengthy process of pricking each cylinder individually.

Next came the integral casting of cylinder arbor supports as part of the bedplate. This was the work of Edmund Fornachon of La Mothe, near Verdun in Switzerland, and was the subject of British Patent No. 6972 of 24 May 1886. This one move not only saved the casting and finishing of the two brass trunnions but eliminated the time-consuming alignment during fitting to the bedplate.

It was only a matter of time before a similar process was applied to the attachment of the motor. First to do this was Paillard, who cast both spring arbor supports integrally with the bedplate, but it was Mermod who first adopted the system whereby the bearing for the spring barrel arbor was only supported on one side by a long bearing-block. By positioning the escapement so that it was actually driven by the spring-barrel great wheel, and by placing that great wheel close to the arbor-bearing face, not only were parts and their fitting saved but also the former close tolerances ceased to be needed. In fact, working tolerances of hitherto unheard of latitude were now admissible. The cylinder no longer required a precise relationship to the driving motor and the spring barrel rotated it by means of an offset driving-peg which engaged in a fork or yoke projecting radially from an extension to the cylinder arbor.

A simplified escapement or train was devised, largely comprising pressed-out or shear-cut components. The stop/start control also became a simple, pressed-out low-tolerance part.

The man responsible for many of these improvements was Louis Campiche, one of Mermod Frères's workers, whose name appears on many patents.

One extremely interesting departure was the abandonment of the form of starwheel and face-cam tune-changing mechanism. The production of this one part was among the most complex of the entire musical box and its setting up called for fitting skills of a high order to ensure that star-point and face-cam combined in the proper position with the height and penetration of the change finger.

Mermod's system dispensed with all this and replaced it with a vastly simplified yet extremely effective system, the key feature of which was a stamped-out steel cam mounted at right angles to the cylinder arbor in such a way that the edge of the cam rested on the edge of the end of the cylinder (see Fig. 27). The cam was prevented from unwanted rotation by physical contact with a simple change/repeat lever, and by a strip-steel spring which pressed against its face. This strip-steel spring also had at its end a projecting arm which could ride just clear of the end of the cylinder surface, held in that position by the in-and-out positioning of the tune-change cam. However, around part of the circumference of the cylinder was situated a raised portion of sufficient size that as the cylinder rotated it could lift the spring clear of the change cam by means of the projecting arm on the spring.

If the change/repeat lever was now set to 'change', this cam would be free to rotate and, as a small radial gulley in the cylinder end contacted the cam, it would now turn, so impelling the cylinder laterally just sufficient for another tune's pins to align with the comb tooth tips. Once again, manufacturing tolerances on this part were much more than on the conventional snail and face-cam.

◄ PLATE 1

An example of the 'added-on' type of musical movement. Although original and coeval with the construction of the clock, the carillon mechanism is arranged at right-angles to the spring barrel and drive wheels of the clock itself. Made in Amsterdam by Allin P. Walker, this 17-bell mechanism is played by 28 hammers.

▼ PLATE 2

A similar, but later mechanism is this London-made clock with 12 bells struck by 21 hammers, each with a hairpin-shaped flat steel spring. Again the musicwork is of the added-on type and driven at right-angles to the clock wheelwork, and once again it is behind the rear plate of the clock. Particularly unusual is the fact that the tune-changing is achieved by moving the whole keyframe sideways while the barrel stays in one place.

◄ PLATE 3

General view of the carillon clock shown in Plate 2. The case, designed by architect Norman Shaw, features a red leather front. Ten popular tunes are played, selection being by turning the tune indicator at the top. A cam wheel moves the keyframe into the desired position.

◄ PLATE 4
Carillon clock made in London by John Taylor.
Fusee-wound and with the musicwork fitted
effectively between the plates and driven in line
with the clock wheelwork, this form of construction
offered far greater precision and a minimum of
backlash in the gearing – a necessity in view of the
considerably greater diameter of the cylinder than
its drive wheel.

PLATE 5 ►
Side-on view of the Taylor clock showing the simplicity of the
12-bell mechanism using only one hammer per bell. The
barrel penetrates the rear plate and is supported on a heavy
cock bracket itself fitted with a dependent bracket carrying a
flat spring pressing on the protruding barrel arbor. This, plus
the width of the barrel drive wheel, clearly shows that it is the
barrel which is shifted in order to change the tune, four of
which are played.

▲ PLATE 6
The limitations of the miniature carillon of bells are
clearly seen in this picture of a fine musical table watch
in an oval, silver-enamelled case. The very flat stack of
nested bells is seen arranged vertically at the left. From
a mechanical standpoint, this means that the hammers
must work in a horizontal plane and must be
spring-cocked.

▲ PLATE 7
A very small gold vinaigrette
dating from about 1805.
Intended to carry a small
sponge steeped in aromatic oils
as a sort of 'smelling salts'
container, this contains a tiny
going-barrel or barellette
musicwork.

◄ PLATE 8
The musicwork of the
vinaigrette in Plate 7. Ten
stacked teeth form the music
from the pinned spring barrel
whose speed is roughly
regulated by a wheel train and
a bare pinion. The stop finger
works in the middle of the
barrel's width.

◄ PLATE 9
Really miniature musicwork – two tiny musical watch keys in two shades of gold highly ornamented and richly enamelled. Each plays one simple tune and, like many other sub-miniature pieces, it is difficult to identify recognisable music on either.

▼ PLATE 10
Sub-miniature cylinder movement in recognisable format, probably used in a musical key or scent bottle. Surprisingly the cylinder plucks the teeth downwards.

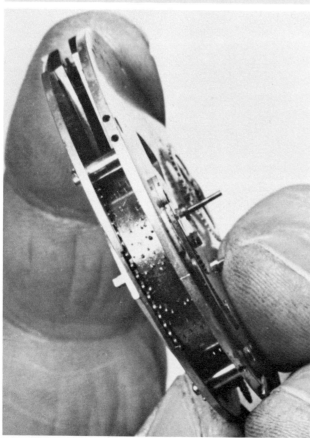

▲ PLATE 11
Rare barillet musical watch made by Henri Capt showing the pinning for the six tuned steel teeth fitted to each plate – they are just visible at the top.

PLATE 12 ►
Teeth tips by the large-diameter pinned barrel. Individual teeth screw holes and locating dowels form two rows above.

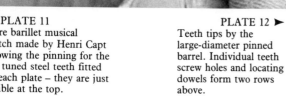

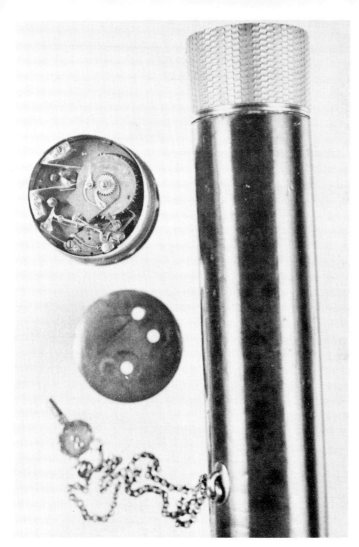

◀ PLATE 13
A most rare musical walking stick, one of only two known. The two stacks of tuned steel teeth can be seen in engagement with the pinned spring barrel. Winding is through the hole in the top plate.

▲ PLATE 14
Early sur plateau movement using a surface-pinned disc and two short combs. In the lower picture can be seen how the tooth tips hook down to engage.

▼ PLATE 15
Nine stacked teeth produce the music on this going-barrel movement. Note the primitive tuning weights on the tooth tips to lower the note pitch.

◄ PLATE 16
Musical watch with sur plateau movement of the type used by Piguet for many years. Two tunes are played by moving the disc, which has a different pin pattern on each side, up or down.

▼ PLATE 17
Detail view of the sur plateau movement showing how, although all the teeth are individually screwed on the one plate, alternate ones are cranked over the disc to engage the upper surface pins.

◄ PLATE 18
Formerly in the Tulace collection of Egypt and King Farouk and pictured here with the aid of a mirror is a Piguet et Meylan gold enamelled snuff-box of about 1810.

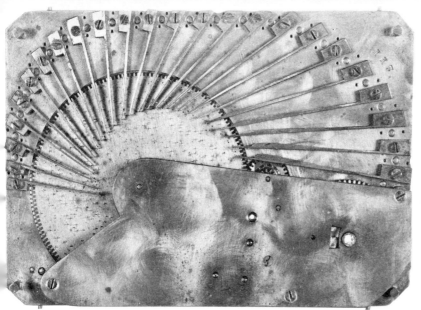

◄ PLATE 21
This Piguet et Meylan sur plateau movement is only fractionally over ¼ in. (5 mm) in thickness, yet it plays two tunes and has 24 teeth on one side and 23 on the other – the screw holes and two locating dowels for each tooth on the other side of the plate can be seen between the fixing screws for the top teeth.

▼ PLATE 22
In this view of another Piguet et Meylan piece (note mark in top right corner) can be seen the flat spring used to move the two-tune disc up and down.

PLATE 19
...ver-gilt snuff-box hall-marked 1814 ...d fitted with a single-tune Piguet-style ...ovement. It plays the tune 'A Sailor's ...ornpipe'.

PLATE 20
...tail of the musical movement which is ...essible through the bottom of the box. ...ere are 20 teeth and, as in all ...vements of this style, the pins pluck ...teeth by moving them sideways so ...t they vibrate in the same plane as the ...:.

PLATE 23 ►
...sical patch-box turned out of ...twood and containing a superb ...gle-tune sur plateau movement shown ...letail overleaf.

◀ PLATE 24
Dating from about 1804, this patch-box movement plays one tune using teeth which are set on either side of the plate and play from pins set on both sides of the disc. There is a total of 25 teeth, the long, bass ones having bellied bodies which serve to lower the pitch of their sounds. These are altogether most complex examples of the watchmaker's art and precision.

▼ PLATES 25 & 26
Musical watch dating from about 1880 and made in the best traditions of the early musicwork using a small cylinder movement. Thirty-one teeth play two tunes, the pinned barrel being shifted laterally to change the tune.

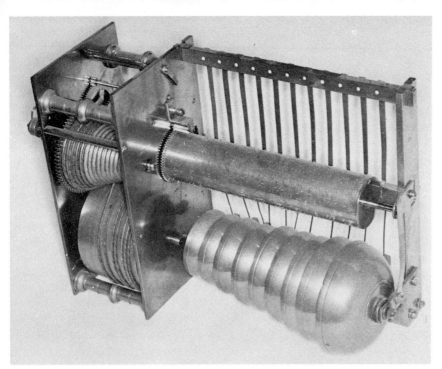

◄ PLATE 27
Fusee-wound carillon mechanism
from a clock showing the early
evolution of a detachable,
separately-powered musical
mechanism with the cylinder driven
in line with the drive wheelwork via a
simple pinion and wheel, in this case
the wheel of the fusee. Dating from
about 1780, 11 hammers play on nine
bells. The music is played after the
clock has struck the hour by means of
a detent which frees the music
clockwork. The earliest carillon clock
to survive is that made by the
Fleming, Nicolaas Vallin in 1598.

PLATE 28 ►
Clock-base musicwork with an
unusual zig-zag comb
arrangement. The teeth, each
screwed on individually, are
arranged in three staggered
rows. Unlike the much-later
three-comb *sublime harmonie*
style, there appears no reason
for this layout as each tooth is
tuned to a different pitch.
Made *c.* 1810.

◄ PLATE 29
Clock-base with musicwork with teeth
in groups of two with the treble on
the left. The stop/start detent can be
seen over the governor block and the
endless screw has a steel top plate in
place of a jewel. The piece is thought
to be French and the controls are in
the form of three push/pull knobs –
the centre one has been removed.
Plate 47 shows how this type of
control rod operates. This piece dates
from *c.* 1815–20.

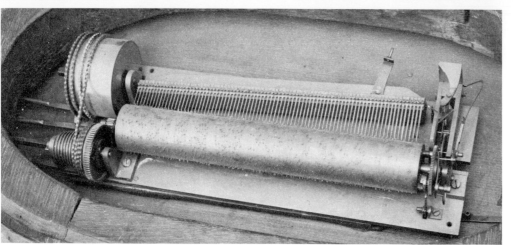

◄ PLATE 30
This clock-base musicwork, also shown in Plate 32, has bracket-mounted spring barrel and fusee, individually-attached teeth and a steel cock-plate for the governor. The cylinder is mounted fully above the bedplate.

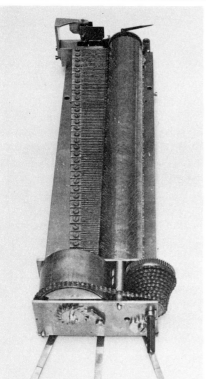

◄ PLATE 31
Unlike the previous clock-base pieces, this is an actual musical box (see Plate 34) featuring plate-mounted spring barrel and fusee. Compare with Plate 27. Other than a small cut-out to clear the fusee chain when it is on the spring barrel, the bedplate is solid.

PLATE 32 ►
For comparison here is the bracket-mounted spring and fusee mechanism of the clock-base movement shown in Plate 30. Compare the winding stopwork. Bracket at top left is for clock detent.

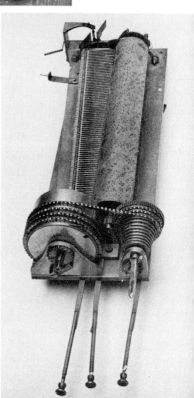

▼ PLATE 33
Underside of movement in Plate 32 showing arrangement of control levers, piercing of bedplate for fusee chain, attachment studs into case bottom, and the two square-headed comb base attachment screws.

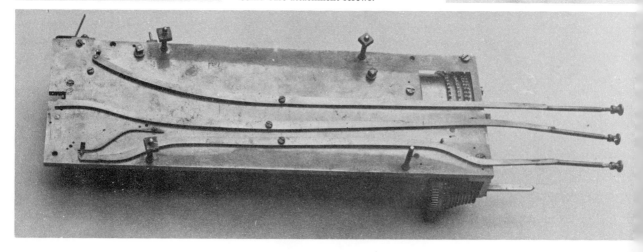

The between-plates fusee-wound movement seen in Plate 31. There is some considerable doubt that this movement and box are coeval: the box has an end-flap (a mid-1860s style) and the brass tune sheet has a hole in it as if it originally fitted round the winding square.

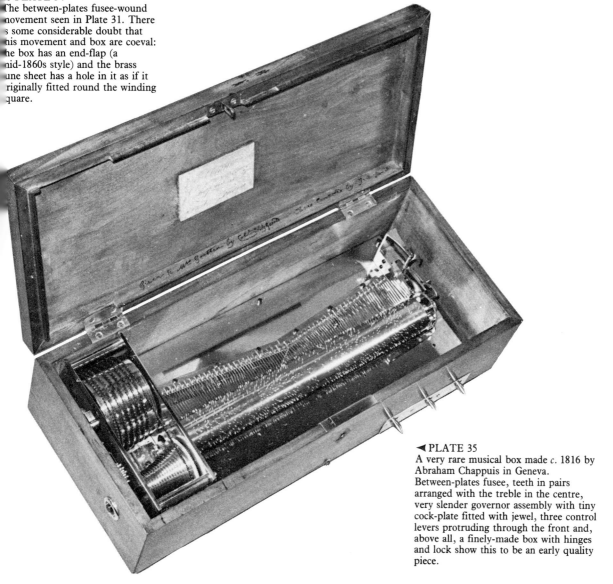

◄ PLATE 35
A very rare musical box made *c*. 1816 by Abraham Chappuis in Geneva. Between-plates fusee, teeth in pairs arranged with the treble in the centre, very slender governor assembly with tiny cock-plate fitted with jewel, three control levers protruding through the front and, above all, a finely-made box with hinges and lock show this to be an early quality piece.

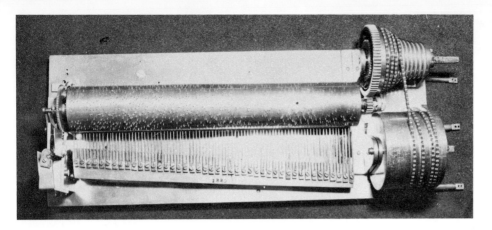

◄ PLATE 36
Bracket-mounted fusee and spring characterise this clock-base movement which has the motor assembly on the right and the comb in front with the treble on the left. The governor assembly has a steel cock-plate for the endless.

▲ PLATE 37
Detail of the clock-base movement of a London-made Parkinson & Frodsham clock.

▲ PLATE 38
Detail of governor of Plate 37 movement. Three wheels mean that the endless screw is driven downwards instead of upwards, so lower bearing has steel bearing plate.

▼ PLATE 39
Register pins protrude slightly from cylinder surface on this *c.* 1810 piece.

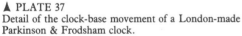

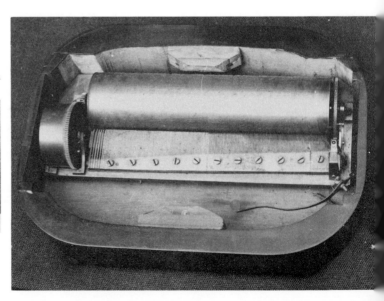

PLATE 40 ►
Superb quality movement by F. Nicole in clockbase. Large cylinder plays long overture programme.

Many other small modifications were embodied to reduce costs. The ratchet pawl for the handle-wound spring motor, for instance, carried a tail against which a small coil spring pressed, so dispensing with the usual form of spring.

The patents covering these improvements were all listed on the stop/start control escutcheon and comprise two American and one Swiss. That of 6 December 1887 is U.S. patent 374410 in the name of Charles H. Jacot, Mermod's U.S. agent. The second patent is number 382292 of 8 May 1888, and this is in the name of Louis Campiche of Ste-Croix. Campiche worked for Mermod and all his patents are assigned to that company. The existence of American patents but not British ones is explained by the fact that Mermod Frères had a strong link with the United States through Jacot and Émile Cuendet, both from Ste-Croix and who together went to America to set up the Mermod agency there.

Mermod Frères was established in the year 1816 at Ste-Croix and were described in the catalogue of the Great Exhibition, held in London in 1851, as high-class watchmakers. The name soon became associated with complex and ingeniously constructed musical boxes and the music on their cylinders was almost always brilliantly set up. The only exception to this was with some of the disc boxes they produced where the melody was somewhat thinly presented.

By 1902 the business was operated by the brothers Louis Philippe, Gustave and Léon Mermod at Avenue des Alpes in Ste-Croix. According to James Hirsch, in 1911 Marc K. Mermod was the New York agent for the company which was still flourishing at that time.

Paillard turned his attention to the spring barrel and, instead of using a brass cylinder sweated into a complicated and costly grooved brass gear-wheel at one end with a sprung lid at the other, he first forged and later stamped the barrel from one piece of steel, requiring only the addition of a separate gear and a simple lid. This was an early example of the 'deep drawing' technique which is still used today by makers such as Reuge, Lador and others for the making of modern musical-box spring-barrels.

An attempt to dispense altogether with the spring-barrel as a separate entity and to return to the early musicwork system of using a pinned going-barrel was made by E. K. Hoffmann (British Patent No. 3241, 7 August 1880). He placed his driving spring inside the end of the cylinder, a system also used later by Bornand. This was not apparently a success and I have only ever seen one such box – a small children's type movement in a painted wooden case.*

Isochronism, long recognised in clocks by horologists yet by no means noticeable to the lay observer, was painfully noticeable to even the most uneducated of musical-box owners. In fact, many of the later parodies of the musical box (such as the popular piano duet referred to in the Introduction) made a feature of this unfortunate characteristic which is simply expressed as being the result of the fact that when a spring is fully wound it exerts more power than when it is almost run down. The audible result is that the musical box runs slower. Louis Campiche of Mermod Frères produced a solution to the problem which he patented in 1890.

The ramifications of Nicole Frères make interesting reading. Research by Dr Cyril de Vere Green, myself and Keith Harding has added much to the history of this illustrious company. Let it be said, though, that much of the charisma attached to this company and its products has been solely due to what today would be called 'good public relations'. Back in the beginning, their agents were always instructed to style their advertisements: 'Suppliers of

---

* Described in *The Music Box*, vol. 8, p. 136, 1977.

the famous Nicole Frères musical boxes' or similar, which served to build up a reputation which no other maker had. There remain many musical boxes made by apparently less illustrious manufacturers which are at least as good – if not better than – many Nicole products.

Having said that, though, it is not to be denied that Nicole products are generally of a high order but the company underwent some sort of hiatus which followed the death of its founders. David Élie and Pierre Moïse Nicole were associated together some time before 1822. David Élie, born in 1792, died in 1871. His brother, Pierre Moïse, was born in 1787 and died in 1857. The business continued until the early 1880s, but between November 1882 and January 1883 the entire business together with the stock of musical boxes was shipped to London where, under the direction of Charles Brun, it continued until an unfortunate excursion into the manufacture of gramophone records in 1904 forced bankruptcy. The company was subsequently taken over by the New Polyphon Supply Company.

What remains something of a mystery is who produced the many boxes marked Nicole Frères sold after the company became London-based, for certainly no manufacture was undertaken in England by the company. A number of clues exist. First is the strong similarity between some of the late 'Nicole' boxes and contemporary products of Paillard. Then there is the coincidence that, after Paillard's invention of the revolver mechanism, Nicole-marked boxes should appear with the same characteristics. Detail points include the shape and style of the governor cocks, bedplate, comb attachment, wheelwork, even the musical programmes. Would it be correct to assume that all post-1883 Nicole Frères-marked boxes are the product of Paillard? Personally, I tend to favour this conclusion but must emphasise that it is but an assumption which awaits incontrovertible evidence. There is, incidentally, a major gap in serial numbers around this changeover period. There remains plenty of evidence to show that many makers supplied component parts to one another and Francois Nicole-marked combs are not infrequently found on mechanisms with names such as F. Lecoultre stamped on the bedplates. Henri Capt (who often Anglicised his name to Henry) made hidden drum and bell boxes, including some playing two tunes per turn, which bore the LF over G^{ve} marks on the comb. Plate 95 would suggest that George Baker, Baker-Troll and Nicole Frères may have had some sort of late joint involvement.

Another 'brand name' about which controversy exists is Charles Ullmann of Paris who seems to have produced large quantities of cheaper style musical boxes bearing his trade mark. The existence of similarities between Ullmann-marked products and those of Manger is interesting, as is the discovery of an Ullmann trademark in the lid design of a Multiphone (a tiny, interchangeable-cylinder manivelle) which is the patented design of John Manger of Mojon, Manger & Co., musical-box makers of Chaux-de-Fonds.

A few years ago, there was considerable mystery about those musical boxes which, according to John Clark, were the product of Thomas Dawkins. It seemed strange that no Dawkins musical boxes were to be found in the United States while at the same time boxes by Ami Rivenc, not uncommon in America, were virtually unknown in England. Evidence was mounting on the activities of the Thomas Dawkins factories and their trading connections with the Swiss makers when the whole business was resolved by Suzanne Maurer in Geneva, who successfully proved that Ami Rivenc was the maker of the Dawkins-attributed boxes. And in the past decade it has been successfully proved by process of deduction and the careful sifting of evidence in archives that those boxes marked and styled 'Thibouville-Lamy' were in fact the work of France's most successful musical-box factory, that of L'Épée.

One mystery at least still remains, and it is a big one. This concerns PVF which is accepted as standing for Paillard, Vaucher, Fils who were most definitely distributors of musical boxes and, apparently, makers. However, there was another company, Paul Vidoudez et Fils which was described as a musical-box maker. This name is still to be seen today on the wall of a building in Ste-Croix. Much more research is still to be done on this mystery before other than these facts can be related.

To revert to Ami Rivenc, he was a maker of great quality and, apart from the bulk production of cheaper boxes which were the mainstay of the business, his full orchestral boxes demonstrate high craftsmanship. He did, for example, go in for the narrow inner glass lid with carved and pierced wood fret behind and central oil painting on glass which was also a characteristic of Bremond and Greiner. He also made fine panelled cases, some of which were actually made dustproof by letting into the upper edge of the case a narrow strip of soft leather all the way round so that the lid closed down on to this. Usually this leather has hardened with age, but it was a very fine touch of class when the box was new.

It was this 'public relations' business that inspired musical-box importers to mark their wares 'Made in Switzerland' as an indication of quality rather in the way that today hi-fi equipment is somehow rated as being preferable if it bears a label saying 'made in Japan'. But Swiss-made boxes were highly thought of and, perhaps with the arrival of the French-made products (which were very good), it was decided to draw attention to the fact. Sometimes the mark was in the form of a steel punch of capital letters, which would be hammered into the front or rear top edge of the case. Sometimes it was a rubber stamp, impressed in the ubiquitous purple stamp-pad ink of the period, and marked upon the tune sheet.

To make it somewhat easier to follow the history of the development of the cylinder musical box, I have taken the salient parts of the musical movement and its case and prepared a short description of each part. In this manner it is hoped that the inquirer will be best able to glean the information he seeks.

THE CASE

Not until around the end of the first decade of the nineteenth century did the first actual musical *box* appear. David Lecoultre is supposed to have introduced the brass cylinder in 1810 according to Swiss records. This at first irrelevant statement apparently indicates that prior to that all musical movements were fitted with going barrels (pinned spring barrels) or *sur plateau* disc-type movements. This is, of course, nonsense since pinned brass cylinders had been in use in bell-playing carillon clocks and even in small organs for a considerable while. The point being made, however, is that prior to about 1810, *and disregarding small musical movements*, the larger type of musicwork was only fitted into the bases of clocks and was intended purely as an adjunct to the timepiece, being contrived to play either at will or on the hour. For this purpose, and since most clocks of the period were to be found under a glass dome, the clock base was oval (or rounded-off rectangular) in plan form. Occasionally, as in the very early Parkinson & Frodsham clock formerly in the de Vere Green collection and now in the Utrecht museum, the clock was rectangular in section and was free-standing on a well proportioned and architecturally styled base.

These early oval bases – not true ovals, being more like either an oval with an extended parallel section front and back, or rectangular with wide-radius corners – were usually of quite roughly hewn wood covered externally with thick veneer in rosewood or walnut. The three musical movement controls (see p. 99, 'Controls') were either of the usual sliding type, or occasionally push/pull type (see Plate 33). The controls pierced the narrow end of the oval which was fitted with a neat escutcheon, sometimes of shaped and engraved brass, but more often of mother-of-pearl and, occasionally, ivory.

Having said that this style predated 1810, it would be wrong to conclude that the practice ceased after that date: musicwork in clock bases continued right the way through to the time of the Great Exhibition of 1851.

After about 1810, the first musical boxes intended to stand on their own as musical interpreters appeared and these were in very plain and often very simple hardwood boxes. The lid of the box in some early instances was hinged using wire eyes and hooks hammered into the wood. A simple hook-and-eye type of catch was provided. The wood of these early boxes was usually heavy and, even with a pine bottom, tended to deaden the sound. This is not to suggest that this type of box should be replaced: always cherish and preserve a piece as it was originally made. These cases were wax-polished to enhance the natural figure and flower of the woods used: French polish was a much later feature.

In the early 1830s, the left end of the case was provided with a hinged flap which opened down to reveal the three control levers (see p. 99, 'Controls'). Three distinct types of end flap may be discerned. The first is the classic type which we can identify as typical of Nicole

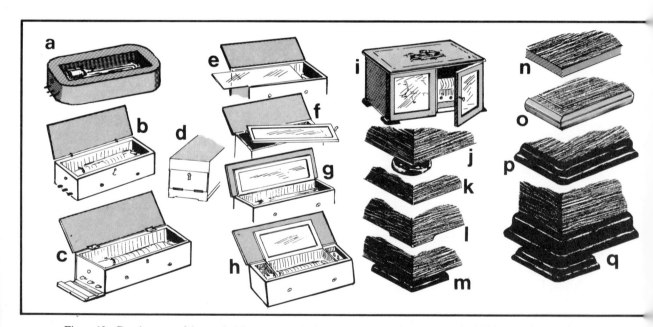

Figure 18 Development of the musical-box case. (a) clock-base style; (b) plain box with wire lid hinges and exposed control levers; (c) hinged end flap to cover levers, proper lid hinges; (d) variation using half-end flap, sometimes lockable; (e) plain glass sliding lid; (f) lift-out full area framed glass lid; (g) hinged full-area inner lid; (h) compartment dividers for winding lever and controls separate from inner lid area; (i) buffet-style with glazed or solid doors; (j) early bun feet) (k) plain case; (l) plain case with simple protrusions; (m) added-on corners as feet; (n) plain case lid; (o) lid with half-round edge moulding having line of central stringing, lid top with stringing inlay; (p) lid with ogee-shaped edge moulding polished black; (q) case lower edge with full ogee base moulding and added-on corner feet.

Frères and, although used by other makers, we can call 'Nicole type'. Here the flap extends the full depth of the case to a point below the levers where it is hinged. The flap is secured in the closed position by a small hook and eye which is only accessible when the lid of the box is opened. The top of the flap extends over the top of the false end or divider in the case and the hook is screwed to this, the eye being on the flap.

The second type we can call the 'Moulinie type', for it appears on only a few makers' boxes, including those by Humbert and by Moulinie. Here the end flap does not extend all the way to the top of the case, but is rather like a small horizontal trap door in the case end. Again it is secured closed from the inside by hook and eye.

The third type we might call 'Lecoultre type' for it appears on some Lecoultre boxes. Once more it is a full end flap of the Nicole Frères type, but, instead of a hook and eye, the top edge of the flap has protruding from it a stud which engages in a hole in the lid so that, with the lid closed, the flap is held securely closed.

About the time the case gained its hinged flap, it also gained a narrow wooden divider which was rebated into the front and back of the case at the right-hand end to make a small compartment for the winding key.

Concurrent with the provision of the end flap, the first use of inlay appeared on cases, usually in the form of narrow boxwood stringing in one or two bands let into the upper surface of the lid and, later, on both the inside of the lid and the front panel of the case itself. Humbert always used a narrow boxwood inlay diamond shape on the lid top and inside, as well as on the case front.

The next significant step in case development came with the introduction of an inner glass lid to protect the mechanism from prying fingers and dirt. In its earliest form, this was just a sheet of glass which rested inside the case on two narrow wooden beads front and back. Then came the routing of two narrow grooves close to the top edge of the case, front and back, into which the sheet of glass could be slipped when the end flap was opened. At this time, the glass lid covered everything within the box: since all the controls and winding were outside the box, there was no reason to provide otherwise. When controls were first moved experimentally to the right-hand side, and the winding changed to push/pull lever inside the left-hand end of the case, the inner glass lid was provided with a wooden frame but still it extended from the left end across to the right-hand case divider. It was not hinged, but rested on an inner case lip and could be withdrawn by two tape tags.

By 1856–8, the definitive form of inner glazed lid was introduced; it was hinged along its rear edge and bounded by the left-hand case divider (which fitted over and round the spring barrel) and the right-hand divider which supported the control-lever plinth.

Shortly before this, possibly in the period 1845–50, marquetry became the main external decorative feature of musical-box cases. As distinct from simple inlay where small strips of other woods are let into the solid surface of timber, marquetry is the building up of a total veneer comprising many small pieces of woods of different colours, textures and grain directions which can be designed to represent a delicate and complex design or picture. The Swiss and German craftsmen excelled at this type of case-making although many musical movements were cased in London-made boxes manufactured in the workshops of craftsmen scattered throughout the city and its environs. The Nicole Frères case of this period, for example, included a marquetry lid and front. Only very rarely were the sides and back of a case given similar treatment; more often they were just left as plain polished base wood. Nicole Frères made a very few musical boxes which featured in place of lid inlays a

93

glass-covered painting or hand-coloured lithograph in the lid. This was framed in a round-ended rectangular beading and the same type of illustration in matching frame was mounted on the case front. One example of this, bearing the serial number 44892 (*c*. 1882), gamme 2883, is a 12-tune two-tunes-per-turn machine with silver tune sheet in the Rita Ford collection, New York.

The edge of the musical-box lid, in keeping with the rest of the lid, was also decorated. A half-round section of close-grained wood was applied and this was embellished with a central line of stringing, again usually boxwood.

Somewhere around 1865–70, and no doubt in an endeavour to lower costs, this lid edging gave way to the familiar ogee-shaped moulding on all sides. The top of the lid retained its marquetry inlay design but the edging was polished black. About the same time came the introduction of crowned or domed lids. Makers such as Heller of Berne, Nicole Frères for their larger orchestral boxes, and Bremond and others went in for crowning in various degrees. As a rule, the larger the box, the more crowned would be the lid. Ami Rivenc, however, almost always crowned lids for even quite small boxes and sometimes this crowning was quite considerable. This is a point to watch for in any repair work as any rubbing down could virtually rub off the crown and cut through the marquetry to the bare wood beneath. The 'buffet' style, with the movement mounted vertically in a case with twin front doors, enjoyed some popularity. Makers included Bremond, Rivenc and Paillard and styles included the Orchestral (see Plate 116).

With the coming of interchangeable cylinders, there had to be somewhere to store the spare cylinders. While initially this was achieved using a plain wooden box which was not intended to be a showpiece, the practice of making the case for the spare cylinders match the musical box in both appearance and quality of workmanship was widely adopted by the time of the Great Exhibition of 1851. The ultimate was, of course, the provision of the matching stand or table for a musical box which could contain one or more drawers to house the cylinders. These stands were not really tables, although many were later adapted as such. So as not to muffle the sound of the musical box, they almost always had a large rectangular cut-out under where the box rested. The style was most often French, Louis XIV being the most popular, often extending to the extensive use of inlay and ormolu decoration in the more expensive pieces.

Bremond was one maker who produced a most pleasing variety of interchangeable-cylinder box and matching stand. Modelled on a small writing-desk – almost a *bonheur du jour* – the musical box was placed at the back of the desk top, the front lid of which lifted up and the front fall of which hinged down to reveal the cylinders.

Another variety was revealed by Paillard with the Amobean series of changeable cylinder boxes. Here there would be either a central drawer actually in the musical-box case (which was very deep) or, with the smaller models, there would be a drawer in each end of the case to hold a pair of spare cylinders each side. Neither of these were intended to have stands. Billon-Haller featured similar styles.

Cases with angled or cut-off corners were features of many of the larger boxes by Bremond, Greiner and Rivenc as well as Ducommun-Girod who may actually have started the fashion. There were two styles: first there was the genuine eight-sided box where the corners were formed of wooden panels mitred in at 45° to the front and side. These were the true representatives of the style. Later and cheaper boxes cashed in on the fashion by literally sawing across the corners of a normal four-sided box virtually to the full thickness of the timber, reinforcing the joint with a corner fillet. While this was reasonably effective, with age these corners invariably split at the feather edge of the front and side pieces, so tearing the veneer and stringing.

Whereas the early musical box was housed in a case of often slender and almost classic proportions, as the era moved into mass-production and cost-cutting so the case underwent several interesting changes. First, it began to be larger than the actual musical movement required. Although this may, in certain circumstances, have been beneficial to sound production, in the majority of instances it served to make a showy exterior for a tawdry movement. Some late pieces with cylinders less than a hand-span in length were housed in cases of quite spectacular proportions. The musicwork would be carried in the case on wide wooden blocks and massive beading.

Around this time – about 1885–90 – the photographic reproduction of designs was perfected and many cheaper musical boxes were treated with a varnish-fixed transfer or decal representing high-quality marquetry decoration. These transfers are extremely good and very realistic – until the unsuspecting restorer tries to clean them and finds that the beautiful inlay on his lid has disappeared revealing coarse pine beneath. BHA was one maker who used such transfers on both his cylinder and small disc musical boxes.

London was very much a centre of quality cabinet-making and quite early on (I suspect as early as 1830 or around the time when the first rectangular-cased boxes appeared in quantity), musical movements were brought in from Switzerland and cased by the importers in London with boxes supplied locally. A list of cabinet-makers used by Paillard in London includes many names in the furniture-making areas such as Shoreditch, Hoxton and Hackney. The caption to Plate 121 relates evidence of this.

Although a number of custom-built and very expensive musical boxes – usually interchangeables – were built by Paillard and Mermod in America right up to the late 1890s and possibly a little later still, quality casework was superseded by the 1875–85 era. These later custom pieces were invariably for the American market, which came into the musical-box field much later than Europe. Often of prodigious proportions and rich in the splendour of Boulle, ormolu, mother of pearl, ivory and silver marquetry, these were very expensive pieces indeed and no two were exactly alike. All the American specimens were contained in American-built cabinets.

Charles Paillard produced some very large full orchestral boxes which were sold widely in the United States in the 1880s and 1890s. These were contained in extremely large cabinets, some of them in the form of mirror-lined dresser-cabinets with an upwards-sliding front panel to reveal the mechanism. The mechanisms featured, from left to right, a drum with eight beaters, lower comb of 20 teeth, reed organ of 28 notes, upper comb of 16 teeth, bells (seven struck by linkages from six teeth), and a six-beater castenet. The power was either a single double-spring motor, or a pair of such motors and winding the powerful springs was achieved using a double-linkage crank. This basic format, namely 8:20:28:16:6:6, was made using reeds of different pitches and one example in the Bellm collection, Sarasota, has 8 ft pitch reeds in the bass which gives the instrument quite a deep sonorous sound.

To revert to musical-box cases, however, there is one small detail which should not be overlooked – the case feet. From the time of the earliest fruitwood-cased, protruding-control-lever musical-box case, small extensions to the case front, back and ends were made to support the box off a surface such as a table or shelf so as to let the sound pass from the soundboard to the open air. These rudimentary feet were created by cutting the sides, front and back about $\frac{1}{4}$ in. (5 mm) all round save for the last inch or two at the corners. At the same time as the case lid became a machine-routed ogee-cornered piece edged in black, so the feet became separate corner pieces which protruded from the case at the bottom and which were also painted black (see Fig. 18).

As the musical box journeyed on to its closing years, decoration was restricted to imitation graining achieved with cheap woods by means of artists' scumble and a graining brush. Transfers (decals) completed the picture. Many of the smaller boxes were fitted with solid wood lids which were not veneered, but which were inlaid, in the original manner, with lightwood stringing surrounding a central applied design. These lids are most prone to warping and, in extreme cases, splitting.

It should be pointed out that Viennese and Czechoslovakian (Austro-Hungarian) musical boxes did not in any way follow the pattern of Swiss development. Since all were key-wound, even up to the early years of this century, cases had no end flaps and inner lids were retained on an inner lip inside the case and could be lifted straight out. Controls were very simple (see Plate 67) and case decoration was elementary, usually just quartered veneer on the top and front. A major case departure was the provision of a thin wooden resonating chamber on which the case proper was mounted. This was of somewhat larger proportions than the box and had sound holes front and back. This type of case was an alternative to the ordinary style described above.

THE BEDPLATE

From the beginning, bedplates were cast in brass and the upper surface planed and polished smooth to act as a level foundation upon which to build the mechanism.

The early bedplates were secured in the wooden case of the musical box by two screws through the front and two screws through the back, these being cheese-headed with hand-cut threads tapped into the bedplate. Small, plain washers prevented the screw heads from cutting into the wood. Later, these screws were provided with countersunk heads and the washers became large and dome-shaped (see 'Attachment').

L'Épée in France, in an attempt to lower the cost of production, successfully changed the bedplate to polished steel which was then dipped in a 'whiting' (tinning) solution which, with age, often appears today to give the impression of gun metal and has a colour which can range from almost blue down to brass. Details of how this process, identified by collector John Hammond, was carried out is contained in *Restoring Musical Boxes*.

Nicole Frères changed over from a smooth polished brass bedplate to a ribbed brass bedplate early in the 44,000 series, according to Patrick McCrossan's investigations. This dates around 1880.* Cast-iron bedplates first appear in the late 46,000 series but brass bedplates continue on some elaborate movements to the end of production. McCrossan cites an interchangeable-cylinder full-orchestral box numbered 52119 as an example of a late brass bedplate.

Some makers, among them Lecoultre, Greiner, L'Épée and Ducommun-Girod, occasionally cast protruding horizontal lugs on their bedplates to extend the width without increasing too much the amount of metal and, in consequence, the weight of the finished box. This was found in particular with early drum and bell boxes, both concealed and otherwise.

* Significantly, perhaps, the time that Nicole Frères became a London-based company and ceased manufacturing in its own right.

Cast-iron bedplates, introduced by Paillard and soon used by Manger and Mermod, were almost always ribbed longitudinally to provide a surface which required the minimum of handwork to prepare for building upon.

Small legs or feet were occasionally cast in to support the bedplate on the case bottom; later these were of iron and were screwed into the brass. Later still, in the era of cast-iron bedplates, they were cast integrally or dispensed with altogether, the movements being seated on wooden blocks in the case bottom (see under 'Attachment').

Paillard, and later Mermod, were among the first to discard the front and rear attachment-screw style and used three countersunk woodscrews – two at one end and one the other – to screw the bedplate down into the case from the inside (see under 'Attachment').

THE COMB

The means of producing sound in a musical box is the comb. Its development, perfection, finishing and fitting were therefore among the most important aspects of musical-box manufacture and yet very little has been written about its progression from a set of individual tuned steel elements into a single-piece comb.

The invention accredited to Favre was for single teeth which had to be small enough to fit into a confined space while at the same time being long and heavy enough to produce a low note – the pitch of the note which a vibrating tooth can produce is a function of its thickness, breadth and length, this last being capable of adjustment by the addition of more weight.

The steel for making combs was always specially made and only available in small quantities, and right up until the 1850s makers of boxes requiring long combs were forced to make their combs out of several pieces of this special steel, soldered together on the brass comb base, and sometimes the join would be stiffened by a rebated steel strip beneath. This explains in part why many earlier boxes featured combs with what appear to be small groups of teeth added on (F. Nicole overture boxes are a classic example of this), but this feature should not be confused with early comb repairs where a new piece of comb has been grafted in.

In all but the very cheapest, late, musical boxes, the comb is pinned to the bedplate with locating dowels before being screwed down. This means that the exact position of the comb relative to the cylinder has been established by the maker who has then drilled both comb and bedplate to take dowel pins prior to drilling and tapping the bedplate for screws. Some makers, instead of this, arranged tapered pointed screws inserted from beneath the bedplate against which the comb was pressed before being screwed down. Although not as reliable as dowels, for they could not be used to restrict sideways movement, these screws allowed a vernier-type of adjustment for, as they were screwed inwards or outwards fractionally, the cone point protruded to a greater or lesser degree, so affecting how far the comb could be pushed up to the cylinder.

The style of dowel pins can often be used to identify maker and date. On some boxes, they are not visible, having been ground off and polished along with the comb. On others, they can be seen, while on yet other types the comb metal is countersunk, so emphasising the presence of dowels.

The securing screws for the comb itself are another form of identification. Early ones were usually very tall; later on the heads became shorter. Early comb screws sometimes had no comb washers; others had brass tapered-edge washers; and later on almost all makers used steel washers. Ami Rivenc used rosette-shaped brass pressings on boxes which he made under his own name and those which were sold under the name of National Musical Box, although it should be pointed out that previous restorers may well have replaced them in intervening years. Francois Lecoultre was one maker who used square-headed screws to secure his early combs, so avoiding the risk of damage to the comb from a slipping screwdriver.* Metert and Langdorff, makers of a massive musical box at the Utrecht museum, used 36 screws in two staggered rows to hold down a 301-toothed comb (this four-overture box is a rare full-mandoline style with each note represented by ten teeth throughout the length of the comb).

Some combs are to be found which have alternate tips apparently broken off. The late John E. T. Clark suggested that this was to enable six-air comb stocks to be used up on twelve-air boxes. This is not correct. The extra teeth, although not capable of being plucked by the cylinder pins, vibrate in sympathy with other teeth which are vibrating. In construction, these teeth have been tuned with as much care as the pluckable ones so as to produce the proper harmonic reinforcement and overtones. It is destructive to try to 'repair' these teeth – they are to be left alone, and they *are* tuned.

The means of lowering the pitch of teeth which was adopted in later years was to solder a block of lead to the underside of the teeth and saw this into strips which remained suspended from each tooth. Tuning was performed by trimming these lead weights to size – the more lead, the lower the note produced.

Early teeth, particularly those of individual manufacture, often used steel weights formed from the body of the comb metal during shaping. These weights are frequently quite small and in some cases no more than a thickening of a tooth towards the tip. These teeth were cut in profile from plate of the same thickness as the tooth width (see Fig. 11). Incidentally, these single teeth were always sealed in position after screwing to the comb base with shellac applied over all the tooth heels and their screws. This should not be removed on cleaning a movement: it is an original feature.

Teeth tips also vary. While treble teeth may be formed from evenly-tapered spike-shaped forms, treble and bass teeth being wider have to be provided with shoulders and a proper slender tip. Most Swiss boxes after 1830 have scalloped shoulders but Austrian combs usually feature asymetric tips which are L-shaped. This is particularly the case in the bass.

Lecoultre was one early maker who used square-shouldered tooth tips, no doubt discarded later on account of the probability of fatigue-cracking at the sharp change of section where the tip joined the tooth body.

Probably no aspect of musical-box comb technology has been responsible for more inadvised writing than the tuning. Until about 1968, restorers and collectors were content to concern themselves solely with the tuning of new teeth but since that time, some have been attempting to retune existing comb teeth to remove what they consider to be tuning anomalies. Naturally this is dangerous ground. There is plenty of evidence to confirm that the early comb makers tuned to the old, unequal temperament, so limiting the number of keys in which tunes could be set or melodies modulated. Once in a while, the 'wolf' of unequally tempered pitch was allowed to come through, and some makers, Ducommun-Girod in particular, stretched the upper octaves to produce a sharpened musical pitch. Today, with our ears 'tuned' to the equalisation of distances between adjacent semitones, we

* So did the earliest epoch of Francois Nicole.

may hear these pieces with an over-critical approach. The pitch of teeth may alter with age, particularly if corrosion products are removed from teeth of small section where the proportions are more critical than, say, in the bass. The subject of tuning is covered in the companion volume, *Restoring Musical Boxes*.

CONTROL LEVERS

The early cylinder movement was controlled by three levers whose short ends protruded through the left-hand side of the case below the hole provided for the insertion of the spring-winding key. These levers ran underneath and were the full length of the musical movement. That at the back operated the tune-changing with a change or repeat position; that in the middle was responsible for starting the movement and for allowing it to stop at the end of the tune. The third lever, nearest to the front, was the instant-stop control by means of which the mechanism might be stopped instantaneously (see Fig. 19).

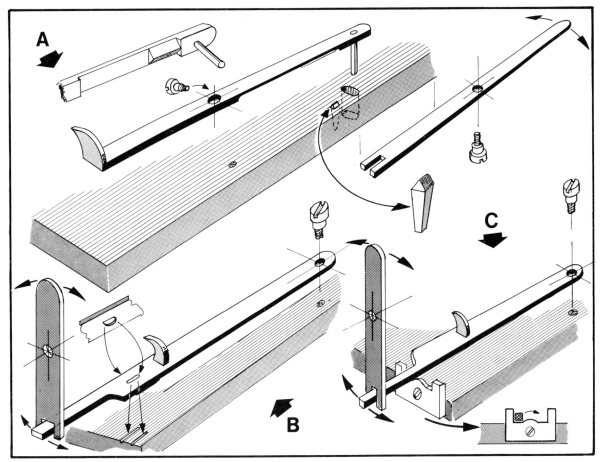

Figure 19   Tune-changing controls. A = the early type worked from the left end of the box. B = later style worked from plinth-mounted lever. C = L'Épée version of B.

The instant stop was a direct-acting lever with a projecting pin so placed that when the lever was set to 'stop' it promptly engaged with the endless screw sprag and stopped the motion. In some early boxes, particularly by Francois Nicole, a fourth control was fitted. This was a direct-acting instant stop and was in addition to the third lever type of instant stop. Because it was obviously intended only for the use of the maker in adjusting the cylinder pins, it was often removed before the box was put on the market. Fitted to the right-hand case divider, it was a simple thumb-lever which slid up and down on two screws engaged in slots. At its lower end, it carried a sprag which moved up and down through a small slot in the divider. With this, the repairman or adjuster could stop the mechanism at once for regulation. Where missing, the clue to its former presence is the tell-tale slot in the divider and two tiny screw holes close by.

The tune-change lever controlled the change finger, allowing it to engage with the change snail on the great wheel, or moving it clear so that the previous tune could be repeated.

The stop/start control centred on the use of a detent one end of which was lodged, when at rest, in a hole, hollow or recess provided for it at one suitable position in the cylinder great wheel, and the other so placed that it engaged in the stop sprag of the endless screw in the governor assembly. When the control was set to 'start', the sprag was freed and the box would play. Even if the control was then reset to the 'stop' position, the mechanism could not cease until the end of the tune when the detent would once more be pushed by a click-type spring into the recess, allowing its other end to engage the stop sprag. This sprag, being a friction fit on the endless, brought the mechanism to a stop within a few turns. Not until the comparatively modern invention of Reuge was the principle of stop operation revised: the Reuge system operates by accepting the end of the stop lever in the cylinder and then drawing it forward until its other end engages the endless fan wings.

Among the earliest musical boxes seen, as distinct from musical movements in clock bases, several have been found having these three controls arranged in a closely spaced line at the back of the box adjacent to the right-hand end. Short push/pull rods directly controlled the functions. An interesting interim box survives in the Nationaal Museum van Speelklok tot Pierement. This has three normally placed push/pull controls. The 24-segment four-tooth comb and slender wheelwork with 'warning' type stop detent (see Plate 45) suggests a date around 1810.

After some time about 1838–42, the end of the case was extended and a hinged flap-end fitted to conceal the levers which now protruded through a false end or case divider, this serving as a locating guide. The levers, a potential source of rattling, were always bowed slightly so that their pivot screws tensioned them against the underside of the bedplate. Further damping was achieved by binding the long brass strips with waxed thread at strategic points along their length. Some of the early movements made for fitting into clock bases still used three controls but, instead of using them as levers, they were employed as push/pull ties, the securing screws passing through slots in each.

Some of the early concealed drum and bell boxes were equipped with a fourth lever mounted a little above the central one of the three. This served to cut out the operation of the drum. No provision was made on these early pieces for silencing the bells. Metert was one who made four-lever hidden drum and bell boxes.

When winding changed from key to lever,* the need for an end flap to the case was not so

* Viennese and Czech musical movements were all key-wound. Their controls, if not detent-operated from a timepiece, are always via push/pull rods.

pressing. The logic of taking the controls the full length of the bedplate to the opposite end of the musical box was now in question and the style which rapidly replaced it was to place all three levers on a platform attached to a wooden divider at the right end of the case. Mounted in the vertical plane, the levers now pointed upwards and resulted in a considerable economy in materials. The operation of the controls was much more positive as backlash was reduced to a minimum. Interior levers of this type were first introduced around the time of the Great Exhibition of 1851. L'Épée made a number, probably but a small quantity, of large boxes having the three control levers supported on three brass extensions attached to the bedplate.

Somewhere about 1870 the instant-stop, or third lever, was dispensed with. Its use, essentially the prerogative of the manufacturer and repairer, was largely redundant and could, in fact, cause damage if used in the middle of a tune by allowing the movement to stop for an unwarranted time with cylinder pins in contact with comb teeth, compressing the dampers and, if the box was jarred, bending them out of alignment or even breaking them off.

Nicole Frères appears to have dropped the use of the instant stop on ordinary production boxes in the 42,000 series (about 1872), but to have retained it on more elaborate boxes as late as the 46,000 series ten years later. Patrick McCrossan* cites a forte-piano numbered 46566.

Musical boxes now had just two controls on a plinth inside. However, there were several short-lived experiments at reviving the third lever, albeit for different purposes. Bremond, for example, made a series of small boxes in which the third lever operated a tune selector by the simple expedient of raising and lowering the tune-change finger (which was made of spring steel) so that it turned the starwheel of the snail cam. Another application was to use the lever for raising or lowering the zither attachment. George Bendon used this system.

Certain types of box dispensed with the formal positioning of controls on a plinth forming the right-hand case divider such as is described above. Makers such as Mermod, Nicole, Baker-Troll and Aubert with their large musical boxes went in for direct-acting controls visibly forming part of the mechanism. This was the era of adjustable speed control (from a large shield-plate on top of the governor cock), tune selection by choice coupled with a tune indicator (a simple pointer which was operated by the end of the cylinder and a spring), and the orchestral effects.

Bells and drums as well as, on larger boxes, castanets, could be taken in or out of play at will by controls which bent up their flexible comb teeth and drew their hammers back from the percussion effects. On some large boxes which incorporated reed organs, the reed organ could even be drawn back out of play by the use of a lever. This was always the sign of a top quality box as, with many ordinary boxes, the pinning of the cylinder for the comb music was somewhat weak and would hardly stand up to being listened to without the organ upon which it relied for musical substance.

SPRING

Musical-box driving-power was developed from that in use in clocks. The earliest examples were fusee-wound with spring barrel and fusee mounted between solid brass plates. Later this was simplified to a pair of brackets to support the spring barrel and a second pair to support the winding fusee.

* *The Music Box*, vol. 4, p. 425.

No clear-cut date can be given for the last use of the fusee-wound spring to normal or 'going' driving barrel, but the going barrel seems to have been in common usage by 1815, a date suggested by the progressive development of other aspects of the musical box. In place of the fixed arbor of the fusee-wound spring, the arbor was now fitted with a ratchet wheel and pawl or, in clock terminology, a click, so that the arbor could be turned with a key to wind up the spring. The power in the spring was retained by the governor through the extended arbor formed by the cylinder itself.

Double or coaxial spring barrels were first used in about 1851 as a means of prolonging the playing time of the instrument. The system is in some ways rather like the fusee in that the first spring barrel becomes the winding medium for the second, the going barrel. The two springs are, in the most usual form, arranged end to end on a common central arbor. The first barrel – that farthest from the cylinder – is wound by rotating the barrel around the arbor by means of ratchet teeth provided on its outer edge. As this spring is wound, it begins to turn the arbor which serves to wind up the second spring in the usual manner. To summarise, in winding the winding barrel is rotated and the winding-barrel spring then winds the spring of the going barrel through the common arbor which unites them. This makes for a very powerful motor which has approximately 85 per cent of the effective energy of two identical going barrels: the reason it cannot possess double the energy is that by doubling the power the friction losses increase sharply.

Occasionally, double springs are found of the parallel type rather than the linear arrangement. Here two going barrels, each rotating in a different direction, are place either side of a central winding gear. Power is then fed to a central pinion at the other end which, in its simplest form, is coaxial with the cylinder, or in the *longue marche* style, drives a layshaft with a very large-diameter wheel which engages with the cylinder drive pinion.

Yet another variety is the four-spring motor, which consists of two parallel pairs of in-line double springs, i.e. a pair of arbors each with a winding barrel and a going barrel upon them. As with the parallel double spring, the pairs of springs rotate in opposite directions to drive the central shaft and to facilitate winding from a centrally situated winding-pinion.

WINDING

Methods of spring winding can be simply divided into two styles – key winding and lever winding. However, it must at once be stated that that is very much an oversimplification of the subject. There were many mutations of winding systems, most of which centred on the years during which the general practice of key winding was replaced by the general practice of lever ratchet winding.

Since the musical movement developed from the clock and was made by clockmakers, it is perfectly natural that winding should have been effected by a key.

The musical box key was virtually the same as the clock key, only more frequently larger sizes had to be used. Since clock keys are of forged steel with a broached square bore which is slightly tapered (the early spring arbors were also tapered over their square-sectioned winding-ends), a given spring size could be wound by one of several sizes of key, but only one size would be right and would safely and tightly engage the square shaft up to the hilt. Sizes were called up in numbers, those from 'six' to 'twelve' being the most common. These corresponded to the across-flats dimension of the arbor as set out in the following table:

TABLE OF MAINSPRING ARBOR SIZES INDICATING WINDING KEY SIZES
(all dimensions in millimetres)

18	17	16	15	14	13	12	11	10	9	8	7	6	5	4	3	2	1
7·35	6·59	6·00	5·60	5·27	4·70	4·40	4·08	3·76	3·58	3·43	3·15	2·93	2·68	2·52	2·30	2·20	2·06

Notes

It will at once be noticed that the steps between these arbor sizes are by no means equal, some being as high as 0·76 mm and others as small as 0·10 mm.

The classification of arbor sizes appears not to have been governed by any hard-and-fast rules; variations are many and marked. The dimension given is that measured across parallel faces at the root of the squared portion of the arbor. The square was always tapered along its length. Since the winding keys were also broached on a taper, several keys could fit on to one size of winding square, the difference being how far the winding square entered the key. Only the right key would take the whole arbor tightly. After the smallest size, i.e. number 1 above, snuff-box, singing-bird and watch keys began again at a fresh number 12 (nominally 1·545 mm across) and diminished to a second number 1. Although the Geneva sizes here were used throughout the era of the musical box, evidence suggests that it was far from universal throughout the early days of the Swiss musical-box industry.

With some of the larger springs it became necessary to introduce half sizes and Ducommun Giron was one maker who produced a number of musical boxes featuring keys which were stamped with the size 16½.

Almost all musical box keys were forged and broached in steel. However, some of the early makers of quality pieces scorned the mass-produced keys which were available from the earliest times of the musical box from the watch and clock sundries houses. These makers fabricated their own keys from brass and these featured necessarily heavy barrels to resist the bursting forces incurred during the act of winding, and a one-piece brass sheet finger grip. This was often of fairly simple shape. These should not be confused with the cheap type of mass-produced brass clock key often found with musical boxes and added inadvisedly at some previous time by a 'restorer' as a replacement for a missing original.

The first ratchet levers of the detachable type which replaced the key as an external winder made use of the broached end of a steel key which was then made up with a simple lever handle and a ratchet wheel and pawl.

For winding miniature musical movements such as watches and snuff-boxes, the key was generally made like a watch-key of a knurled brass-bodied type without finger 'wings'. To aid professional watchmakers and repairers, the so-called star key was produced. This was a centre piece, circular in later ones, to which were fitted three or five different-sized key barrels, each being denoted by a number.

103

Around 1860, the ratchet lever was gradually introduced. In its developed form it fitted neatly and simply on the winding arbor of the spring with a brass bushing to increase the bearing area. The brass lever carried its own click and clickspring in addition to the usual one attached to one of the motor attachment brackets (the outermost). Both clicks engaged in a square-bored ratchet wheel on the spring arbor. As the lever was pulled forward, its click engaged in the ratchet wheel, allowing it to be turned, so winding the spring while the click on the bracket allowed the wheel to turn. At the end of the stroke of the winding lever, the bracket click dropped back into place, allowing the lever to be pushed forward to allow another winding stroke. This is shown in Fig. 20.

It is worth analysing the records of Nicole Frères since, as they numbered their boxes, we have a fair idea as to the dates when changes in style were adopted. The change from key to

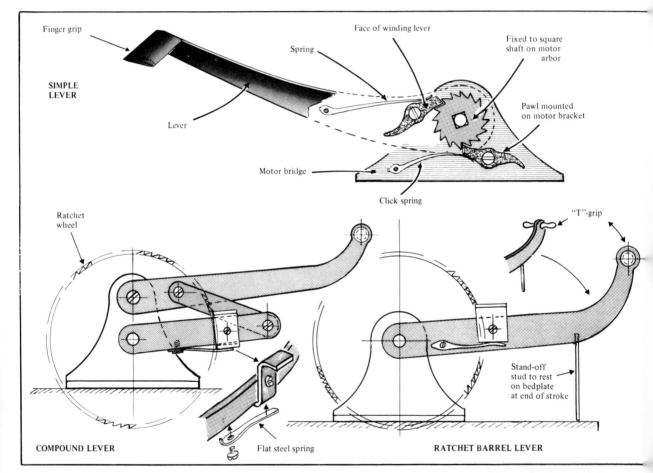

Figure 20   Ratchet lever winding. Top: common form of lever winding system. Below: schematic diagram showing principles of lever winding applied to co-axial spring motors where the winding is achieved by rotating the barrel of the first spring to wind up the arbor of the second spring. On the right is the simple form in which the barrel ratchet teeth are engaged by a right-angle steel pawl. On the left is the compound form used by Paillard for winding movements with two or sometimes four very strong springs.

104

lever winding happened at the end of the 39,000 series – about 1863. But Patrick McCrossan has rightly deduced that this only applies to the standard production 4, 6, 8 and 12 air boxes. Lever winding appeared about five years earlier on the more elaborate types of movement. He has recorded seeing a hidden drum and bell box and a six-overture box in the 34,000 series which both feature an internal three-lever control platform and lever winding. Furthermore, I have seen a key-wound forte-piano box in the 42,000 series. A key-wound musical box with an engraved brass tune sheet bearing the name Berguer & Fils, Geneva, appeared in a Sotheby's Belgravia sale in March, 1977. This bore the engraved date 15 Juillet 1863.

Until the definitive lever was adopted by all makers (except Viennese and Czech*), there were several varieties. First was the key-type lever. This was virtually a key end attached to a ratchet handle rather like a modern socket spanner and wrench. The handle was made of wood, the box still had an end flap, and the lever was applied to the end of the arbor in the same manner as a key, winding being by pushing the handle backwards and forwards. This style has been seen on boxes marked Moulinie Aîné and Metert as well as Nicole Frères.

An unusual style of interim lever has been seen on a box marked F. Lecoultre wherein a very slender lever is provided with a freely pivoted drop arm carrying at its extremity a shaped spade end. This serves as a winding ratchet and on the return stroke passes loosely back over the ratchet teeth under its own weight. Yet another style is to be seen on a box marked Golay Leresche in the Dr Burnett collection. Here the slender winding lever is double-jointed, with a second lever having two scolloped finger guides on it. This allows much easier winding because of the effectively greater lever length.

The internal ratchet lever as evolved from all this resulted in a simplified design of case (see page 92 'Casework') since it dispensed with the hinged end-flap. The lever normally had a cranked top pointing to the left but some makers bent their levers over towards the right so that they were over the spring barrel. The advantage of this is that it economised on space inside the case. Makers who did this appear all to have been French and both L'Épée (Thibouville-Lamy) and Adre Soualle followed this style. Some L'Épée boxes had wooden lever ends instead of the more usual brass.

With larger musical movements which used twin spring motors mounted on the same axis, the winding lever was employed in a slightly different way. Instead of being connected through its ratchet and pawl so that it wound up the spring from the arbor, it had to rotate the barrel of the second motor. To this end, this second motor was provided with an external ring of stout ratchet teeth and the lever, freely pivoted on the arbor end, turned this by means of a spring loaded pawl or winding bracket half way up the length of the lever. On very large mechanisms with four springs mounted in coaxial pairs, the force of winding would have been beyond the resources of the average owner, so the lever was re-styled so that its pivot was above that of the spring arbor, a second lever connected by a link actually performing the winding. This double lever considerably reduced the winding force required and was first used by Paillard in its large orchestral boxes.

Crank-winding from within the case as distinct from lever-winding, was tried by Bremond at one time but this appears to have been a somewhat short-lived exercise around the mid-1860s. The left-hand motor bridge was provided with two bearing blocks for a vertical shaft and a pair of bevel gears to transmit rotary motion of the winding handle in the horizontal plane into winding power for an otherwise conventional spring motor. Another

---

* These retained key winding through to the end.

maker who used this system was the 'German-Swiss' company of Karrer of Teufenthal in northern Switzerland's Aargau. Karrer's version, introduced somewhere about 1890, came at a time when the company products were already demonstrating the strong influence of the cheapening styles of mechanical musical instruments. Cases, for example, were now being mitred into reinforcing corner columns rather like the Ariston organettes being mass-produced by Ehrlich in Leipzig. Karrer's spring motor was made with a gearwheel having teeth angled at 45°. Into this was meshed a winding wheel, about two-thirds the diameter of the barrel wheel, also with angled teeth. This was attached to the end of a vertical shaft mounted in simple bearings and having at its top end a spelter handle cross-hinged like a sewing machine handle so that it could be folded down out of the way when not in use.

One maker who went in for a very fine, well engineered handle-winding system was Henri Capt who seems to have scorned the changeover from key to lever for his large and expensive boxes. Capt made a number of orchestral boxes characterised by their most expensive, serpentine-fronted cases and metal tune-sheets with scolloped edges. Over the spring motor was placed a metal plate through which protruded a hinged handle, again of sewing machine style but of infinitely superior fabrication. The knob of the handle was contained in a recess when the handle was folded down. Winding was again achieved by turning the handle in the horizontal plane.

Both Paillard and Mermod later went on to gramophone-type handle-winding using a detachable handle which was plugged into a hole in the side of the case to connect with the spring arbor. These usually had their motors placed on the right-hand end of the bedplate to allow right-hand winding.

The musical movements which were contained in the bases of automata and in musical pictures, usually small ones, were generally wound using a brass pulley fitted on to the spring arbor and provided with a cord protruding at some convenient part through the case. When pulled it would wind up the spring: during playing, the pulley would gradually rewind the string.

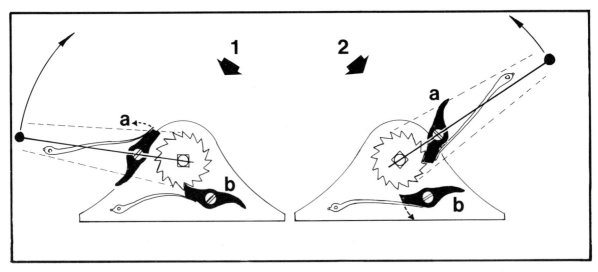

Figure 21 The operation of the simple musical box winding crank showing how to let down the spring power.

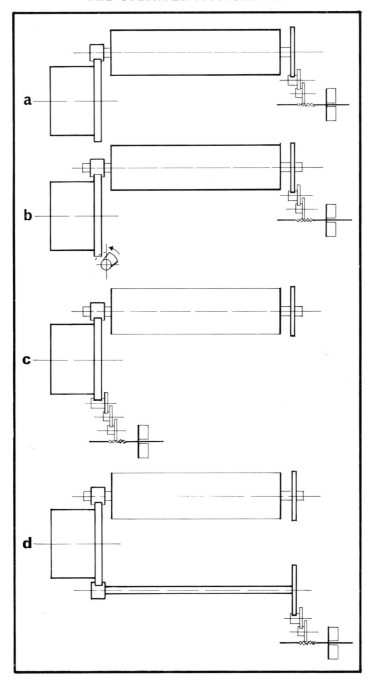

Figure 22   Power train of the cylinder musical box. (a) the standard form with spring at the left and governor and endless screw at the right, power being transmitted through the cylinder; (b) early form of changeable cylinder mechanism whereby the spring power is locked by a worm so that the cylinder can be removed; (c) developed interchangeable cylinder mechanism wherein the cylinder plays no important part in the power train: also found with intermediate layshaft between spring barrel and cylinder, the final drive to the cylinder also driving the governor; (d) Paillard 'Gloria' system wherein the governor remains at the end of the cylinder but is quite separate being driven by a second shaft.

But the most eccentric winding method of all must surely lie with Cuendet Develay Fils when, in 1891, it produced its patented interchangeable-cylinder box for the ham-fisted, the stupid and the non-respecter of mechanisms. This incredibly robust mechanism with its one-tune cylinders and 'patent undestroyable dampers' was wound by, of all things, a big capstan wheel mounted vertically in place of the conventional lever and which the user could only turn one way.

Silent winding, later to be employed quite widely by the Swiss disc musical-box makers and a few of the German makers, was also used in a limited way on cylinder instruments. Although a fairly early invention, it was no doubt brought about by attempts to avoid the clattering of the winding ratchet if a box had to be wound during play. Later Paillard and Mermod cylinder musical boxes, particularly those which were wound by handle, featured this. The system was simply achieved: as pressure was applied to the winding handle, the pawl or click on the ratchet would be lifted clear of the ratchet teeth by means of a cage pivoted loosely to the motor frame. But as soon as winding pressure was removed from the handle, the pawl would at once re-engage itself – all done quite silently. Louis Ducommun was granted a British patent, number 1766 of 6 July 1871, for a method of winding musical boxes without the use of a pawl at all but using instead steel rollers which were so placed as to form a geometric lock when under pressure from the wound-up motor. Mermod used a 'silent' ratchet comprising two knurled wheels and a free roller.

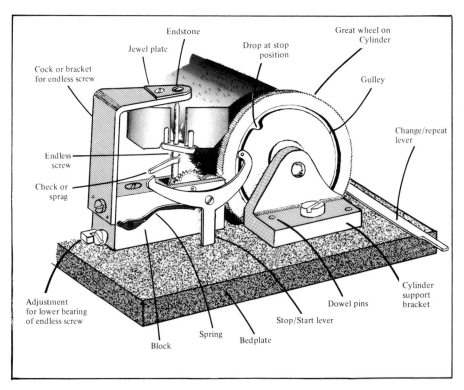

Figure 23   The governor end of the musical box showing the stop/start and change/repeat mechanism.

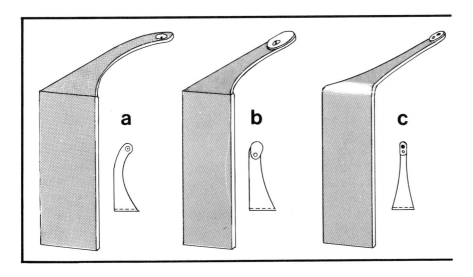

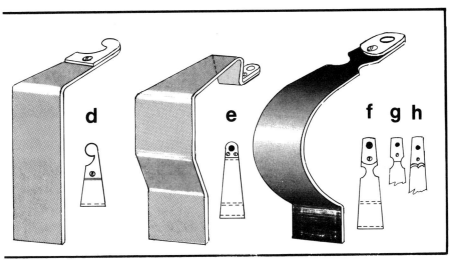

Figure 24   Types of governor cock. (a) very early style with plain bearing, the endless being driven downwards. (b) very early type with plain steel cock plate, the endless being driven upwards. (c) early type with the first use of the endstone or jewel and featuring a very small steel jewel plate. (d) early plain steel top bearing. (e) jewelled cock used by Henri Capt on movements with large fan blades. (f) standard type of production cock, the scolloped sides allowing screwdriver access to screw securing governor to bedplate (early ones were usually screwed up through the bottom). (g, h) variations on the last-mentioned, the style (h) being Charles Paillard.

THE GOVERNOR

The power of the musical-box spring is let down and regulated by means of the governor assembly, which comprises a train of gears driven by the spring barrel, through the cylinder (which acts as nothing more than an extended arbor between drive pinion at the spring end, and the great wheel at the other) and terminating at an endless screw or worm which carries an air brake or fan. The speed of rotation of the cylinder is governed within broad limits by the power of the spring and the ratios of the wheels as determined in design. Fine adjustment is possible by regulating the span of the wings of the fan, often termed the 'butterfly', but more properly described as an air brake. The governor parts are shown in Fig. 23.

This fan comprises a cross tee staked to the upper portion of the endless screw to which are riveted two brass wings. The span of the wings is adjustable – with care – by pivoting them on the securing rivets. It is interesting to note that musical movements of Austrian and Viennese style in particular have no such 'user-adjustable' speed control, the fan being of fixed span.

With larger musical movements, the fan must be considerably wider than might conveniently be accommodated in the gear train block. For this reason some makers such as Paillard shape the cock or endless bracket so that it is bowed and can locate a wide-span fan. Another type of adjustable fan is that used on some Paillard boxes; it comprises a horizontal cylinder into which are located the wings. The securing rivets pass through circumferential slots in this little cylinder so that they can be twisted to oppose to a greater or lesser degree on the air.

Large movements, particularly those of organ boxes, require a more regular power than is obtainable from the normal fan and so the attachment for the wings, instead of being just a tee-piece, is a small brass flywheel. Some of these movements proclaim on the tune sheet, the words 'Volant compensé', or compensating speed control (Fig. 25). Because the drag of the fan is not required as the drive spring overcomes initial friction to start the mechanism in motion, but is required as it speeds up, the volant compensé employs such a flywheel to which the wings – usually three – are quite loosely secured but held normally closed by small flat springs. At the moment of starting, they present the smallest amount of drag: as the movement speeds up, so they move outwards and into action.

Some makers believed that a more regular speed – and a slower fan rotation – might be achieved by the introduction of another wheel and pinion into the gear train and so occasionally this feature can be observed. It is also usual to find this additional stage in the gearing used in conjunction with the organ-type form of movement and it is an extension of this middle wheel arbor which carries the eccentric drive for the bellows.

Gustave J. Jaccard of New York took out an American patent number 395440 (1889) for an improved stop-motion for musical boxes which did not have a fan or air-brake. Speed control and regulation was achieved by means of a pressure plate which bore down on the ends of two adjacent endless screws. Although this system undoubtedly would have worked, it deprived the gear train of the essential flywheel qualities of the fan-type of air-brake and would have made regular, smooth speed difficult to maintain. Other makers such as Paillard and in particular Nicole Frères used a speed control system which was independent of the need to adjust the fan wings. This was similar to the Jaccard patent in that pressure could be adjusted on the end of the endless, but regular speed was ensured by the use of a conventional fan. On Nicole Frères boxes, this device was called the 'Moderateur'.

110

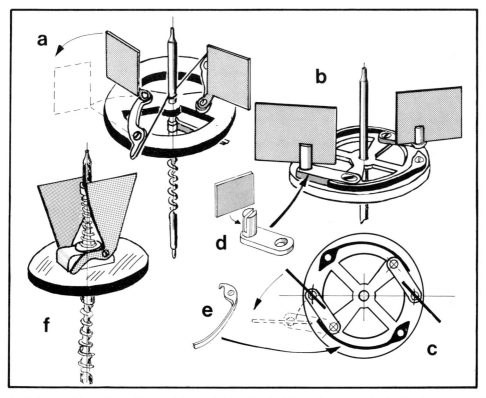

Figure 25 A feature of the orchestral box and the musical box fitted with a reed organ section is the *volant compensé* form of air-brake. Three types are seen here, (a) being the common form with sprung arms holding the wings. (b) is a variation of this form which is shown in detail in the plan view (c). In (d) is the style invented by Langdorff in which the centrifugal governor effect causes the wings to fly outwards as the speed increases.

Whereas the greater majority of makers went in for conventional layouts for their governor assemblies, Junod patented a musical box (the 'Orphea' style) which had the motor and the governor under the bedplate and therefore out of harm's way. Only the cylinder and comb was visible – and there was no airbrake to flick if it would not start first time!

Another variety is that used by Mermod Frères. Here the endless screw of this maker's interchangeable-cylinder boxes was arranged horizontally and driven direct from the spring barrel. This most characteristic feature of Mermod was always used in conjunction with the Parachute Safety Check (see next section).

SAFETY CHECKS

Right from the earliest days of the musical movement, it was appreciated that any accidental damage to the governor assembly – itself in a vulnerable position – would unquestionably cause very serious damage to the entire mechanism. At its least, it would be very costly to repair: at its very worst it could virtually destroy the piece. A broken endless or a damaged pinion or a wheel not properly depthed could at once unleash the full power of the spring,

111

NO MORE RUINED MUSICAL BOXES

WITH JACOT'S

PATENT ✳ SAFETY ✳ CHECK.

JACOT'S PATENT SAFETY CHECK.

Figure 26 Jacot's, one of the several different forms of safety checks devised to prevent the cylinder spinning destructively should the governor be broken or disengaged.

Musical boxes are operated by one or several powerful springs, the speed being controlled and regulated by a series of wheels and pinions terminating in a fly-wheel. Now if the fly-wheel be broken or removed, or any of the wheels get loose from the pinion when the spring is wound, the cylinder will revolve with lightning rapidity, causing the partial or complete ruin of the instrument, by bending and breaking the pins on the cylinder as well as the teeth of the comb, as illustrated on page 22.

causing it to whirl the cylinder round at very high speed, ripping off pins and fracturing comb teeth and sending them flying in all directions. This is called 'a run'.

To prevent this from happening, several makers contrived simple attachments which could be fitted to musicwork for the purpose of containing spring power if the gear train became deranged. Each worked on some application of gravity or centrifugal force. Jacot's Safety Check, probably the most advertised, was a gravity mechanism. A ratchet wheel of large diameter was affixed to the end of the cylinder and against this rested a special double-toothed pawl with a weighted arm. As the box played, this arm alternately engaged and disengaged pawls. However, if the motion of the cylinder speeded up, the weighted pawl would jam in the ratchet wheel, so holding the cylinder firm. Mermod's Parachute Check, another well-known model, worked on the same principle, only here the rocking pawl became a feature of the nickel-plated movement by being fitted with a shield which bore the Mermod Frères trade mark (see Fig. 26).

A variant which worked on the centrifugal force exerted by a weight on an arm was used by Paillard, among others. Here a small pinion was positioned so that it was rotated by the cylinder great wheel. This pinion turned a shaft through which was bored a cross hole. Through this hole was fitted a loose rod with a steel ball on one end and a compression spring and securing washer on the other in such a way that the ball and its rod could be slid back and forth through the shaft but, when at rest or turning slowly, remained in equilibrium at a central position by virtue of the small coil spring. The whole assembly was held in a bracket of such proportions that the slowly rotating ball and rod had just sufficient room to turn. However, if the cylinder should have cause to speed up suddenly as would be the case if the endless screw were to be broken, then the ball would at once fly out through centrifugal force and jam its shaft against the attachment bracket.

Without any doubt, these safety checks saved a number of musical mechanisms from destruction through carelessness or accident.

THE CYLINDER

The cylinder is the musical programme of the movement and comprises a delicate brass shell which, with its surface displaying a profusion of tiny steel pins, is free to move laterally on its steel arbor or axis. It is keyed to the rotational movement of the axis and restrained from unwanted radial movement (backlash) by a drive pin which protrudes from the great wheel.

The normal single-cylinder movement is an integral unit with its arbor, drive pinion and great wheel. With the advent of the interchangeable cylinder, described in the next section, the drive pinion normally remained part of the movements and the cylinder became located in special bearings, taking its rotational drive from an eccentric drive spigot.

Although the greater majority of cylinders were put on the market just as they left the makers' workshop, i.e. plain brass which could (and did) ultimately tarnish, some later pieces by Paillard were nickel-plated. Mermod also went in for plated cylinders. While this certainly improved the looks of the movement, it is impossible to convince oneself that a good silver-looking box plays any better than a good tarnished brass one!

Musical movements were measured by the length of the cylinder in *pouces* and its diameter in *lignes*. This information was, with later boxes, written on the tune sheet. It is interesting to note that this system of measurement is itself an anachronism since it was superseded when the metric system which we know today came into use by law in France on 2 November 1801. But musical-box makers were no doubt slow to change and so, right up to the end, they followed the system in which 1 *ligne* equals 12 points, 12 *lignes* equal 1 *pouce*, 12 *pouces* 1 *pied* and 6 *pieds* 1 *toise*, or 1·949 metres.

The *ligne* equalled 2·256 mm (0·0895 in.). Twelve *lignes* or 27·072 mm (1·065 in.) equalled 1 *pouce*.

CHANGEABLE CYLINDERS

The restricted programme available with the normal cylinder musical box led to the development of the movement with changeable cylinders. Such pieces were styled *pièce à rechange* and at the time the mechanism was built, a number of changeable cylinders were manufactured any one of which could be inserted into the mechanism and played at will. Interchangeability meant that the owner could select his programme of music from the cylinders which were supplied with the box.

The earliest examples of this variety date from around 1850 and I have seen two specimens. The first was marked Ducommun Girod and included a 16-note reed organ accompaniment at the left end of the cylinder. There were six cylinders with this instrument which were housed in a plain, rough wooden box. To change the cylinder at the end of the tune, two very large levers which were normally pressed down by heavy leaf springs had to be raised, so freeing the cylinder arbor ends. In a special compartment by the side of the mechanism were

113

two small hooks rather like glove hooks or crochet hooks with well fashioned wooden handles. These were inserted into recesses in the ends of the cylinder, so allowing it to be lifted out, set on one side and the hooks employed in lifting another cylinder out of its storage case and placing it into the mechanism. It is this system of special hooks for cylinder changing which gives this type of movement its cognomen – the glove-hook changeable-cylinder box. A second example in much grander form was sold at Christie's South Kensington in 1977.*

The high risk of damage to the comb teeth and the cylinder pins during changing cylinders remained to the forefront in the minds of the makers of these early systems. Francois Charles Lecoultre devised an interesting and, as far as the musical box was concerned, unique application of barrel organ technology in his system (British Patent No. 1941 dated 26 June 1869) which specified the withdrawing of the cylinder through the right-hand end of the case (which was provided with a large let-down flap) on a carrier. The actual removal of the cylinder from its safety locks was thus carried out actually outside the box and well away from the delicate comb tips and dampers. The British Patent is one year later than its Swiss counterpart so this implies that Lecoultre was experimenting with this system as early as 1867–8. A box making use of this system and complete with internal vertical winding, is preserved in the Rita Ford collection and is illustrated on page 34 of Bower's *Encyclopedia of Automatic Musical Instruments*. A second example, this time incomplete, is in the Hughes Ryder collection in Cranford, New Jersey.

Another variety of early changeable-cylinder box features special handles formed from the cylinder arbor extensions. One example, unmarked, also sold by Christie's, is shown in Plate 87. A virtually identical specimen of this last-mentioned style is in the Murtogh Guinness collection, New York. This one has the bedplate stamped 'Karrer & Ce à Geneve' (sic) and an engraved brass tune sheet signed 'Henry Capt à Geneve' with the legend 'Musique Mandoline et a Expression avec Cinq Cylinders de Rechange' (sic). Its single comb plays on long and short cylinder pins as a *piano-forte* style. This same system has been seen on a much larger *piano-forte* box bearing the name Moulinié Ainé stamped on the bedplate and with the letters ML stamped into the combs, signifying that these were made by Metert and Langdorff. This partnership ran from 1844 to 1852 and since this particular box is wound by a ratchet handle, it would appear to date from the very early 1850s. The style of the two combs is also very much Metert – see Plate 64.

It fell to Amédée Paillard to perfect the first practical changeable-cylinder mechanism in the mid-1860s. With his invention of a much safer and less potentially damaging means of changing cylinders came the possibility of manufacturing cylinders on their own – in other words, by standardising the size of a musical mechanism and by building to jig-set tolerances it would be possible to produce cylinders which would fit into any movement of that size and so dispense with the need to justify replacement cylinders to a particular movement. So was born the interchangeable-cylinder musical box. From a list of possible tune programmes, the customer could now select those he preferred in the certain knowledge that they would instantly fit his musical mechanism. The process by which this was achieved was to use a *gabarit* or full-sized assembly jig in which the cylinders were produced and justified within common limits. The *gabarit* was the invention of Amédée Paillard who was a member of a most ingenious and prolific family of musical-box makers and was subsequently respon-

---

* This was fully described in *The Music Box*, vol. 8, p. 71, 1977.

sible for many improvements in the manufacture and later mass-production of pieces.

Numerous systems to improve the interchangeable appeared over the years, with particular emphasis on not just the ease of operation, but the protection of the mechanism. A carelessly manipulated cylinder could so easily smash the comb or otherwise break the delicate musical mechanism. Many patents were taken out for systems, but one which was quite novel was that invented by G. F. Beutner and A. A. Lateulere in 1886. The mechanism had a fixed arbor for the cylinder which at all times remained in place. The cylinder itself was not really a cylinder at all but was saddle-shaped with a long slit down the whole length through to the centre. This strange-shaped musical programme was dropped over the arbor and locked in place for playing in the usual way. These mechanisms were put into production by Paillard but must be considered rarities. The 'cylinders' themselves were always filled solidly with cement.

It has already been explained how the train of gearing from spring motor to governor uses the cylinder arbor as one vital link in the system. Take away the cylinder arbor, and the spring power was unbridled and would at once dissipate, probably with destructive force. In the movement mentioned above as sold by Christie's in London, the power of the spring was retained while the cylinder and arbor were removed by the use of a special pinion rod which locked the spring barrel teeth firmly in a stationary position.* J. Billon-Haller used a similar system in his production boxes for a while, but the problem was not overcome until Paillard thought to move the governor to a different position so that the mechanism could run safely with or without the cylinder in place. Paillard's simple improvement was to drive the gear train from a great wheel on a short shaft carrying the cylinder drive pinion in mesh with the spring-barrel teeth. The cylinder itself was driven by a dog spigot in a position external to the gear train. This one move advanced the perfection of the movement a considerable way.

No doubt in an effort to avoid the patent problem, Alfred Junod in conjunction with Jules Jaccard and Paul Calame-Jaccard made another variant in which the spring barrel and the governor retained their former relative positions at either end of the cylinder, but both were mounted underneath the bedplate and linked together by a long steel shaft. The cylinder fitted in the usual type of mechanism above, but again was quite independent of the whole power-train system.

It was also Junod who was responsible for the unusual Alexandra system of interchangeable-cylinder musical boxes (see next chapter). Patented in 1890 (British Patent 12170 dated 2 August 1890 (French patent 207352; US patent 445699 issued 3 February 1891)), the Alexandra was a cheap movement with completely hollow cylinders which were

---

* The development of the practical changeable-cylinder musical box was indeed one fraught with problems and many makers produced experimental systems, most of which were technically inferior and not provided with any fail-safe device to prevent accidental derangement of the mechanism. One prototype system by Billon-Haller survives in the Nationaal Museum van Speelklok tot Pierement in Utrecht. The endless assembly is mounted to a separate bedplate extension to the left of the twin mainsprings, its drive being taken by means of a layshaft passing in front of the spring barrels. The bedplate is pierced for an endless in the normal position, its screw hole and dowel-pin holes showing that the bedplate was a 'standard' casting. The cylinders retain their great wheels which, of course, serve no purpose. The problem of separating the cylinder from the power train in this way is that the cylinder is free to amplify any normal backlash in the gearing and so turns rather jerkily. This was later overcome by providing a special drive wheel and dog spigot for the cylinder. The endless, instead of being driven separately by the spring as in the Billon-Haller prototype described above, was driven directly from the shaft powering the cylinder drive spigot, effectively removing all backlash.

open at one end and had a sort of hand grip at the other. There were three sizes of instrument: one with a cylinder 7 in. long with a playing length of 5¾ in. (style number 7); one with a cylinder 10⅛ in. long with a playing length of 8⅞ in.; and a small one with a 4¾ in. cylinder which differed in that it was open at both ends. The cheap-style musical movement featured a detachable arbor on which was fixed a plain brass tube on to which the cylinder was slipped and a recess engaged in a dog set in the end. The arbor was then replaced in the mechanism. The tone of these instruments was poor; a zither and tune-indicator were standard attachments. The transfer-decorated case had inside a number of black-painted wooden columns on to which the cylinders could be securely held when not in use. Style number 2 with 7 in. cylinders had two rows of three at the left while style number 7a, with the same size cylinders, had one row running along the back.

The revolver mechanism, described in the next chapter, was another invention of Amédée Paillard. This offered the advantages of cylinder interchangeability without the inconvenience of requiring separate cylinders. The penalty was one of cost.

Another low cost interchangeable style was the Ideal made by Mermod Frères. Here the tune changing was achieved in a much simpler manner than before by using an automatically rotated cam in place of the usual *limaçon*, or snail-wheel and cam.

TUNE CHANGING

The use of the snail for tune changing goes back to the earliest times of the musical box and was applied from the practice and experience of clockmaking and, in particular, the tune changing on bell-playing clocks.

This tiny but important piece of precision engineering is mounted off centre on the great wheel of the cylinder arbor between the wheel and the cylinder in such a manner that an adjustable peg protruding from the end face of the cylinder is in contact with its face (see Fig. 27).

In the very early musical mechanisms, the tune change wheel comprised a very narrow form of lantern pinion, the inwards-facing side of which was the snail cam. Each engagement of the tune-change finger indexed this slender lantern wheel by one division. Later on, though, the comparatively neat lantern style gave way universally to the one-piece wheel and cam.

The wheel itself is star-shaped and provided with as many points as there are tunes on the cylinder, i.e. as many times as the cylinder must be shifted. When a metal finger, located on the bedplate of the musicwork, is moved into the proper position,* it will cause the starwheel to be turned through one division each time it is brought round with the great wheel.

Upon the face of the starwheel, and providing the surface on which the cylinder peg contacts, is a stepped cam giving the whole assembly the general appearance of a snail. It is this which gives rise to its soubriquet. Each time the starwheel is indexed one point, the face cam causes the cylinder to be shifted laterally so that another set of pins, representing another tune to be played, is brought into alignment with the tips of the comb teeth and those of the previous tune or tunes allowed to pass silently between the teeth.

---

* On the Swiss and French movements, the finger moves in and out at right angles to the cylinder, but on later Czech movements the finger slid parallel with the cylinder into engagement and out of it. All movements of this type used push/pull rod-operated controls in place of the familiar sliding lever.

116

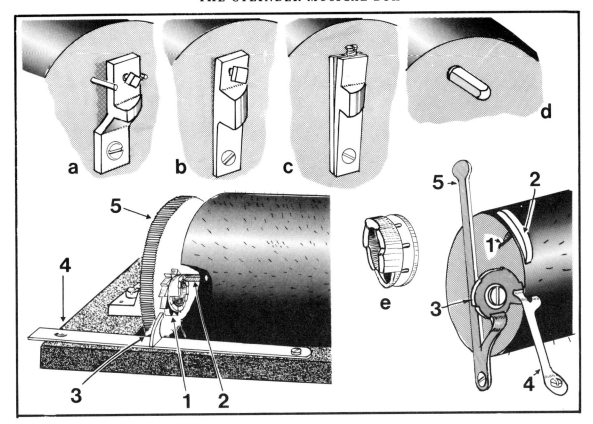

Figure 27   Tune-changing and registration systems. The means by which the cylinder is brought into register with the change snail, seen lower left, vary from the adjustable wedge (a, b and c) to the later screwed peg (d). Lower left shows the later production type of change: 1. star-wheel with as many points as there are tunes on the cylinder on the face of which is a snail cam of the same number of steps. Register peg (2) is moved by the snail. Tune change lever (4) carries a finger (3) which can be placed to turn the star-wheel which is freely pivoted on the cylinder great wheel (5). The sketch at (e) shows the very early form of change snail in the form of a lantern pinion. Bottom right is the late form of tune-change devised by Mermod using a stamped steel face cam (3) either held tight in the 'repeat' position by lever (5), or released so that it catches in cleft (1) and, when spring (4) is lifted by cylinder cam (2), is rotated one step by the cylinder to the next tune position.

It will be appreciated that the snail must be rotated through a much greater distance on a box playing only a few tunes than on one playing a large number. For instance, a 4-air movement requires that the snail rotate through 90° for a single change, but a 12-air movement will call for only 30°. There is also a minimum feasible lateral distance which each change of the snail must impel the cylinder horizontally. This is governed by the width of the teeth which itself regulates the distance between the points. A coarse-combed 4-air movement, for example, demands a much greater lateral shift of the cylinder during tune changing than a fine-combed 8-air example.

These considerations were all taken into account during the design of the musicwork, the more so in the early period when the dictates of watchmaking ensured that the mechanism was built to extremely close limits, not just as regards dimensions but also as concerned the

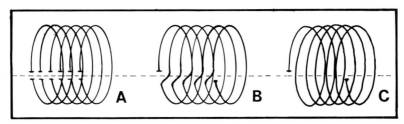

Figure 28 Principles of single-play and extended-play musical-box cylinders. At (A) is the normal, six-air cylinder playing one tune per turn. At (B) is the semi-helicoïdal where the cylinder is pinned over the change position, so advancing normally through some 340 degrees of rotation and then being shifted for the remaining 20 degrees to the next snail step. The totally smooth spiral-moving cylinder is represented by the full helicoïdal sketched at (C).

driving power and the reduction of friction. This last concern – friction – was paramount in the minds of builders and one point which had to be considered was the extra power needed to effect the shift of the cylinder at tune changing and to overcome the frictional resistance of the parts. Of course, the change sequence came at the very worst time from a mechanical standpoint – between tunes and when the movement was starting up from stationary.

Matters are somewhat eased in that during the change sequence, the mechanism is not normally playing – I say normally because, in the case of the semi-helicoïdal and plerodiénique, it is still in play. This means a reduction in the resistance afforded to the movement by the cylinder pins contacting the comb. Even so, on movements with large, long and heavy cylinders the inertia to be overcome is considerable. For this reason some musical movements, both of the early genre and also, significantly, of the later period, change the tune position before the mechanism comes to a stop at the end of the preceding tune. When the mechanism is set to play again, the cylinder is already in position and start-up resistance is minimal.

The higher the standard of quality of a movement, the less the radial distance needed for the snail to effect the lateral shift to the cylinder.

Later, mass-produced movements were forced to allow quite a wide gap between tunes, clearly seen on the cylinder, to allow the snail to shift the cylinder through the necessary lateral distance by means of a gradual slope on the cam. Early movements do not demonstrate that such a need existed. The snail is engaged with the change-lever finger and starts to rotate well before the end of the tune. The duration of the actual change period is very short, the snail cam being quite steep, and the gap between tunes as viewed on the surface of the cylinder is quite narrow.

While discussing tune-changing, another difficulty facing the constructors of these movements was how to bring the cylinder back from the end-of-programme position (tune 6 on a 6-air movement) to the tune 1 position again. Whereas the later manufacturers of street pianos recognised the problem and so arranged their 8-tune cams so that the cylinder progressed 1, 3, 5, 7, 8, 6, 4, 2, so avoiding a large return distance to be retraced by the barrel, this was not a feature found in the cylinder musical box. However, I have seen just one box, maker unknown, with a 6-air mechanism and a 12-point snail allowing the tunes, somewhat disturbingly, to be played forwards, and then in reverse order. This was mechanically a neat idea, but a commercial white elephant unless the tune sheet was provided with a cautionary note to the user!

On the majority of musical movements, the cylinder is returned under the pressure of the spring on the other end of the arbor and this naturally results in a slight bang as the stud on the end of the cylinder falls off the highest point of the tune-change cam and strikes the lower point. Normally this distance is little more than one-tenth of an inch, but even so, with a large, heavy cylinder and a necessarily strong spring, this is sufficient to cause a shock which might result in damage. Because the snail is driven only in one direction and is otherwise loose, it was impractical to adopt the system used on large orchestrion organs, which was to angle the drop into a steep slope, so allowing a rapid but not instantaneous shift. Where the style of box suggested that damage might occur, some makers overcame this by transforming the transition into two closely spaced jumps. The snail cam would have a short, inter-mediate step half-way down the drop so that the cylinder peg would lodge momentarily on this.

A variation exists on some very small musical movements. Some 3-air miniature move-ments (with cylinders about 3-4 in. long) employ a 6-pointed starwheel giving a systematic shift up the cam and then down it again not unlike the street piano system mentioned just now. Again, some later small movements of the type used in photograph albums have an automatic tune-change system through a fixed change-finger and a snail cam which moves 1, 2, 1, 2, and so on continually. Others use an automatic changer in the form of a rectangular cam which is constantly in contact with the end of the cylinder and is changed by a groove in the cylinder end (Mermod's style is illustrated in Fig. 27).

The accurate registration of the cylinders to the combs, particularly on the interchange-able models, was one hurdle which evidence suggests gave the most problems to many makers. The normal snail change impels the cylinder asymetrically from one side at some distance from the arbor. A few moments of thought will reveal that unless the cylinder can slide perfectly smoothly on its arbor, the slightest friction can prevent the easy translation from one lateral position to the next. In severe cases, arbor bearing wear can occur which will end up making accurate snail cam operation impossible.

As the cylinder musical box developed, the refinements and improvements in operation centred more and more on the elimination of problems from asymmetric shift rather than on the elimination of asymmetric shift itself. Both Mermod and Paillard in their later mass-produced interchangeable boxes ended up driving the cylinder from a pin on a faceplate while the snail was so arranged on the faceplate that the actual cylinder arbor was able to ride the snail. This way, the lateral force was applied to the cylinder in a mechanically ideal way. In the United States, one maker (believed to have been Jules Cuendet) solved the problem in another way. He used a normal form of change snail but duplicated it so that instead of having one snail at the radius, he had one on each side of the arbor on a diameter. The two snails were united by three small gears so that as the single change finger turned one, so the other also turned, impelling the cylinder evenly from either side of the arbor. One such mechanism can be seen at Sarasota in the Walt Bellm collection.

Miniature musicwork tune-change systems are covered extensively under Chapter 3.

NUMBER OF TUNES PLAYED

Very occasionally, an interchangeable-cylinder box would have cylinders pinned with unequal numbers of tunes. For example, I have seen a PVF Mandolin Expression six-cylinder box playing thirty-four airs, one cylinder having only four tunes.* This was by virtue of the fact that some tunes would be represented on two turns of the cylinder. This would not be achieved in the same way as with the helicoidal type of movement, but by having, say, two variations of the same tune under one title. This is the same system as was featured in some of the early boxes where, for example, an overture (usually 'William Tell'!) would be fitted on to two separate revolutions of the cylinder, the convenient linking slow passage between the two sections of the overture forming a natural break as the barrel shifted. In modern times, this selfsame characteristic is to be found on quality movements from Reuge with melodies such as the 'Harry Lime Theme' represented on three revolutions of a three-air-type movement.

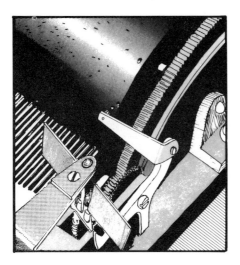

Figure 29　The ability to play tunes of different lengths is a characteristic of the mechanism sketched here. Invented by F. Lecoultre, the mechanism could be made to stop anywhere by providing a small hole in the cylinder surface for the point of the trail to drop into. Used in conjunction with normal snail tune-changing, it allowed one revolution to comprise for example one long and one short tune to make up the full turn.

TUNE SHEETS

The list of tunes affixed inside the lids of later musical boxes is generally called a tune sheet, although, in contemporary parlance, tune sheet was the name also given to the disc for a disc-playing musical box.

The very earliest boxes appear not to have bothered too much over the titles of the music played. Then came the practice of writing the titles in manuscript on the bare wood, sometimes on the case bottom or on a piece of wood inside. Plain labels were then used, these being stuck on the bottom or along the inside back of the case. By the late 1820s, the first tune sheets proper appeared – simple printed labels with, in some cases, the initials of the maker engraved in the design. Within a short while, tune sheets became more and more involved as the art of the engraver paved the way for decorative calligraphy. Almost without exception, these early tune sheets were printed black on white or buff paper, occasionally on thin card. By 1850, colours had been introduced and the printing was done in blue or brown on

* One interchangeable box in the Murtogh Guinness collection, New York, has five four-air cylinders and one eight-air.

coloured card. Still, though, only one colour was used. The programme of music was then handwritten in the spaces provided.

Highest-quality boxes were often provided with brass or sometimes silver tune-plaques upon which the titles were engraved; Henri Capt made fairly common use of brass tune sheets, as did Nicole Frères, usually through their agents such as T. Cox-Savory.

In most instances, the tune sheets were affixed under the lid using four domed-headed brass pins, but occasionally they were fixed into the back of the box. Most elaborate and often beautiful designs were adopted by some manufacturers and the coming of lithography in colours produced some very fine chromolith tune sheets in the period 1870–90. Prior to this, though, motifs were generally classical, garlands and wreaths twisting round columns and balustrading, and interwoven with the names of famous composers.

The progress of the tune sheet was an interesting one because soon it became more of a decorative feature of the box and by the end of the century it was a bright and somewhat gaudy device of unnecessarily large proportions – sometimes as big, almost, as the lid itself and often proclaiming almost everything except the titles of the tunes upon which its existence apparently depended!

The early changeable-cylinder boxes used plain handwritten cards for listing the tunes and these would be selected from the pack of six (or however many cylinders the box played) and the appropriate one inserted in a little holder at the back of the movement. In later years, one big tune sheet was used upon which was listed the entire musical programme broken up under headings, 'Cylinder No. 1', and so on. On the Karrer/Capt early changeables, the titles of the tunes were stamped into the cylinder surface itself before pinning.

Tune sheets came in many sizes and styles. Nicole Frères, for example, produced a great number, among them some which were printed with their main agents' names and addresses. Among the early Nicole styles are found similar sheets printed on white card, blue card and green card. For some while it has been believed that the blue cards indicated an inferior mechanism or programme. There appears no truth in this whatsoever and the significance of the cards of various colours seems of little consequence. Bremond for a time used a diamond-shaped tune sheet, and I have seen a C. Lecoultre six-air part-mandoline box with a similarly shaped tune sheet. However, these were probably isolated departures from the practice which suggested that all tune sheets should be rectangular, be they long and narrow, such as those used by Nicole in the early days and by the Viennese makers, or almost square such as the ones used by David Lecoultre.

While most were printed sheets, a few were embossed, these being of the early period. One style, with two embossed medallions, is attributed to Karrer of Teufenthal, the German-speaking part of north Switzerland. Another, used by Henriot, featured a symmetrical design of four motifs, one centrally in each side. A selection of types and styles appears in the Appendix.

With the large-size tune sheets of later production, it was not unusual to find three different styles of handwriting used to itemise the musical programme – one for the title, one for the opera (or style of music such as march or dance), and the third for the composer. Quite often one finds mistakes not just in identification of music but complete mis-titling.

Billon-Haller, with a tune sheet stating just the style of the box, wrote his tune titles on strips of red-edged white paper which were stuck along the length of the cylinder at the change position. Ullmann typed his tune details, then printed copies on a jelly duplicator using blue or mauve ink.

ATTACHMENT

The manner in which musical movements were attached to their boxes can tell us a lot about the date and period of the box. All the early movements were held in place using four hand-cut metal screws, two through the front of the case into the fore edge of the bedplate, and two through the back of the box into the rear edge of the bedplate.* Some early movements were mounted in cases with detachable bottoms, that is to say, the bottom was not an integral part of the box. With these, the movement was put into the case from underneath and located by two strips of wood attached to the front and back of the box. After the two front and two rear securing screws were put into place, the bottom of the case was screwed on. On some early Francois Nicole boxes, the two front securing screws were partnered by a single down-screw at the back of the bedplate which fitted into a case block and held the bedplate secure with a brass nib-piece. With all these detachable-bottom cases, the movement was not maintained in contact with the base of the box at all.

Quite early on, and possibly as a result of the progress of the musical movement in the bases of clocks, it was found that if the bottom of the case was firmly secured into the case by chamfering its edges and wedging them into grooves routed out of the lower parts of the case sides and ends, the sound output was improved. The brass bedplates were now fitted with four steel legs which rested on the bottom and acted, to a certain extent, as sound posts. As the four movement-securing screws were put in, there was a tendency for the case front and back to pull in if there was too much clearance. This had the effect of jamming the inner glass lid (where fitted) and, in bad instances, of preventing the main case lid from closing properly. To keep the movement tightly in position, special U-shaped metal wedges were driven down, where necessary, between case side and bedplate at the point of screwing so that the screw passed between the two legs of the U wedge.

Nicole Frères, typical of many makers, retained the front and back case screwing and the four legs for most of their existence. But Paillard and, later, Mermod realised that, whereas four legs could not be guaranteed to rest evenly on the bottom, three stood a better chance. So came to be introduced the tripod mounting in which the movement was secured into the case with three large woodscrews passing down through the bedplate into special wooden case blocks either end, or by metal bolts which passed down through the case bottom and formed a positive means of contact between bedplate and case. It was this form of attachment which finally came to be adopted by the majority of cylinder box makers.

I have seen one very early Ducommun-Girod box which has two metal screws passing through the front of the case into the fore edge of the bedplate and one only centrally in the back – an odd and probably short-lived experiment. This box is in the Hughes Ryder collection, New Jersey.

DECORATION

Under this heading I am including aspects of musical-box embellishment both of case and mechanism. External decoration in the better-quality boxes did not stop at marquetry but often extended to parquetry and the inlay of other substances such as metal and tortoiseshell, ivory and mother of pearl after the style of Boulle work (not, please note, Buhl which is a common and incorrect Germanic spelling of the name of André Charles Boulle). Most

* Humbert Brolliet used *six* screws – three front and three back.

frequently, inlays were of brass, occasionally silver and even pewter. Coloured enamels were also let in and some of these boxes presented a truly magnificent appearance.

Internally, some makers went in for carved work, particularly those such as Bremond in their organ-accompaniment boxes. Here the full depth (front to back) of the box would be divided into roughly one quarter and three-quarters, the rear, narrow section being in the form of a fixed, carved screen backed by coloured silk and provided so as to allow the sound of the organ to escape. On some large boxes, this screen portion of the inside would be in two sections with a miniature painting in its centre, usually on glass and always very finely executed. The subject seems invariably to have been Geneva and its environs. L'Épée was very fond of fixing large gilded spandrels on the inside of the box lid and also inside the case of his biggest boxes. These were punched out of thin metal and often look like later additions. They are, though, original. Ami Rivenc always cross-banded the veneer round the frame of the inner glass lid – a nice touch and a mark of this maker's quality.

As for the mechanism itself, bells were often chased and tooled as were motor spring barrels. Usually the motor barrel treatment would be to turn a pattern of wavy lines around the circumference and occasionally the face of the barrel gear would be engraved or otherwise tooled. The top of the zither was another area which received the ample attention of the embellisher and, whereas the early ones were quite plain, by the 1880s and 1890s, these were often a riot of design.

Detail decorations ranged from making the strikers of bell-boxes in the shape of enamelled bees, butterflies and moths down to chamfering the edges of the cock-plate. A favourite style of box, apparently introduced by Paillard, was the 'mandarin' bell-box, wherein the bells were struck by maces held in the hands of nodding mandarins.

Control levers are frequently found with decorative escutcheons, and special boxes – particularly presentation items – often had brass or sometimes silver tune sheets engraved in script. Paillard was among the few to make a range of highly decorated boxes as can be seen from the plerodiénique shown in Plates 121 to 123. This has finely chiselled brass mouldings, inlays into ebony (parquetry), and a heavy bevelled-edge mirror inside the lid.

MUSICAL-BOX MANUFACTURE

Musical-box making was essentially a cottage industry in the early days and large numbers of outworkers, separated by their style of country living in an area where communication was a toilsome task, contributed to the construction of one box. It is a sobering thought that, by virtue of this style of work, many who made musical-box parts never saw the fruits of their own labours, let alone were able to hear them.

Actually how musical boxes were designed and put together has for many years been one of those enigmas of the most infuriating type – there was an end product with little clear-cut indication as to how it was devised. One has only to listen to an 1830 musical box playing, note perfect, a complex piece of music to comprehend some measure of the task facing its manufacturer.

The most demanding procedures were the making of combs and cylinders and both were carried out by absolute specialists who worked on nothing else.

Today, with allegedly better tools, better knowledge and the evidence of the past to go on, many amateurs have attempted to build a musical box. To my knowledge, several have succeeded in making new combs, making spring barrels and governors, even casting bedplates. And one member of the Musical Box Society of Great Britain has actually completely manufactured a cylinder musical-box mechanism. All but one have stopped short at the final stage which transforms a mute engineering marvel into something which is a delight to listen to – pinning music on the cylinder.*

Not that there is anything impossible about this – the skills are well recorded in textbooks which go back two centuries and I myself published a modern treatise on the subject not half a dozen years back. The problem lies in the complete miniaturisation of a delicate operation whereby four, six, eight or even more tunes may be pinned with a high degree of accuracy to the cylinder.

Assembly of the musical box from the parts delivered from the outworkers, who were all poorly paid, would be undertaken in a finishing shop. The final man in the whole chain would most carefully listen to each tune over and over again, making minute adjustments to pins by bending them slightly forwards or backwards. He was termed an improver and his job was to ensure that all the notes and their intervals were correct, that all the notes in a chord fell at exactly the same moment, and that there were no wrong notes. His work was carried out with the aid of a watchmaker's tiny hollow drift.

Making the combs was a highly skilled operation, starting with the actual comb steel which was of a special 'mix' the equivalent of which is no longer produced. It approximates most to what engineers call 'ground flat stock', 'tool steel', or 'silver steel'. The first operation was to cut out the blank to the over-all size required. This was then ground down to the thickness required for the teeth, with care being taken to allow the full thickness of the metal over the places where the lead weights would later be soldered and where the steel dampers would subsequently be pegged into place.

Once the comb was ground, it would be slit with a jeweller's saw to produce the number of teeth required, and the tooth tips shaped by grinding wheel and file. The holes for the fixing screws and the damper wires would be drilled at this stage. Next would come the heat treatment, a most precise and carefully controlled process of heating in a muffler furnace and then gradually cooling to impart a hardness and ring to the teeth. A block of lead from which the lead weights might be fashioned was then soldered carefully to the section of the comb left unground at the teeth ends. After rough trimming, leaving it oversize somewhat for tuning purposes, the cast brass base for the comb would also be soldered into place.

The comb teeth would now be re-sawn, this time to cut only through the lead. Some makers experimentally used brass instead of lead and Lecoultre used steel in at least one instance – a small musical snuff-box in the Utrecht museum. The next step was to hone the tooth tips to the correct angle, polish the upper surface of the comb and fit the dampers in position in their anvils. The tuner now attended to the comb and, working from a master comb which sounded the correct notes, he proceeded to tune the new comb.

With the comb clamped in a hand-vice, he would work on one tooth at a time using snips for the lead weights, and a series of small, angle-handled files. Removing weight towards the tip would raise the note; removing metal from the middle of the tooth would lower the note. By balancing most carefully his treatment of the comb teeth, he could produce a comb wherein all the teeth performed with equal strength and tonality.

---

* Mr G. T. Mayson has built in 2,000 hours of spare time a musical box which plays four tunes – Schubert's *Die Forelle* and three of the Quintet variations. His masterpiece, whose music was arranged for his comb by Mr Robin Timms, was exhibited at a Society meeting at Stratford-upon-Avon in December 1977.

Cylinder pinning was, initially, a process developed from that of pinning carillon clocks, an established part of the clockmaker's art. The plain brass barrel would be scored off in evenly spaced divisions around the circumference, each indicating the line traced around the cylinder by one tooth tip when aligned for the first tune position. Occasionally, to produce a deeper bass note, the bass teeth of the comb would be allocated a progressively wider spacing with the very last (lowest) tooth appreciably wider than those in the rest of the comb. This feature would be indicated by this ruling off of the cylinder surface. Some makers at this early period then ruled off the cylinder surface longitudinally so as to produce what looked very much like a chequer-board surface. Each division was equal to one semibreve or whole note. This immediately indicates that each tune played on the cylinder must be of the same length in semibreves, or performed in double time or in half time. For this reason, this form of notation is termed 'rigid notation' in that it is dependent on and is governed by a rigid framework. For the early makers, this apparently was an advantage and was a more practical method of working. From the standpoint of pinning a cylinder today, this system is to be recommended to the novice, for at least he can see precisely where he is in every tune which he is pinning on the surface of the cylinder.

A close examination of a musical-box cylinder will show that the pinning does not extend all the way around the circumference* but that a narrow strip of unpinned surface is left. This is to provide a projection-free area during the tune-changing operation so that as the cylinder moves sideways slightly it does not interfere with the comb teeth or, more important, the dampers.

An even closer look will reveal that there is a line of tiny dots (centre-pop marks) which coincide with the position of all the comb tips relative to the cylinder at the first tune position. At one or two places on the cylinder, it may be seen that the line of dots has been filled in to provide one little pop mark for the location of a tooth tip at each tune position. This feature is usually indicative of the work of an early repairer.

The purpose of the dots was to align the comb accurately since the smallest degree of tilt or twist relative to the cylinder would spoil the precise playing of the music.

In earlier times, before the advent of the one-piece comb, the problem of alignment was even greater and each individual tooth had to be shaped and secured so that it was in the proper position. For this purpose, special registration pins were provided in the cylinder. The line of centre-pop marks was drilled through and a normal cylinder pin inserted. These pins would be *in situ* during the normal procedure of pinning the cylinder and would be ground off to the same height as the playing pins of the tunes. Then each was hammered in a fraction further using a special depth punch so that now they stood a few thousandths of an inch below the level of the musical pins. The difference in height between the pins was the normal distance by which the comb teeth engaged the musical pins in order that they could be plucked: if they did not interfere one with the other, there would be no plucking action.

That done, each individual tooth was held in place and pressed against its respective register pin. The angle of the tooth was adjusted by delicate filing at the heel and then it would be screwed firmly into place and the next tooth given similar treatment and so on until all the teeth were in place. At this point, the register pins would either be hammered flush with the cylinder so that they were out of the way, or would be tapped down only fractionally so that they were just clear of the tooth tips.

* There is an exception here: this is the helicoidal and semi-helicoidal type of movement outlined in the next chapter.

If you examine an early musical-box cylinder under a powerful eye-glass you will see this line of pins, either tapped flush with the surface or, in very early works, left marginally proud. These pins can be seen clearly in Plate 39.

With the coming of sectional combs, i.e. teeth in groups of two, three, four, five or more, there was still a need for register pins but this time only for the first and last tooth in each group. And so on these boxes you will usually see only a few register pins. The early one-piece combs still used register pins, but usually only one at each end and possibly one or two in the middle to check against comb twist. The centre-pop marks of later production boxes are, in every way, a legacy of these register pins.

The pinning of the cylinders remains something of a mystery, in particular with the early ones with complex music. The task is, in theory, easily accomplished with the aid of a dividing head and a divided stage to indicate the different note positions. But the method of achieving such great accuracy in pinning music for a comb with up to 250 teeth leaves me, at least, speechless. In order to allow teeth proper time in which to be damped before being sounded again, each note was normally allocated more than one tooth – up to eight or more on a mandoline box – so the problem must have been even more taxing. It is known that the pricking of a cylinder – this was the name given to the provision of the tiny dots on the cylinder surface which represented each note – was a long and tedious process requiring the utmost concentration, quiet and lack of interruption. Obviously, if the pricker was distracted from his work, he had little choice but to retrace his work through from the beginning to continue from where he left off. In the early days, this work was undertaken solely by hand, using a special lathe and divider. In later years, though, attempts to speed up the process included a special cylinder-pricking machine which, according to John Clark who saw one (but was never allowed to watch it in operation), looked 'like a big typewriter'. Other developments included the many endeavours towards duplicating cylinders so that the time-consuming pricking could produce a large number of cylinders. Copying methods, judging by the patents available for examination in the Patent Office, range from the desperate to the ingenious, indicating the frantic search for a method of saving time as the industry became more and more competitive in the 1880s.

After pricking, the cylinder was placed in the hands of unskilled female labour where the job was to drill through each prick mark on the cylinder surface using a watchmaker's bow drill. Then came the eye-straining task of pinning and cylinder finishing. Since this task is the same as that undertaken by restorers today, this is described in greater detail in *Restoring Musical Boxes*.

Many importers bought in musical boxes in knocked down or component form and employed their own finishers to reassemble them and fit them into locally made cases – this saved on shipping costs. The majority of musical boxes originally sold in America, for instance, appear to have been cased in that country. See caption to Plate 121.

MANUFACTURING SUB-CONTRACT WORK

As the musical-box industry became more organised, so it began to see the importance of specialisation, in particular in an attempt to cut down costs and hence improve its competitiveness. It took a leaf out of the clock and watch industry and began to polarise into specialist workshops. Before 1880, there were workers who were supplying more than one manufacturer with their products. Wheelcutters who could blank and cut teeth automatically served the industry at large and some evidence suggests that whole governor assemblies were fabricated on a sub-contract basis for disposal through several makers. Screw-cutting, platework and the manufacture of details became the production province of numerous bulk-supplying small workshops.

One of the earliest and best known of such workshops was that of Jean Billon. Thanks to the researches of Suzanne Maurer we know that Jean-Joseph Billon established a factory for the manufacture of castings for musical boxes as early as 1844 at Cluses, Savoie in France (a mere twenty-three miles to the south-east of Geneva, close to the French Alps). The closure of this factory in 1852 prompted Jean-Joseph's son, Jean, to shift the business to Geneva where it remained until financial difficulties caused its final closure as recently as 1905. It was, though, back in October 1862 that Jean Billon, together with Louis Jules Isaac, a clockmaker born in 1830, founded the Société Billon et Isaac. Their initials, SBI, are to be found raised out of the metal in many a musical box bedplate and comb base. Rough castings from this workshop went to just about every Geneva manufacturer and even to some further afield in the Jura.

Another name associated with part-work is that of Gueissaz Frères. Based at La Sagne, Chaux-de-Fonds, the name Gueissaz is to be found scratched on the bedplates of many small musical movements made by others such as Paillard in the 1890 period. Clark believed that this might indicate that the movements had passed through the hands of Gueissaz Frères for repairs, but asserts that it could just as well be an indication that the movements were at one time sold and not made by them. It was not unknown for a smaller maker to be supplied with movements and materials by the larger ones since usually the larger makers could produce the pieces at a lower price. At nearby Ste-Croix it is known that André Gueissaz was at work making musical boxes and the trade directories list Gueissaz Fils & Co. of L'Auberson as musical-box makers between about 1890 and 1904. This name has been seen on an expensive and complex interchangeable-cylinder musical box believed to have been the one supplied to the Shah of Persia in 1896 (see p. 71). The possibility remains that Gueissaz were component factors or distributors. On a large *voix céleste* box attributed to PVF, the top of the organ component was stamped 'Gueissaz'.

A maker in his own right who supplied completed combs to other makers was Conchon and a number of boxes by other manufacturers bear combs which are stamped with Conchon's name.

By the end of the cylinder musical-box era, sub-contract work was so widespread a practice in the industry that it becomes extremely difficult to identify the individual characteristics of makers because of component similarities. There is also the situation concerning relationships between makers and agents, discussed on pp. 89–91 with particular reference to the post-1882 period of Nicole Frères, Charles Ullmann, Thomas Dawkins and Thibouville-Lamy.

Musical boxes which were originally sold in the United States from new display certain characteristics which render them different from those boxes seen in Europe. To begin with, the majority of musical boxes imported to America were sent in caseless and were fitted with locally made cabinets – the same as the greater number of Swiss boxes sold in England. These cases were finely made and demonstrate the use of American woods and taste. Marquetry and inlay was less popular than in Europe. However, by the time that many Swiss musical-box manufacturers were advertising a range of spare parts (among them Nicole, Mermod and Paillard), it became feasible for a 'manufacturer' to buy-in the majority of the ancillary components and fit these to his own cylinder/comb assembly. Import duty on musical-box parts was also much lower than on complete boxes and for this reason it seems that makers in the States such as Jacot, Paillard and Gautschi bought in a stock of components from a wide variety of Swiss suppliers and used these parts in their musical boxes. This explains why some boxes found in America have the appearance of having been assembled from a large number of other makers' components: they have!

THE NEW "AMOBEAN" MUSICAL BOX,

WITH INTERCHANGEABLE CYLINDERS AND THE CHARMING ZITHER ACCOMPANIMENT.

THIS MUSICAL BOX differs from the ordinary Musical Box in this most important particular, that you can be supplied at a merely nominal cost with an unlimited number of Cylinders, playing an unlimited number of Tunes, without requiring to send us the original Box to be fitted with the Cylinders. This new system will be admitted by all lovers of the Musical Box to be a great advantage over the old sytem of Musical Box with fixed Cylinder.

THE PERFECT INTERCHANGEABLE MUSICAL BOX.

This splendid Musical Box has been made up specially of the very best material and workmanship, the Mechanism also being equal to the finest clockwork, and the melody of the various Tunes harmonised to perfection.

With Six Cylinders 6½ in. long, 2 in. diameter. Inlaid Fancy Wood Case, with Two Drawers to contain the Cylinders; Zither Accompaniment, Nickelled Movement, winds up by means of a Detachable Crank Lever from outside, instead of the old style of Lever Winder. 36 Tunes with 6 Cylinders, 6 Tunes each. Price only £8 8s.

ENORMOUS DEMAND LAST SEASON FOR THIS SPLENDID BOX.

"A Thing of Beauty and a Joy for Ever."

THE NEW AMOBEAN Musical Box PLAYS THIRTY-SIX TUNES.

Testimonial.

Broadhayes Farm, Stockland, Honiton, Devon, 1894. Gentlemen,—The Amobean Musical Box arrived quite safe, and I am highly delighted with it. It is a perfect work of art, and it plays the various tunes, 36 in all, to perfection ; the tone also is really splendid.

I am, yours truly,
GEORGE NEWTON.

THE NEW AMOBEAN Musical Box PLAYS THIRTY-SIX TUNES.

Testimonial.

Strathearn Lodge, Crieff.

Dear Sirs,—Miss Bainbridge wishes me to write and inform you that she duly received the New Amobean Musical Box safe and sound, and she is very much pleased with it. Its charming music gives her every satisfaction, and thanks you very much.

I remain, yours truly,
JOHN EWBANKS.

Inlaid Fancy Wood Case, with 2 Drawers to contain the Cylinders, Nickelled Movement, 36 Tunes, with 6 Cylinders, 6 Tunes each. Price only £8 8s.

Carriage Paid to any Address in Great Britain with the following Coupon.

Cut out this.

CAMPBELL'S PRESENTATION MUSICAL BOX COUPON.

Entitles the holder to the above-described Musical Box, playing 36 Tunes, with the New Tune Indicator, ZITHER) and 6 Cylinders playing 36 Tunes, on receipt of P.O.O. for £8 8s. (ACCOMPANIMENT. This Coupon is not available after 30th September, 1895.

Cut out this.

THE ABOVE BOX PLAYS ALL OF THE FOLLOWING TUNES.

SACRED SONGS. CYLINDER No. 35.	FAVOURITE SONGS. CYLINDER No. 36.	FAVOURITE SONGS. CYLINDER No. 40.
Jesus of Nazareth.	Robin Adair.	Oft in the Stilly Night.
Tell Me the Old Story.	Annie Laurie.	Kate Kearney.
Hold the F rt.	Ye Banks and Braes.	The Harp that once thro' Tara's Hall.
The Gate Ajar for Me.	Scots wha ha'e wi' Wallace bled.	The Minstrel Boy.
Sun of My Soul.	Auld Robin Gray.	Garryowen.
Sweet Bye-and-Bye.	Bluebells of Scotland.	The Tar's Farewell.
CYLINDER No. 47.	**CYLINDER No. 28.**	**CYLINDER No. 19.**
Awake, My Soul.	Star-Spangled Banner.	Bay of Biscay.
Glory to Thee, my God.	Kathleen Mavourneen.	Rule Britannia.
Old Hundred.	In the Gloaming.	The Harmonious Blacksmith.
From Greenland's Icy Mountains.	Last Rose of Summer.	Home, Sweet Home.
A Few More Years Shall Roll.	Blue Alsatian Mountains.	The British Grenadiers.
Onward, Christian Soldiers.	Auld Lang Syne.	Ehren on the Rhine.

A LARGE ASSORTMENT OF OTHER POPULAR TUNES NOW READY.

Sold only by CAMPBELL & CO., Musical Instrument Makers, 116 Trongate, Glasgow.

CHAPTER 5

Cylinder Musical-Box Classification and Makes

During the one hundred and ten years or so of cylinder musical-box production, a very large number of styles and types was produced which afforded some variety on the original basic concept of a pinned cylinder and tuned steel teeth.

The production of improved and modified varieties of instrument largely came about as a result of the burgeoning market around the middle of the nineteenth century. Indeed, the Great Exhibition of 1851 saw the large-scale introduction of what today we would tend to call gimmick names for musical boxes. Earlier there had been ordinary musical boxes and those which were marked 'Overture'. Now came the start of a technological and largely publicity-minded explosion which carried with it into the pages of musical-box history names such as Polytype, Longue Marche and Flutina. While many of the earlier (pre-1885) styles really did have something to contribute to the development of the musical box, such as sublime harmonie, forte-piano and orchestral, many were no more than a linguistic twister to try to sell a cheap, mass-produced and probably musically inferior piece to a receptive market.

And so it came to pass that the cylinder musical box, which nobody had ever thought justified any sort of cognomen, began to earn itself a measure of product individuality as a number of manufacturers coined names. Within a short period, Geneva found itself unwittingly responsible for the eponym which became adopted in France and Germany as indicating a cylinder musical movement – 'Musique de Genève' which simply meant mechanical music after the style invented in Geneva.

There follows a conspectus of the more common names after which I will describe each in some degree of detail. Included in this list are those names which occasionally head up a tune sheet and which help to define the maker or the programme type. Makers' names, however, are excluded – these can be found in Chapter 11.

Alexandra
Amobean
Bells in Sight see *Bells in View*
Bells in Vue see *Bells in View*
Bells in View

Columbia
Colibri
Concertino
Concerto
Diva Harmonic

Duettino
Duplex
Étoile
Excelsior
Flute see *Jeu(x) de Flûtes*
Flûte Voix Célestes see *Vox Celeste*
Flutes Celestial Voices
Flutina see *Vox Celeste*
Forte Piano
Fortissimo
Gem Sublime Harmonie
Gloria
Gloriosa
Grand Format
Guitar Zither
Harmoniphone
Harp see *Zither*
Harpe Éolienne
Harpe Harmonique
Helicoidal
Ideal
Jeux de Flûtes
Longue Marche
Mandoline
Musique Expressive Musique Symphonique
Multiphone
National
Orchestre (Orchestra)
Organ Celeste see *Vox Celeste*
Organocléide
Orphea
Overture
Peerless

Piano Forte see *Forte Piano*
Piano Forte Mandolin
Piccolo
Pièce à Oiseau
Plerodiénique
Polytype Revolver
Polytype Zither
Qualité Superextra see *Excelsior*
Quatuor
Rechange
Revolver
Semi-Helicoidal
Simplicitas see *Helicoidal*
Specialité
Sublime Harmonie
Sublime Harmonie Fortissimo
Sublime Harmonie Longue Marche
Sublime Harmonie Octave
Sublime Harmonie Piccolo
Sublime Harmonie Tremolo
Superextra
Tambour et Timbres en Vue
Timbres see *Bells in View*
Tremolo Harmonique see *Sublime Harmonie Tremolo*
Tuyaphone
Universal
Variation
Victoria
Visible Bells see *Bells in View*
Vox Celeste
Volutina
Zither

ALEXANDRA   A mechanism patented by Alfred Junod, Jules Jaccard and Paul Calame in the year 1891, the Alexandra was a late attempt to produce an interchangeable-cylinder musical box and, for what it was, it must be considered a success. The musical movement was provided with a removable cylinder which was quite plain and served as a mandrel for the musical cylinder which was sleeve-shaped. The pins were set in the surface of this and it was slipped over the mandrel and then replaced in the movement. Three sizes of Alexandra have been seen, although the middle size is known in several styles of case. Lengths of the sleeves are $4\frac{3}{8}$ in., 7 in., $10\frac{1}{8}$ in. The spare sleeves are stored on wooden phalli which are arranged either at the back of the case or to one or both sides of the movement.

AMOBEAN   A name used by Paillard to describe their later, mass-produced interchangeable-cylinder musical boxes style 700–711.

BELLS IN VIEW   Probably the most trite and obvious piece of terminology no doubt inspired by the fact that early musical boxes, when fitted with bells, always had the bells concealed under the movement (see list of styles). Paillard was probably the first to adopt this type of name on which there are numerous variants such as 'Timbres' (literally clock-bell), 'Bells in Vue', 'Bells in Sight', 'Visible Bells', etc. The type of box which displays this sort of title usually has three bells, sometimes only two and occasionally five. Usually they are not tuned and all play approximating the same note and not very purely at that. Very cheap-quality boxes attached the bell-striking linkage directly to the underside of the normal comb teeth instead of making use of a separate bell-playing comb. This was no doubt intended to look impressive, but effectively muted the bass comb teeth – a characteristic no doubt effectively replaced by the tinkle of the bell. Some very impressive – and musical – movements were made with bells, but these are not among them.

COLUMBIA   This is the trade name of one style of normal late-production cylinder musical box manufactured by Paillard and registered by them as such. There appears nothing outstanding or different from an ordinary musical movement.

COLIBRI   An unusual style of box produced by Ami Rivenc. At first appearance, it resembles an organ-type box with two short combs and three levers in the centre operated by pins and bridges in the centre of the cylinder length. Behind the cylinder is mounted a bird; in one type, two birds. The tune sheet proclaims 'Chant No. 1' and so on up to number six and this is just what this is – six comb-played representations of birdsong. The cylinder is pinned to reproduce the trills and glissades of a bird and plays no 'normal' music. The levers serve to move the bird and to add verisimilitude to the performance. A late product, c. 1890, and a novelty. Can be classified as a rarity, but remains something of a gimmick mechanism.

CONCERTINO   Name used by Paillard on boxes mainly, it seems, intended for the American market. This type of mechanism has two combs, one spanning more than three-quarters of the cylinder and a short one covering the remainder. This is one of the so-called accompaniment movements, where the teeth proportions of the shorter comb are such that they produce a different tonality from the teeth of the main comb and so can be used to produce some interesting tonal variations. Similar to the piccolo (q.v.) but *usually* a unison comb.

CONCERTO   Name used on large musical boxes by F. Conchon.

DIVA HARMONIC   Name used on some late operatic boxes probably made by Heller in Switzerland.

DUETTINO   This was the name given by Baker-Troll to six-air musical boxes having a special arrangement of two combs. The first and main comb was deep-toned and resonant and the second comb only had sixteen teeth. This comb was a piccolo comb, tuned an octave above the main comb and used in the same manner as that in the piccolo (q.v.) style.

DUPLEX   Patented by Alfred Junod c. 1887. Characterised by playing two cylinders simultaneously and identified in two forms, the first and more common with the cylinders and their combs arranged parallel one behind the other, and the second playing two cylinders and combs mounted in line, usually with the governor assembly in the centre between the two. Not to be confused with the plerodiénique (q.v.). The musical arrangement on the cylinders was identical as was the tuning and timbre of the combs. Apart from sheer spectacle – these are very rare boxes – little was achieved musically which was not obtainable with the sublime harmonie (q.v.). There is a third and even rarer style of Duplex, the reversed, counter-rotating parallel. This is an interchangeable mechanism in which the two cylinders are parallel. However, the cylinders rotate in opposite directions and the comb for the front cylinder is in the front, that for the back is at the back. A picture of this most unusual mechanism is contained as Figure 230 in *Histoire de la Boîte à Musique* by Alfred Chapuis. Charles Paillard made a number of extremely large linear duplex cylinder musical boxes (i.e. two cylinders mounted on a common axis) with changeable cylinders. These gargantuan instruments were in sublime harmonie format, the extreme right-hand of the four combs generally being provided with an adjustable zither attachment. The governor assembly with a very large, double-scalloped air brake, was mounted in the centre between the two cylinders and the change lever, also mounted centrally, was yoke-shaped since it had to operate a change snail on each cylinder. That on the left cylinder was in the usual position at the right end, while that on the right cylinder was on the left end, so allowing a symmetrical change yoke to be used. The twin parallel drive springs for these mechanisms were so powerful that the female stopwork had to be mounted to the spring barrel face by a screw in double shear, a top plate or bridge being secured over it. The cock of the endless was engraved 'C. Paillard'. Ami Rivenc made some unspectacular, low-cost examples.

ÉTOILE   The name used by F. Conchon on his helicoidal (q.v.) musical movements. The star became his trade mark.

EXCELSIOR   *Qualité Excelsior* and *Superextra* are characteristics of musical boxes sold under the Charles & Jacques Ullmann name. The Ullmanns went in for somewhat flamboyant descriptions of their boxes, although, except in the cases of the scarcer, larger instruments, they were fairly ordinary, simple and non-spectacular. *Excelsior* is also a style name used by Paillard. See comment on makers of Ullmann-marked boxes on p. 90.

FLUTES CELESTIAL VOICES   One of the more ridiculous of musical-box style names, this one used by George Bendon for a musical box with vox celeste or reed organ accompaniment. The celestial voices (?) were attributable to the double reeds which produced a slight vibrato.

FORTE-PIANO   Sometimes seen as *piano-forte*, literally a musical movement which can play soft or loud but, unlike the 'soft-loud' of Cristofori, the opportunity to alter the volume of sound lay solely with the arranger of the music on the cylinder. Said to have been invented by Nicole Frères, who certainly made very many of them early on, in 1840, the style was soon adopted by others.* Perhaps not surprisingly in view of his association with Nicole

* The Nicole style is very distinctive: the larger *forte* comb has the bass at the left, and the treble on the right as usual, but the *piano* comb has the treble on the left and the bass at the right.

Frères, Henri Metert also made some very fine specimens. Musical boxes of this type generally have two combs (see p. 114), the first being longer than the second. The teeth of the first or predominant comb are voiced to sound loudly; those of the other comb are tuned in unison but are voiced to sound much quieter. Some very fine movements were made and some outstandingly beautiful effects could be achieved by this type of movement. The combs require careful setting up if the full effect is to be achieved. A very unusual and much rarer variety is the single-comb forte-piano movement in which, as the name implies, there is only one comb. The effect of soft and loud playing is achieved in this type by varying the length of the pins in the cylinder. Precisely how this was done is uncertain. A theoretical solution to the problem would be to use a cylinder of slightly thicker metal, to pin all the 'soft' music first, to skim the cylinder in a lathe to get all these pins the proper height, and then to repeat the procedure for the louder music. All this would of course have to be done before cementing the cylinder, hence the need for thicker metal to support the uncemented pins. Another solution and, although equally laborious, probably the one used, was to pin the cylinder in the normal way and complete it. On adjusting the movement, the arranger would then be called upon to re-depth the pins for the softer music using a shoulder punch. Probably the operation would be completed by softening the cement in the cylinder by heat and re-cooling. At all events, single-comb forte-piano movements – Malignon was one who made them, and Lecoultre & Granger another – are rare and are something of a curiosity as to their realisation. For the cylinder re-pinner, they present a formidable challenge.

FORTISSIMO   A style devised by Paillard which featured comb teeth of short length but appreciably wider than usual. This produced a very loud tone without harshness and for the household with a very large drawing-room, or an owner who was hard of hearing, must have afforded untold pleasures.

GEM SUBLIME HARMONIE   A style of interchangeable-cylinder musical box produced by Paillard to patents taken out by Henri Metert, Louis Gagnaux and Eugène Tuller. This style was produced around 1895 (the patents predate this by up to eighteen years) and was a very cheap type of interchangeable-cylinder movement with the cylinder driven by a yoke and spigot.

GLORIA   Patented in Switzerland in 1889 by Eugène Tuller of Ste-Croix and manufactured by Paillard, the Gloria was another attempt at simplifying the interchangeable-cylinder musical box. It afforded a mechanism which still provided the motor at one end and the governor at the other, but instead of relying on the cylinder to transmit motion between the two, which would call for isolating the power during the removal of the cylinder, the cylinder was bypassed in the drive cycle. A layshaft ran beneath the bedplate to transfer power to the endless, leaving the cylinder as an independent, driven accessory instead of an important mechanical link. The stopwork was operated by the drive wheel on the layshaft which drove the cylinder from a great wheel on the cylinder arbor. There was no usual cylinder drive pinion at the motor end.

GLORIOSA   Name used by J. C. Eckardt of Germany to describe musical Christmas-tree stands and the name was sometimes used on the musical movements within them.

GRAND FORMAT   This was a very large musical movement, usually with a cylinder between 18 in. and 22 in. long and from 4½ in. to 5 in. in diameter. As made by Heller and by Nicole Frères, these were very good quality pieces with excellent tone and volume and could play from largely unabridged scores. Lecoultre made some considerably larger grand format boxes up to 6 ft in length but as the movement gained in size so its musical and artistic capability seemed to diminish. Added to which, these very large pieces did not sell well. They were ideally suited to exhibition purposes and indeed a number were created for this purpose. Sometimes *Grande Format*.

GUITAR ZITHER   A part-mandoline movement fitted with a zither.

HARMONIPHONE   A name used by Louis Ducommun to describe his vox celeste (q.v.) cylinder boxes fitted with reed organ accompaniment. The variation 'harmoniflute' is probably a name used by L'Épée for his similar style of boxes.

HARPE ÉOLIENNE   A style invented by Conchon in which two combs were used. In many ways rather like the *forte-piano* but nowhere near so sophisticated, the *harpe éolienne* had one comb of relatively stiff teeth which played loudly in conjunction with a normal comb. Instead of a 'soft-loud', this was more of a 'normal-loud' and a main feature was that the shorter comb was usually at the bass end and was provided with a zither which, in some boxes seen, operates under the comb. The movements are fairly small, the comb teeth fairly coarse, the tone not all that impressive.

HARPE HARMONIQUE   A style of musical box patented by Weill & Harburg.

HELICOIDAL   The idea of the helicoidal was to remove the limitation on the length of the tune which a cylinder musical box could play, allowing it to perform quite long pieces of music by the simple expedient of using the characteristic of the orchestrion barrel organ – the continual advancement of the cylinder during playing. Instead of making one revolution and then being changed between tunes by a snail-cam, the helicoidal advanced steadily in a very precise spiral for, usually, eight revolutions. There was no clear area on the cylinder coincident with a 'start' and 'stop' position and for this reason, in order to return the cylinder to the 'start' position at the end of its performance, it was first of all necessary to back the cylinder away from the comb tips to avoid damage. Only when the cylinder had moved away from the comb was it allowed to shift laterally, whereupon it would advance towards the comb and the start of play position. Francois Conchon is said by L. A. Grosclaude to have made the first helicoidal in 1878. However, Grosclaude also made this type and, when Switzerland first opened its patent office in 1889, some patents were issued, no doubt retrospectively. One, dated 23 March 1896, was to Arthur Junod-Turin of Ste-Croix. Numbered 12243 it referred to a style named 'Simplicitas' stamped on the governor. Two further Junod patents exist in the US patent office: 366325 of 12 July 1887, assigned to Emile Cuendet of Hoboken, and 367409 of 2 August 1887, assigned to Jacot & Son in New York. A similar mechanism, but differing in one important detail, was the semi-helicoidal (q.v.). See Fig. 28.

IDEAL   Name given to a range of interchangeable-cylinder musical boxes produced by Mermod Frères. Some are single-comb models, others two-comb, such as the Ideal Piccolo which uses the treble end of the right-hand comb as an octave on the melodic line. Another is the Ideal Excelsior, which has shorter comb teeth to produce a louder tone; another is the Ideal Guitare, which is softly-voiced and is part-mandoline. The Ideal Sublime Harmonie is self-expressive; Ideal Sublime-harmonie Piccolo is a combination of the sublime harmonie and the piccolo; Ideal Soprano is a sublime harmonie again but here the melodic line is performed on one comb only as a solo to the accompaniment of the two combs. The Ideal was considered the better-quality cylinder box produced by Mermod, the other being the Peerless (q.v.).

JEUX DE FLÛTES   A most rare type of box which is, in fact, a small barrel organ with orchestral accompaniments. The cylinder is pinned to play a rank of flute organ pipes. Three short combs are also provided but these are purely for the operation of drum, tuned steel bells and castanets. Of necessity a very large and heavy box. There is another variety which was made by B. A. Bremond which had thirty-six organ notes comprising eighteen flute pipes and eighteen reed notes. Another variety exists wherein the organ pipes are provided with a tiny manual keyboard on which the user is able to make up his own pipe organ accompaniment to the music pinned on the cylinder.

LONGUE MARCHE   Characterised by the interposition of a layshaft between spring barrel and cylinder drive pinion, the longue marche was intended to increase the playing time of a musical movement by allowing a much stronger spring to be used in the motor. Several inventors worked to this end, but the one to use the name 'longue marche' was Daniel Aubert. He was granted British Patent number 3711 dated 16 September 1879 (in the name of Aubert & Son), and US patent number 238326 of 1881 (in his own name). The provision of a very large, slender wheel on that layshaft to further increase the playing time was patented in America on 28 December 1886 by Heinrich Zumsteg assigned to Mermod Frères. On 17 July 1886 A. Karrer of Teufenthal was granted British Patent number 9024 for the same system. The majority of longue marche movements have very wide bedplates which are supported some distance above the bottom of the case so as to allow the super-great wheel to pass through the bedplate. Musically speaking, and although they often benefit from the large resonating space provided by the box, they are not over-spectacular. A name used by Paillard for a coaxial double-spring long-playing movement was *sublime harmonie longue marche* (q.v.). Mermod Frères made a number of *longue marche* boxes, as did Cuendet-Develay.

MANDOLINE   A true *mandoline* box – and some are marked thus which are not – has at least eight teeth on the comb tuned to each note or to the tones used in the tunes played so that by plucking each tooth in rapid succession a fair representation can be achieved of the sound of a mandoline. As might be expected, the comb of a mandoline box has very fine teeth to allow the large number needed if the box is to sound effective. The cylinder is readily identified by the very obvious angled lines of pins grouped in its surface, particularly in the treble register where the mandoline effect is required to be most pronounced. Some boxes of a later period were produced with the name 'mandoline' on the tune sheet but which offered far fewer than eight notes per tune – usually six, sometimes fewer still.

135

These can be termed pseudo-mandoline inasmuch that the effect is nowhere near as well brought off as with a proper mandoline box. Other and later varieties included the mandolin expressive and mandolin percussion. 'Mandolin' is found spelled with and without the final 'e'.

MUSIQUE EXPRESSIVE   A single-comb piano-forte musical box has been seen bearing this title. The box is marked 'Lecoultre & Granger à Genève', and plays three overtures and one waltz.

MUSIQUE SYMPHONIQUE   A name used on tune-sheets issued by M. J. Paillard in New York and indicating nothing very special other than that the repertoire of the box was based on the classics.

MULTIPHONE   Without much doubt the world's smallest interchangeable-cylinder musical box, the Multiphone comes in two versions – a hand-cranked *manivelle* and a bottom-wind contrate-wheel-driven powered model. It was manufactured to a patent taken out on 16 February 1886, in London (number 2241 of that year) in the name of John Manger who was described as a musical-box importer and connected with Mojon, Manger & Co. There is also a connection of some sort with Charles & Jacques Ullmann in that their initials appear as part of the lid design of the manivelle box and stamped on the comb of the powered one. Each of the tiny cylinders plays just one tune and measures $1\frac{3}{4}$ in. (44·5 mm) long.

NATIONAL   The National musical box was manufactured by Ami Rivenc and distributed by the National Fine Art Association in London. See under this name in Chapter 11. Oleographic tune-sheets printed in rich colours with an angled panel with the name 'NATIONAL' therein. All boxes seen have designs of flowers on the tune-sheet. Other than that, nothing in any way is spectacular about these boxes. Formerly believed to have been made by Dawkins who was Rivenc's UK distributor.

ORCHESTRE or ORCHESTRA or ORCHESTRAL   Following on the popularity in the late 1860s and early 1870s of musical boxes with visible bells, the cylinder musical box looked at the other effects which it could adopt to supplement the comb. The drum, the castanet (a hollowed-out hardwood block struck in the same way as the drum by a number of hammers), a reed organ, the inevitable bells and zither, and, in some cases, even a triangle, were all built in to form the style dubiously termed the orchestral box. Usually these were interchangeable-cylinder movements and all were both large and heavy. With everything in play, they produced a sound more often stupefying than melodious. The careful and sympathetic owner could, however, select which features he wanted to bring in or out by the use of control levers. Some particularly fine specimens were created which were very musical and far from offensive. The full orchestra style has everything; the part orchestra usually settled for bells, drum and castanets. Impressive boxes to observe and, occasionally, very impressive to listen to. Some styles were made in upright format, i.e. with the musical movement mounted upright so that, with the cylinder still horizontal, the bedplate was supported vertically in a drop-front or glazed double-door front case. This was called the *buffet* style.

ORGANOCLÉIDE Whereas the mandoline (q.v.) type of movement has repeated notes in the treble which allows the equivalent of a sustained note to be produced, the organocléide has this feature throughout the length of the comb, with particular emphasis being placed on the bass notes. The effect of these rapidly repeated bass notes is to give the impression of a long, low note rather like a pedal note on a pipe organ. The overall tonal scale of the organocléide is quite different from that of a normal musical box in that it is pitched a whole octave lower and plays a programme of music best suited to its basso profundo.

ORPHEA Brand name of musical boxes made in America by Junod and distributed by American retailers. Both the motor and the governor assembly are mounted underneath the bedplate. The mechanism is covered by American patent 445699 (1891), British patent 12170 (1890), and French patent 207352 in the name of Société A. Junod.

OVERTURE Sometimes spelled the French way, *ouverture*. A musical box with a programme devoted entirely to operatic overtures. The early ones were of outstandingly high quality and are much prized. They are characterised by very large diameter cylinders and extremely fine combs. Not infrequently in the case of the better-quality instruments, the tune sheet is made of brass or even silver. Top-quality makers of the period were Lecoultre, Nicole Frères, F. Nicole, Falconnet, Moulinie Aîné, Bremond, and many others. Some of the larger instruments had between 200 and 300 teeth in the comb and were able to reproduce faithfully virtually every note of the original score. Of necessity, due to the slender proportions of the comb teeth, these top-quality boxes played very softly but with an extremely pure tone.

PEERLESS Name given by Mermod Frères to its range of cheaper-style musical boxes. Styles included the Peerless forte-piccolo, made with and without zither. Like its more expensive variant, the Ideal (q.v.) the Peerless had interchangeable cylinders, and was a mass-produced item.

PIANO-FORTE MANDOLIN Just as with the piano-forte or forte-piano movement, the piano-forte mandolin worked in the same manner with two combs, one to play loud, the other soft. However, the soft comb would be arranged as a part-mandolin (i.e. about five or six teeth tuned to each tone) and the soft-toned part of the cylinder pinned accordingly. This type of movement is unusual.

PICCOLO Another two-comb type of movement, this has one very short treble-end comb. This would be tuned to the octave above the melodic line and, because the teeth were somewhat thicker, would impart a distinctly bright accompaniment to the air on the main comb. The effective use of this comb would not be to arrange it in play all the while, but only to use it in occasional phrases to strengthen either melodic line or counter melody.

PIÈCE À OISEAU There is often confusion between *pièce à oiseau* and *oiseau mécanique* – and the confusion appears contemporary as well! For this reason I will deal with both under the same heading. The *pièce à oiseau* is essentially a large musical box, usually a rather grand-looking piece with a long cylinder, multi-barrelled motor, reed organ and, sometimes, bells as well. Behind the cylinder and in line with the organ is a rustic scene created out of painted twigs and artificial leaves and in the middle of this rests one or sometimes two artificial birds. As the musical box plays, these birds move and apparently sing, their motion and song coming from the organ linkages via the special pinning in the middle of the cylinder. Several linkages or keys will be set aside for operating the bird movements and these will easily be identified by the different style of pinning in the barrel. *Oiseau mécanique*, or to give it its full name *oiseau mécanique sous medaillon* is similar in almost every respect except that the bird is mounted in a glass-fronted bull's-eye window in the front of the box and is therefore visible even when the lid of the box is closed. Makers of these styles included Conchon, Troll & Baker and Jules Cuendet.

PLERODIÉNIQUE   One of the most interesting and rare types of musical movement is this, the so-called 'telescopic' type. The idea was to be able to perform very long pieces of music on a cylinder musical box. Another solution to the same problem was the helicoidal (q.v.). The plerodiénique was devised by Albert Jeanrenaud who was granted an American patent number 266826 on 31 October 1882. This was assigned to M. J. Paillard in New York. The comparable European patents are assigned to Paillard in Switzerland who was responsible for the construction of these unusual pieces. The first showing of the style was at the Industrial Exhibition held in London in 1862, when it was described as 'the largest and most ambitious musical box yet seen' in England. Two cylinders were mounted on a common shaft end to end with a small gap between them. Each cylinder was arranged to stop playing and change via its own snail change cam, but at a different radial position. This meant that both cylinders would play together, when one stopped playing (but not rotating) and changed to its second tune position, the second cylinder would still be playing. Then as the first cylinder came back into play, the second would stop playing and change. In this way, a long, continuous piece of music could be played as, to the casual observer, the cylinders, their separating gap covered by a metal sleeve fixed to the right hand one and thus appearing as one long barrel, would systematically grow shorter until, at the end of the entire playing cycle, they would expand one at a time to the full length for starting again. It was this feature which gave the piece its erroneous sobriquet 'telescopic'. The plerodiénique was always a long and expensive box and few are known to collectors today. See Fig. 28.

Because of the musical set-up, quite frequently with both cylinders playing in unison, the instrument operated for extended periods during the revolution of its cylinders as a *sublime harmonie*. However, the engineering of the box called for most careful adjustment, in particular the radial registration of the cylinders. Whereas it was sufficient to drive one cylinder in the usual way with an offset drive pin, the necessary precision demanded a somewhat more accurate means of driving and adjusting the second cylinder. For this reason, the second cylinder was driven by a dog located in a special brass block on the cylinder end. This had a screw adjuster at each side and allowed very accurate radial registration of one cylinder with the other. To ensure that the movement started and stopped only at the end of the total number of cylinder revolutions, the normal interchangeable-type drive sub-shaft carried on a suitable wheel a count-wheel type of mechanism. Built into one of the sub-shaft support brackets was a starwheel with as many points as the cylinder had to revolve to complete its programme, i.e. six points. This starwheel was indexed by a protruding pin on the sub-shaft wheel. Riding round the body of the starwheel was the stop/start detent. At the completion of the sixth step, a hole in the starwheel body would be aligned with the detent which would drop in and stop the mechanism.

138

POLYTYPE REVOLVER   Probably the rarest of all the revolver-box variants is this extraordinary instrument, only one example of which has so far been recorded. Of necessarily massive proportions, the Polytype Revolver has four cylinders, each mounted on its own bedplate and with its own combs. Changing the musical programme consists of rotating the four mechanisms within the main bedplate, so bringing another into playing position. A glazed opening in the lower front of the base is provided to show the next musical movement awaiting rotation into place. The enormously complicated and very heavy musical box may at first sight appear to bristle with redundant components; in truth, although a cumbersome way of doing it, it offers the advantages of four quite separate musical boxes in that each cylinder-bedplate-comb assembly is of a different type. The first is a *sublime harmonie piccolo* with three combs; the second is a mandoline; the third is a *forte-piano* and the fourth yet another arrangement. The sole example recorded is said to play five tunes on each cylinder. The maker is unknown but from appearance it would appear to be Paillard.

POLYTYPE ZITHER   Paillard, Vaucher & Fils introduced the polytype zither to endeavour to offer an even wider tonal variety to a single-cylinder musical box than had hitherto been possible. This was late-style, crank-wound, with the motor at the right-hand side of the case. The $13\frac{1}{2}$ in. cylinder played six airs on two combs, basically sublime harmonie in style. However, the tunes were arranged in differing manners, two being sublime harmonie, two as piccolo zither, and the final two being tremolo zither.

QUATUOR   A name first said to have been used by David Cadet of Sainte-Suzanne in France for a four-comb movement which he made. The style quatuor came to be used for a number of four-comb boxes including PVF with Quatuor Expression Piccolo.

RECHANGE   Early name for a musical movement with interchangeable or changeable cylinders. Full title: *Pièce à rechange*.

REVOLVER   This fascinating mechanism is claimed to have been invented by Amédée Paillard of Ste-Croix in 1870, but there is evidence that a similar system was perfected by Henri Joseph Lecoultre who was also responsible for the interchangeable cylinder system. The mechanism comprised two large-diameter hoops between which were mounted three, four, five or six cylinders. By rotating the whole cylinder assembly with its hoops, any cylinder could be brought into alignment with the comb whereupon it was automatically locked during playing. Each cylinder played in precisely the same way as a normal fixed cylinder in that it was pinned with up to eight airs and had the normal type of snail and cam change. These movements were so expensive that it is economically not surprising that the majority made were of the six-cylinder variety and that even these are a rarity. The most common make was Paillard but, during the closing years of their business in Geneva, Nicole Frères also made some fine specimens. They were ousted, technically speaking, by the interchangeable-cylinder mechanism which could be produced cheaper and had far less to go wrong with it. The sheer weight of the cylinder assembly in a revolver box necessitated a very heavily-founded mechanism. One variety of revolver mechanism is known only by an example auctioned in Surrey in June 1977. This behemoth model did not rotate its cylinders into place against the comb, but actually rotated four complete bedplates with cylinders and combs. Each cylinder played five tunes and an off-centre window in the case front revealed some of the complexity of this even heavier and more complex style. See *polytype revolver*.

SEMI-HELICOIDAL   Like the *helicoidal* (q.v.), the *semi-helicoidal* was intended to allow the playing of longer pieces of music then possible with a normal mechanism. Whereas with the helicoidal the cylinder was impelled sideways all the while it played, so that it moved in a spiral, the semi-helicoidal moved in exactly the same way as the cylinder in an ordinary single-play type of box. A normal change snail and cam was used, although so arranged that its effect on the cylinder was slightly more gradual. The cylinder pinning, instead of being in a spiral as with the helicoidal, was once more in plane with the diameter for about 350° of the revolution (see Fig. 28). Then, as the cylinder began to shift under the influence of the snail cam, the pinning would be continued over the gap, the effective line being joggled as the cylinder moved laterally. As regards the mechanism, this was little different from the full helicoidal in that it was still necessary to back the cylinder from the comb at the end of the programme. However, the system did make it theoretically easier to pin, say, two or maybe three tunes on to a cylinder – one being of, say, four revolutions duration, the others being normal single-turn tunes or a two-turn tune. Bremond was a maker of semi-helicoidals which, although musically very effective and with well-arranged tunes, were far from fail-safe in terms of their design and engineering. This interchangeable box drove its endless from the usual type of spigot faceplate wheel which also provided the stop/start yoke with its gulley and drop. The gulley-drop, though, was protected by a starwheel indexed by a projection fitted to the bedplate. This turned the starwheel one degree on each cylinder revolution, covering the drop and so keeping the mechanism in play. At the end of the programme, a gap in the starwheel aligned with the drop, allowing the box to stop. Each turn of the cylinder also moved a countwheel under the cylinder by one increment. At the completion of the programme, this countwheel operated a lever which pushed the cylinder away from the comb before it shifted to the bottom step of the change-snail. At this position, it also rather cleverly withdrew a safety lock from the cylinder locating clamps, so allowing the clamps to be opened, if required, to change the cylinder. Whereas in a perfect mechanism this countwheel would have been connected to the tune-change lever so that accidental repetition of one step of the snail would automatically disconnect the indexing mechanism, this was not developed with the result that this action is readily put out of alignment. The inventors of various other styles have, it is believed, all been listed under the helicoidal heading, but D. Allard & Cie of Geneva made some very fine examples.

SPÉCIALITÉ   Name of a long-playing style of musical box made by Mojon, Manger & Co. of Chaux-de-Fonds. This had a double spring and would play from 20 to 150 minutes on one winding.

SUBLIME HARMONIE   Without doubt the most effective of all the comb arrangements was the invention of the sublime harmonie. Charles Paillard was granted two patents, an American one (number 161055 dated 23 March 1875) and a British one (3697 dated 26 October 1847) for a 'musical box having several combs each of short teeth to give notes of shorter duration and also to allow slight dissonance'. The principle of the sublime harmonie was that slight

140

dissonance between two notes of ostensibly the same pitch would produce a rich and fuller sound. In this style, two and occasionally three combs were arranged in line so that the music being played was represented by cylinder pins presented to comparable teeth in each comb. In other words, the music was repeated in the span of the cylinder to play two similar but not identical combs at the same time. The style was used widely by many makers and was later to find its way into the disc-playing boxes made in Leipzig and Berlin. A word of warning: boxes with more than one comb may not automatically be sublime harmonie or anything else. Sometimes on a large or long box the supply of suitable lengths of comb steel dictated that the comb might have to be made in two or more pieces. The sublime harmonie is identifiable because the centre of the cylinder is marked by the treble end of the first comb and the adjacent bass end of the second comb.

SUBLIME HARMONIE FORTISSIMO   A sublime harmonie movement in which the combs have shorter teeth than normal, which produces a louder and more strident tone. See also under *fortissimo*. Necessarily, the combs would be of somewhat coarse pitch and scale.

SUBLIME HARMONIE LONGUE MARCHE   This was Paillard's name for a sublime harmonie movement fitted with a double coaxial spring motor which gave a very long playing time on one winding. See also *longue marche*.

SUBLIME HARMONIE OCTAVO   Basically a sublime harmonie having the second comb tuned one octave higher than the first to produce a full-compass brightness.

SUBLIME HARMONIE PICCOLO   This was a combination of the sublime harmonie with a piccolo comb at the right end which heightened still more the sounds produced.

SUBLIME HARMONIE TREMOLO   A deep-voiced sublime harmonie with the addition of a piccolo comb in the treble.

SUPEREXTRA   Name used by Charles & Jacques Ullmann. See under *Excelsior*.

TAMBOUR ET TIMBRES EN VUE   A form of orchestral (q.v.) box comprising, as the name suggests, visible drum and bells. Introduced fairly early on, the style was known at the time of the Great Exhibition of 1851 where it was shown.

TUYAPHONE   A style of musical box devised by George Baker & Co. and first exhibited at the Exposition Nationale Suisse of 1896. In addition to sublime harmonie combs, an octave and a half of tubular bells is provided which are struck by hammers operating from nineteen teeth on a special bell-comb in the centre of the normal musical combs, i.e. from the middle of the cylinder. A similar style was made by Ami Rivenc but without the name.

UNIVERSAL   Patented in 1891 by Cuendet-Develay Fils et Cie of Ste-Croix, the Universal was intended to be the closest thing to an 'undestroyable' musical box – a term proclaimed on the tune sheet which announced that the box had 'undestroyable dampers'. The spring was mounted underneath the bedplate and wound by a large capstan wheel. Each cylinder played just one tune using pins of such proportions that it was impossible in normal use to damage them. The dampers were forked and engaged with a pin which pierced each comb tooth tip. Not very musical but certainly very robust. Several sizes were made, including one with three bells. This played cylinders (usually zinc-plated) 7½ in. (190 mm) long.

VARIATION   The variation style is one of the most interesting from a musical standpoint. Usually the programme of a variation box comprises just two tunes, each played on two turns of the cylinder, making four airs in all. The simple air is stated on the first revolution, then on the next revolution it is embellished with variations. A master of this form was Nicole Frères. A scarce and much cherished type of musical box.

VICTORIA   Style of musical movement produced by BHA and normally contained in a vertical cabinet like a disc-playing musical box.

VOX CELESTE   The addition of a small reed organ to the comb-playing musical box goes back to the 1850 period. Initially, the organ would be arranged at one end, usually the left end, of the cylinder and would comprise about two octaves of single reeds. These were styled 'flutina' and the early makers included Ducommun-Girod, Kimmerling and Grosclaude. In later boxes, the organ was moved to the centre and the comb was divided into two parts, the bass part being on one side, the treble on the other. The number of reeds played went up to twenty-four or even more on some models and another important change took place. This was the introduction of double reeds mounted side by side on the same windway. Each pair of reeds was tuned to a slight, slow beat and this was the true voix céleste which when in perfect order could produce a very beautiful sound. The names used by various makers were numerous and included organ celeste, flutina, flûte voix céleste and so on. Bremond, Greiner, Heller and Paillard were among makers. Bremond, Paillard and George Bendon produced instruments which were full-organ boxes, i.e. without musical combs. Early mechanisms of this type had French feeders, that is to say, the upper board and the lower board of the bellows were both fixed and arranged to form a V between which a movable board was lifted up and down. It thus compressed wind on the upper stroke in the upper section of the V, and compressed wind on the downward stroke in the lower chamber. The reservoir was spring-loaded and was also arranged like a V when open. Wind was admitted to the reeds by external circular pallets which were opened and closed like the keys of the clarinet by stickers from the organ levers. Later on, the French feeder was replaced by the slightly more efficient cuckoo feeder with a rocking feeder which compressed wind in chambers to each side of the centre on alternate halves of the same stroke. The reservoir was now parallel-rising using an upholstery-type spring for compression. The reeds for the organ now received their impulse to sound via proper internal pallets opened by wire stickers which passed down from the top surface and were operated by the organ levers. The word 'vox' is found spelt both this way and as 'voix'.

VOLUTINA   A name used on some of the larger movements sold under the name of Charles & Jacques Ullmann. Characterised by the very large box with a relatively small (11 in. cylinder) movement inside, 'volutina' might be thought to derive from the Latin in which case it is something about rolling around and jingling. Maybe that's what they meant!

ZITHER   It is said that the zither attachment to cylinder musical boxes was invented about 1878 – Jaccard gives this year and names the worker who contrived it as Marel. It

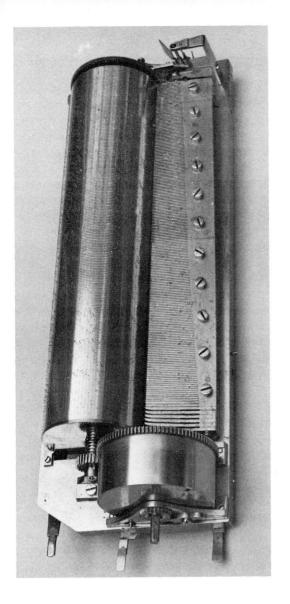

◄ PLATES 41 & 42 ▲
The F. Nicole movement from Plate 40 showing comb in three sections with the addition of six bass teeth screwed on from the end – a characteristic of maker's period as is rigid notation and cylinder alignment grooves (see Fig. 10).

▲ PLATE 43
The case of an unusual musical box marked with the name Lecoultre and shown in detail in Plate 44.

◄ PLATE 44
Lecoultre box with sectional comb in groups of five, three control levers protruding from the front, steel cock-plate and plain paper tune sheet. Note the simple wire case hinges and the lid catch and compare with Plate 35. Later styles directed that movements should be the other way round in cases.

◄ PLATE 45
Steel cock-plate also distinguishes this fine early box. Note the two wedge-shaped gaps between comb-section segments for the locating dowels. See page 100.

▼ PLATE 46
Detail of motor end of the above mechanism showing exceptionally slender cylinder arbor and trunnion brackets, also one of the comb-base dowel cut-outs.

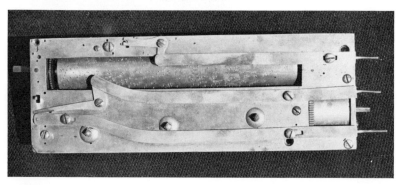

▲ PLATE 47
The movement in Plates 45 and 46 is worked by pull/push controls and this view of the underside shows how they operate. Note bedplate now has rectangular cut-outs for cylinder and spring barrel.

PLATE 48 ►
Nicole Frères clock-base movement number 28529 with the comb stamped F. Nicole. This format became the standard for most that followed.

◄ PLATE 49
Fine early musical box attributed to Lecoultre and dating from about 1820. Four tunes are played. A narrow divider at the right-hand end of the case, now missing, formed a slender compartment for the winding key. The comb screws have no washers beneath their heads – usually at this period small brass washers would have been used – and the movement is secured with four small screws, two through the box front and two behind.

PLATE 50 ►
An unusual tune sheet, so far unidentified, is the only clue as to the maker of this *c.* 1830 musical box. It is nevertheless a classic example of the simple early mechanism with three control levers protruding through the left case end and a hole for the winding key. One tune is from Mercadante's opera of 1821 *Elisa e Claudio.*

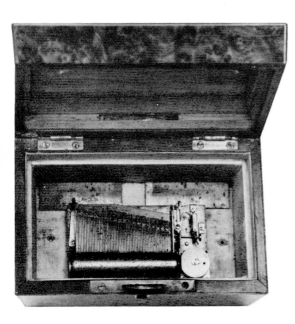

◄ PLATE 51
Musical jewel casket in the Sheraton style with comb teeth in groups of three. Movement plays two airs and dates from about 1820. Note the early-pattern straight cock bracket and the cylindrical spring barrel – the female stopwork is missing. The treble is on the left when the cylinder is viewed from the conventional position.

▲ PLATE 52
This small movement has, among other unusual
characteristics, the governor gearing on the right
and the endless driven on the left via an
under-comb shaft.

▲ PLATE 53
Fine early movement from a snuff-box featuring a
chevron comb of sections of three with the treble in
the centre.

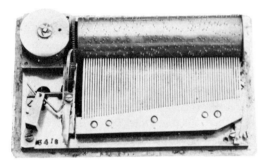

▲ PLATE 54
From about 1840 is this early single-piece comb
snuff-box. Long and slender teeth suggest
Alibert or Capt.

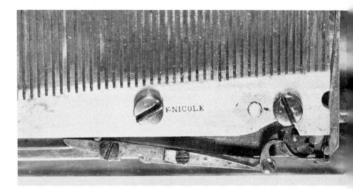

▲ PLATE 55
Most unusual horizontal snail tune-changer on a
F. Nicole snuff-box movement. Usual cylinder
shifting fork is controlled by the cam profile.
(See page 58.)

▼ PLATE 57
Typical late mass-produced movement used in photograph
albums and other novelties. This simple two-air
manually-changed movement bears the name of Hamburg
distributor Detmering.

▲ PLATE 56
Miniature *sublime harmonie* snuff-box-type movement made by
Hermann Thorens. One tune played – there are four
altogether – is *Come take a trip in my airship*.

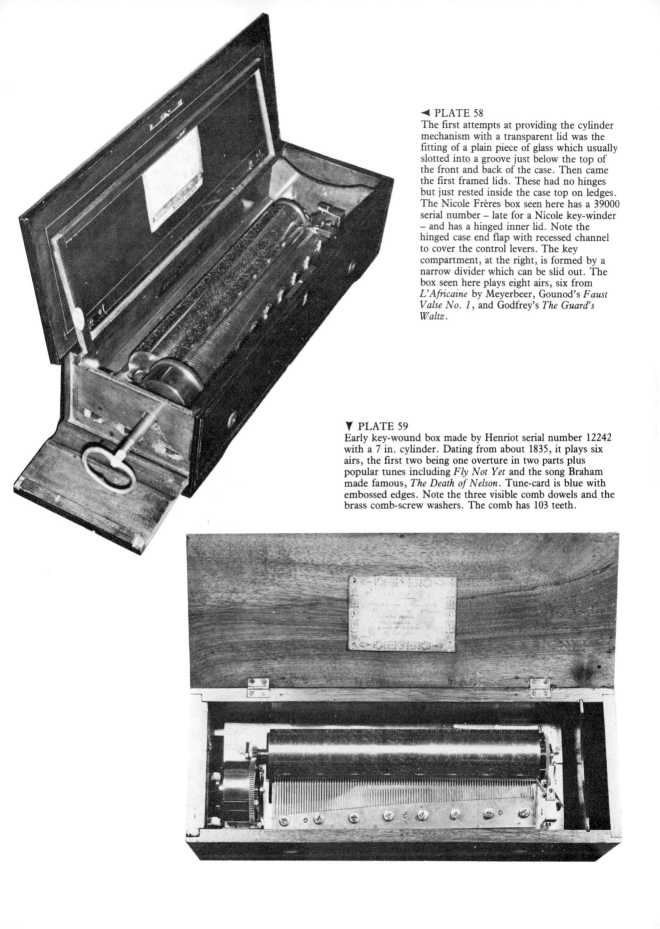

◄ PLATE 58
The first attempts at providing the cylinder mechanism with a transparent lid was the fitting of a plain piece of glass which usually slotted into a groove just below the top of the front and back of the case. Then came the first framed lids. These had no hinges but just rested inside the case top on ledges. The Nicole Frères box seen here has a 39000 serial number – late for a Nicole key-winder – and has a hinged inner lid. Note the hinged case end flap with recessed channel to cover the control levers. The key compartment, at the right, is formed by a narrow divider which can be slid out. The box seen here plays eight airs, six from *L'Africaine* by Meyerbeer, Gounod's *Faust Valse No. 1*, and Godfrey's *The Guard's Waltz*.

▼ PLATE 59
Early key-wound box made by Henriot serial number 12242 with a 7 in. cylinder. Dating from about 1835, it plays six airs, the first two being one overture in two parts plus popular tunes including *Fly Not Yet* and the song Braham made famous, *The Death of Nelson*. Tune-card is blue with embossed edges. Note the three visible comb dowels and the brass comb-screw washers. The comb has 103 teeth.

◄ PLATE 60

Case decoration began with a simple line of stringing around the edges of the case lid and the front. Centre lid inlay motifs came later still. This box has a simple inlay of darker wood around the top of the lid and also the front panel. The tune sheet is made of brass and inscribed with the name Berguer & Fils together with the date *15 Juillet 1863*.

PLATE 61 ►

This style of box and tune sheet has been seen bearing the name Bruguier. However, this example has the name Scriber stamped into the brass bedplate. So far, the maker has not been identified. Eight popular airs are played and the box dates from about 1850.

◄ PLATES 62 & 63

On the far left is a box with an unusual sculptured case lid edge. It is a *piano-forte* style made by Ducommun-Girod. Note the arrangement of the two combs. Only Nicole Frères and Bruguier adopted the style using bass teeth at the outer edges (see Plate 82). Immediately left is a key-wound box attributed to Karrer – the tune sheet is missing from the lid.

◄ PLATE 64
Bearing the stamp of H. Metert on the bedplate, this *forte-piano* box is of pleasing proportions. The tune sheet is sealed to the lid with a wax seal presumably to prevent its being removed. The cylinder is only 8 in. long and the serial number is 4444.

▼ PLATE 65
Cylinder movement made by Ami Genoux. Every part is stamped with a dagger mark. Note the very unusual female stopwork on the spring barrel. Clearly visible here are the two recesses in the underside of the brass comb base to enable a screwdriver blade to be inserted to aid removal of the comb.

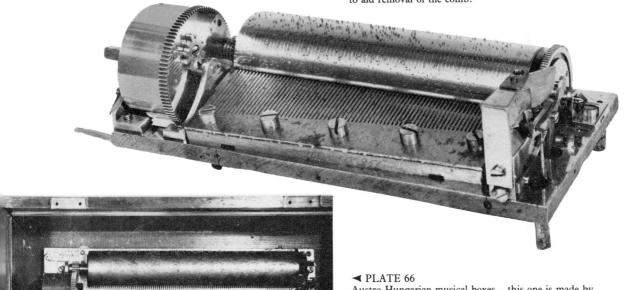

◄ PLATE 66
Austro-Hungarian musical boxes – this one is made by Gustav Rebicek in Prague in what is now Czechoslovakia – have many distinctive characteristics. The comb is always 'reversed' with the bass on the right, and the proportions of comb teeth are as seen here. The governor fan is large-diameter and of fixed span.

PLATE 67 ►
The movement in Plate 66 dates from 1870–90. This one by rantisek Rzebitschek, father of Gustav, is about 1865. Both ve the same general format including the short, symmetrical ner (right-hand) motor support bridge or bracket. This one is ted with a resonating chamber base to enhance its volume of und. All musical boxes of this type have plain, simple cases th mitred corners, all play very well and all are key-winders.

PLATE 68 ►
Four-air small box probably by Perrin-Chopard playing
Arditi's *Il Bacio* and an aria from Verdi's *Il Trovatore*
thus dating the construction as after 1853. Notice that
although still a key-winder, the stop/start and
change/repeat controls have moved to a plinth
developed from the key compartment divider.

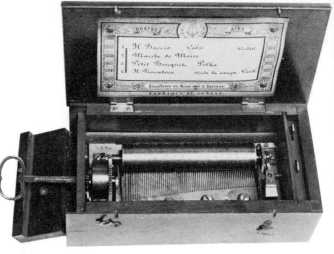

▼ PLATE 69
A most interesting box is this 12-air box made by
Bruguier. It plays two tunes per turn but is specially
geared so that the cylinder turns very slowly and each
tune is of normal length for a box of this size. One of
the tunes played was composed by Bruguier himself.

PLATE 70 ►
Very popular during the 1860–1885 period was the musical Swiss
chalet style. Many of these were produced by Bremond – or at least
the musicwork was by Bremond. This is a particularly fine specimen
complete with water-colour painting. The three control levers can be
seen left.

◄ PLATE 71
This Nicole Frères style was known as *Grande format*
and is numbered 45850. It plays 12 airs on a cylinder
23 ins. long and 3¼ in. in diameter. Note the somewhat
coarse comb, the early Nicole type of tune-indicator at
the left end of the cylinder, the twin-grip winding lever
and the three control levers on a brass-topped plinth.
A fourth lever at the back of the plinth operates a
tune-selector. Engraved brass tune-sheet.

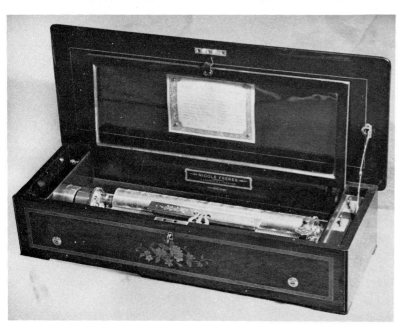

◄ PLATE 72

The word *gamme* means gamut or programme. Many boxes bear both a serial number and a *gamme* number and one maker who almost always listed both was Nicole Frères. This fine oratorio box, dating from the period after the company had become London-based, bears the serial number 51361 and the *gamme* number 5161. Eight airs are played on the 17¼ in. long cylinder. The double or coaxial spring is lever wound from a separate compartment accessible without opening the inner lid, and the governor has a speed control adjuster on top. Only two control levers are used. The comb is fitted with a zither attachment.

PLATE 73 ►

This Nicole Frères *piano-forte* oratorio box plays ten airs. Note the arrangement of the soft and the loud combs with the highest, treble notes where the combs meet. Brass engraved tune sheet shows serial number 46512 and *gamme* 2674. Distributor Keith, Prowse's name is also shown. Box has special stay hinges.

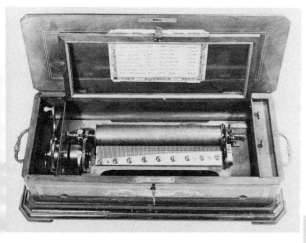

▲ PLATE 74

Early changeable cylinder box by Nicole Frères number 47495, *gamme* 3297 a & b. The coaxial twin spring motor has power locking via lever next to the barrel gear to facilitate changing.

PLATE 75 ►

French-made musical box by L'Épée for Thibouville-Lamy and with the latter's tune sheet. Characteristics are the bedplate of tinned polished metal with prominent case-fixing lugs, parallel cock to the governor, wooden-gripped winding lever reversed over the spring barrel, and the full lid which covers the motor. The glass can be slid out through one end of the lid frame. This specimen is number 26000 and bears the mark SW in an oval (See Fig. 45).

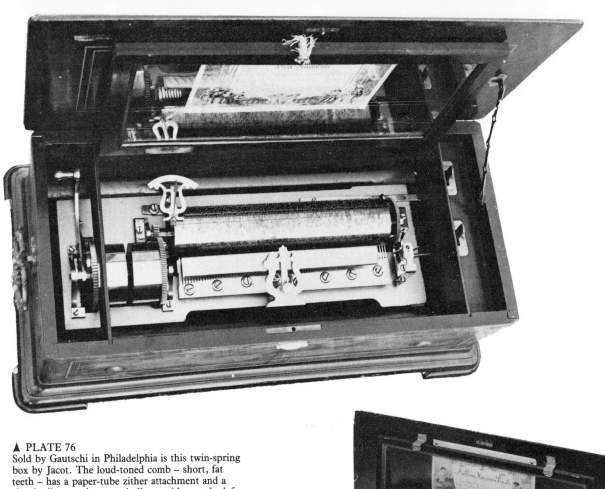

▲ PLATE 76
Sold by Gautschi in Philadelphia is this twin-spring
box by Jacot. The loud-toned comb – short, fat
teeth – has a paper-tube zither attachment and a
simple direct-acting tune-indicator rides on the left
end of the cylinder.

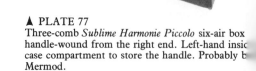

▲ PLATE 77
Three-comb *Sublime Harmonie Piccolo* six-air box
handle-wound from the right end. Left-hand insid
case compartment to store the handle. Probably b
Mermod.

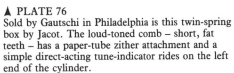

◄ PLATE 78
Built by Reuge in Switzerland as a limited edition to commemorate the 25th
anniversary of the Musical Box Society International, this 1974-vintage
piano-forte box demonstrates the best of recreative craftsmanship. Note the
enlarged variant of the snuff-box-type spring housing.

◄ PLATE 79
Marked on the silver tune-sheet 'François Nicole', this 3-air overture box bears the serial number 3. Compares with Plates 41 and 42. This altogether outstanding box ranks among the earliest known of the sought-after overture-playing breed. The case has mitred corners, a feature usually seen of Viennese or Austrian pieces. The comb is stamped Franc⁵ Nicole and the very last tooth on the comb, during the playing of the first tune, overhangs the end of the cylinder. Nevertheless, it is brought into play just at one point by a solitary pin mounted in an individual brass block screwed to the end of the cylinder. Lecoultre-pattern cylinder registration using a tiny steel comb and left-end cylinder grooves are used.

◄ PLATE 80
Many of the earliest overture boxes played three works and this one, made by Lecoultre et Falconnet, is no exception. Bellini's overture *Norma*, Rossini's *Guillaume Tell* and Bellini's *I Puritani* form the repertoire of this piece which dates from between 1835 and 1840. Interesting features include the mitred case corners, the basic cut-outs for the lever ends in the hinged case flap and the fact that this has been converted from key-wind to reversed-lever winding using a lever which barely fits the case. The original inner glass lid and key-compartment divider are now missing.

PLATE 81 ►
While the Lecoultre et Falconnet box above had an inner glass lid by *c.* 1840, the large Nicole Frères seen here and dating from about 1842 did not. Serial number is 23398 and the programme is somewhat unusual. Ostensibly it is an eight-air box playing two tunes per turn. However, the programme comprises two overtures which are played on full revolutions plus four popular tunes, each played on half a revolution.

◄ PLATE 82
A most compact
little box is this
Nicole Frères
eight-air
two-tunes-per-turn
piano-forte box. The
cylinder is 9·3 in.
long and the serial
number is 28618
with *gamme* 1055.
The box has its
original dark blue
tune-sheet listing the
tunes which include
Balfe's *Light of
Other Days*, *God
Save the Queen*, *Rule
Britannia*, *Alice Grey*
and *Yankee Doodle*.

PLATE 83 ►
High-quality four-overture box
made by Nicole Frères, serial
number 27801, *gamme* 1235. Note
the extremely fine comb teeth,
and the silver engraved
tune-sheet. This piece also shows
an interesting transitional stage
between key and lever winding for
the handle incorporates a ratchet
so that it only has to be moved
back and forth in order to wind
the spring. When not in use, the
handle is stored in a separate
compartment at the right of the
cylinder which has its own hinged
lid.

comprises a tube of thin paper which can be lowered on to the top (occasionally it is raised against the underside) of the comb teeth so that when they are plucked, they produce a buzzing sound a little like a Jew's harp and nothing at all like a zither. It was even styled by makers who were keen to upstage the ordinary mass-producers of movements with zithers as 'harp', an instrument which its sound resembles even less. The metal bar, usually with a wooden holder screwed under it, which actually pressed the paper on to the comb was often very ornate and finely marked. Better-class makers sometimes engraved their names on the top. Since most sane restorers in the intervening years have discarded these dubious additions, and only recently have we learned that we should preserve the good along with the bad, there is always the chance that the zither may not be the original one, so if it has a name on it it may not indicate that it and the rest of the movement came from the same parent. Some zithers were intended to operate only on certain parts of the comb, or, in the case of a multi-combed movement, on one particular comb. Cheaper boxes, though, followed the maxim that the larger the zither the more impressive it would look – and never mind what it did to the music.

In addition to these tune-sheet styles, there were various formats of the mechanism which were not otherwise listed. Mechanical styles such as Duplex and Plerodiénique were usually written on the tune sheet, but there were others which never were accorded such distinction. Some have self-explanatory titles. They included the following:

Two tunes per turn
Three tunes per turn
Four tunes per turn
Irregular-length tunes
Single-comb piano-forte (see under *forte-piano* in previous listing)
Custom-built
Custom programme
Concealed drum and bells
Coin-operated

TWO TUNES PER TURN   Many of the large, fat cylinder musical boxes played two tunes per turn. This was achieved by having two stop drops in the gulley of the cylinder great wheel. However, because there was only one change snail, if one wanted to repeat the first tune, then the cylinder would have to play the second tune to complete the cylinder revolution before the first could be heard once more. Nicole Frères made a number of these. Charles & Jacques Ullmann made some late, small movements with this characteristic.

THREE TUNES PER TURN   The foregoing words apply with obvious modification to this style, which is not all that common.

FOUR TUNES PER TURN   Again, another variant of the two-per-turn mechanism, this one with four stop drops arranged at 90° positions around the cylinder great-wheel gulley.

IRREGULAR-LENGTH TUNES   A somewhat ambitious and very early arrangement was pioneered by Lecoultre to enable a mechanism to play, if required, a tune of only a few seconds' duration, one taking up a full turn, or one taking up some other fraction of the

155

whole. Out of a whole programme potential of, say, four complete revolutions of the cylinder (four points to the change snail), virtually any number of tunes could be played so long as the mechanical dictates of maintaining a plain strip across the width of the cylinder at the moment of cylinder-shift was adhered to. The way in which this was done was ingenious, but prone to disorder. Instead of allowing the stop trail to ride round the cylinder great-wheel gully seeking a drop (which, of course, would stop the mechanism at the same position on every tune position), the stop trail was so arranged that it ran round the surface of the extreme end of the cylinder. At suitable points on the cylinder's outside, and corresponding to the stop trail's position, a small hole would be drilled in the surface. The trail was encouraged to drop into this, so bringing the mechanism to a halt in a normal way. The only example seen is marked F. Lecoultre, has a cylinder 7 in. by 3 in., and plays a 124-tooth comb (see Fig. 29).

CUSTOM-BUILT   Occasionally musical boxes were produced to the special order of a wealthy customer. One maker who specialised in this type was Paillard, who made some impressive and large movements in exotic cabinets. M. J. Paillard in New York took orders for a number of such pieces, but they were also made by Mermod and Nicole Frères. With the exception of some of the gargantuan cabinet models by Paillard, which seem to have been made in very small batches, most are unique. These boxes would also feature in many cases the custom programme.

CUSTOM PROGRAMME   A special-order musical box was often provided with a list of tunes which were beloved of the intended purchaser. Custom programmes are usually identifiable by their odd assortment of melodies.

CONCEALED DRUM AND BELLS   When these percussion effects were added to the musical box, it was normal that they should be hidden out of sight underneath the mechanism. Identifiable by the extra depth of the case below the musical movement, these almost all predate about 1855 and, in general, are musically good with well tuned bells which were nested to take up less space beneath. The drums were sometimes fitted with large resonating chambers and had skins of thin brass sheet. The earliest drums were screwed inside the case bottom so that the movement was supported above the drum. A screw protruding through the case bottom would be provided to raise or lower the drum to make it sound soft or loud. There were several variations on the style such as Ducommun Girod's 'Hidden Bells, Drum and Castanets', usually lever-wound and hence c. 1862.

COIN-OPERATED   Coin-freed cylinder musical boxes were introduced for use in public places. There were two basic styles: the first was the large animated scene comprising dancing dolls and other movements which were sufficiently visual to be used as a sideshow or spectacle on its own in an amusement arcade, and the second was the usual-format table-top model provided with a lockable glass lid through which the mechanism might be watched while in play. The former type was made by a number of makers including Mermod and Paillard, but it seems that the glass-lidded conventional style was mainly made by Mermod. Most of the surviving examples can be attributed positively to this maker since all are fitted with the Mermod style of horizontal endless.

Mention should briefly be made of the musical novelties which incorporated cylinder movements. Besides clocks and pictures there was also the musical praxinoscope with a three-air Bremond movement and of course the ever-popular Swiss chalet, again usually Bremond (see Plate 70).

This listing covers the majority of commonly-found types and styles of cylinder movement. Those omissions will usually be identified readily from a knowledge and awareness of the foregoing.

MUSICAL BOXES, First Quality.
Rich Case, "Cabinet" Style.

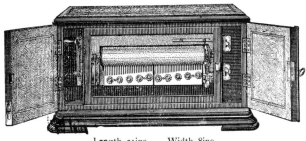

Length 21ins.   Width 8ins.

Numbers.				£ s. d.
5161	Musical Box, cabinet style, **Forte Piano**, 2 combs, 8 airs, 10¾ins.	each		11 10 0
5163	,, ,, ,, **Mandolin Zither**, 6 airs, 10¾ins. ...	,,		12 10 0
5164	,, ,, ,, ,, 8 airs, 10¾ins. ...	,,		13 10 0

MUSICAL BOXES WITH ACCOMPANIMENT,
Extra Quality.

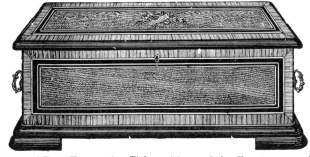

			£ s. d.
5170	Musical Box, **Expressive Zither**, rich case, 6 airs, 8ins. ... each		5 5 0
5171	,, ,, ,, ,, ,, 8 ,, 10¾ ,, ... ,,		6 12 0
5172	,, ,, ,, ,, ,, 10 ,, 12¾ ,, ... ,,		7 5 0
5173	,, ,, ,, ,, ,, 12 ,, 14¾ ,, ... ,,		8 8 0
5175	,, ,, **Guitar Accompaniment**, rich case, 6 airs, 8ins. ,,		10 0 0
5176	,, ,, ,, ,, ,, 8 ,, 10¾ ,, ,,		12 0 0
5178	,, ,, ,, ,, ,, 12 ,, 14¾ ,, ,,		17 5 0
5182	,, ,, **Zither Mandolin, Piccolo**, rich case, 6 airs, 12¾ins. ... ,,		12 12 0
5183	,, ,, ,, ,, rich case, 8 airs, 17ins. ... ,,		17 5 0
5189	,, ,, **Sublime Harmony, Forte Piano, Zither**, 2 combs, 6 airs, 12¾ins. ... ... ,,		13 0 0
5193	,, ,, **Sublime Harmony, Forte Piano, Concert Piccolo**, 3 combs, 6 airs, 12¾ins. ... ... ,,		14 0 0
5206	,, ,, with double spring box, sublime harmony, forte piano, 8 airs, 17ins. ... . ,,		18 10 0

CHAPTER 6

The Disc-Playing Musical Box

The cylinder musical box suffered from one major shortcoming, namely the brevity of its repertoire. Although interchangeable cylinders had been evolved to afford a measure of variety, and various systems had been employed to extend the playing capabilities so that long pieces of music might be played without interruption, the unalterable fact remained that the quality cylinder box was an expensive luxury whose inflexible programme of music could work out as expensive as £5 per tune or, in the case of the largest overture boxes, considerably more. Its sale, therefore, was restricted to those who had ample money to indulge in such luxuries.

Obviously there was scope for a 'people's musical box' which might at once do away with the economic limitations of the ruling type of mechanical musicwork. First a comparatively low-cost box had to be made. Second, it had to allow the purchaser to select his own favourite music – and add to it as the will took him.

The earliest attempt at meeting this requirement was made by a man from Haiti about whom virtually nothing is known other than his name, Miguel Boom. Obviously inspired by the long-used principle of the carillon cylinder which could be repinned with as many tunes as the carilloneur had patience using a spanner on the nuts of the removable, adjustable barrel pegs, Boom devised a machine which retained the essence of the musical box – the tuned steel comb – but which played music from a rotating wheel or disc. This disc was formed with a large number of concentric grooves into which could be set small pegs to pluck the comb teeth as it revolved. In theory at least, here was a machine which could perform any music at all, once the pegs had been properly arranged in their grooves in the disc. Sadly, the system had severe shortcomings, for it demanded that the owner be possessed with sufficient knowledge of music, mathematics and mechanics to be able literally to make his own music. No examples of Boom's instrument are known to have been made; although his principle has been used many times in children's musical toys, and also in the Musik-Baukasten described on page 183.

The early 1880s were packed with blossoming musicwork technology and in Leipzig F. E. P. Ehrlich was designing, patenting and building a number of organettes using discs with various forms of perforations or projections representing the music to be played. What happened next is not too precise but it would appear that Ellis Parr, a musical-instrument dealer and inventor in London, had the idea of using a perforated disc as a means of playing a musical-box comb. He was granted two patents – 16320 dated 11 December 1884 and 10944 dated 15 September 1885 – for musical instruments played by a rotating disc. It must be said that both these patents were for mechanisms which could not really be called disc musical boxes; in fact the former was related more to cylinder boxes, and the latter to musical spinning-tops. In an interview which Parr subsequently gave to the *Pall Mall Budget* for 16 February 1888 (reproduced *in toto* in *Clockwork Music*), he described how he later went to the Leipzig Fair where he learned that a German, Paul Lochmann, was making a musical box played by a disc. Parr, who it must be remembered had not yet created a musical box which could be played by a disc, but had thought up the disc as a means of playing related instruments (and this must have been inspired by the Ehrlich patents), at once saw fit to publish the following notice in the London magazine *Musical Opinion* for 1 December 1886:

NOTICE. HAVING OBTAINED A LETTERS PATENT, No. 16320 (1884) and No. 10944 (1885), in the United Kingdom, &c, for IMPROVEMENTS in the METHOD of PRODUCING TUNES in MUSICAL BOXES by the use of Changeable Metal Bands and Discs, and it having come to my knowledge that Musical Boxes are now being offered for sale in the United Kingdom which are an infringement of my said Patents, I HEREBY GIVE NOTICE that LEGAL PROCEEDINGS will be taken against all persons manufacturing, selling, or using such instruments. All communications to be addressed to Messrs. EDWARDS & CO., 35, Southampton Buildings, Chancery Lane, E.C.

ELLIS PARR.

The musical box which played discs thus arrived in England with threatened court action to greet it. This was the first of many such legal wrangles about the instrument. However, Parr and Lochmann remained at loggerheads only a short time, for Parr must soon have realised that Lochmann's machine (patented in England as number 11261 on 22 September 1885) was a practical realisation of what could only have been an idea in his head. Similarly, Lochmann was probably shrewd enough to see that Parr could be the first distributor in England particularly if the trade had been frightened off by Parr's haughty threats. The two men entered a trading arrangement and Parr subsequently said:

. . . the Symphonion is made at Leipzig where my co-patentee, a German gentleman, is at the head of our factory. Of course I should employ English labour, if such were possible, but as yet we have not the necessary skill in this country. It requires a long and thorough education before the work can be done, and workers skilled in this particular handicraft are not to be found in England. We employ about 120 hands in the factory at Leipzig, besides a number of girls who prepare the discs at their own homes . . .

When Parr was interviewed by the *Pall Mall Budget*,* he claimed to have taken out a patent for the Symphonion and told his interrogator:

As a curiosity it may perhaps interest you to know that Mr. Lochmann, my German co-patentee, made precisely the same invention only a week after I made mine. I was on my way to Switzerland without knowing anything about him, when at the Leipsic [*sic*] fair I heard of his invention. At first I took action against him to prevent his interfering with the

* Article 'Music by Machinery', facsimile reproduction in *Clockwork Music*, by Ord-Hume, pp. 113–15.

sale in England, but eventually we became partners, and are now both trying to improve our instrument in every possible way, till it shall be quite perfect.

This is contrived to put Ellis Parr in the superior position, yet there is nothing to substantiate Parr's claim to have, by inference, produced an instrument 'precisely the same', and his patents are general enough in terminology to be barely relative. Parr certainly became a collaborator with Lochmann, yet Lochmann was very much the inventor and innovator throughout the burgeoning days of the Symphonion.

Of Parr not a great deal is known. His business, Ellis Parr & Co., was established in 1809. He dealt in pianos, holding the agency for Schiedmayer & Söhne and Haake and, by 1889, the Packard reed organ. In the early 1880s, his business was at 97 Wigmore Street with a branch at 17a Duke Street. In 1889 he was at 99 Oxford Street close to Berners Street. Parr patented a number of minor musical accessories – a musicleaf turner was one, an improved portable, adjustable, attachable pianoforte music and table desk another.

It is unlikely that we are looking at one man if his business was founded as early as 1809, but on the other hand he may have bought into an existing, 1809-founded business. Certainly, as an importer of musical instruments and a dealer in pianofortes he seems an unlikely person to have forestalled the disc musical box in so detailed a manner as he claimed.

What happened to Parr is something of a mystery, for his business seems to have quietly faded away and soon others were proclaimed 'sole agents and importers' for the Symphonion, among them Henry Klein and Ernst Holzweissig. By 1900, Symphonion opened its own London office at Ely Place. It therefore seems that Parr ceased business somewhere shortly after 1899.

As a piece of mechanism, it is all too easy to refer to the early disc musical box as a 'primitive' instrument without qualifying what one means by this terminology. This was indeed very far from the truth. The musical comb was already well established, tonally perfected, and thoroughly understood. The acoustic properties of the wooden case which enclosed a musical movement were appreciated (although the knowledge of this facet of musicwork was subsequently to be extended far beyond the experience of the mid-1880s), and the technicalities of arranging music for mechanical playing were fully mastered.

This is not to suggest that, although the disc musical box posed such dramatically different operating conditions, their solution was a simple matter. The technique of transferring the programme of music into the proper plucking of the comb was a major hurdle, and equally complex was the solution of the problem of damping the vibrating comb tooth prior to its being plucked again. It was in these details of realisation that the first disc musical boxes could be described as 'primitive'.

The early Lochmann musical box had two vertically mounted combs across the top of which was placed a stationary perforated cardboard disc. The combs were rotated by clockwork. Obvious problems with the card discs, developed from the organette-type disc devised by Ehrlich, led to metal discs being substituted and so, by 1887, zinc discs with rudimentary projections had been invented and, because the rotating combs were in no rigid way connected to the case, stationary combs were introduced which improved the volume and tone of the music produced. One problem still remained and that was the difficulty of plucking the teeth directly from the disc. In 1889, a Symphonion engineer named Paul Wendland patented the starwheel which acted as an intermediary between the disc and the combs – it appears to have been used for several years prior to this date however. The

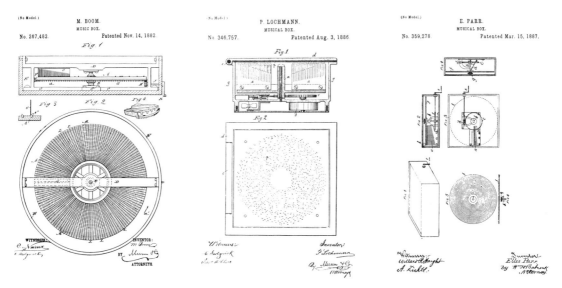

Figure 30   Three early patents covering the invention of the disc-playing musical box. The first, that of Miguel Boom, was for a repinnable disc. Next is Paul Lochmann's 'square disc' system beneath which the musical combs were rotated. Ellis Parr's patent was in many ways similar.

projections formed on the underside of the music disc now connected with one point of the starwheel and, in turning it, allowed another point to lift and pluck the relevant comb tooth. The disc and the comb could now be mounted in the same plane, i.e. parallel to each other. Prior to this, the disc had always had to be at right angles to the comb so that the projections could do their job directly on the comb tooth.*

The concept of the disc machine was simple. The instrument was large and ornate, and was made to fit into the home of the period. It could also be fairly expensive without detracting from its merits, which lay in the fact that one could play any music on it by the simple expedient of buying a metal disc to fit the machine. Discs were priced from a few pence up to several shillings.

The impact of this invention on the musical-box industry was a foretaste in many ways of things to come, and for the other musical-box manufacturers, it was clearly a case of 'beating

---

* It is worth charting the progress of the disc musical-box through the British patents. Patent number 11261, dated 22 September 1885, was taken out in the name of Paul Lochmann for a musical box having two combs on a vertical axis which were rotated against a tune sheet attached to the underside of a cover. Case resonance must have been nil on this mechanism, hence Lochmann covered himself by stating that the tune sheet might also rotate against stationary combs. The disc projections were called upon to pluck the combs directly. Patent number 6391 of 12 May 1886 appeared under the name of F. E. P. Ehrlich for a musical box with combs operated by a perforated tune sheet with an intermediary plucking system. Ehrlich was joint patentee with G. A. F. Müller on Patent number 9742 of 28 July 1886 for a musical box with combs ('or tuning forks') mounted vertically under a rotating tune disc having projections which once again were expected to pluck the comb directly. Patent number 5442 dated 29 March 1889 was taken out in the name of Paul Lochmann for a method of plucking and damping musical-box teeth using a starwheel. Although the actual patent does not make it absolutely clear, it seems likely that the patent retrospectively covers the starwheel but specifically relates to its use in connection with dampers and brakes.

them or joining them'. Within a few short years, very many other disc musical boxes were being made, and the cylinder box rapidly degenerated in quality in a forlorn attempt by its erstwhile advocates to hold their own.

But we are ahead of the story. Paul Lochmann's factory in Gohlis, a Leipzig suburb, was gradually gearing up to production of the Symphonion. Foreman for the Lochmann firm was Gustave Brachhausen. He was not altogether happy with the Symphonion, had a disagreement with Lochmann, and left, taking with him Paul Riessner, a brilliant engineer and a forward-looking young man to boot.

The two men decided to go into partnership and produce their own disc musical box. Setting up in business in a large private house practically on Lochmann's doorstep, they formed the Polyphonmusikwerke and began producing the famous Polyphon, probably the best known name in the annals of the disc musical box.

Lochmann was naturally perturbed, and accused Brachhausen of infringing his patents, in particular with regard to the shape of the disc projections. Lochmann's discs had a characteristic double-lipped projection, one half being bent back to support the other, very much like a letter P when viewed edge on. Brachhausen used a slightly thicker metal for his discs and formed his projection from one bent up tag.

Lochmann sued Brachhausen. For many months, the names Symphonion and Polyphon were bandied about in court and the case was indeed a complicated one. Meanwhile, the now vast Polyphon and Symphonion plants continued turning out machines in all shapes and sizes. Some were horizontally mounted table models, others vertically mounted models for hanging on the wall, standing in the four-ale bar or assuming pride of place in the drawing-room.

Litigation suddenly ceased, judgment was found in favour of Polyphon, and there were great festivities. From then on, the two companies appear to have at least tolerated one another, even using the same type of single-strip disc projection.

No sooner was this action out of the way than another and much more basic court action was started in Leipzig. Paul Ehrlich, the maker of the Monopol disc musical box, was claiming for his company (the Leipziger Musikwerke) a monopoly in the use of starwheels for mechanical musical instruments.

The case had come up in the summer of 1896 and Ehrlich had lost. He now appealed to the Court of Naumburg against the earlier decision. Considerable weight of objection to his appeal had been lodged by the house of Lochmann (which denied to the Ehrlich factory all rights to forbid anybody to use starwheels as plectra for the tongues of musical-box combs) and other factories both in Leipzig and Berlin. It was, in fact, correctly claimed that other makers had been using starwheels much earlier than Ehrlich. The court subsequently dismissed the appeal, but with heavy costs against Ehrlich. In 1904, Ehrlich sold the company to Wwe Emilie Buff-Hedinger, the new name being Neue Leipziger Musikwerke A. Buff-Hedinger at Herloss-sohnstrasse 1–4, Leipzig-Gohlis. As well as making Ariston organettes, the business made player pianos, player organs, orchestrions and the Toccaphon xylophone piano. The mushrooming industry was accompanied with the inevitable trappings of prosperity – business take-overs, the speculators and the troublemakers. Then, as now, money made by far the loudest noise. But there were other problems which hinged on trade restrictions, duties and tariffs. In 1895, for instance, the Austro-Hungarian finance ministry decided that piano-orchestrions were to be taxed as 'finger-board instruments' at 20 florins per hundred kilos for the countries with whom commercial treaties existed, and

THE DISC-PLAYING MUSICAL BOX

double that for the others! And in America McKinley's attitude towards imports was more than just short-sighted. A valuable decade of European intercourse was lost.

It was now Polyphon's turn to be taken to court. In 1898, the firm of Henry Litolff's Edition of Brunswick sued the manager of Polyphon for the unauthorised transcription of 'Marche Lorraine', composed by the Frenchman Louis Ganne, on to tin discs. The case was a particularly interesting one for several technical reasons regarding the interpretation of the copyright law, the Berne Convention and the involvement of a French national's work. However, it suffices to say here that the case went against Polyphon and, in spite of an appeal, the court decision was upheld that all discs, together with master plates, appliances for the production of the discs and so forth, should be confiscated, whether in the hands of Polyphon or their agents anywhere in the world. Polyphon acted accordingly, and 'Marche Lorraine' was officially impounded and destroyed. However, a number of the discs had already been sold and had been available for several years; thus copies of this banned disc do exist and I have one in my own collection.

A strange piece of trade impudence was tried by a certain William H. Hoschke of 680 Broadway, New York, who, in November of 1894, issued a circular to all people in the musical instrument trade warning them not to buy or make automatic musical instruments fitted with a 'star or spur wheel' in consequence of patent rights dated 8 April 1889. This gentleman, who went on to acquire further patents on musical boxes in 1894, was obviously unaware that the Fabrik Lochmann'scher Musikwerke (Symphonion) had taken out an American patent several years earlier for precisely this system.

During this time, Polyphon had moved into a huge factory at Wahren, Leipzig; by 1899, the factory had been enlarged to accommodate a thousand persons. However, the growth of the company suffered a setback when, during the night of 6 July that year, fire broke out in the joinery department. Fanned by a high wind, the fire gained hold with great rapidity and soon the whole building was engulfed, part of the roof falling in and the outer walls collapsing. Since most of the factory was devoted to the manufacture of the fine, ornate cases, immense wood stores aided the flames. By good fortune, the large machinery halls formed a fire break and these were saved from extensive damage as were the steam engines which drove the factory plant. The most valuable part of the works, the machine shops where all metal parts were made, were situated in the basement and these escaped damage. An adjacent building housing the disc-stamping department was also saved. Fire-fighting was hampered by the shortage of water and soon water carts were forced to draw from the distant river Elster. The military authorities were also called in to help, but by all accounts it was a sad sight that greeted the 780 workers the next morning. It was decided not to lay off any employees, and immediately all hands were put to salvage operations, temporary buildings were set up in the extensive factory grounds, and production of the Polyphon continued with little delay.

The arrival of the disc musical box had naturally been greeted by other makers of musical boxes with perturbation. Most were quick to realise that the disc box had obvious selling advantages which they could not possibly hope to challenge. And so began the trickle of other makers' disc boxes which soon became almost a flood.

The Leipzig manufacturer, Friederich Ernst Paul Ehrlich, who had been making paper and cardboard music-playing organettes, including the widely known Ariston, since the early 1880s, produced the Monopol disc musical box quite early on. It was in production by 1896, making it at least as old as Polyphon as a production disc box. This was a good

163

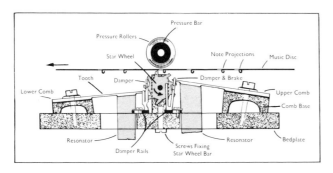

Figure 31 The principles of the disc-playing musical box as exemplified by the Polyphon.

machine, in very many ways similar to the Symphonion and, in fact, some sizes were interchangeable and played the same discs. Monopols ranged in size from small hand-cranked manivelles playing discs $5\frac{3}{4}$ in. in diameter up to models which played, in addition to musical combs, dulcimers, bells and percussion from a disc 32 in. in diameter. Not that the gargantuan disc was to be found solely on Monopol: all makes produced giant models, some which were disc-operated piano orchestrions in that the instrument comprised a strung piano back, drum and cymbals and no musical combs at all.

Other makes included the Kalliope, the smaller models of which are distinguished by their centre-spindle winding; the Orphenion which, instead of punched-out disc projections had zinc discs with scoop-shaped indentations; the Adler and later its matching sister, the Fortuna with its acoustic cabinet; and the sweet-toned Celeste.

To begin with at any rate, the Symphonion and Monopol (Ehrlich) patents were so tightly

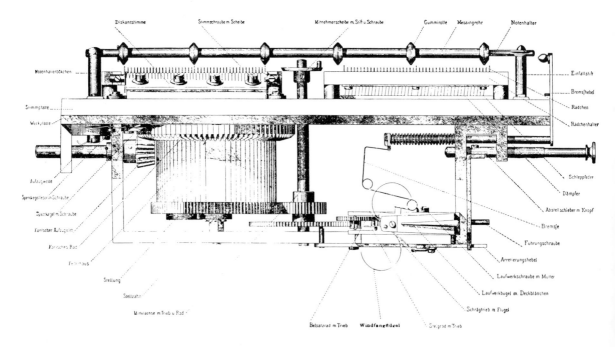

Figure 32 Mechanism of the Symphonion table model and detail of the air-brake and governor assembly.

164

guarded that other makers had to find a way round at least two of the salient parts of the disc-playing mechanism – the dampers and the disc projections.

Many methods were tried in the quest for a practical way to damp the vibrating tooth. They included felt (a singularly useless approach no doubt inspired by the knowledge that felt works well as a damper in a piano), catgut, cam levers and friction wires. Significantly, the only one which really worked was the cam lever, used by Polyphon and Regina. Among the numerous early attempts was one by Lochmann (he invented many systems) which had a comb of thin metal teeth with felt-covered tips. This was mounted under the musical comb so that the damper tips projected upwards and outwards at an angle of about 45° to stop short of a protruding anvil under the tooth. As the starwheel rotated, its first task was to press the spring-loaded felt damper onto the tooth tip. It was not a success.

Disc projections also came in all styles with some, such as that invented by Bruno Ruckert for the Orphenion, impractical due to the rapid rate of wear. Others demanded complex tooling and the consequent incurring of a high maintenance cost. Some types are shown in Fig. 33.

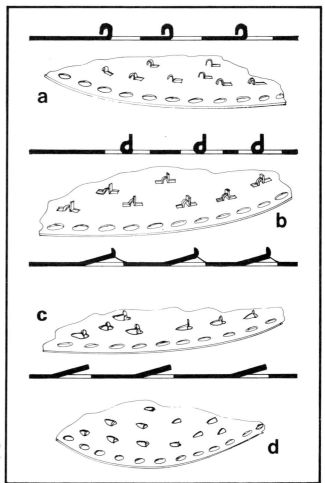

Figure 33 Different types of disc projection; (a) basic form first used by Polyphon; (b) the Symphonion form; (c) Swiss Mira style with dimple and projection; (d) Orphenion type.

165

Discs without projections were obviously far simpler and cheaper to make and offered the added advantage that they were easier to store: trying to force a disc into a storage bin was always achieved at the cost of broken or bent projections which, of course, meant that the particular note intended to be sounded by that projection would never sound again.

As early as March 1892, Brachhausen and Riessner took out patents (British Patent No. 4451 refers) for a disc punched with plain slots. Of the several types of projectionless disc-playing musical boxes ultimately manufactured, the best known and the most successful was the Stella made by the Swiss musical-box manufacturer, Mermod Frères, which naturally adopted a star as a trademark for the box (the original Mermod trade mark, a shield, is illustrated elsewhere). When for some reason Mermod decided also to produce a disc machine with projections, they followed their liking for Latin names and called it the Mira. The Mira in many cases used the same cabinets as the Stella and was also specially manufactured for sale in the United States under the name of Empress through the Chicago company Lyon & Healy.

Coming late in the relatively short-lived era of the disc musical box, Mermod had to challenge the undoubted leaders of Polyphon and Symphonion and, as we shall see, the aspiring Regina. That they succeeded in doing this is some indication of the quality and often superior finish of the boxes which Mermod produced. The heavy, Teutonic case styles of the Leipzig and Berlin products were quite different from the light, attractive and (then) modern Stella cabinet. Soon, needless to say, the Germans got the message and the following generation of disc boxes was produced with a broader eye to the world-wide commercialism of the commodity. Mermod was also probably the only European company to market an electrically driven disc machine – the 26 in. Orchestral Stella.

The factory of Symphonion was slightly smaller than the giant Polyphon plant which its former employee sired. The Symphonionfabrik employed about 400 workers. Both companies obtained their comb tuners from Switzerland and, since these workers obviously had to work in a quiet place, they were established away from the main workshops. Symphonion comb tuners worked in a large house where they could work undisturbed.*

Also from Switzerland, Paul Lochmann acquired the services of Octave F. Chaillet who had lived in Ste-Croix. Chaillet was a musician who had arranged, transposed and pricked the cylinders for several of the Ste-Croix musical-box makers including the makers of the large reed-organ-accompanied musical boxes. Now as an employee of Symphonion, he set up music to be transferred to discs.

Many of the products of both Symphonion and Polyphon were exported to America and Brachhausen took out patents to protect his inventions in the States in 1889 and onwards.

Higher import tariffs plus the increasing opportunities open to the musical-box market in America led first to the Polyphon company and then Symphonion establishing American divisions, which soon became autonomous in operation. In 1892, Brachhausen sailed for America in company with three machinists and two cabinet makers. At the end of that year, when thirty-five years old, Brachhausen established the Regina Music Box Company in a small rented factory in New Jersey. Initially, almost all parts for instruments were imported from Polyphon in Leipzig and assembled and cased in the plant at 20 Morris Street, Jersey City. The discs were Polyphon stampings as well and, even after Regina had started indigenous production, discs were still made in Germany for several years.

---

* Initial production Symphonions made use of imported, Swiss-made combs.

Within a year, the Regina had made a tremendous impact on the American public. Demands for their musical boxes were so enormous that Brachhausen sought a larger, permanent location. A building of 25,000 square feet, previously occupied by a printing and publishing concern, was acquired in Rahway, New Jersey. More than sixty German and Swiss musical-box specialists were brought from Polyphon and Symphonion.

An amusing anecdote is recorded concerning the Swiss comb tuners who sat side by side along a bench running the length of one room. Brachhausen allegedly became annoyed at the amount of talking which went on among the tuners. Believing that less talk would mean more work, he erected barriers between the men so that each had his own private cubicle. The talk diminished, but so did the work, for the whole group walked out and flatly refused to return until the barriers were taken down. Brachhausen conceded and work was resumed.

Discs could not for ever be obtained from Leipzig. Brachhausen hired Octave Chaillet from Symphonion and established a disc-stamping shop at Rahway. Not long after, Regina published a catalogue listing almost two thousand titles.

The Regina was most probably the finest disc musical box ever produced, both in tone and musical arrangement. The standard of manufacture and case style was of the highest order, being the result of all the best of Polyphon and Symphonion, plus the Swiss musical knowledge of several generations. Brachhausen explored the sounds of a musical comb and possibly did more to enhance both tone and volume than any other maker. A late model of the Regina played $15\frac{1}{2}$ in. (39·8 cm) discs and featured a special short bedplate and a clever arrangement of soundboards. The tone of this was quite remarkable, being loud enough for use in a large room without sounding in any way harsh, brash or unpleasant. In 1977, this model was put back into limited production by Dwight Porter in America under the brand name 'Porter'.

In the same way that large Polyphons and Symphonions were now being built in Germany which were coin-operated and which could be used in places of entertainment, cafés and public houses, so Reginas were made for nickel-playing in cafés and speakeasies. By employing mass-production techniques including standardisation of component parts, many thousands of machines were made ranging in price from a few dollars to several hundred. Much business was in the form of special orders for custom-made cases.

Hydraulic presses were made which could stamp out ten discs simultaneously from one master, and disc sizes ranged from 8 to 32 in. in diameter. The two popular models were the $15\frac{1}{2}$ in. size and the 27 in., these dimensions being the diameters of the discs. The 27 in. Regina had double combs encompassing rather more than seven octaves, and played for two minutes on one revolution of the disc. Piano-type sounding boards were used in the upright models, which gave a surprising volume to the instrument.

In 1897 came the next significant improvement in disc machines, the self-changer. Gustave Brachhausen invented this as the answer to the need to keep changing the discs. Was there not in this perhaps an inkling of the growing laziness of Man, later crystallised in the labour-saving devices of the twentieth century?

The self-changer, whose history is described in detail further on in this chapter, was a major achievement put into production almost simultaneously by Polyphon in Leipzig and Regina in New Jersey. Two big clockwork motors were used, one to operate the changing mechanism and the other to drive the disc while playing. The discs, twelve of them, were stacked in a frame rather like a toast rack in the lower part of the instrument. A selector lever was provided so that the owner could choose which disc he wanted to play. Alternatively, the instrument would play through the whole programme until the clockwork ran down. Later models dispensed with the weight and costly installation of twin motors and, in place, fitted a coil-spring motor which stretched from side to side of the case behind the bedplate. This was used by both Polyphon and Regina and became a feature of the later self-changer models by these makers.

This mechanical marvel would select its disc, methodically lift it up to the playing spindle, clamp it on, play it, then unclamp it, lower it back into the toast-rack and be ready for the next. The self-changer was produced in large numbers, particularly by Regina, and they are not uncommon today although they are highly prized collectors' items. Other makers who devised self-changers made in such limited quantities that their products are extremely rare.

The disc musical box had become the father of the modern juke box and along with its development into a new entertainment medium so had to be created the whole panoply of an outside service team and distributors who could rent out machines, maintain them and change the discs regularly. The lessees were allowed a percentage of the takings.

There is an interesting side story concerning the Regina self-changer. Styled the Corona, this has a curved front door with hinges at the left, case lock to the right. A feature of the hinges is that they protrude sufficiently to allow the hinge-pin to be withdrawn by any person hell-bent on forcing open the door to steal cash from the cash-drawer (in truth barely possible). To prevent this, Regina introduced a novel security catch. Inside the left side of the case was screwed an alloy casting resembling a simple door catch. Fitted to the inside of the left side of the door was another alloy casting, this one in the shape of a curved finger. As the door closed, this finger passed round the case casting in the horizontal plane, so trapping the door against being opened even if the hinge pins were removed.

Of those other makers who patented self-changers, among them Thorens and Barnett Henry Abrahams, only one other seems to have entered production and this was Symphonion with its largest machine. This cannot have been a great success since the total number of machines known to collectors today is two!

But to return to Regina, between the years 1892 and 1919 the company turned out some 100,000 musical boxes and at one time about 325 employees were engaged in building them. In 1901, there was a general business recession, but business soon recovered. However, in 1903 there was a serious plunge in sales from which the company never recovered. Brachhausen had never been owner of the Regina company, for it was financed by a German bank which now tightened its control. Brachhausen was relegated to the position of factory manager.

The impact of the phonograph, already felt in Europe, was making itself known in America. Regina began making a hand-pumped vacuum cleaner as early as 1902, following it with an electric one in 1909; and from then until 1922 an assortment of products were made including player-pianos, printing presses and so on. The last musical box was made in 1919. Three years later, the firm was bankrupt. Most of the musical-box production machinery, together with stocks of unused parts, was dumped into the river. What remained, including some master discs and a hand-operated disc press, plus a quantity of Regina spares, was acquired by Lloyd G. Kelly of Massachusetts, who for some years produced new Regina discs from original masters. In 1976, the Regina Music Box Company was acquired by J. Harry Carmel of Illinois who now holds title to the name. Reorganised as the Regina Corporation, the Rahway firm re-entered business in 1924, making floor polishers and cleaners. It is still in existence today, but there are no musical boxes to be seen. Brachhausen was disillusioned over the end of the musical-box era but stayed with the company as a tool and die maker. He had sold out his interest in the company for around $1 million in 1915 and returned to Germany. Here he lost his fortune and his marriage ended in divorce. In 1919 he returned to Regina as a benchworker. The last musical box was made around that time and the final one sold was from inventory in 1921. In 1922 the company went into receivership and a new managment took over. Still Brachhausen worked on the bench until, too old for his task, he became night watchman for the now-styled Regina Corporation. On 2 October 1943, he died at the age of 86. Octave Chaillet's daughter had been his second wife.

Although Regina did not cease musical-box production until 1919, the majority of the other European makers had long ceased production, a move largely forced upon them by the 1914–18 war, which not only eroded the workforce of companies, but also alienated the major market areas.

Earlier I mentioned that Symphonion also had set up in America. For a business which produced some really spectacular disc musical boxes, the fact remains that very little is known today about the company which occupied a fine brick building at Bradley Beach near Asbury Park in New Jersey. Styled the Symphonion Manufacturing Company and with products named 'Imperial Symphonion', the company set up its manufacturing facilities about 1897 but seems to have disappeard soon after 1902. According to estimates by Q. David Bowers* no more than between 5,000 and 10,000 musical boxes were made – and he thinks that this may even be on the high side.

Symphonion in Leipzig underwent some fundamental changes, too. After its foundation as the Symphonion Musikwerke by Paul Lochmann, it became Symphonion-Fabrik Aktiengesellschaft (a limited liability company) in 1889. By that time, however, its directors were Franz Thumen and Hans Kanitz, Paul Lochmann having severed his connections to establish the Original Musikwerke Paul Lochmann GmbH founded in 1900. Symphonion's first address was at Braustrasse 13–19 in Leipzig's Gohlis suburb, but by 1909 it had moved to Schkeuditzer Strasse 13–17b. The company went on with musical boxes and the manufacture of electric pianos until about the outbreak of the First World War, when it moved to Gera, Reuss, and changed ownership to concentrate mainly on phonographs.

Paul Riessner founded the Polyphon Musikwerke in 1890; the first Polyphon was made in 1887 and serious production was in hand by 1895 – note that this period is the earliest in which Polyphons were made and only Symphonion can predate 1887.† The company diversified during the early years of the present century and produced motor cars (the Polymobil was one) and typewriters (the Polygraph). Its best move, though, was to buy up the then financially stricken Deutsche Grammophon record company. With the technology which this acquisition brought the company, it produced gramophone records under the Polyphon label (even using the selfsame Polyphon girl trademark). However, time was to dictate that the Deutsche Grammophon company was to become the stronger party and by

---

* Article: 'Imperial Symphonion', *The Music Box*, vol. 7, pp. 86–90, 1975.

† Keith Harding (*The Music Box*, vol. 3, p. 260, 1973) has found a connection between the dates stamped on the spring rivet on 19⅝ in. (50 cm) Polyphons and the serial number stamped on the top motor plate. He suggests that this might form a guide to the numbers made. The fifteen dates he lists are: 1.10.87 = 7831; 1.6.98 = 15000; 6.6.98 = 15145; 24.7.98 = 16986; 22.8.98 = 17160; 18.9.98 = 18707; 5.12.98 = 21098; 16.12.98 = 21408; 28.4.99 = 25801; 11.5.99 = 25350; 18.5.99 = 25995; 7.9.99 = 27728; 28.9.99 = 29699; 27.3.00 = 32444; 15.6.00 = 35432.

1929 the company, restructured as Polyphonwerke A.G., was a division of DGG and based in Berlin at Markgrafenstrasse 76.

So passed the era of the disc musical box, although Thorens in Switzerland remained in business producing small, cheap disc musical-box novelties until fairly recently. In the space of twenty years or so, the disc musical-box industry had been born, had blossomed – and then faded. During its short life, it reached a high degree of perfection, turned out many thousands of instruments in a great variety of styles, and exported them to every corner of the world through a surprisingly well organised network of distributors. The story of just one of these distributors, that set up in London, will give some idea of trading methods and conditions of the period.

Back in 1898, if you wanted to travel, you needed no passport or other travel documents – you just put on your hat and went. For nineteen-year-old Arthur Ficker, the family business of cotton millers at Zschopau just outside Dresden in Saxony held little charm. Besides, he was more interested in commerce and the possibilities afforded by the new German musical-box industry. Among his wealthy bachelor uncles he secured promises of cash to help him set up in business; his father, Hermann Ficker, also promised to see his son right. A letter of introduction to the manager of the Polyphon Supply Company in London was also forthcoming, and so off he set for England.

The Polyphon Supply Company had enjoyed a somewhat chequered history. The first London distributors had been the Polyphon & Regina Company established by Nicole Frères at 21 Ely Place in 1896. At this time, Nicole Frères was already a London-owned company, having been taken over by Charles Eugène Brun who joined it originally as manager in October 1881.

The subsequent formation of the Polyphon Supply Company endeavoured to take a large share of the mushrooming disc musical-box business away from the Nicole company's offshoot. Manager was a young German named Curt Herzog. Although Ficker had never met Herzog before, Herzog also came from Zschopau close to the Czech border. In fact his father was the village schoolmaster. Four years Ficker's senior, Herzog had already been in London several years trying his best to run the Polyphon Supply Company, which was largely financed by businessmen from Saxony.

The first address for the PSC (until 1898) was 3 Bishopsgate Street Without, London EC, but then it moved into the same building as Henry Klein & Co.

The story is more than usually complicated, for Henry Klein was the biggest wholesaler (trade distributor) of Polyphons in London and as such his company was sole consignee for the Leipzig agents H. Peters & Co. Peters, founded in 1887 at Theaterplatz 1, Leipzig, was one of several principal shippers of Polyphons to England. Klein's business was at 84 Oxford Street.

When the Polyphon Supply Company moved into rooms at Klein's Oxford Street address to serve the retail trade and to rent instruments to public houses and amusement arcades, it was obvious that confusion would soon arise. Indeed the righteous Klein was forced to insert a notice in the trade papers to the effect that his trade was quite separate from that of the PSC. These notices are to be found reprinted in *The Music Box*, vol. 5, p. 322. The PSC obtained its instruments from another famous Leipzig distributor, Hugo Popper & Co., founded in 1891 at Reichsstrasse 33–35, but also bought, probably unwisely, from Peters via Klein.

The Polyphon Supply Company was a strangely organised operation. Perhaps the word 'organised' is to place too fine a point on its management for there was a lot of personal pocket-filling going on and the business, although obviously doing good trade, was not making money – for the shareholders at any rate. Herzog was fighting a losing battle with his own supervisors.

It was with this unbusinesslike situation with its undertones of animosity from Klein and the trade that Arthur Ficker found himself. The two men from the far off Saxony village decided that they should try to do something about it. They surveyed the Polyphon Supply Company as it tottered on the brink of dissolution brought about by the greed of its top operators. Herzog and Ficker discovered that most of the shareholders in the company were friends and it was soon agreed that the old company should be disbanded, the shares sold at par and the two Saxonians given the chance to try to reorganise the business back into a state of profitability.

Arthur Ficker took up 7,362 shares in the new venture, and Herzog 1,000. Ficker's father in Dresden took up 375, and various other relations back home added their contribution. A fresh company was registered – the New Polyphon Supply Company – at 1, 2, and 3 Newman Street, Oxford Circus. Number 1 was later to be hived off. Other shareholders in the business were G. Reicheldt (Hermann Ficker's father-in-law), May Ficker (Arthur Ficker's wife), Anna Marie Herzog (Curt Herzog's wife) and other family members and industrialists, mostly from the Dresden area.

The whole musical-box business was now in its closing phase and, as so often happens at this period in the history of an industry, there were some massive changes and expansions to take place before the final crunch. Nicole Frères had made its disastrous venture into the gramophone record business (see *The Music Box*, vol. 5, pp. 338ff) and, as a result, found itself bankrupt. In October 1906, the NPSC acquired all that was left of the once famous Ely Place musical-box company. Earlier that year, Henry Klein had retired from business. At that time he was operating at 142 Wardour Street and his assets, too, were gobbled up by NPSC. On the company letterheads it now proclaimed: 'Incorporating Henry Klein & Co. late of Wardour Street; Nicole Frères, late of Ely Place'. And, just to add some reflected respectability by way of age, a line was added which said 'Established 1815'.

Business thrived for the two Germans. They covered large areas of the country on bicycles collecting the coppers from their hired-out Polyphons. The persons who rented machines were allowed 20 per cent of the takings. One day, Curt Herzog was cycling through a wood near Salisbury Plain when he was set upon by a Victorian mugger. He fought off his would-be attacker, laying him out cold with a swipe round the head with his bag of pennies!

Little by little over a period of years they made new deals with public houses and, in certain cases, sold them instruments. The business became very profitable. Its secretary was an able accountant by the name of Sidney H. Dixon.

Prior to 1914, they met and were joined by a man named Louis Sterling of Clerkenwell Road. Louis (later Sir Louis) Sterling was to become a legend in his own lifetime. Born in a New York slum in 1877, he started as a newsboy, came to Britain in a cattle boat with just £6 in his pocket, once spent a night in London's Vine Street police station because he got drunk, and later headed up the giant gramophone company which bore his name. Sterling began his career in gramophones by joining His Master's Voice as an office boy, was closely involved in the Columbia organisation and became chairman of Electrical & Musical Industries until he resigned in 1939. He died in 1958. But as far as Herzog and Ficker were concerned, their meeting and subsequent friendship with Louis Sterling was to prove extremely felicitous.

171

Meanwhile, war had broken out. To begin with, Ficker and Herzog were not worried. Their business was well away from matters of a hostile nature. In any case, they were now well established in England, However, the Trading with the Enemy Act of 1914 and its Amendment (1916) were inescapable. German-owned companies were to be sequestered, their Teutonic operators to be interned as aliens for the duration. In due course, the long arm of the law stretched out, Ficker and Herzog were arrested and the NPSC sold under the Alien Properties Act. The two men were interned in, of all places, London's Alexandra Palace, which had been hastily converted as a wartime detention centre. They were imprisoned in the tower which later became the building from which the BBC transmitted all its television programmes until the 1950s. Ficker became elected spokesman for the Germans in his section. Herzog was later transferred to Holland on an exchange basis for British prisoners of war.

With the NPSC sold off, a new name came to the fore – Robert Willis. It was he who re-formed the business as the British Polyphon Company at the 2 and 3 Newman Street premises, with a branch at 27 Jamaica Street, Glasgow. His son, Gordon, later joined the management team.

Early in 1917, the BPC sold off its entire stock of automatic pianos, electric pianos, band organs, Polyphons, Symphonions and tunes for same to Keith Prowse & Co., the then makers of automatic pianos. Years after the war was over, Louis Sterling introduced Ficker and Herzog into radio and electrical wholesaling and their descendants run the business which resulted to this day.

Earlier I said that there was a certain common appearance among the German-made disc musical boxes. Some, like the largest Komet, were housed in massive, overpowering and architecturally ornate cases. Funnily enough, although the Swiss probably led the revolution in case design for table models, when BHA produced the Britannia, one case style at least was so closely influenced on the Leipzig form as to out-uglify the ugliest! A number of German makers adopted cabinet styles which were so similar as almost to suggest a common cabinet-maker – a postulation which we know to be unfounded. This is not without precedent: the London church and chamber barrel-organ industry of the 1790–1850 period also tended to follow very definite case designs.

Styles of case were very varied, and often makers advertised the same instrument in a choice of cases. Regina offered oak or mahogany cases, plain or carved. Symphonion offered, in addition to their richly turned and embellished mahogany cases, a table model of the $11\frac{3}{4}$ in. (30 cm) disc size in a most ornate case, apparently carved from solid wood. This was, in fact, very cleverly pressed out of sawdust and glue with a thin veneer of surfacing wood. How this was achieved is unknown, but the outside surface gives every indication of solidity and the pattern is deeply incised.

Another characteristic is that, generally speaking, all German-made machines (and, consequently, American) rotate their discs in a clockwise direction (with the exception of the smallest models in some ranges such as Polyphon), and all Swiss disc boxes played anti-clockwise. The Swiss makers included B. H. Abrahams (who made the Imperial and the Britannia), Mermod (who made the Stella, Mira and the Empress), Thorens (who made the Helvetia and the Edelweiss) and Billon (later Société Anonyme), who made the Gloria and the Polymnia. Mermod's larger machines, however, all moved clockwise.

With the cylinder musical box, we have seen how all manner of additions were incorporated to the basic instrument in an endeavour to enhance its sales potential and sound output. So it was with the disc musical box.

The fitting of a zither to the combs, comparatively easy to accomplish with the cylinder box, was harder to achieve with the disc machine where only limited space existed between the top of the comb and the underside of the disc. Small Symphonions were made with paper tube zithers of the same style as that fitted to the cylinder box, but acting on the underside of the comb. These were invented in 1896 by C. Landenberger. Monopol perfected an ingenious linkage of levers and felt-padded arms which slid up over the combs and which occupied very little of the slender space available. A similar system was used by Symphonion, Polyphon and Regina (Fig. 34). One 15½ in. Regina in a New York collection, however, has a paper-tube-type zither which acts on the underside of both combs.

Mention has already been made of the Concerto Automaton built both by Polyphon and Regina, which played a 32 in. diameter disc. This did not play on combs, but on piano strings, drums, triangle and cymbal. The Regina Concerto was a self-changer.

The majority of the disc musical-box makers produced models which, in addition to the musical comb(s), played tuned steel bells, tubular dulcimers or bar glockenspiels. Some models, usually the smaller styles, played the bell notes in unison with either the bass or the treble end of the comb. Others used special discs which were provided with a portion of the projections expressly for sounding the bells. In these instances, the bells were struck via a linkage which resembled one point of the starwheel, i.e. it did not have a rotating starwheel between disc projection and hammer. One example of this style is the 22 in. Polyphon which plays discs set up in virtually the identical manner to the 19⅝ in. model, with an outer addition to operate the bells. The same applies to the 14⅛ in. diameter Polyphon which plays discs which are the same as the 11 in. model with bell notes added.

Bells were usually hemispherical, occasionally elliptical in section. Tubular bells were mounted on a frame in silk suspensions, and the flat steel bar glockenspiel supported at the nodal points by screws.

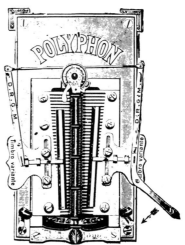

Prices for Nos. 45, 103, 47, 104, 118, 105, 159, I.
10/- 11 6 13 - 13 - 13 - 16/- 16/- 16/-

Figure 34 Polyphon advertisement for a zither attachment.

One of the largest disc-playing musical boxes made which played on tuned steel combs was the $33\frac{5}{8}$ in. Komet. This was driven by a motor about 15 inches wide with a spring 4 inches deep and of $\frac{1}{16}$ inch thick steel. The instrument had ten combs of broad steel and there were fourteen tuned bells played from the disc.

The connections between the musical box and the clock have already been mentioned. During the early part of the nineteenth century, clocks and mechanical music tended to go their separate ways, but by the 1890s the coupling of disc musical boxes and clocks was in vogue again. Polyphon, Symphonion and Regina made large instruments which incorporated clocks.

The actual timepieces were not of particularly good quality (usually mass-produced Lenzkirch clocks) and did not measure up to the standard of either the musical component or the casework. Polyphon and Symphonion made 'long-case' clocks which stood over nine feet high. These tended to resemble umbrella stands rather than long-case clocks, as only the top and bottom portions (the latter containing the musical works), were boxed in and the centre was simply a back panel with richly turned wood columns between. It is doubtful whether these were ever good timekeepers. The musicwork, as well as the clock, was weight-powered – it had no spring motor – by chains supporting brass-encased lead weights.

The musical works were usually 11 in. or $15\frac{1}{2}$ in. in the case of the Polyphon, or $11\frac{7}{8}$ in. or $14\frac{3}{4}$ in. in the case of the Symphonion. Whilst these were free-standing giants, both companies also made smaller variants for screwing on to the wall.

The $20\frac{3}{4}$ in. model of the Regina self-changer was also made with a clock pediment and arranged so that it would play a tune on the hour by command of the clock. Only one example of this particular model is known. The timepiece incorporates moonwork and it is probably custom-made. It is at present in the Rita Ford collection, New York.

An interesting diversion was the Regina Chime Clock. Not really a musical-box mechanism at all, this looked like a standard weight-powered hall clock. A set of fourteen tuned steel bells provided with tubular resonators was struck by hammers given sequence and motion from a special $12\frac{1}{8}$ in. diameter disc. The musicwork was powered by a clockwork spring motor. Some of the bells had two hammers to aid repetition of notes. Each steel disc played four tunes, the disc making one quarter of a revolution – to coincide with the quarter-hours – to play each tune.

The $24\frac{1}{2}$ in., 22 in. and $19\frac{5}{8}$ in. Polyphons were also made with clock pediments, the clock being an integral feature of the decorative top. Whilst the hall clocks were arranged so that the clock tripped the musical mechanism to play on the hour, these last-mentioned variants were completely separate from the musical works.

Disc machines were also made which had plinths for dancing dolls and simple automata inside. These were not of good quality, and are today very rare – partly, one must imagine, due to the temptation for children to remove the gaily coloured figures from their support wires.

Perhaps the kudos for the most diversified disc musical box which retained the comb as the principal sound-producer (many very large disc-operated piano-orchestrions were produced in the early years of the present century) should go to Zimmermann of Leipzig. Zimmermann acquired the ailing Adler musical-box factory and produced a 26 in. (66·5 cm) disc-playing model of the Adler/Fortuna which not only played twin 118-tooth musical combs, but also a five-clapper snare drum, a fourteen-note reed organ – and a triangle. Each of these accessories was provided with a lever to disengage it at will after the same manner in

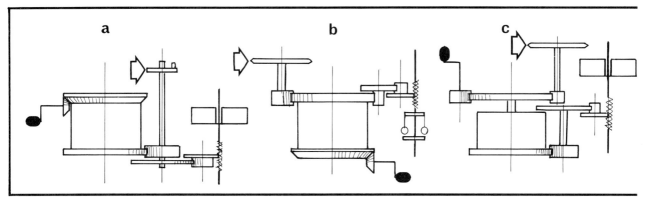

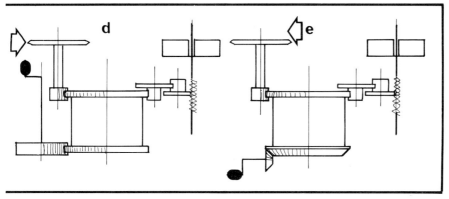

Figure 35   Power train for the disc-playing musical box. Five styles of train used in upright models and, with minor adjustments, table styles. In each case the open arrow indicates the point of disc drive and the black blob the winding handle.

which cylinder boxes were usually equipped. The organ was silenced by the simple expedient of opening a big valve in the air bellows.

During the summer of 1900, Jules Heinrich Zimmermann introduced into Britain his twin-disc Fortuna which played two of these 26 in. (66·5 cm) discs simultaneously complete with all the accessories. It stood 6 ft (1·82 m) high and was 5 ft (1·52 m) wide. Selling price was £90 and it is not known how many were sold – none is known to exist today.

Metal discs were originally made in zinc. Although zinc does not rust, the projections tended to break off easily. A large number of Polyphon and Regina discs up to $15\frac{1}{2}$ in. in diameter were made of zinc in the early days, but eventually every manufacturer made steel discs coated with a special lacquer to ward off rust.

The comb arrangements used on disc machines were again varied. Whilst some Symphonion models, including the $11\frac{7}{8}$ in. and up to the 25 in., had one comb at one side of the central spindle and a second comb the other side, models were also made of all but the $11\frac{7}{8}$ in. with two combs mounted side by side, thus playing discs which, although similar in size, were quite different in manufacture. Polyphons produced models with two combs of fine teeth, each starwheel plucking two teeth at once, one in the lower comb and one in the upper comb.

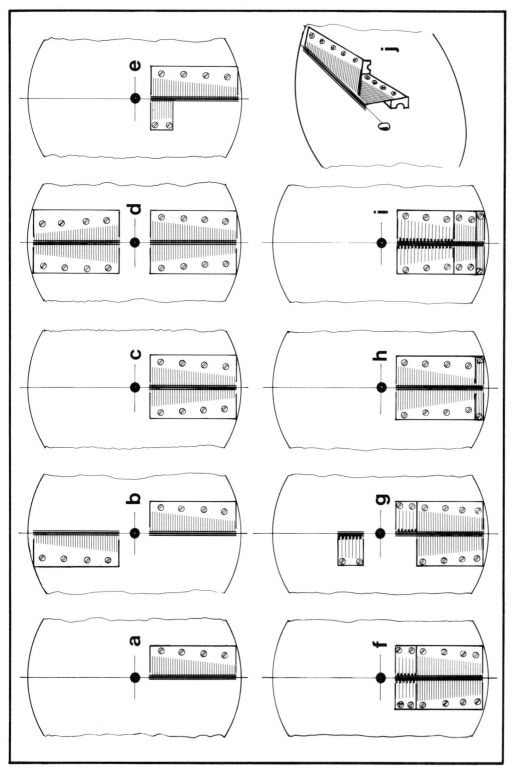

Figure 36 Different styles of comb arrangement used on disc-playing musical boxes. (a) single-comb, bass at centre; (b) *sublime harmonie* (do not confuse with some styles of Symphonion which have this apparent arrangement, but in fact comb one runs from lowest note centre up the scale outwards while comb two continues the scale from its outside end upwards to reach a treble position at the centre); (c) double comb, made with narrow teeth played in unison, and broad teeth played alternately; (d) four-comb *sublime harmonie*, each comb pair plucked in unison; (e) single comb with extra bass comb, bass teeth plucked in unison; (f) two main combs plucked in unison plus two bass combs plucked alternately; (g) same arrangement as (f) but bass combs situated either side of centre spindle; (h) two combs in unison plus bell combs plucked alternately; (i) two combs in unison plus two sets of percussion combs (bells, drums or glockenspiel bars) plucked alternately; (j) Stella arrangement with two combs mounted at right-angles plucked in unison.

176

They also made models with two combs of broad teeth where the starwheels plucked alternate combs. Sometimes, they used a single comb augmented with a short secondary comb at the base end. Comb arrangements are shown in Fig. 36.

The methods of driving discs differed too. Generally speaking, discs measuring up to about 12 in. in diameter were driven from a small central turntable. Larger discs were driven with a toothed wheel which engaged in perforations around the outer edge of the disc. As we have come to expect in the world of musical boxes, this is not a hard and fast rule and there are exceptions both sides of the arbitrary 12 in. The $9\frac{1}{8}$ in. diameter Britannia disc is driven peripherally whilst one model of the $14\frac{3}{4}$ in. Symphonion is driven from a central turntable through two drive pegs.

The discs themselves were ingenious. The music was initially transferred to a thick steel master plate in the form of holes. This plate was then fixed into a press and the master plate holes used as guides for the actual projection punches which set up the projections on the disc. The demand for discs necessitated the employment of mass-production techniques, and presses were made which could stamp ten discs at a time from the master; they were mounted in tiers one above the other. Disc stamping was traditionally carried out by women. After stamping, the number of the disc, corresponding to the tune it was set to play, was usually scratched on to the back and the disc sent to be printed. The title and number, together with trade marks, other designs or wording, were then printed on. Some discs also had coloured transfer designs or trade marks affixed at this point. Polyphon, for example, used a large gold and black trademark transfer on their earlier discs, and later switched to a small impression printed in black with the tune titles. After printing, the discs were painted with a lacquer to ward off rust, and were then lightly oiled and wrapped in greaseproof paper for distribution. For transit, they were packed in circular wooden caskets or containers which were not unlike a garden riddle in general appearance.

Titles were usually printed on the disc in three languages, English, French and German, but sometimes in only one of these languages. The range of tunes was very great and popular foreign airs were available; hence titles appeared in Russian, Greek, Spanish, Italian and so on.

The wording of the disc titles was not always correct and many discs show names with mis-spellings. Discs with entirely incorrect titles are not uncommon, a slip-up obviously having occurred in the printing room. Quite often, manufacturers attributed the wrong title or composer to a piece of music. A common error was to amalgamate two different tunes. Where two arias from an opera were run into one, it was understandable (an instance of this is the $19\frac{5}{8}$ in. Polyphon rendition of 'She is the Belle of New York' which also incorporates 'When We Are Married', both tunes being from the musical *The Belle of New York*). However, sometimes music from different operas, even by different composers, was linked into one piece for the disc. Many smaller disc machines performed drastically abbreviated tunes which were sometimes so severely chopped that it was difficult to recognise them.

At one time, certain sizes of Polyphon discs were printed with the title, number and trademark before being stamped out and, where stocks of a disc title were slow moving (perhaps through poor sales or over-ordering from the print room), the blanks were turned over and given another title. Thus one sometimes comes across these palimpsest Polyphon 11-inch discs which have a different title on each side. A classic example is a disc which was to have been 'Nearer My God to Thee', turned over and issued as 'Beer, Glorious Beer'. Discs are also sometimes found bearing printed advertising slogans. The circumstances surrounding these, again 11-inch Polyphon, are unknown. And in the collection of Bob Glasgow, White Plains, is a zinc Regina disc, 15½ in., printed (as usual) on both sides, yet never punched.* True silent music!

The storage of discs by the customer was also a point considered by many makers. The larger Polyphons, Symphonions, Reginas and Fortunas had disc storage compartments beneath them. Mermod's Stella had a shallow drawer beneath the table instruments, large enough to hold a surprising number of their smooth, projectionless discs. Monopol made boxes to match their smaller instruments in which discs could be kept.

Lochmann, in 1892, patented special albums in which Symphonion discs could be kept. Each disc was secured to its page with metal clips and the volume, with its leatherette binding, could take its place on the bookshelf. These were made for the $11\frac{7}{8}$ in. disc size and smaller, and each held twelve discs. These albums are illustrated in Fig. 37.

Polyphon also went in for separate storage cabinets. These were produced either as small cupboards to match the instrument, or as a base upon which to stand the machine. They also made a range of disc storage racks, some of ornate wrought iron, others of wood and wire, into which the discs might be slipped. These resembled the now familiar gramophone record stands but were, of course, somewhat larger, and due to their cumbersomeness few have survived.

* It is a feature of many Regina discs that they bear the title and decoration on both sides.

Figure 37 Albums for storing Symphonion discs were available for several of the smaller disc sizes.

178

Bad storage of discs led to bent or broken projections and, whilst this was probably good for business at the time, it undoubtedly led to many frustrated owners parting with their machines because the discs were spoiled, jammed on the machine or just would not play.

I once bought a fine disc musical box with a large stock of discs. I had been told that the instrument would not work properly. The many discs had been jammed into a small cupboard and each time any was taken out or pushed in projections were damaged or destroyed. Removal of all the discs from their closet revealed a pile of small, rusted metal curls on the floor.

The smaller disc machines were set in motion by a knob or lever connected to a trail on one of the wheels in the gear train. After the disc had made one revolution, this trail dropped into a hole in the appropriate wheel. As it did so, a sprag on the endless fan would strike the trail and bring the mechanism to a standstill. The action of setting the box in motion lifted the trail clear of the stop hole, thereby freeing the fan on the endless screw.

Larger machines could be either coin-operated or manually controlled. The coin variants were used in public places. A penny dropped down a chute into a tray or pan fixed to a pivoted arm. The arm was counterbalanced and carried on it a form of cam-follower which travelled round the edge of the great wheel of the spring cage as it rotated. When the coin entered the pan, the coin tray arm was depressed sufficiently to allow the projecting sprag to fall free of the endless screw sprag, so setting the works into motion. Towards the end of the tune, a cam on the great wheel would depress the coin tray against a stop, tipping out the coin. The counterweight on the arm then lifted the arm until it contacted the endless sprag and brought the machine to rest again.

The public-house Polyphons were equipped with a special lever which could be set by the landlord so that the instrument would play twice for one penny. This was intended, no doubt, to drum up business on slack days. Similar devices are made today for juke boxes which, if they are not played for fifteen minutes, either play a tune for free or issue a spoken reminder from a special record. This 'charity lever' moved a second gear-wheel into place and it was important that this lever only be touched when the instrument was at rest, otherwise the start and stop position of the discs was thrown out of register.

For domestic use, it was hardly right to have a coin-operated machine, although I do have one from a Norfolk public house in my own home, into which visitors are happy to empty their small change in return for a tune. However, the manufacturers produced models for stately homes which could be worked by the turn of a small key at the side. This operated the same type of lever as the penny did in the coin-operated models.

The difference in tone between various machines is quite marked. Polyphons produce a pleasing tone, particularly the 24½-inch model, which has an almost bell-like sound. Although the *modus operandi* of all disc machines tended to be the same and although the plucking of a tooth featured in them all, the shape of the teeth, the arrangement of the sound-boards in the case, and the general design of the box all influenced to a greater or lesser extent the type of noise given out. The depth of tone and sonority of the Regina larger musical boxes is totally different from others in the field. All the smaller boxes tended to sound alike, for there was not much that could be done to enhance the sound of a small instrument with but a few teeth. An exception was the Britannia which had a cabinet with reasonable acoustic properties that produced a crispness of sound quite different from that of other boxes. Indeed, the larger Britannias had a piano sounding-board back which was separated from the back of the case by a space of several inches. Two long thin doors in the sides of the case could be opened to allow the full tone to be produced.

An interesting point concerns the Stella. As related earlier, the Stella was usually made with a thin drawer under the base in which discs could be stored. This drawer, if filled with discs, acts as an effective sound damper, and emptying the drawer, or taking it out altogether during playing, yields a marked difference in sound output. In later models, the drawer had no bottom panel, just battens of wood to support the discs.

A box with a really delightful tone and one which is far better than its Polyphon counterpart, is the $19\frac{1}{8}$ in. Symphonion. This has a tone of great purity and is as good as, if not better than, the 25 in. Symphonion and the $24\frac{1}{2}$ in. Polyphon on this standpoint.

The Orphenion, made only in limited numbers, has a characteristic tone which is very mellow and, certainly on the 11-inch model, surprisingly deep.

Any account purporting to be a résumé of the history of the disc musical box cannot be considered complete without reference to a handful of unusual variants which appeared. These were instruments which were not disc machines although, by the same dictum, they were not like any other form of musical box. They employed the basic principles of the disc machine and one at least even had starwheels and projections on a rotating programme to turn them, but there the similarity disappears.

The first of these, and quite the best known, was a product of the F. G. Otto Company of New Jersey in America. The Otto brothers were friends of Gustave Brachhausen of Regina; in fact they lived just across the road from him. We may conjecture that they were interested in making a musical box, seeing the obvious success which their illustrious neighbour was making in the business. Brachhausen and the Otto brothers no doubt discussed this; and Brachhausen, friend and neighbour though he was, was nevertheless justifiably unwilling to foster competition. The Ottos then designed an instrument and formed a company to produce it. The box was called the Capital and, for reasons that will become obvious, has been dubbed the Capital 'Cuff Box'. How much of this was Brachhausen's idea and how much the Ottos' is uncertain, but sufficient to say that it was cleverly designed so as in no way to infringe either Brachhausen's jealously guarded patents or Regina's market.

The box did not play discs. It played tapered cylinders of thin metal into which were stamped disc-type projections. The cylinder was threaded on to a mandrel on the instrument and, as it turned, it operated starwheels in exactly the same way as, say, a Polyphon. This method had been patented in May 1894 by E. Paillard, who was later to become the sales agent for the machine. Strong similarities between parts of this mechanism (particularly the combs) and the Regina led to a court action when Paillard, as sales agent, was sued by Regina for patent infringement.*

Several sizes of this instrument were produced and although the Capital sold well in America for a short while it is today very uncommon, no doubt due to the widespread habit of permanently discarding obsolete family acquisitions (as compared with the 'tuck it in the attic' nature). The Capital 'Cuff Box' was never sold in England and thus remained virtually unknown until within the past few years when several collectors imported specimens from the United States, where they are scarce to say the least.

---

* Even so, the combs of the $15\frac{1}{2}$ in. Regina and the starwheels appear interchangeable with Otto products of the same size even down to the positions of screw holes. Were these parts made by Regina and sold to Otto – or was it a 'back door' operation?

The other unusual variants were those which we might collectively term the 'lever-pluckers'. In these, the music was represented by an endless band or a concertina-like folded book of perforated card similar to that used in fair organs. The mechanism comprised a set of sliding levers or fingers which engaged in the musical note slots of the card. The lever would then be carried forward a short distance, bringing one part of the lever over the end of the comb tooth. At the limit of its sliding travel, the lever would be depressed by the music, plucking the tooth and flying back to the rest position again.

These lever-pluckers were an interesting breed and, indeed, had certain great advantages over both the cylinder and the disc musical box. They could, for example, perform pieces of music of variable and almost limitless length. Since the music was a parallel strip rather than a circular disc, the speed of plucking the notes at either end of the comb was constant. This considerably eased the design of dampers since the damping force and speed of operation was equal from one end to the other. It will be appreciated that with a disc machine the outside of the disc is moving at a greater speed in inches per second than the centre and thus the treble starwheels are turned more briskly. The speed of music was usually about four feet per minute (1·22 m per minute).

The lever-pluckers did, however, have two major drawbacks. First of all, there was a tendency towards a mechanical clicking as the levers sprang back after the note sounded. Secondly, the card music was not durable enough to counter the resistance of dragging the metal levers through the motion with each note.

Many patents were taken out for this system both in America and Germany and the name of F. E. P. Ehrlich (builder of the Monopol disc machine and the Ariston organette) appears frequently in the lists of patentees. Other designers include Keile; Johann Schünemann of Berlin; Carl Albert Roepke, who came from Berlin to Manchester, and manufactured the unusual and interesting book-playing musical box bearing his name; and J. L. Muller. The

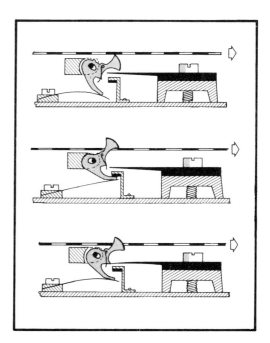

Figure 38 Adolf Richter's patent for the lever-plucking mechanism of the Libellion.

181

only inventor to persevere in this field seems to have been Freidrich Adolf Richter of Rudolstadt, Germany, who took out a number of patents between 1885 and 1900 and, in the first years of this century, produced a remarkably fine-looking instrument called the Libellion (see Fig. 38 and Plate 159).

The other examples of this type of instrument include the Arno, made in America to patents by Arno and A. E. Paillard, and the Unikon, produced in Germany. Both these were small with combs of about forty teeth and, again, the mechanism tended to outlive the music material.

The lever-pluckers were an interesting concept, spoiled by lack of suitable material from which to make the music and stifled by coming on the market too late in the musical-box era. Richter's Libellion was being offered for sale at the same time as the first phonographs were entering the market. Examples of this breed are very rare today.

There was, however, an eminently successful variant of the lever-plucking concept. Although it was used in conjunction with a zinc disc as compared with a punched book, it marked such a novel departure from the standard type of disc musical box to warrant special mention. Patented by Louis Hössly of Ste-Croix and assigned to the manufacturers, Hermann Thorens, the system looked very similar to a normal disc-playing musical mechanism with two combs and a central gantry of comb-pluckers. However, in place of plucking starwheels, Hössly used short double-ended levers which when engaged by a plain slot in the disc, would pluck both combs. But there was another feature. The levers were contained in a stepped slot in the gantry so that they lay at a tangent to the plane of the disc when at rest. Besides rocking in the conventional manner under the influence of the projectionless disc, each lever had to be aligned with the comb at the time of each pluck, being allowed to swing tangentially away from the comb teeth tips when out of play. This tangential motion was effected by the shape of the disc slots which had, in appearence, one side of the trailing end truncated. In action, the lever, double-ended and spring-loaded, engaged the disc slot, moved over into comb-tip alignment, plucked the tooth (or, in the case of twin-comb boxes, teeth) and then the lever was depressed and allowed to swing sideways from the tooth tip. Patented in the United States (number 588433 of 17 August, 1897), Thorens used this style on the Helvetia and the Edelweiss. There was one other novel feature. While playing, it was possible to silence the mechanism by moving a lever which held down all the levers, so allowing the disc to turn in silence. See *The Music Box*, vol. 9, page 114 *et seq*.

The disc musical box developed along some particularly interesting lines, certainly as regards what we generally call the table model, which plays its disc horizontally.

DEVELOPMENT OF THE INSTRUMENT

The first production Symphonion featured a diagonal bedplate in a small square case. This was soon altered to a rectangular bedplate arranged centrally across the broadest width of a rectangular case. This allowed small soundboards to be screwed either side of the bedplate. The first Polyphon – the smallest – had a square case with a full-sized, square bedplate which deflected the sound through the bottom of the box.

Just as cylinder boxes very rapidly acquired feet to allow the sound to pass via the case bottom to the open air, disc machines also acquired feet of one form or another – some being attractively turned, others being rudimentary extensions to the case sides.

In all instances, the clockwork motor was underneath the bedplate. When the first upright machine was made with the clockwork placed below the musicwork bedplate rather than interposed between it and the case base (or back in this instance), the improvement in tone was marked and it did not take manufacturers long to appreciate the tonal advantages to be gained from leaving clear space between bedplate and case.

Probably the first to put theory into practice was Bruno Ruckert with the Orphenion, wherein, although the motor remained below the bedplate, the bedplate was now extended to bring motor and governor to one side of the case. This same style of extended bedplate was to become a feature of the Swiss Stella and Mira as well as the larger Regina and Polyphon machines.

While some manufacturers were experimenting with soundposts to provide a direct acoustic connection between bedplate and case, the Adler (significantly built in Bruno Ruckert's old factory after his business had closed) was the first to develop the proper acoustic case wherein a deep, well finished box was equipped with a musical movement screwed firmly to a soundboard bottom, and the spring driving motor was separated in a compartment to one side, usually the right. What had been created was virtually a horizontal upright musical box and, if you stand such an instrument on its side, with the motor compartment downwards, you will see that the machine is nothing more than a horizontal arrangement of a vertical model. This is very different from the earlier table models where you had a horizontal juxtaposition of components which was quite different to that used in the vertical machines.

The increase in volume which this arrangement produced led other makers to adopt the acoustic cabinet and after the Adler (and with it Zimmermann's other box, the Fortuna) came the superb tone of the Lochmann Original and the larger sizes of Kalliope.

The acoustic cabinet also featured in Regina, with the $15\frac{1}{2}$ in. short-bedplate model being best known to collectors today. Even so, it would seem that Symphonion continued to rely on the silvery tones of their normally arranged table models, enhanced by the *sublime harmonie* arrangement of their combs. Similarly, Polyphon never went in for acoustic design, preserving in production the mid-1890s construction and design styles.

Polyphon among others always advised users of upright models to stand them against a wall and tip them slightly so that the back was pressed against the wall and the weight was taken on the front case feet. A wooden cross member was provided to this end near the top of the case back. This way, the wall could be used to reflect the sound and improve the volume and frequency response.

As the disc musical-box era drew towards its close, there was one strange hark-back to the very earliest days of the instrument. Miguel Boom's idea of a pin-it-youself disc musical box – patented in 1882 – was revamped by a German called H. Graf. He designed an instrument manufactured in Berlin by Liebermann and called Graf's Musik-Baukasten. Patented in 1910 and the subject of British Patent No. 11617 of 1911, Graf's instrument was very similar to a normal disc box as regards the disposition of its component parts. No motor was provided, the disc being turned by a crank handle in the case side. This drove a central turntable on which was placed a thick steel plate provided with a large number of holes into which the user could insert separate steel pegs. These were held in place by a second, unperforated cover plate of metal placed on top.

Where Graf did score, though, unlike Boom, was in providing printed charts showing where to put the pegs in order to produce certain tunes. Even so, Graf's idea was not greeted

183

with open arms by a public which, by that time, was becoming less and less enchanted with musical boxes of any kind, let alone those which produced music via labour-intensive means. Only one complete Musik-Baukasten has so far been located; it was the subject of a detailed article in *The Music Box*, volume 8, pp. 146–50, 1977.

To conclude this chapter on the development of the disc musical box, there are three general classifications which we ought to consider. These concern instruments which were made to play two or more discs at once; instruments which automatically changed their own discs; and instruments which could also play gramophone records. Chronologically, I have set out the order in which they appeared.

MULTIPLE-DISC MUSICAL BOXES

The most renowned multi-disc machine is without question the Symphonion Eroica which played no fewer than three discs at once. This instrument was patented by Oskar Paul Lochmann and his British Patent is number 18356 dated 30 September 1893. It was introduced to the British market by London agent Henry Klein at Christmas, 1895. This spectacular upright musical box with its three hundred comb teeth arranged in six combs, two per disc, was expensive at 65 guineas (£68.25). Three 14 in. (35·5 cm) discs were used and these could either be three copies of the same disc or specially made sets of three marked A, B and C. Large numbers were made and the type is not uncommon throughout Europe. American-made models survive but are not so prolific.

In America, the Symphonion Manufacturing Company also produced a triple-disc machine, only this played its three discs side by side in a piano-style cabinet. This used three $17\frac{5}{8}$ in. (44·8 cm) in diameter and again discs were produced in sets of three. These are unknown in Europe and very rare in America.

As well as triples, Symphonion in both Leipzig and Asbury Park made twin-disc models. The Leipzig product was a table machine which used $11\frac{7}{8}$ in. (30 cm) discs mounted horizontally side by side. This was also made in America for a time, but the philosophy which produced Imperial's vertical side-by-side triple was used to create a similar-styled twin-disc version which also used $17\frac{5}{8}$ in. (44·8 cm) discs. Due to the short-lived production of the Imperial Symphonion, these models are very rare in America and are unknown in Europe. The Leipzig-style table twin survives in small numbers in Europe while the Asbury Park model of the same style survives in very small quantities in America.

Polyphon made a twin vertical side-by-side version of the $24\frac{1}{2}$ in. (62·5 cm) but none is known to survive. The same can be said of the Fortuna Orchestrion, a twin version of the 26 in. (66·5 cm) model. This was produced under both Adler and Fortuna names. This appeared in London in 1900, stood six feet high, five feet wide and cost a staggering £90 – 32 per cent higher than the three-disc Eroica. Few can have been sold at that price.

Lochmann's 'Original' was produced as a double which played two $24\frac{3}{8}$ in. (62 cm) discs. This was in 1903. However, of all the multiples made, one was radically different from all others. This was the Monopol Gloria; only one example of it is known and this is in the collection of J. B. Nethercutt. The instrument plays two $26\frac{3}{8}$ in. (70 cm) discs vertically, one above the other, from a common drive-wheel with contrate teeth so that the discs rotate in opposite directions.

A brand new twin-disc machine is Brian Etches's Jubilee which plays two $19\frac{5}{8}$ in. Polyphon-type discs at once. New also is Keith Harding's Gemini twin-disc Polyphon.

SELF-CHANGERS

The first patent for a musical box which changed its own discs came relatively early on in the history of the disc machine. British Patent number 17113 of 24 September 1892 was taken out by E. and C. Stransky for a coin-operated disc musical box which changed its tunes. Nothing then happened until 1896 when E. P. Riessner of Polyphon received British Patent number 11469 dated 26 May 1896 for a tune-changing device for a coin-operated disc musical box.

Next came E. Breslauer with British Patent number 9308 dated 22 April 1898 for a similar device upon which he improved with another patent granted on 4 October 1898 – number 20913. Gustave A. Brachhausen was granted British Patent number 5569 dated 14 March 1899 for a self-changer which was obviously the Polyphon. British Patent number 9688 of 8 May 1899 was granted to the agent of Hermann Thorens for a disc changer, and number 16883 was granted to W. A. Drysdale for a changer and tune counter on 19 August 1899.

E. P. Riessner's British Patent number 23200 of 21 November 1899 was unusual in that it covered a changeable-disc mechanism whose discs had radial slots from centre to periphery so that the disc could be taken off and put on without moving the pressure bar. British Patent number 24877 of 14 December 1899 went to Fabrik Lochmann'scher Musikwerke for a self-changing Symphonion. On 29 May 1900 G. Varrelman was awarded Patent number 9913 for a self-changer as was Gustave Brachhausen for an improved system on 20 September 1900 with British Patent number 16794. Barnett Henry Abrahams of Ste-Croix received a similar patent (number 21215) on 23 November 1900 and the following year, on 12 July, Fabrik Lochmann'scher Musikwerke was granted British Patent number 14249 for an improved self-changing Symphonion. The company received another patent, number 2583 dated 31 January 1902, for a horizontal self-changer.

A number of these patented inventions seem never to have seen the light of day. For example, no self-changing Britannia is known, nor is there a self-changing Edelweiss – at least, nobody has found one so far. Models which do survive, however, include Regina (large numbers), Polyphon (scarce), and Symphonion (a mere four or five). Bill Edgerton of Darien, Connecticut, unearthed an extraordinary prototype auto-change table Symphonion with a mechanism so remarkably complex that its failure to go into production (or even be completed as a one-off) is not surprising. Called Drysdale's Automatic Symphonion, it bears a patent number 670771 and the year suffix 98 which suggests a German patent of 1898. Perhaps somebody may complete this masterpiece. It does, though, conform to British Patent number 16883 of 1899, referred to above.*

Regina changers were styled Corona, the smallest being the $15\frac{1}{2}$ in. (39·8 cm) Regina Corona. Next was the $20\frac{3}{4}$ in. (52·4 cm) Sublima Corona and then the 27 in. (68·6 cm) Orchestral Corona. The 32 in. (81·3 cm) piano orchestrion was also a self-changer using the same disc-change system.

Polyphon changers began with several models of the $15\frac{1}{2}$ in. (39·8 cm) which are today very rare, the $19\frac{5}{8}$ in. (50 cm) model which is rare; the $22\frac{1}{2}$ in. (56 cm) model, several of which are known; the $24\frac{1}{2}$ in. (62·5 cm) model, several of which are known.

Symphonion listed two different types of disc changing 14 in. (35·5 cm) instrument. Both were horizontal machines. The first style played through twenty-five discs, discharging each

---

* See *The Music Box*, vol. 9, pp. 66-8.

one after playing, allowing them to pass through a slot in the back of the case on to the table (or floor) behind. The second operated along more conventional principles although this, too, was a table machine. This stored eight discs in a horizontal rack. The lid of this model had a clear glass panel in it so that the mechanism could be watched. None of either model is known to survive. Several styles of the 21¼ in. (54 cm) upright self-changer were made, each containing basically the same changing mechanism, similar to that used by Regina and Polyphon. Only two of these are known to survive.

PHONOPECTINES

Disc-playing musical boxes incorporating a means of adjusting the mechanism so that gramophone or phonograph recordings could be played I have styled 'phonopectines'.* The best known of the breed and the one which survives in largest quantities is the Reginaphone. Regina musical boxes which could be fitted with attachments for playing phonograph discs comprised the 12¼ in. (31·2 cm), which came as either a table or a console model with the extra items totalling $25; the 15½ in. (39·8 cm) available in several styles of table model and consoles; 20¾ in. (52·4 cm) table models in different style cases; the 27 in. (68·6 cm), one style in massive console-type cabinet, of which, according to Bowers,† only ten were made. Maybe the smallest phonopectine ever made was the experimental 11 in. Reginaphone. A prototype example survives in a United States collection in the hands of a one-time employee. The record turntable is 7 in. in diameter.

The Swiss-made Mira was also produced as a phonopectine and, so it seems, sold well in America although none appears to survive. Lochmann made provision for optional attachments to his 'Original Concerto Piano' disc musical box.

Two models of the Polyphon were also so provided. In Germany these were known as Polygraphons but in English-speaking areas they were named Gramo-Polyphon. Both 15½ in. (39·8 cm) and 24½ in. (62·5 cm) models were available but none is known today (Fig. 39).

The principle of operation varied. Some of these were belt-and-pulley-driven turntables which were carried on fixed pivots fitted to the bedplate, others used spigoted turntables which engaged with a dogged spindle which formed an extension to a suitable wheel arbor in the gear train. At all times, though, the spindle for playing the record on was not the same as that used for the comb-playing disc for the simple reason that the latter was too large in diameter and rotated at the wrong speed. A tone-arm and diaphragm sound-box was provided which engaged with a suitable opening in the case. With the early, smaller instruments, the entire sound-producing part was very much an add-on affair, tone-arm, sound-box and large wood or metal horn being carried on a special bar which had to be clamped to the sides of the musical-box case. The Reginaphone used the space under the musicwork bedplate as an acoustic box or amplifier which served equally well for gramophone record and musical-box disc and, certainly as a musical box, these sounded extremely good.

---

* Should anyone question the etymology of a word that is half Greek (*phonos* = sound) and half Latin (*pectin* = comb), then he should consider the word 'television'!

† *Encyclopedia of Automatic Musical Instruments*, p. 202.

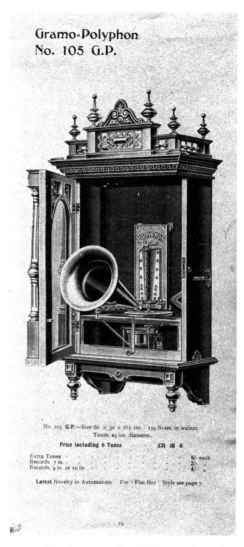

Figure 39 Two models of the Polyphon phonopectine.

Nevertheless, an instrument modified to serve two fundamentally different functions can seldom be expected to perform either function perfectly. At best the phonopectine must have made either a poor gramophone or a poor musical box. Maybe Reginaphones came closest to a common perfection, but the need to proceed with the perfection of the mechanism died almost immediately with the era of the disc musical box.

CHAPTER 7

Disc Musical-Box Classification and Makes

A great number of different disc boxes were produced between 1885 and 1910. Many consider the genus 'disc box' as embracing only the products of Symphonion, Polyphon and Regina and presume to give the impression that all other brands were inferior. Even some of the leading auction rooms have been known to describe a disc musical box as 'a Polyphon by Britannia', a didactic statement of alarming ignorance if ever there was one!

I cannot claim to have collated the entire product of the disc musical-box industry. I have, though, included 73 names, covering 51 identifiable types of box, in the list which follows and for each of these I have itemised the disc diameters which have so far been determined. To complicate matters, however, there are several instances at least of stencil-branding, that is the making by one manufacturer of an instrument expressly for another outlet and so having a different name. The style may be identical to that of the original, or may have received cosmetic treatment at source to customise it.

In cataloguing and classifying disc musical boxes, stylistic and design features have to be taken into consideration. The direction of rotation of the disc (usually anti-clockwise on Swiss machines and some small-sized German ones) is an important consideration, as is the diameter of the disc and the method of driving it. This last may be achieved centrally from a small turntable with offset drive pegs, peripherally by means of a toothed wheel forming part of the motor mechanism which engages in holes or indentations arranged around the edge of the disc, or from the edgewise engagement of the disc with a pinion having the same directional axis as the centre spindle. In the last-mentioned case, the edge of the disc is serrated and meshes with the pinion as a wheel and is termed 'pinion-drive'. This is a characteristic of some very small machines and in particular the small Swiss-made manivelle styles. As for the diameter of discs which a musical box plays, this is sometimes an arbitrary measurement thanks to the long-standing rounding-off of both metric and Imperial units of measurement.

The disc itself can be of one of two basic types – with projections or without. If with projections, there are many different forms which these can take and some of these were discussed in the previous chapter.

A basic classification is the method of plucking the steel comb – by rotating starwheel as in, say, the Polyphon, or by sliding lever as in the case of the Libellion (not strictly a disc musical box but employing common technology). The starwheel classification can be further divided into those systems where the starwheel rotates on a fixed axis and is operated by a disc projection and those where the starwheel is encouraged to rotate on a free, sprung axis and is operated by a slot in the disc as distinct from a projection, such as is used in the Stella.

Dampers are another identification point. There are so many systems ranging from felt to slender wires pressed on to the vibrating tooth tip that these, too, become vital points of identification. These, also, are discussed in the preceding chapter.

Zither attachments, where fitted, usually take one of three forms. First there is the simple, small zither used on some Symphonions, where the movement of a lever presses a narrow U-sectioned strip of metal containing a roll of thin tissue paper to the under surface of the comb teeth. Then there is the system used by Polyphon and Kalliope (among others) which slid out along the comb tooth's upper surface a felt-covered metal bar. When out of play, this was drawn back along the comb to lie just short of the root of each tooth. Used on parallel combs, this type of zither was controlled from one lever connected to both comb zithers via a pantograph linkage (Fig. 34). The third system was a version of this, but operated on the underneath of the comb, and was used by Regina.

After the diameter of the discs and their direction of rotation, the second main characteristic of the disc musical box is the arrangement of the combs. If we tabulate the fundamental types, we find there are seven main styles, portrayed in Figure 36, each of which may be subject to changes pertinent to one make or size of box. These are:

1 Single comb (i.e. arranged as a radius to the disc).
2 Single comb plus harmonic bass (i.e. a short extra bass comb).
3 Twin comb (i.e. mounted either side of one set of starwheels).
4 Twin comb sublime harmonie (i.e. one comb to each of two sets of starwheels arranged to form a diameter to the disc with the disc pivot or spindle in the centre).
5 Twin comb sublime harmonie plus harmonic bass (see 1 and 4 above).
6 Four comb sublime harmonie (i.e. style 3 set out as style 4).
7 Split comb (i.e. two combs with their own starwheels arranged either side of the central spindle as in 4 but tuned chromatically with bass notes at one end of the diameter, treble at the other).

Any of the above styles may include provision for strikers for bells, dulcimers, glockenspiels, drums or cymbal, or keys for reed organ pallets.

A word on bell tones. These were produced in three ways: conventional, musical-box-type hemispherical bells; flat steel bars like a xylophone and referred to, mistakenly, as dulcimers; and tubular glockenspiels, which were lengths of metal tube tuned by cutting to a predetermined pitch length.

By far the greatest majority of disc musical boxes – probably 99·99 per cent, played one tune per complete revolution of the disc. Many of the larger-size machines would set the tune on half of the revolution and then immediately repeat it to complete the disc, so playing the tune twice per turn. Occasionally, the second half would include a variation or perhaps a shake or appogiatura to bring the music to a close. On some discs, it seems almost as if the music arranger miscalculated in his work and ended up with his melody almost finished, and a good measure of disc left to fill. I have several discs in my own collection where the tune is intentionally slowed right down or spread out to fill.

Then there were just three boxes which played two tunes per disc, each on one complete revolution, by the simple expedient of shifting the disc. Although a convenient method of enlarging the repertoire without doubling the number of discs, this meant that the starwheels had to be narrow enough (or the concentric rings of projections widely enough spaced) to allow one set of projections to pass between each pair of starwheels in the same manner as the pins for five tunes must clear the teeth tips on a six-tune musical box of the cylinder type. This had the same effect as a coarse comb in that it reduced the number of playing notes possible. However, of the three types of box made with this feature, the Tannhauser, Sirion and New Century, only the last two seem to have survived in numbers.

Such mechanical wonders as Ehrlich's helicoidal or spiral 'discs' posed immense production problems and cannot have been produced in numbers. None is know to survive and certainly the demand for long-playing musical movements was better answered by the book-playing movements such as Libellion and Roepke. As for the complex and unique programmable self-changing Symphonion conceived by Philadelphian William Atlee Drysdale (see p. 185) this could never have been considered as a serious production machine.

Although Polyphon, Regina and Symphonion remain undoubtedly the best known and the most prolific makes of disc boxes, let it not be thought that the products of lesser manufacturers were automatically inferior. I can name a dozen makes which, in my opinion, produce a sound more charming than that of the $19\frac{5}{8}$ in. Polyphon and can suggest several which obviously attached more than average importance to the accuracy and arrangement of their music.

On the larger-size Polyphon musical boxes ($19\frac{5}{8}$ in. and upwards), hymns and sacred songs are invariably treated to two verses and frequently the second half of the disc is a projection-for-projection repeat of the first half. Occasionally it differs only in minor details such as closing cadenzas, harmony or a treble embellishment. A variation is the $19\frac{5}{8}$ in. disc of 'The Golden City' (number 5556) which states the air in less than one-third of the disc and then produces two further verses in variation form. How very much more satisfactory is the performance of this tune on the smaller $15\frac{1}{2}$ in. disc. An unusual disc, and one which I personally find extremely beautiful, is 'Little Slumber Song' on $24\frac{1}{2}$ in. whereon the entire melody is expressed in the treble and only towards the conclusion of the music does the arrangement descend into the bass.

Popular musical shows were the mainstay of the disc musical box and so one finds large numbers of once-favourite songs from shows such as *The Belle of New York*, *The Three Little Maids*, *The Bohemian Girl*, *The Geisha* and many others. Advancing technology also touched the disc repertoire and disc number 58558 on Polyphon was 'Oh! Flo!', described as a 'Motor Car Song'.

Polyphon's disc numbering system was interesting. All 11 in. diameter discs were four-figure groupings in the 2000 from 2001 to 2999 and then followed forty discs numbered 20001 upwards. These were all interchangeable with the 11 in. Regina. Discs of $14\frac{1}{8}$ in. diameter bore the same numbers as the 11 in. but with the prefix '1', so Suppé's march 'Boccaccio' is 2031 on the smaller and 12031 on the larger.

By far the largest series of Polyphon and Regina discs were those of $15\frac{1}{2}$ in. diameter. All were interchangeable. The first series of discs began with number 1001 and extended to 1999. Of these, all discs up to and including 1160 were titled identically with Regina, two exceptions being 1026 'God Save the Queen', which is known in America as 'My Country 'tis of Thee', and 1040 'Les Cloches de Corneville' which was translated for Regina discs as 'The

190

Chimes of Normandy'. From this point onwards, initially we find a few Polyphon and Regina discs bearing the same name (or the American name), but soon the Regina list hives off completely to conclude at around 11361. Meanwhile, Polyphon's $15\frac{1}{2}$ in. discs entered their second series at number 10001 and the last number found is 10602.

For the $19\frac{5}{8}$ in. Polyphon discs, the first series began at 5001 and went to 5999. The second series began at 50000 and ran to 50999. For 22 in. discs, the first digit was replaced by a 9 so that 5032 'The Mikado Waltzes' became 9032. For $24\frac{1}{2}$ in. discs, the digit 5 was replaced by a 4 so the same piece by Sullivan became 4032. *

Symphonion discs came in a very wide range of sizes and styles. The $5\frac{3}{4}$ in. size were all in the 5000 series; the $7\frac{11}{16}$ in. diameter discs were all in the 7000 series. The three popular sizes, $8\frac{1}{4}$ in., $9\frac{1}{2}$ in. and $10\frac{5}{8}$ in. all bear a 'family' numbering system. The smallest starts at number 1 and extends to 658. The middle size becomes 1001 to 1658 and the largest begins with 2001 and runs to 2658. The popular $11\frac{3}{4}$ in. size are all in the 3000 series extending to 3827. The $13\frac{5}{8}$ in. discs are in the 6000 series to 6747. For the Eroica style, discs were all in the 8000 series to 8163. For $19\frac{1}{8}$ in., the discs were numbered in the 9000 series up to 9090. It seems that comparatively few discs were produced for this, one of the best toned of all Symphonions.

Almost all German-made discs were titled in English, German and French and sometimes Russian (see p. 177). The translations were not always accurate nor the spelling ideal. Nicolai's popular overture becomes on Polyphon 'The Jolly Wives of Windsor'.

Another weakness in disc titling concerned composers and a classic example is Thomas Arne's 'Rule Britannia!', which Polyphon awards to L. Zampa, Symphonion to Handel and Monopol to Leghorn. Mermod credited the composer of its Stella disc correctly, but called the tune 'Rule Britanna!'

The method of operating the mechanism was normally by small projections thrown up on the back of the disc and these projections were the subject of much litigation initially (see previous chapter). They varied in complexity from the double-stamped projection of the early Symphonion to the simple scoop-shaped indentation of the Orphenion but in all cases their form and durability was of prime importance. Sadly some manufacturers either placed but scant value on durability or were forced through outside factors to select material which was unsuitable for the purpose. Many early discs were made, for example, of soft zinc and these even include some of those made for Regina in America. Apart from their poor resistance to accidental removal during storage, the zinc disc projections easily snapped off or wore badly and this was probably not more so than with the sweet, mellow-toned Orphenion.

A tin-plate shortage in the later years of the German musical-box industry, which also hit the tin-toy business in which Germany also excelled, and a sharp rise in price no doubt was a cause for great concern to musical-box makers and there is a surprisingly wide variation in both thickness and quality of material. Although the mechanism of the projectionless disc musical box was more complex and needed more manufacturing operations, the discs were cheaper to produce since the dies had only to pierce instead of punch and form.

The type of clockwork used is another important point of classification. Some disc-playing Polyphon and Symphonion hall clocks, for example, had no spring-driven motor at all, but were operated via weights and an escapement – the true clockwork as used in any weight-driven German clock.

* Sullivan's music on Polyphon is a rarity. One wonders if he had some disagreement, maybe concerning copyright, with the company.

Where coiled springs are used, these may be of two types. The first is the familiar flat spring as used in the majority of instruments and now anachronistically called by some repairers 'gramophone springs'. The second is the torsion spring made of coiled wire wound loosely upon a long arbor. This type was used in some large disc machines.

Flat springs form the basis of the so-called 'waggon-spring' power unit used in some models of F. G. Otto's Capital.

In defining a disc musical box, the following sequence of statements of characteristic should always be adhered to:

1 Disc size
2 Make of instrument (if known)
3 Style of instrument (i.e. table, upright, self-changer)
4 Style of comb
5 Special features.

The following examples should suffice to illustrate how this is used:

a $24\frac{1}{2}$ in. Polyphon, upright, parallel unison combs, gold leaf design on door, complete with disc bin and 22 discs;
b 11 in. unknown make, table model, single fine comb fitted with zither attachment, discs have floral design and play anti-clockwise, 17 discs;
c $11\frac{7}{8}$ in. Symphonion Eroica, triple-disc, sublime harmonie combs, etched glass in door, complete with 15 sets (45 total) of discs in hinged bin.

There follows a listing of so far identified disc musical boxes, each of which will be described and annotated in the form of a subsequent essay. Contained in this listing are some boxes which employ similar or related technology such as the cuff-playing and book-playing instruments. Boxes which are known by more than one name, or which are otherwise connected, or which have more than one spelling to the name are also included and cross-referenced as necessary.

Adler
Alexandra – see Britannia
Ariophon
Arno
Britannia
Calliope – see Kalliope
Capital
Celesta
Celeste
Chevob
Chocoladenmühle – see Novelty Makers, p. 239
Comete – see Komet
Corona – see Regina
Coronation – see Junghans
Criterion
Diorama

Edelweiss
Empress – see Mira
Euphonia
Euphonion
Euterpephon
Ehrlich
Fidelio
Fortuna – see Adler
Gemini
Gloria
Gloriosa – see Kalliope, Monopol also Novelty Makers, p. 239
Grand – see Stella
Harmonia
Helvetia
Illusions-Automat – see Fidelio, also Symphonion

Imperator
Imperial – *see* Britannia
Imperial Symphonion
Jubilee
Junghans
Kalliope
Komet
Libellion
Lipsia
Lochmann Original
Lyraphon
Mira
Miraphon(e) – *see* Mira
Monarch
Monopol
New Century
Oberon – *see* Novelty Makers, p. 239
Olympia
Original – *see* Lochmann Original
Orphenion
Orpheus
Perfection

Polygraphon – *see* Gramo-Polyphon
Polyhymnia
Polymnia
Polyphon
Porter – *see* Regina
Regina
Reginaphone – *see* Regina
Roepke
Saxonia
Silvanigra – *see* Junghans
Sirion
Spiegel
Stella
Sun
Symphonion
Tannhauser
Thorens – *see* Edelweiss
Triumph – *see* Monarch
Troubadour
Unikon
Victoria – *see* Komet

ADLER (Ard-la) *From German* Adler = Eagle.
The Adler was introduced and manufactured by Ernst Malke and F. H. Oberländer of Leipzig-Gohlis* and first shown to the trade on 9 March 1896. A report in *Zeitschrift für Instrumentenbau* says that 'both owners have great experience', which might suggest that Malke and Oberländer had formerly worked with another musical-box producer. Certainly the quality of the instruments was extremely good and the musical arrangements pleasing. The initial factory was at Halle'sche Strasse 125–7. By the beginning of 1897, the two men had been joined by a third, named Schlobach, who apparently injected capital into the enterprise. At the same time, showrooms were opened at Nuemarkt 23.

Malke and Oberländer were granted four patents in England. The first was 23232 dated 4 December 1895 and was for the characteristic slanted drive slots in the periphery of Adler discs. The second, a consecutive patent, was for a winding mechanism which took its drive via a toothed wheel engaging in holes in the motor barrel (this was produced in several variations for the smaller models). The third consecutive patent – all were of the same date – related to the playing of two or more musical movements together, connected by sprocket wheels, chains or perforated steel bands. On 13 March 1896, a fourth British patent was granted, this being number 5684, which covered a method of preventing overwinding disc musical-boxes and also a means of making disc projections. One US Patent was granted to Ernst Malke – number 598323 of 1 February 1898 – which covered the same specification as British Patent No. 23233. The company trademark – the Eagle – was registered in Germany on 3 January 1896.

Almost from the start, a wide variety of models was introduced which included wall-mounted, free-standing and table versions.

* The early history of the Adler has been researched by Hendrik Strengers: see *Bulletin*, MBSI, Vol. XXI, p. 208.

In September 1897, a twin-disc Adler was shown in Leipzig, an instrument which 'is capable of playing almost twice as long as formerly; it is now possible to reproduce music with a considerable length, truer to the original'.* A year later, the factory removed to Sedanstrasse 5–7, the former factory of Bruno Ruckert who produced the Orphenion (q.v.). The business was known as the Adler German-American Musik Works, although the correct meaning of 'German-American' is not known. The *Zeitschrift* for 11 September 1898 says: 'The workshops of the factory have been supplied with the most select and perfect machines. Besides the factory, the owners have rented in nearby premises two storeys, for a showroom and a room for the comb-tuners.'

The Adler exists with two different styles of disc projections. On the smaller models – the $11\frac{1}{2}$in. model is instanced – zinc discs were made having initially Orphenion-type dimple projections which most probably were made on Ruckert's old equipment. Later, narrow, single-punch, Polyphon-style projections were employed.

At the start of 1900, Adler introduced a large machine which in addition to musical combs featured a small harmonium, a drum and a triangle. Within a few months it was announced that the Adler Music Works had changed hands and that from the first day of April the business would be operated by Jules Heinrich Zimmermann. Zimmermann founded his business in 1886 as a maker of pianofortes and harmoniums under the trademark 'Fiedler'. It is not known for certain whether there was any connection with the Leipziger Pianoforte-fabrik Gebruder Zimmermann A.-G. established nine years later in another area of Leipzig, Molkau. However, J. H. Zimmermann had company offices at Querstrasse 26 and 28 and rapidly grew to become a large distributor of musical instruments and accessories.

Within two months of assuming control of the Adler works, Zimmermann registered a new trademark, the name 'Fortuna'. The name Adler was retained for a year or so, but gradually it was suppressed in favour of Fortuna. Zimmermann's influence was first applied towards the restyling of some of the overtly Teutonic designs of the Adler cases – some of the upright models featured ridiculously proportioned broken-arch pediments shaped like stylised eagles – and here he had the benefit of some fourteen years of Leipzig musical-box production designs to fall back on for reference. But it was in the table models that his styling was most apparent, with a transition from the accepted square box style to much plainer cabinets with rounded corners and lids to suit.

Other than such cosmetic exercises, it seems that musical box production was basically unchanged following Zimmermann's takeover, the big difference being that the name of Adler was replaced by Fortuna. The largest model produced was an improved version of the disc-operated musical box, harmonium and drum which Adler had marketed first in 1900. It was given the name Fortuna Marvel. Devolving from the Malke and Oberländer patent of 1895, the Marvel mechanism formed the prime unit of an enormous twin-disc instrument which was styled the Fortuna Orchestrion. This played a total of 236 comb teeth, 28 harmonium reeds (a unison 14-note organ), two drums and a pair of triangles. The discs were 26 in. in diameter.

During 1902, a hand-cranked organette called the Orgophon was introduced and in 1906 the company joined the fast-growing ranks of the phonograph-followers and produced a talking-machine with the name Kantophon (or Cantophon).

How widely the Fortuna and Adler musical boxes were sold is uncertain. Strange to say, there seem today to be far more specimens of the Adler than the Fortuna, in Germany at

* *Zeitschrift für Instrumentenbau*, 21 September 1897, p. 924.

least. One would feel that with Zimmermann's fast-growing distributive trade (he advertised branches in St Petersburg, Moscow and London) he would have been in a better position to have made a sizeable impact on the market. This, however, seems not to have been the case.

Disc sizes

Marking	Diameter (in.)	Diameter (cm)	Numbering
B	$7\frac{1}{16}$	18	1001 onwards
C	$8\frac{1}{4}$	19·5	9001 onwards
D	9	21	2001 onwards
F	$10\frac{3}{8}$	26·5	12001 onwards
H	11	28	3001 onwards
K	$14\frac{9}{16}$	37	7001 onwards
M	$16\frac{1}{8}$	41	4001 onwards
O	$18\frac{3}{4}$	47·5	11001 onwards
R	$21\frac{1}{4}$	54	5001 onwards
T	$25\frac{3}{4}$	65·5	8001 onwards
Z	26	66·5	6001 onwards

The more popular tunes were available on all sizes of disc and the numbers were always the same, only the series differing, e.g. the 'Faust Waltz' on size H was 3029, on M it was 4029, on O it was 11029 and on Z it became 6029.

These were always quality musical boxes, musically fine and mechanically satisfactory, although on this latter point clockwork engineering had progressed beyond its best period.

ARIOPHON (Ar-eye-oh-phon)
This was a book-playing lever-plucking musical box similar to the Libellion and Roepke (q.v.). Unlike those others, though, it aimed to reduce the wear on the cardboard music strips by employing motion-assisted starwheels which were friction-driven from a continuously rotating shaft. This system was conceived in several forms, one by Pöllnitz and Bauer of Komet Musikwerke. However, the Ariophon was apparently the design of Wilhelm Alfred Seifert, described as a merchant of 9 Post Strasse, Leipzig-Plagwitz. He was granted a British Patent number 14666 of 1893, which would have been exactly a year after a comparable German patent. (See *The Music Box*, volume 7, pp. 258–62.)

ARNO (Ah-no)
The Arno was a most unusual instrument, only one example of which is known to survive and that is in the Horngacher collection. The instrument is a true mutant, being neither one thing nor the other. Its sound is produced in the usual way from a musical box type comb, yet its system of plucking is pneumatic, being operated by a perforated paper tune-sheet which served as a sliding valve to control the collapse of small bellows which in turn operated a tooth-plucking mechanism. The paper roll of music thus operated on the principle of the player piano.

The instrument was the invention of Oliver Hilton Arno, 16 Green Street, Boston, Massachusetts, who was granted four US Patents for various inventions concerning pneumatic actuation. These were numbers 10279 (18 December 1883), 361200 (12 April 1887) and 361201 of the same date, and 596768 (4 January 1898). He was granted one British Patent during this period in conjunction with co-patentee, Alfred Eugene Paillard, whose address was given as 680 Broadway, New York. This patent, number 5343 dated 12 April 1887, covered the design of a tune-sheet-operated musical box playing both air-blown free reeds and musical-box type comb. Bowers* asserts that Arno was associated with the Massachusetts Organ Co. and other firms but offers no further comments.

The chances of other examples of this obviously rare and no doubt largely experimental model turning up are indeed small, certainly in Europe.

BRITANNIA
The musical-box manufactory of Barnett Henry Abrahams was founded at Ste-Croix in 1857 and subsequently continued by his sons. The business was still operating as late as 1903, but

* *Encyclopedia of Automatic Musical Instruments*, p. 248.

Figure 40   Early model of the Swiss Britannia disc-playing musical box.

had ceased functioning between then and 1909. An English emigrant, Abrahams produced large numbers of cheaper-quality cylinder boxes, usually with bells, and subsequently introduced the Britannia and Imperial disc machines. The address in Switzerland was Rue des Arts 3, Ste-Croix, and in 1886 there was a London office and wareroom at 128 Houndsditch. The Britannia appears to have been distributed almost exclusively by the Star Silver Depot based in East London.

With the familiar trade initials BHA, the company seems to have been a latecomer to the disc musical-box market. First to be introduced was the Imperial, the earliest reference to which appears in the August 1905 trade catalogue of musical instrument distributors Barnett Samuel & Sons of 32 and 34 Worship Street, Finsbury, London (see Fig. 40). It therefore may have been introduced in late 1904 but probably not much earlier. The name Imperial was cast into the silver-painted ribbed cast-iron bedplate and four sizes were initially marketed playing discs $8\frac{1}{2}$ in., 9 in., $11\frac{3}{4}$ in. and $17\frac{1}{4}$ in. in diameter. The two smaller were virtually the same discs only the first was driven from the centre and the second had peripheral drive holes.

The Britannia was virtually an identical instrument with the similarity extending to the case styles. A smaller model playing 5 in. diameter discs has been recorded* and two further sizes noted – $19\frac{5}{8}$ in. (which will also play on the similar-sized Polyphon) and 25 in. A popular model with collectors today is the so-called 'smokers cabinet' 9 in. vertical which is called the Alexandra and which was possibly named after Queen Alexandra, wife of Edward VII, who came to the throne on the death of his mother, Queen Victoria, and whose coronation, delayed by illness, took place on 9 August 1901. Cabinets have been seen which bear a transfer (decal) depicting, in colour, the royal coat of arms of King Edward VII.

All Britannia boxes seen have the name and that of the Star Silver Depot cast into their bedplates. All have a strident tone, none more noticeable than in the Alexandra model, which is very loud. The musical arrangements tend to be on the thin side, a defect which is ably compensated by the volume of sound.

Discs were all decorated with the name 'Britannia' in silver or red outlined in black, although – strange to say – on a specimen of the larger size contained in the Greenacre collection the name on the front of the cabinet is spelled 'Brittania'. Frank Greenacre commented that, in keeping with some other disc boxes, the bass comb teeth are broad-toothed for loudness, changing to duplex fine teeth for the middle and treble registers. Cases for table models seem to owe much in style to the cylinder musical-box and decoration of richly figured inlay and cross-banding is nothing more than a cleverly contrived transfer (decal) applied to painted wood.

CAPITAL

The Capital was a unique instrument embodying an amalgamation of the technology of the disc musical box with that of the cylinder phonograph to create a thoroughly fresh approach to the production of mechanical music from comb via a projection-studded surface.

The research into this company is almost entirely the work of Hughes Ryder,† who likewise recorded the history of the related instruments (Criterion (q.v.), Olympia (q.v.), Regina (q.v.) and Pianette).

* F. S. Greenacre, article in *The Music Box*, Vol. 1, No. 7, p. 29.
† Hughes Ryder, 'The Capital Self-Playing Music Box', *The Music Box*, Vol. 3, 1967, pp. 35–48.

197

Frederick G. Otto started his company, F. G. Otto & Sons, in Jersey City, New Jersey in 1875 to manufacture surgical instruments. His sons were Edmund, Gustav and Albert, and the factory premises were at 48 and 50 Sherman Avenue. The Ottos lived close by at numbers 96–101 Sherman Avenue, an address all the more significant because it was directly opposite the home of Gustave Brachhausen of Polyphon (q.v.) fame, who had come to America to set up the Regina (q.v.) musical-box manufacturing organisation. Brachhausen lived at Sherman Avenue during 1893 and 1894.

One of Otto's workers, a pattern maker named Henry Langfelder, was subsequently charged with the design of a musical box which could be patented: the result was US Patent number 519816 dated 15 May 1894.

This instrument, subsequently named the Capital, employed comb and starwheels in the normal manner, but instead of a disc it played a hollow thin-walled metal cone retained on a mandrel carrying locating discs for the cone which could be slipped on and off. This feature led to the sobriquet 'cuff-box' being given to the Capital, a name attributed to the resemblance of the conical tune sheet to a cuff. The practical form of this was the invention of foreman Ferdinand Schaub, whose US Patent number 532290 dated 8 January 1895 refers.

Some models of the Capital use a novel form of mainspring invented by Otto (US Patent number 525717 refers) and employing a series of short elliptical springs compressed between long guides by a fusee-type chain wound around a drum on the main gear. A further type of spring was a coiled wire spring located on a wooden dowel. These two novel varieties survive in fewer numbers than Capitals powered by normal spring-barrels.

The Capital appears to have entered production in 1895 and was sold through M. J. Paillard of 608 Broadway, New York City. Production is thought to have terminated about the end of 1897, possibly due to the acceptance of the fact that the public appeared to prefer the instruments playing flat discs rather than the cumbersome cones. The outcome of this was the Criterion (q.v.).

The comb of the Style C Capital was virtually identical with that of the $15\frac{1}{2}$ in. (39·4 cm) Regina and the tone of the instrument is good with the music well set up. The Style F instrument used parallel unison combs with the 'cuff' recessed to a greater or lesser degree so that it could engage with the starwheels from the opposite side to the comb. Capital 'cuffs' were made in three sizes to suit eight styles of box, all being of horizontal, table format. The dimensions are given in the following order: overall length of the cone, diameter of the larger end, diameter of the smaller end, and each size will be preceded by the style of box which it fitted.

Style O, A = $4\frac{1}{4}$ in. (10·8 cm) × $3\frac{3}{8}$ in. (8·6 cm) × $2\frac{1}{4}$ in. (5·7 cm); Style C, D, E, F = $7\frac{3}{4}$ in. (19·7 cm) × $4\frac{1}{4}$ in. (10·8 cm) × $3\frac{1}{4}$ in. (8·25 cm); Style G, B = $5\frac{1}{2}$ in. (14·0 cm) × $4\frac{1}{4}$ in. (10·8 cm) × $3\frac{1}{2}$ in. (9 cm).

CELESTA (Sel-estar)

The Celesta was a fine-toned instrument produced in at least four different sizes by Pietschmann & Söhn of Brunnenstrasse 25, Berlin, during the mid-1890s. At least two table and two upright models were made and the discs were stamped 'Made in Leipzig'. Projections were very similar to those of the Polyphon but the method of damping was quite ingenious, making use of weighted levers carrying flat wire dampers to be pressed against the vibrating teeth by the rotation of the starwheels. The air brake was also unusual, comprising a fixed rectangular plate to the extremities of one side of which were pivotally attached two brass wings. These are normally held closed by springs but when the assembly rotates, the wings move outwards against the spring tension.

The smaller discs have what appears to be a semicircular drive hole punched out near the centre: this serves no purpose at all. Disc sizes found comprise: $8\frac{1}{4}$ in. (21 cm); $11\frac{3}{8}$ in. (29 cm); $15\frac{1}{2}$ in. (39·4 cm); $19\frac{5}{8}$ in. (50 cm). This last-mentioned size is interchangeable with the Polyphon of the same size.

CELESTE (Say-lest)
The Celeste, not to be confused with the Celesta, was marketed about 1901–2 by Heinrich Hermann at Weinbergstrasse 9, Bernau near Berlin. I say 'marketed' rather than 'made', for I have a sneaking suspicion that this may turn out to be another stencil brand musical box. Two sizes have been determined: 11 in. (28 cm) and $19\frac{5}{8}$ in. (39·4 cm), both being the same size as Polyphon and apparently interchangeable. In addition to the name 'Celeste' on the discs, a distinctive trademark was affixed. This consists of a simple and rather crude drawing of two five-spoked cartwheels, slightly overlapping each other, framed by a sort of heart-shaped jawbone-like frame, the lower part of which is cut off by a banner reading 'Trade-Mark'. The whole design is surmounted by a beetle and the whole thing is drawn with no finesse. This is the Pietschmann trade mark (see p. 263).

Hermann was a maker of organettes primarily and this leads me to suspect that the Celeste was bought in to add to the range in order to be able to offer all types of music. At some date prior to 1909, the Hermann business, which was established in 1901, was absorbed into the Leipziger Musikwerke 'Euphonika', a company formed in 1895 at Friedrich-List-Str. 11, Leipzig, for the manufacture of organettes.

CHEVOB (Shev-ob)
The discovery of a $15\frac{1}{2}$ in. (39·4 cm) table disc machine bearing no marks other than a label reading 'Chevob et Cie, Geneva, Successors to Baker-Troll' sounds very much like the discovery of a stencil brand, for the box is surely a Polyphon in disguise. Chevob was in business at 6 rue Bonivard and claimed to be a manufacturer of singing birds and orchestrions. An advertisement clearly states that the business was formerly known as Baker-Troll (the makers of cylinder musical-boxes) established in 1873. The telegraphic address, by means of supporting the claim, was 'Baktrol'. Subsequently, a cylinder musical box has been seen bearing this name and the definitive date 7 September 1907. Rather as Brun took over Nicole Frères in London and claimed still to be a manufacturer, I believe that Chevob took over Baker-Troll, but no longer manufactured instruments. The absence of any further references and thereby the establishment of the skills to produce this disc musical box in Geneva leads me to suspect that this is but a Polyphon.

CRITERION
Following on the Capital (q.v.), the New Jersey firm of F. G. Otto & Sons introduced the Criterion, its first conventional disc musical box. The invention was that of Ferdinand Schaub, shop foreman and son of Otto's head bookkeeper Adolph Schaub. Ferdinand Schaub had already invented and patented the unusual truncated cone tune sheet for the Capital. By February of 1895, according to researches by Hughes Ryder, Ferdinand Schaub had filed a patent application for a flat disc musical box with a centre-wound spring on the

same principle as that employed by the smaller-sized Kalliope (q.v.) instruments. This system was not used by Otto, however, possibly due to the realisation that patent infringement might be claimed.

In November of 1896, however, the Criterion was first marketed, the sales agent being M. J. Paillard in New York, who had handled the Capital. During the first five months of production, Paillard alone handled between eighty and a hundred instruments a month.

Unlike the Capital, which used steel for its tunes, the Criterion used zinc for the majority of its discs, steel being used only for discs of the smallest model, which was centre-driven. The drive holes for the zinc discs (which were peripherally-driven) were rectangular in shape and formed by trefoil punching and folding so that the bearing surfaces were twice the base metal thickness. Three sizes were produced: $11\frac{5}{8}$ in. (29·5 cm; $15\frac{3}{4}$ in. (40 cm); and $20\frac{1}{2}$ in. (52 cm).

The makers of the Regina (q.v.) subsequently sued F. G. Otto & Sons through their agents, M. J. Paillard & Co., for patent infringements, a case which was heard in the New York courts during 1896 and 1897 and which resulted in the instrument being withdrawn some time late in 1897. In the following year, Otto introduced its successor in the shape of the Olympia (q.v.).

DIORAMA (Dye-oh-ram-a)
This instrument was advertised in the late 1880s by B. Kirsch, Bei der Burg, ob Schmeidgasse 16/18, Nuremburg. The Kirsch business, managed in 1909 by Wwe E. Kirsch, was founded as early as 1862 and handled all kinds of musical instruments and musical boxes. It is not certain whether Kirsch was actually the maker of the Diorama which was an upright disc machine with a flipping-card stereoscopic picture display mounted at eye level and viewed through two openings in the door. Five models were listed in the 1898 Ernst Holzweissig catalogue: Model 501 Diorama Musik-Automat with 79-note ($52\frac{1}{2}$ cm) Troubadour musicwork; Model 501A with 90-note (41 cm) Adler musicwork; model 501S with 106-note ($48\frac{1}{2}$ cm) Symphonion musicwork, and two slightly larger versions, 505A and 505S again with Adler and Symphonion musicwork respectively. In all instances, the moving pictures comprised a band of 18 pictures.

EDELWEISS (Ed-el-vice)
There are two distinct types of disc musical box to bear this name, both made by Hermann Thorens of Avenue des Alpes, Ste-Croix, Switzerland. The first, patented by Hössly in 1897, was a disc-playing lever-plucker of sophisticated design. Identical in mechanism to the Helvetia (q.v.), it was made in at least three sizes: $12\frac{1}{16}$ in. (30·5 cm); $15\frac{1}{2}$ in. (40 cm); and $22\frac{1}{4}$ in. (56·5 cm). All these are twin-comb machines peripherally-driving discs with lozenge-shaped drive holes. See also p. 182.

The second type is a bright-toned simple little musical box made to fit inside photograph albums, cigar boxes and so on. Two other makers produced similar movements – Symphonion (q.v.) and Junghans (q.v.). All Edelweiss and Helvetia machines rotate their discs anti-clockwise.

Three sizes of the little Edelweiss have been seen: the little $4\frac{1}{2}$ in. (11·4 cm) playing a disc which has a serrated edge, being pinion-driven. Then comes the $7\frac{11}{16}$ in. (19·5 cm), and the $8\frac{1}{16}$ in. (20·5 cm), which also has two bells.

EHRLICH (Air-leek)

Friedrich Ernst Paul Ehrlich of Gohlis, Leipzig, first produced his Ariston organette in the late 1870s and had secured such a success with it that his business was assured the financial stability to encourage invention and development along further lines. For Ehrlich, the cardboard disc punched with plain slots was a perfect means of supplying the musical programme and so it is natural that when he first looked to the manufacture of a disc-playing musical box he should automatically consider punched card discs as the music.

Obviously plain punched card posed certain design restrictions on the comb-plucking mechanism and this he set out to overcome with his first patent for a lever-plucker disc machine, British Patent number 6391 dated 12 May 1886. His next patent, taken out in conjuction with G. A. F. Muller, was British Patent number 9742 dated 28 July 1886. This bore a similarity to Lochmann's first patent for the Symphonion (q.v.) in that it described a vertically mounted comb pointing upwards under a rotating disc with projections. But it was to his third related patent that production ultimately began. This was British Patent number 1086 dated 24 January 1888 which covered a mechanism very similar to Richter's Libellion (q.v.) system.

The Ehrlich disc musical box with its Ariston-like card discs seems not to have been accorded a great deal of success. It must be remembered, though, that Ariston production and the manufacture of other organettes was keeping the production facilities fully stretched and the mechanism of the Ehrlich was nothing if not labour-intensive. By the late 1890s, Ehrlich had developed the Monopol (q.v.), an undoubtedly superior instrument, and so the Ehrlich card disc machine was dropped. One specimen is known in Britain.

Only one size of Ehrlich has so far been determined: this plays a 47-note comb from a card disc 11¼ in. (28·6 cm) in diameter. The delicate nature of the instruments and the friability of the card discs together suffice to make this an instrument which may be classed as rare.

The manufacturer, Paul Ehrlich & Co. A.-G., was founded in 1877. In about 1886, the business became the Fabrik Leipziger Musikwerke under the control of Paul Ehrlich. The address was Mockernschestrasse 30d, Leipzig-Gohlis.

EUPHONIA (You-foan-ear)

The New Jersey musical-box manufacturer F. G. Otto had entered the disc musical-box business as early as November 1896 with the Criterion (q.v.) but found himself in trouble with patents due to the similarity with the Regina (q.v.). The Euphonia was a later development of the Criterion put out in an attempt to redress the situation. Some form of arrangement seems to have been agreed between the parties concerned, for all the patents under which the Euphonia was manufactured were duly listed inside the lid!

The instrument itself was the invention of Gustav Otto and Ferdinand Schaub, who were the co-patentees listed on US Patent number 700550 dated 20 May 1902. A legend inside the lid of the 15¾ in. (40 cm) disc-playing machine read: 'The Euphonia, No. 54, Pat. No. 700,550. Pat. Sounding Board.' Discs are numbered in the 4000 series.

The patents listed comprise: 290697; 401187; 401188; 417650 (issued to O. P. Lochmann and covering dampers); 474520 (issued to Samuel Cuendet); 500371 (issued to G. A. Brachhausen and P. Riessner); 538033; 538468 (issued to Ferdinand Schaub).

It would appear that the Euphonia only appeared in the 15¾ in. (40 cm) disc size.

EUPHONION (You-foan-i-yon)

The Euphonion appears to demonstrate that stencil-branding was practised in the 1890s musical-box industry for there seems to be every indication that the Euphonion is nothing more than a custom-made line from Polyphon (q.v.).

The instruments were allegedly manufactured by the Euphonion-Musikwerke Sperling & Wendt, Enenkelstr. 26, Vienna XVI/4, yet this company appears to have been nothing but a distributor.

Three sizes have been determined: 11 in. (28 cm); 15½ in. (39·5 cm); 19⅝ in. (50 cm), all these being Polyphon sizes. All discs are interchangeable. Bowers* says: 'Other Euphonion boxes use non-Polyphon types of discs, however', but does not elaborate further.

EUTERPEPHON (You-ter-pee-fon)

This is something of a mystery marque. Only two examples have so far come to light. The first is an incomplete specimen in the Mekanisk Musik Museum, Copenhagen. A table machine, the plain bedplate has a single comb mounted on the right-hand side. No discs survive but it appears to play a 30 cm disc although, according to Q. David Bowers, an 11 in. (28 cm) Polyphon disc will play 'quite well' on it, suggesting that it has the same tuning scale and tooth spacing. Inside the lid is a picture of the robed muse Euterpe blowing two trumpets, one facing to the left and the other right. The box is handle-wound from the right side with a stop/start knob on the left as in table Symphonions. The second machine is in good order and plays discs 12⅛ in. (30·8 cm) in diameter. So far no clue as to its maker has been found.

FIDELIO (Fid-ay-leo)

Max Levy established his Fidelio Musikwerke in 1907 with addresses at SO.16, Neander-strasse 8 and 43 Neue Konigstrasse in Berlin. The speciality was the 'Illusions-Automat' instruments. These were large, upright-style cabinets which contained a Swiss-made cylin-der musical movement plus a complex automaton scene. One such model was described in the company's catalogue in the following terms: '52 steel tongues, 3 chinese beating 6 bells, interchangeable barrels of music, 7½ × 2 inches, double spring, self-acting piece-marker [tune-indicator]. During the play a door openes [sic] itself and by electric light, which changes three times its colour, a ballet of about 100 dancers begin to performe. – Most effectful show. – Case of walnut highly finished and of best workmanship. In case that this automaton shall be set in connection with an existing electric stream please mention this when ordering; the price will in this case 30 shillings less.'

Some models of this marque were fitted with disc movements but, as with the cylinder movements, they were not made by Fidelio but were bought in from Leipzig. The Illusions-Automat No. 150 was fitted with a 19⅛ in. (48·5 cm) disc movement by Symphon-ion (q.v.) which also included this model in its catalogue. The Fidelio company cannot have remained long in the musical-box business for within the short space of four or five years Illusions-Automat machines were being made with phonograph movements and later still the business resolved into the selling of gramophones and radio sets.

GEMINI (Jem-in-eye)

Name used by Keith Harding for his 1978 version of twin 19⅝ in. Polyphon.

* *Encyclopedia of Automatic Musical Instruments*, p. 246.

GLORIA (Glor-ear)
Made by the Société Anonyme Fabriques Réunies, formerly at 12 rue Bonivard, Geneva, and later at 18 Quai de St Jean. This consortium, which comprised the three businesses of Ami Rivenc, Langdorff Fils and Billon, was formed in 1896 (it was not, however, incorporated until July 1902) in order to try to stem the decline in the Swiss musical box caused by the German disc musical box. The idea was to dispense with the middle-man in marketing and to sell their own machines direct to the public. The SAFR chose to meet the German threat fair and square with, initially, two products. The first was the Gloria, then there was a clockwork organette. Later they marketed the Polymnia (q.v.), but the Société was disbanded in September 1905.

The Gloria was made in two styles – table and upright. Both are characterised by the fact that the comb assembly is angled to the bedplate. Two sizes have been determined: $11\frac{3}{4}$ in. (30 cm) table; and $18\frac{1}{4}$ in. (46 cm) upright. Disc rotation is anticlockwise, and the drive holes in the discs are rectangular in shape.

HARMONIA (Ha-moan-ear)
The Harmonia was a short-lived Swiss attempt to usurp some of the German market for the disc musical box. Manufactured in Auberson near Ste-Croix by the Société Anonyme Harmonia, the Harmonia first appeared in 1897 and was factored by several agents including Nicole Frères in London.

The founder of the Harmonia S. A. was August Bornand-Galaz. The Ste-Croix area was the home of the Bornands (see list of makers in Chapter 11) and it seems that the Harmonia was a Bornand invention. The similarity between certain features of the Harmonia and the Stella (q.v.) might in some measure be due to the fact that one member of the Bornand family, Joseph, left Ste-Croix to work in New York for Paillard when he opened his New York factory in 1883 (the first Paillard showroom opened in 1850 in New York). Paillard was involved with the close-knit Swiss musical-box fraternity in New York and hence Joseph Bornand may have fed back technology to Bornand-Galaz. This involved intelligence might be overly cumbersome, especially since Mermod was manufacturing at Ste-Croix close to Harmonia S.A.

The Harmonia used projectionless discs and sprung starwheels but other than that was sufficiently different to indicate no real connection with Mermod.

Three sizes have been determined: 8 in. (20·3 cm); 10 in. (25·4 cm); and $16\frac{1}{2}$ in. (42 cm).

HELVETIA (Hel-vee-sha)
This is the second of the disc musical boxes made in Ste-Croix by Hermann Thorens, the first being the Edelweiss (q.v.). Both Edelweiss and Helvetia are similar in most respects, the names having been used no doubt to suit different markets. In the earlier, larger machines, they are lever pluckers with the Hössly patented action and have the ability to be silenced while playing by moving a lever. In the later, smaller styles, conventional starwheels were used and on the $8\frac{1}{16}$ in. (20·5 cm) size, the discs have a start arrow printed pointing inwards to the centre. Other disc dimensions are as listed under Edelweiss.

IMPERATOR (Im-pear-ah-tor)
Friederich Adolf Richter of Rudolstadt took out a number of patents for mechanical instruments between 1893 and 1900 which together accounted for two rather sophisticated

203

musical boxes. One was a disc instrument and the other was a book-playing mechanism included here because of its closely related technology and appearance.

The Richter business was at Schwarzbergerstrasse 56 in Rudolstadt and was established in 1876 (some sources say 1896, which is incorrect) by Dr A. D. Richter, Councillor of Commerce, and subsequently operated by Adolf Richter jun. A large and wealthy business, it was also a diversified one, and part of a large combine known as the Leipziger Lehrmittel-Anstalt which produced scientific apparatus, 'appliances for teaching', electric motors, soap, and a remarkably detailed model building brick kit from which accurate scale models of famous German buildings could be constructed. The company exhibited extensively at the 1900 Paris Exposition and was awarded a medallion which was subsequently modelled on its later musical boxes. The Imperator disc musical box bore the trademark of a flaming torch of knowledge.

Some seventeen patents are on the British files covering Richter's two musical boxes. These are as follows: 5060 dated 8 March 1893; 17528 dated 18 September 1893; 9446 dated 12 May 1894; 11234 dated 9 June 1894; 14380 dated 26 July 1894; 17041 dated 7 September 1894; 5951 dated 21 March 1895; 16000 dated 26 August 1895; 17317 and 17318 both dated 17 September 1895; 14450 dated 30 June 1896; 15675 dated 15 July 1896; 18049 dated 14 August 1896; 25354 dated 11 November 1896; 25552 dated 23 December 1899; 9427 dated 22 May 1900; and 11816 dated 29 June 1900. These relate exclusively to musical boxes and there are other patents concerning coin-feed apparatus and relating to other forms of amusement. Many of the musical-box patents refer to the Libellion (q.v.) which was a book-playing lever-plucker.

The Imperator has been identified in three sizes, the Style 27 with a $5\frac{1}{2}$ in. (14 cm) disc, the Model 52G playing a $10\frac{1}{4}$ in. (26 cm) disc and a much larger model, the Style 49, which plays a 21 in. (53·5 cm) disc.

IMPERIAL SYMPHONION

The Imperial Symphonion was the name given to instruments produced by the Symphonion Manufacturing Co. at Bradley Beach near Asbury Park (originally called Neptune Township), New Jersey. The Symphonion (q.v.) was produced by the Symphonionfabrik, more properly known in its early days as Kuhno-Lochmann and later as Symphonion Fabrik Lochmannscher Musikwerke A.-G. at Braustrasse 13–19, Leipzig-Gohlis. With the growing market for musical boxes in America, it was decided to set up an American branch of the business. The date of the establishment of the Bradley Beach Plant is, regrettably, unknown but it was *circa* 1896–7. Initially, as with Regina (q.v.), instruments were imported from Leipzig, the majority being without cases and locally made cabinets being provided. Wholly American-manufactured instruments followed soon afterwards and by 1898 advertisements were acclaiming 'the new American-made Symphonion' as 'The First Perfect Music Box'. During 1902, however, the company ceased trading.

The first difference between Leipzig-made and American-made instruments lay in the design of the case, which now followed closely eclectic American trends. Significantly, it seems that only table models were built with the exception of the so-called piano-style-cased uprights. These, sired in Leipzig and developed under the Imperial name, were produced in limited numbers and were made with one, two or three disc movements, the multi-players having their discs arranged side by side vertically.

While early German-built Symphonions naturally represent the range offered and can be found listed under Symphonion, the sizes produced exclusively at Bradley Beach appear to have been $11\frac{7}{8}$ in. (30 cm); $17\frac{5}{8}$ in. (44·8 cm); 20 in. (50·8 cm); and $27\frac{5}{8}$ in. (70·2 cm). All American-made models had cast into the bedplates in capital letters 'Symphonion/Mfg. Co./N.Y.'.

JUBILEE

This is the name given by Keith Harding and his team to their recreation of the $19\frac{5}{8}$ in. Polyphon which is an exact copy of the original in every respect and was first unveiled at the Musical Box Society of Great Britain's summer meeting in London in 1977. The same name has been used by Brian Etches in his brand new twin-disc table-style musical box which plays two $19\frac{5}{8}$ in. Polyphon discs at once. This instrument, in a Louis XVI style glass-topped cabinet, is electrically driven and features a nickle-plated bronze bedplate assembly and a novel adjustable helical gear which can 'register' both discs while playing. Special discs in 'A' and 'B' settings, rather like those for the Symphonion Eroica, can be made for this. At present existing only in prototype form, the Etches Jubilee was unveiled at the summer meeting of the Musical Box Society of Great Britain in 1978.*

JUNGHANS (Yong-uns)

The disc musical boxes with which this manufacturer is best associated comprised movements fitted into clocks and so much of the story of these is tied up with the history of the manufacturer. It was in 1843 that F. Haller started his clockmaking business in Schwenningen in the Württemberg Black Forest. Haller specialised in alarm clocks and carriage clocks characterised by their extraordinary cheapness. Known somewhat derogatorily as 'tin clocks', they were the product of the first serious attempt at mass-production of clocks in Europe. The second attempt at this goal was the work of Erhard Junghans who, with his brother Xaver, founded the Junghanssche Uhrenfabrik at Schramberg in Württemberg in 1861. The business thrived and soon overtook that of Haller until at some period in the 1880s Junghans took over Haller to form the Vereingte Uhrenfabriken Gebr. Junghans und Th Haller A.-G. Schwenningen, only a small village, sported a number of musical clockmakers and the former Haller company continued in business under the Junghans brothers. Meanwhile, at Schramberg, Junghans began producing disc-playing musical clocks and between 1889 and the start of the First World War a wide range of low-cost clocks, mostly 'tin clocks', was produced containing $4\frac{1}{2}$ in. (11·5 cm) disc movements. Some of these were pinion-driven, Thorens style, but others used a centre-driven disc characterised by a black-printed design covering not quite half the disc which included a circle containing an eight-pointed star with the large letter 'J' within. All the disc numbers were prefaced with the letter 'S', e.g. S.28.

British Patent number 26806 was granted to A. Junghans on 16 November 1897 for a disc-playing musical mechanism operated by a clock on the alarm principle.

There is some controversy as to who made the movements and/or the discs, for both bear strong family resemblance to the smallest Symphonion (q.v.) and the discs, when compared, appear absolutely identical, except that the Junghans trademark is replaced by 'Symphonion' and the lyre trademark. Even the style of numbering, e.g. S.28, is identical. Did Junghans make this particular size for Symphonion, or vice versa?

* The Etches Jubilee is illustrated in Plates 48–50 of *Restoring Musical Boxes*.

There is also a small conventional-style table musical box which plays the selfsame Junghans-marked disc. In Germany this was marketed under the name Silvanigra which is a derivation of the old Latin name for the Black Forest, *nigrae silvae*. This same box also appeared in England in 1904 under the name The Coronation. The style is very similar to the Style 20 Symphonion but, unlike that instrument which is handle-wound from the side, this one is wound by a lever operating in a slot across the front of the case.

The connection with the Symphonion is strengthened by the fact that the Junghans musical clock also featured in the Symphonion range, this time branded Symphonion. Was there a reciprocal arrangement between Junghans and Symphonion? I personally think it likely, particularly since Schwenningen-style clocks feature in Symphonion musical boxes.

KALLIOPE (Kal-eye-oh-pee)

A latecomer to the disc musical-box market, Kalliope successfully entered the field where others had tried and failed. This was done with a wide range of instruments most of which characterised the change which had overtaken the eclectic cabinet styles of the 1890s. In the larger Kalliope machines we find clear, if as yet but tentative steps towards a more functional appearance with just a hint of what we now call Art Deco. Loudness was another characteristic which former Polyphonmusikwerke employee Emil Wacker sought when, in 1895, he formed the Kalliope Fabrik Mechanischer Musikwerke Espenhain, Wacker und Bock at Dorotheenstrasse 20 in Leipzig-Gohlis. Hendrik Strengers has identified the original founders as Emil Moritz Anton Wacker, Christian Heinrich Richard Bock and Gustav Max Espenhain. By 1897 the business was reconstituted as Kalliope-Musikwerke A.-G. and, later on, Max Espenhain operated his own company as the Apollo Musikwerke. Kalliope opened a large corner factory at Bitterfelder Strasse 1 in Leipzig. This is where all the Kalliope machines were made. The instrument was advertised as 'made in Saxony', of which Leipzig is a principal city. By 1909, the business was run by Emil Wacker and Hugo Zetsche.

Right from the outset, Kalliope Musikwerke prospered and this must have been due to an early and thorough distributorship tie-up. For the French market, however, the name 'Kalliope' had to be altered to 'Calliope' – the French seem to have difficulty with words beginning with the letter K as there are only half a bucketful in the French dictionary. (See also how Komet became 'Comète'.)

A feature of the later small table model Kalliopes which is at once noticeable is that the disc is driven by the centre shaft which itself is the mainspring arbor, the spring being mounted vertically. Winding is achieved by slotting a handle into the top of the shaft (it can be done while the disc is playing) and turning. This system was patented by the company in 1901. Other table models retain the vertical spring, but are wound from a vertical hole in the bedplate next to the disc. One other table model which has double combs is wound from the left side of the front, the motor being arranged next to the disc but on the left side – the opposite side to that selected by Adler, Orpheus, Fortuna and Lochmann.

The upright model Kalliopes were made, as indeed were some other makes of instrument, with single combs, double combs and broad-toothed double combs (alternate plucking). Naturally the broad-toothed combs (referred to as 'extra-wide teeth') called for a different tuning scale to the normal or narrow-toothed combs which were plucked in unison. For this reason at least one diameter of disc – the 24 in. or 61 cm – comes in two styles, classified as 'new series' and 'old series'.

Bells are another feature of many Kalliope instruments, usually hemispherical but sometimes flat metal glockenspiel type. It is a small Kalliope with bells which formed the basis of the 1974 Symphonion made by Studio Oyen (q.v.).

Another Kalliope product was the Gloriosa musical Christmas-tree stand, a rectangular cabinet which played 7 in. (18 cm) discs. Some models were coin-operated and were fitted with bells. A very large Kalliope Christmas-tree stand has been seen which includes a $9\frac{1}{4}$ in. (23·5 cm) disc movement complete with six bells.

Early in this century, Kalliope moved into the talking-machine business and in October of 1903 introduced the Odeon phonograph.

The Kalliope company survived the 1914–18 war and in 1919 it merged with Menzenhauer & Schmidt, Henry Langfelder's company at Rungestrasse 17, Berlin, where the Guitarophone was produced.* Shortly afterwards, Kalliope was engaged in the manufacture of phonographs bearing this name. Prior to the First World War, the company had produced some combination musical box/phonographs under the name Kalliophon. Reflecting the passion which some souls have for equestrian gambling, as early as 1903 the company had produced the Kalliope Panorama, an upright musical box playing $22\frac{3}{4}$ in. (58 cm) discs and incorporating a coloured panorama of racing horses accompanied by the advice that 'Bets can be paid off with prizes of beer, cigarettes, etc.'.

These are all good-quality musical boxes which, in the smaller examples at any rate, feature simple, uncomplicated musical arrangements produced with ample volume to attract attention.

There are 13 definable disc sizes as follows: $5\frac{5}{8}$ in. (14·5 cm); 7 in. (18 cm); $9\frac{1}{4}$ in. (23·5 cm); $9\frac{3}{4}$ in. (25 cm); $13\frac{3}{8}$ in. (34 cm); $14\frac{1}{8}$ in. (36 cm); $17\frac{3}{4}$ in. (45 cm); $18\frac{1}{4}$ in. (46·5 cm); $20\frac{5}{8}$ in. (52·5 cm); $22\frac{3}{4}$ in. (58 cm); 24 in. (61 cm) (made in two series); $25\frac{3}{8}$ in. (64·5 cm); $28\frac{5}{8}$ in. (72·5 cm); $29\frac{1}{2}$ in. (75 cm).

A phonopectine was produced under the name Kalliophon.

KOMET

The Komet survives today in extremely small numbers and one reason for this must undoubtedly be the imprudent introduction of so many different sizes of machine, each with its inventory of discs. According to Bowers (*Encyclopedia of Automatic Musical Instruments*, p. 112), the Komet was manufactured in Leipzig by Weissbach & Co. and the period of production of instruments seems to extend from about 1898 to 1900. However, an examination of British Patents reveals that patent number 13940, dated 22 July 1895, was granted to Hans von Pollnitz and Franz Louis Bauer of the firm of Komet Musikwerke, Pollnitz & Bauer, Manufacturers, of Friedrichstrasse 4, Plagwitz-Leipzig. This patent covers a musical box playing a projectionless tune sheet and the motion-assisted starwheels (see under ARIOPHON). This would seem to establish the existence of a company called Komet as early as 1895 and to define the inventors of the instrument. Where and when Weissbach came into the picture remains to be seen.

The smallest of the Komet machines were in table-style cases but there were also small upright models for free-standing or wall-mounting which were produced under the name Komet Victoria. The larger instruments were uprights in typical Germanic cases. The largest model, with eight musical combs plus fourteen bells with butterfly strikers, plays a disc

---

* Bowers, *Encyclopedia of Automatic Musical Instruments*, p. 108.

$33\frac{3}{8}$ in. (84·8 cm) in diameter and this is believed to be the largest disc ever made for a normal comb-playing disc musical box.

No fewer than eight sizes have been determined as follows: $10\frac{3}{8}$ in. (26·3 cm); $13\frac{1}{8}$ in. (33·3 cm); 17 in. (43 cm); $20\frac{1}{2}$ in. (52 cm); $21\frac{5}{8}$ in. (55 cm); $24\frac{1}{2}$ in. (62 cm); $25\frac{1}{4}$ in. (64 cm); $33\frac{3}{8}$ in. (84·8 cm). The $24\frac{1}{2}$ in. (62 cm) size will play on a Polyphon (q.v.) of the same size, but the tuning scale is different. The $13\frac{1}{8}$ in. (33·3 cm) and the $10\frac{3}{8}$ in. (26·3 cm) sizes both use projectionless discs. All but the smallest are peripherally driven; the smallest is centre-driven.

The Komet trademark is a figure in peasant costume blowing a brazen horn, standing on a curved sort of ski which has a spur-like star at the forward tip. On the discs this figure is shown facing left. Where the trademark appears on the actual instrument such as on the Komet Victoria models, it faces right.

For the French market, the instrument was styled as COMÈTE and the discs so lettered. Otherwise the same.

LIBELLION (Lee-bell-eon)

The Libellion was the second of the two comb-playing musical boxes devised by Friederich Adolf Richter but unlike the Imperator (q.v.), which was a disc machine, the Libellion operated from folded cardboard music.

Richter's numerous patents for musical boxes, which include the complex system of sliding levers which comprise the mechanism of this lever-plucker, are listed in the section under Imperator. However, the Libellion was specifically manufactured under the following British Patents: number 17041 dated 7 September 1894; number 17317 dated 17 September 1895; number 11816 dated 29 June 1900. The following US Patents also applied: number 532585 dated 15 January 1895; number 551789 dated 24 December 1895; number 560283 dated May 1896. The Libellion was awarded numerous medals according to information on the instruments, including Chicago, 1893, and at the Paris Exposition of 1900.

Two styles were manufactured, the first being table format and cased rather like any other similar format musical box playing discs. The second was in upright format and was built into vertical cases, in the one example known, surmounted by a clock. Two sizes of table model have been recorded, the smaller playing cardboard $7\frac{7}{8}$ in. (20 cm) wide, and the second $9\frac{3}{4}$ in. (24·7 cm). The solitary upright example plays music $11\frac{9}{16}$ in. (29·1 cm) wide.

An example of the latter size survives in Holland's Nationaal Museum van Speelklok tot Pierement in Utrecht. The instrument plays five octaves and a fourth on two combs, chromatically disposed with fifty teeth each side of the central cog which drives the cardboard music. This particular instrument has a repertoire centring on long operatic pieces and well-known songs with variations and the playing length of the books varies from five to fifteen minutes. One book differs from all the others in that it comprises a large number of short pieces and is arranged to be set in motion automatically by the clock which surmounts the upright cabinet. The music is arranged to play hourly by the release of a detent engaging with pins on the locking wheel of the clock's striking train. The music itself is stopped and started by a small lever one end of which engages with the stop sprag on the governor of the music-driving clockwork motor. The other end rests on the underside of the music sheet adjacent to the central drive-wheel. At suitable positions corresponding with the end of each tune, the metal reinforcing strip along the centre of the cardboard (and into which are punched the square drive holes) has a rectangular hole into which the lever can rise. When

◄ PLATE 84 a and b
Also with a to-and-fro handle lever wind is this
Nicole Frères *Grande Format* four-overture box
serial number 31021, *gamme* 1396 dating from
about 1850. The cylinder is 16·4 in. by 3·8 in. and
one revolution allows almost three minutes of
playing. The comb has an incredible 230 teeth and
the governor fly features a brass ring flywheel.

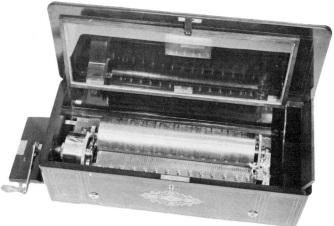

PLATE 85 ►
Another François Nicole overture box is this superb specimen
whose 10½ in. by 2¾ in. diameter cylinder plays on two combs
having a total of 200 teeth. Three airs are played, two Rossini
overtures each taking a full turn, and two shorter arias each
taking up half a revolution. As on the box in Plate 79, there is
a single extra pin fixed beyond the cylinder limits, and the
cylinder register comb is used. This piece has a very fine case.

◄ PLATE 86
The Nicole Frères *Grande Format* style
remained in vogue for a long while. Here is a
lever-wound example dating from about 1862.
The three control levers are plinth-mounted to
the right of the cylinder and the very fine comb
is made in two parts. Auber and Mozart is
played.

This piece is thought to be an experimental changeable-cylinder box. No maker's name has been found on it, but it appears as a perfectly normal key-wind box of the 1850–60 period. No doubt because of an arthritic owner, some clockmaker has, in the past, added a pair of extra winding pinions to make it easier to wind the spring. The problem in changing the cylinders in a musical movement of conventional format is that the governor is at one end of the cylinder, and the spring at the other. Remove the cylinder, and there is nothing to hold the spring power. The maker here provided a small index with a pointer which, as it turned, locked into the spring barrel teeth to hold the power and at the same time removed the locks on the cylinder arbor end clamps. The cylinders each play four airs and are 11 in. long. A virtually identical box in the Guinness collection bears the name Henri Capt on the brass tune sheet and the bedplate is stamped 'Karrer et Ce [sic] à Geneve'. Both boxes play cylinders stamped with tune titles before pinning. Moulinié Aîné has been seen stamped on similar items.

PLATE 88 ►

Before the advent of the interchangeable cylinder box, replacement cylinders had to be made expressly for one particular box and for this reason they were called *changeable* cylinders and the repertoire was only available at the time the box was made. This fine specimen, complete with flutina or reed organ, is in a case style associated with the hand of Greiner and also Bremond – a box on a small desk containing drawers for the spare cylinders. The piece seems to date from around the 1850s. The governor assembly is driven by a great wheel on the end of a short layshaft situated coaxially with the cylinder and so arranged that the cylinder can be lifted out without disturbing the power train. Lifting the cylinders in and out was achieved on these early pieces using two small hooks fitted with handles and for this reason they are styled 'glove-hook' boxes. This specimen has six cylinders each playing six airs.

◄ PLATE 89
Sublime Harmonie six-cylinder interchangeable box complete
with matching table containing the cylinders. Probably made
by Conchon, boxes such as this would be considered desirable
items of furniture and elegant pieces for the living room.

▲ PLATE 90
As distinct from the table-mounted interchangeable-cylinder musical
box, some were produced which were fitted with legs, spare cylinders
being stored in separate cases. This Nicole Frères instrument plays
cylinders 19½ in. long by 2½ in. in diameter and has no fewer than 15
spare ones.

◄ PLATE 91
The massive proportions of the mechanism of the Nicole Frères box seen above
can be appreciated from this interior view showing the two pairs of
parallel-mounted coaxial spring barrels, the *longue marche* style drive wheel, the
tune indicator and, at the right-hand end of the cylinder, a tune-selector. The
governor assembly is mounted by the short layshaft which is driven by the
large diameter slender wheel at one end and which drives the cylinder at the
other. The top of the endless is fitted with a speed regulator.

PLATE 92 ►
Interchangeable cylinder musical box made in Geneva by Baker-Troll. This two-comb *sublime harmonie* has three 11 in. cylinders each playing six airs. Coaxial spring barrels are fitted for long playing. The tune-indicator is engraved 'Troll & Baker, Geneva' and there is also a tune-selector.

▼ PLATE 93
Two-comb eight-air *sublime harmonie zither* three-cylinder interchangeable bearing the tune sheet of Junod. Governor has air brake with double-scolloped wings similar to Paillard style, and a horizontally-placed tune-indicator.

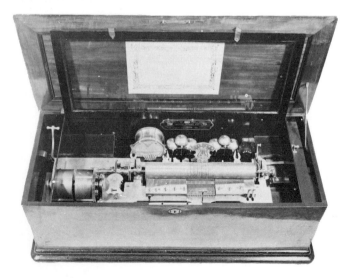

▲ PLATE 94
Paillard's *Gloria* interchangeable box *Mandoline zither* was a bold attempt to mass-produce this style. Although the governor assembly was at the right of the cylinder, it was driven by a shaft under the bedplate and was thus independent of the cylinder.

◄ PLATE 95
Nicole Frères *Imperial* orchestral interchangeable number 52809 has a 31-key reed organ. Compare with Plate 13, *Restoring Musical Boxes* and note many common factors such as the shape of the winding handle and also the fact that the organ is retractable. This box was made by George Baker (Baker-Troll).

▲ PLATE 96
Most ornate and complex interchangeable orchestral box probably made by Mojon, Manger and featuring twin coaxial springs, 18-note flutina reed organ and three sets of bells, the outer sets being struck by birds and the centre pair by a seated mandarin. At the far end of the right-hand comb can be seen the lever for disengaging the bells.

▼ PLATE 97
Mermod's style of interchangeable cylinder box is characterised by this instrument. Handle-wound from the right, the motor has a silent winding ratchet, visible far right front of spring barrel, a horizontal governor and endless, and the patented Parachute check, a device for locking the power in event of endless damage.

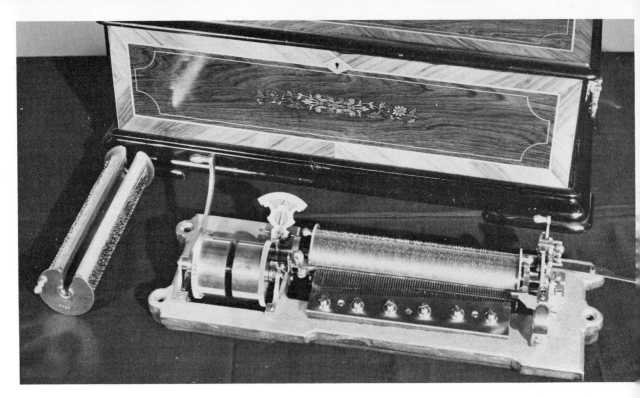

▲ PLATE 98
Detail showing the unusual arrangement of Paillard's Style 601 and 602. The instruction sheet for performing the changing routine was reproduced in the book *Clockwork Music* by the present author.

▲ PLATE 99
With the advent of the imitation-wood transfer or decal, became possible to decorate an entire musical-box case i very cheap, quick manner. This fine-looking musical bo is of plain wood with a transfer decoration!

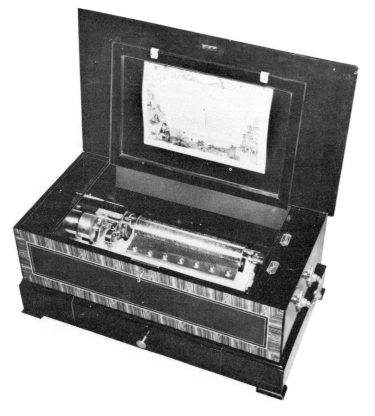

◄ PLATE 100
Another view of the transfer-decorated interchangeable cylinder box seen above. It is probably French and mad by L'Epée. The case has survived without too much damage to spoil the surface.

▲ PLATE 101
The revolver box seen here is a six-cylinder model made by George Baker, formerly Baker-Troll of Geneva. This complex and heavy mechanism features also a speed regulator, tune-indicator and tune-selector as well as an ornate case.

▲ PLATE 102
There were three sizes and numerous styles of the sleeve-playing Alexandra. This one stacks all its spare sleeves, each playing four tunes, at one side.

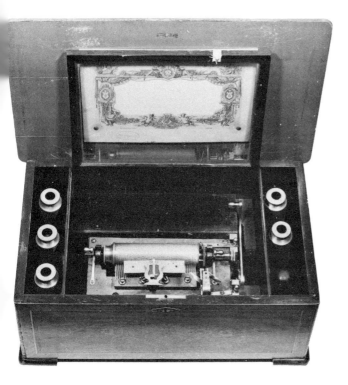

◄ PLATE 103
Another style of the Alexandra with the spare cylinders or sleeves stacked on wooden trees at each side. These instruments did not produce a very good sound although the mandrel for the sleeve was fairly solid.

◄ PLATE 104
Percussion accompaniments to musical boxes such as
drum and bells were originally concealed underneath
the bedplate where they could be heard but not seen.
This fine piece made by Henri Metert dates from
between 1850 and 1860 and has ten bells, nine of
which have two hammers each so allowing
quickly-repeating notes to be played. There is also a
drum with ten strikers – the drum head is vellum and
the damper is a triangular shaped piece of wire. Being
a very early example, the force of the hammer strokes
is very slight. This enables softly sounding, mellow
bells to be used which complement the music very
greatly – a quality so often lost in later boxes. The
drum is provided with a control lever to disengage it if
desired. The bells, however, are in play all the while.

PLATE 105 ►
In this view of the mechanism of the
Metert box can be seen the arrangement
of the bells and the drum. The bell
hammers all have adjustable heads and
the drum is provided with an extra
resonating chamber, not visible in this
picture. Many of these early boxes
featured drums which were mounted in
the case bottom and which could be
moved closer or further away from the
hammers by means of a screw. This
enabled the owner of a box to have the
volume of drum sound adjusted to his
taste.

From hidden accompaniments, by the changing of public tastes manufacturers gradually brought the bells into visible location. This sparked off a whole new breed of musical-box type names such as *Visible Bells*, *Bells in View* and so on, purely highlighting the fact that whereas boxes were available without bells which could be seen, some were now made with bells you could watch! This one has nine nicely-graduated bells which can be disengaged at will by the lever at the far right of the comb. Give the customer a feature – and then provide him with a means of disregarding it!

PLATE 107
Heller of Berne made some very fine orchestral boxes in later years. This piece, from about 1870, plays on six graduated bells.

▲ PLATE 108
This *Flute-Voix-Celestes* box features a simple, single-reed 16-note organ accompaniment and two coarse combs. There are 12 tunes.

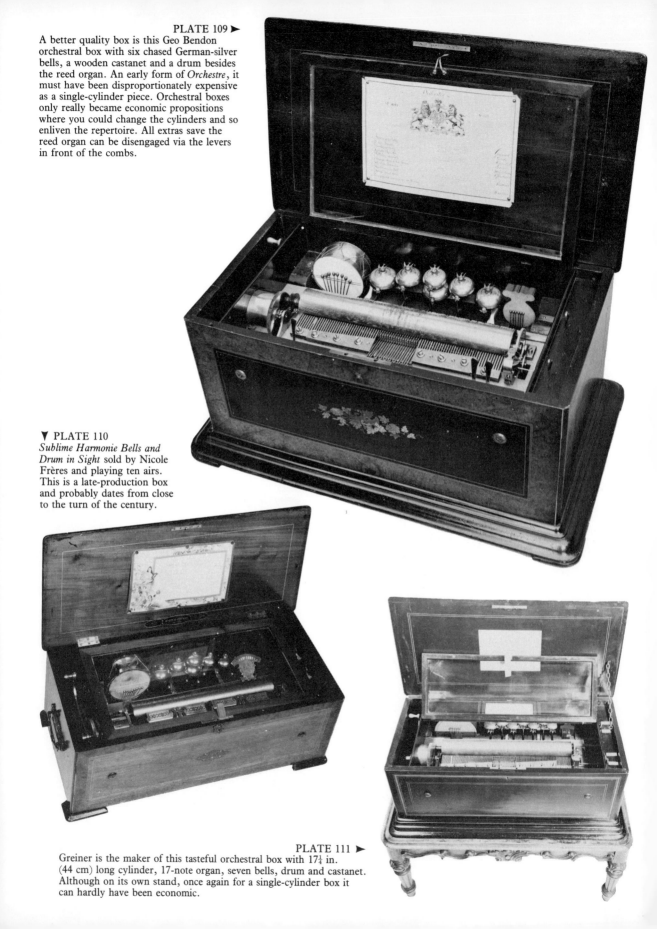

PLATE 109 ►
A better quality box is this Geo Bendon orchestral box with six chased German-silver bells, a wooden castanet and a drum besides the reed organ. An early form of *Orchestre*, it must have been disproportionately expensive as a single-cylinder piece. Orchestral boxes only really became economic propositions where you could change the cylinders and so enliven the repertoire. All extras save the reed organ can be disengaged via the levers in front of the combs.

▼ **PLATE 110**
Sublime Harmonie Bells and Drum in Sight sold by Nicole Frères and playing ten airs. This is a late-production box and probably dates from close to the turn of the century.

PLATE 111 ►
Greiner is the maker of this tasteful orchestral box with 17¼ in. (44 cm) long cylinder, 17-note organ, seven bells, drum and castanet. Although on its own stand, once again for a single-cylinder box it can hardly have been economic.

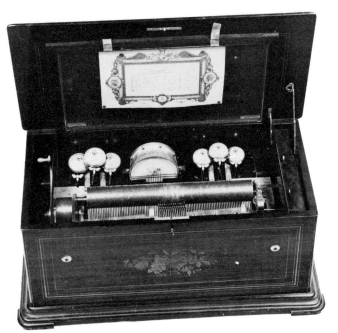

◄ PLATE 112
Made by Paillard, Vaucher, Fils, this eight-air orchestral
box has a 16 in. cylinder and plays a 15-note reed organ,
six bells (which have bee strikers) and a drum. The bells
are decorated with engine-turning. Ornamental strikers
such as these are often found finely enamelled in several
colours. Butterflies, bees, doves and moths are frequent
subjects for representation in metal as strikers.

▼ PLATE 113
This closely-packed orchestral mechanism offers six bells,
drum with eight strikers and castanet with six strikers.
Note that the cock-plate on the governor bracket has, in
addition to the jewel-retaining hole, a close-by oil hole.

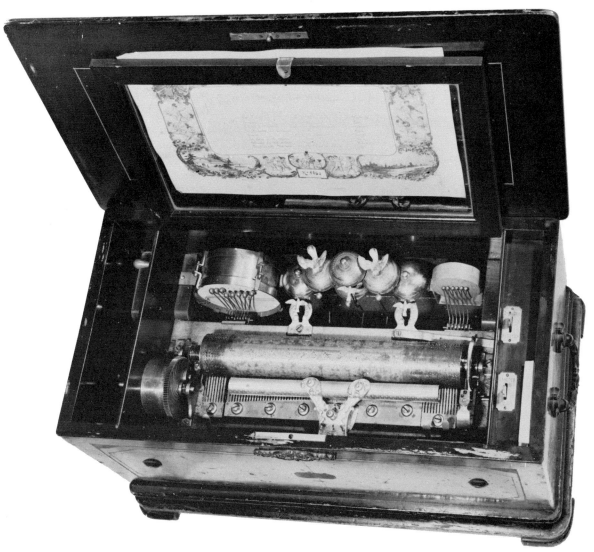

▲ PLATES 114 & 115 ►
Junod's unusual interchangeable *sublime harmonie* has motor and
governor under the bedplate and percussion accessory combs at centre.

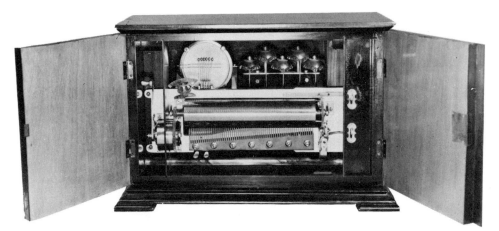

◄ PLATE 116
Upright style of orchestral
musical box, known as
buffet after its two
cupboard-style doors.
These were popular around
1895–1900 and were made
by Paillard, Ami Rivenc
and others. This one is a
Paillard Orchestra.

◄ PLATE 117
Mojon, Manger & Co. *Sublime-Harmonie Longue Marche* playing
12 tunes. The parallel twin coaxial motors – four in all – justified
a plaque on the bedplate reading: *This Musical Box Is Guaranteed
to Play Two and a Half Hours When Once Fully Wound Up –
Patented September 1879*. This was Aubert's British Patent
number 3711.

PLATE 118 ►
An unnecessarily complex way of extending the volume of
sound into a sort of super sublime harmonie was afforded by
the massive Duplex which played two similar cylinders on two
similar combs at once.

this happens, the other end of the lever stops the mechanism. The clock itself is an outstanding eight-day Lenzkirch movement with a Graham dead-beat escapement.

Libellion musical boxes are an undoubted rarity and, apart from five table models and the one clock variety, the marque appears extinct. Their delicate mechanism of sliding and sprung plectra and the friable card music probably accounts for their rarity.

LIPSIA (Lip-seer) (the Latinised name for Leipzig, City of the Lime Tree)
The Lipsia remains something of a mystery. A surviving example is in the Mekanisk Musik Museum, Copenhagen. It plays a $17\frac{3}{4}$ in. (45 cm) diameter disc and is contained in a stylish cabinet which is indicative of the first decade of the twentieth century. The door carries a painting of a nymph holding a shield bearing the initials W & R. Although several possibilities have been put forward (*The Music Box*, Vol. 7, p. 105), no definite information has yet come to light.

LOCHMANN ORIGINAL
At some time after early 1900, Paul Lochmann, founder of the company which made the Symphonion (q.v.), severed his connections with the company and, with Ernst Luder, established the Original Musikwerke Paul Lochmann GmbH at Am Bahnhof, Zeulenroda (Thuringia). The date of foundation of the company is given as 1900. By 1902, an office had been opened in Leipzig at Thomasgasse 4, Leipzig II and this was run by Paul Luder. By 1909 the address was Querstrasse 15–17.

The product of the Original Musikwerke was a developed form of the disc musical box which, while owing much to Symphonion technology, also incorporated the very best of eclectic technology in not just mechanical instruments but musical acoustics as well. These musical boxes were all called the Lochmann 'Original' written in just that style with the word 'Original' in inverted commas. The instruments incorporated spruce soundboards and, on the larger models, a shaped bridge or sound-bar linked musical movement bedplate with soundboard to produce a greater volume and purity of sound than was capable of being produced by most other contemporary instruments.

The small sizes of table instrument incorporated a transverse winding-shaft which meant that the spring could be wound by inserting the handle into either side. The $8\frac{1}{4}$ in. (21 cm) size was centre-wound from the disc spindle and the 11 in. (28 cm) table model was wound from inside the case via a vertical spindle close to the edge of the disc. Larger table models had the spring motor and controls all mounted inside the case to the right of the disc. The acoustic case with its recessed soundboard and sound-bar (it could not be called a sound-post) meant that this had to be a separate compartment with a cover in the same manner as with the Adler (q.v.), Fortuna (q.v.) and similar. However, unlike these other musical boxes which allowed the clockwork to remain visible through glazed covers, Lochmann concealed the 'Original' clockwork beneath polished wood covers.

Tubular bells feature in a number of the larger table instruments as well as some of the upright and wall-hanging variants. Hemispherical bells were also used on some of the largest models, as were glockenspiel bars. Discs had Polyphon-type, standard projections and the disc edges were beaded for stiffness. The start position was usually indicated by a long slender arrow pointing to the edge of the disc and punched out of the metal.

Lochmann later went on to produce a number of large, disc-operated piano orchestrions and then made barrel-operated piano orchestrions and phonographs.

Nine different disc sizes have been determined but the tenth size, for piano-orchestrion without musical comb-work, is included in the identification. The sizes were: $5\frac{1}{8}$ in. (13 cm); $6\frac{15}{16}$ in. (18 cm); $8\frac{1}{4}$ in. (21 cm); 11 in. (28 cm); $15\frac{3}{8}$ in. (39 cm); $16\frac{15}{16}$ in. (43 cm) with 8 dulcimers; $21\frac{3}{8}$ in. (55 cm); $24\frac{3}{8}$ in. (62 cm), same as preceding size as regards musical arrangement but includes 12 dulcimers; $29\frac{1}{8}$ in. (74 cm) includes 12 dulcimers, bass drum, spare drum and cymbal; 32 in. (81 cm) piano-orchestrion. This model was also available with a phonograph-playing attachment.

Case styles were generally more modern in appearance than those of Symphonion and the use of marquetry and appliqué fretwork featured on some of the largest instruments.

Tonally, the Lochmann 'Original' is pleasing, loud without being brash, and rich in case-induced resonance. Musically, the discs are well set up without over-embellishment. Lochmann uses his bells, as with all other musical-box makers, to double the top melody line. Only rarely does the bell play any harmonic or contrapuntal part.

Manufacture of the Lochmann instruments ceased with the outbreak of war in 1914. Sadly, coming as it did at practically the end of the disc musical-box era, due acknowledgement in terms of success never came the way of the 'Original'. Ousted by the challenge of the gramophone and the rising market for barrel orchestrions, it cannot have remained in production more than a few years. However, it would seem that large numbers were made and they are not all that uncommon in Germany today. Whereas all small musical boxes tend to sound alike, it is in the larger sizes that the Lochmann 'Original' scores and justly earns praise for its excellent sound.

LYRAPHON (Li-ra-fon)
Two specimens only of the Lyraphon appear to be known – one in the Bornand collection, New York, and the other belonging to Mrs Mark Davis of Toledo, Ohio. A manivelle, i.e. hand-cranked with no drive spring, it plays a $6\frac{1}{2}$ in. (16·5 cm) disc in a shallow case and is wound from the front. Inside the lid is a printed card reading 'Lyraphon No. 3 PATENT' but providing no reference as to which patent. There is a resemblance to the Orphenion manivelle both as regards layout and proportions as well as the style of the printed card. Were there, one wonders, Lyraphons Numbers 1 and 2?

MIRA (Mee-ra)
After the introduction of the Stella (q.v.), the Swiss manufacturer Mermod Frères of Ste-Croix appears to have had fresh thoughts about disc machine mechanisms. Certainly the Stella, with its sprung starwheels, unusual comb attachment – one was mounted vertically under the starwheels – and projectionless discs, was an uncompromisingly complex piece of machinery and, although it remained in production for a long while, Mermod probably felt that it could capture a larger section of the market if it introduced a disc musical box along more conventional and thereby cheaper lines. The result was the Mira, introduced in 1902.

With the slogan 'Unequaled [sic] for Sweetness, Harmony and Volume of Tone' and the legend 'Best in Construction', Mermod's Mira reverted to standard technology for much of its mechanism. The Stella-style disc pressure bar was retained, but a conventional juxtaposition of the duplex combs was used along with normal starwheels and discs with projections. The discs themselves were reinforced around the periphery by a circumferential bead and the drive holes were formed by swaging to produce a disc which was both very stiff and strong.

222

Similar to the Stella (only the largest model of which was available as either a console model or vertical), the Mira was available as a table model for the small sizes and as a console model for the larger variants. Although the advertisements for the Stella made a feature of the projectionless discs, saying that the absence of 'pins' allowed a greater playing time, the Mira was claimed also to play 'at least one-fifth longer than any other music-box of same size'. Presumably the presence of 'pins' was not as much of a hazard as Mermod had at first considered!

The Mira was manufactured without case and shipped to the distributor who was responsible for the fitting of the mechanism into locally made cabinets. European-made and American-made cases were just not of Mermod manufacture. Expressly to the order of Chicago music-dealers Lyon & Healy, the Mira was also manufactured under the stencil-brand Empress; all machines marked Empress are therefore Mira machines sold through Lyon & Healy.

Seven sizes were made: $4\frac{1}{2}$ in. (11·4 cm); 7 in. (17·8 cm); 8 in. (20·3 cm); $9\frac{1}{2}$ in. (24·1 cm); 12 in. (30·5 cm); $15\frac{1}{2}$ in. (39·4 cm); $18\frac{1}{2}$ in. (47 cm). The $15\frac{1}{2}$ in. (39·4 cm) model was also available as a phonopectine with gramophone attachment for playing Victor phonograph records. This was called the Miraphon or Miraphone (for the English and American market).

MONARCH (Mon-ark)

It seems strange that two musical boxes, both very similar, should be produced so late in the musical-box era, and in New Jersey to boot, with so little information to be found concerning either. Yet this is the case with the two instruments made by the American Music Box Co., Hoboken. Hughes Ryder of Cranford, N.J., has researched the company and found that it was capitalised for $150,000 in 1896. Émile Cuendet, who had come from Ste-Croix to America to work for the Jacot company in New York, took up fifty of the $100 shares and was president. Isaac Ingleson was treasurer.

The design of the Monarch and its successor, the Triumph, fell to Cuendet and Frank J. Bernard, who between them, individually and severally, were granted a number of patents assigned to the AMBC. US Patents number 554906 dated 18 February 1896; 570898 dated 10 November 1896; and 572950 dated 15 December 1896 were all in Bernard's name and 577839 dated 2 March 1897 is in the joint names.

The one instrument seen plays a disc $15\frac{1}{2}$ in. (39·4 cm) in diameter and bears a strong resemblance to the similar-sized Regina (q.v.). Disc drive is by scoop-shaped peripheral openings on one type of disc which also featured normal Regina or Polyphon-type projections but with a tiny top-surface 'pip' at the tail, yet on another disc of the same size the projections are formed by the punching up of a 'leg-and-foot' form of projection. An examination of two discs of the same piece of music for a Monarch and Regina and featuring the common form of projection revealed an identical arrangement of music and the discs appeared to have been punched using the same master. The discs seen are in the 2000 series.

The second machine which the company made was the Triumph, which again was made to play a $15\frac{1}{2}$ in. (39·4 cm) Regina-compatible disc. This instrument, though, has a different form of projection created by first bending up at right angles to the undersurface of the disc a small rectangular tab of sufficient length to operate the starwheels. Behind this and at right angles to the first projection, a second projection is punched up. This one, a quarter-circle in shape, supports and adds strength to the first.

Both the Triumph and the Monarch use combs which are identical and very similar in tone and style to that of the 15½ in. (39·4 cm) Regina. The instruments themselves feature plain cast-iron bedplates devoid of any name, but externally the cases look similar to the Regina table models.

MONOPOL (Mono-pol)

After his first and largely experimental disc musical box, the Ehrlich (q.v.), Friederich Ernst Paul Ehrlich perfected a more conventional form of instrument playing metal discs with perforations and using combs and starwheels similar to the Symphonion (q.v.). This instrument he called the Monopol and production appears to have begun not later than 1892 and possibly as early as 1890. Other than the patents described under the section devoted to Ehrlich, the other traceable patent relating to comb-playing musical movements was British Patent number 10515 dated 29 May 1893 and related to a design for a tune sheet with projections and a machine for making it.

Monopol machines were produced in a wide variety of styles including a number of hand-cranked manivelles of various types. Larger boxes comprised table, wall-mounting and free-standing models. The 7½ in. (19·5 cm) size was also used in 'Gloriosa' Christmas-tree stands as an alternative to stands made with Kalliope (q.v.), Polyphon (q.v.) and Symphonion (q.v.) movements. Discs were usually of a golden-brown lacquered steel, sometimes in blue, and almost always with a complex golden-yellow design silk-screen-printed on the surface. Some late Monopol discs are plain brown lacquer with the title and the word 'Monopol' screen-printed in small yellow letters. Disc drive methods varied widely. The smaller sizes were virtually identical with similar-sized Symphonion discs with the exception of the 7½ in. (19·5 cm), which was peripherally dimple-driven. The Monopol Excelsior played 21¾ in. (55·2 cm) diameter discs and this, too, employed a dimple drive. The drive holes on the 17³⁄₁₆ in. (43·6 cm) were dumb-bell-shaped, i.e. a waisted rectangle.

Twelve sizes have been determined as follows: 5¾ in. (14·6 cm) manivelle; 7½ in. (19·5 cm); 8½ in. (21·6 cm); 9⅜ in. (23·8 cm); 11⅞ in. (30·2 cm); 13⅝ in. (34 cm); 14⅛ in. (36 cm); 17³⁄₁₆ in. (43·6 cm); 20½ in. (52 cm); 21¾ in. (55·2 cm); 26⅜ in. (70 cm); 32 in. (81·3 cm).

A most unusual model was the giant Monopol Gloria Musik Automat which played two 26⅜ in. (70 cm) diameter discs at once, each on parallel unison combs. The unusual feature lay in the fact that both discs were driven by the same large-diameter drive-cog mounted parallel to the plane of the discs with contrate teeth so that the discs rotated in opposite directions. This was the only twin-disc machine ever to operate on this principle. To operate, the two disc pressure bars were hinged to a common axis supported above the contrate wheel and locking on the disc centre spindles in the normal way, one at the top and one at the bottom for the two discs.

The Monopol remained in production by the Fabrik Leipziger Musikwerke (formerly Paul Ehrlich) at Mockernschestrasse 30d in Leipzig-Gohlis until about 1903, when the Fabrik Leipziger Musikwerke was reconstituted following the departure of Paul Ehrlich. Re-established in 1904 as the Neue Leipziger Musikwerke A. Buff-Hedinger with Wwe Emilie Buff-Hedinger in charge, the business was expanded to Mockernschestrasse 29–33 and Herlosssohnstrasse 1–4 for the production of the Premier piano-player and player piano, the Primavolta electropneumatic player piano and another instrument which incorporated a piano and xylophone called the Toccaphon. Meanwhile, Paul Ehrlich's son, Emil, founded in 1903 a company called Ehrlich's Musikwerke Emil Ehrlich at Magdeburgerstrasse 13 in Gohlis, where he produced the Orphobella piano player and an organette called the Ehrlich Instrument.

At the most, Monopol musical boxes were produced for only twelve years yet they were manufactured in large quantities and were well made with good tone and well arranged music. A characteristic of almost all models was the rich decoration cast into the bedplates in the form of arabesque design.

NEW CENTURY

The New Century is a highly sophisticated musical box which in many ways is superior to the Sirion. It is believed to have been devised using the Sirion's mechanics as a base upon which further development was made. A line of design continuity exists in that there is a strong resemblance between the New Century and the technology of the Sirion with its Mermod association. Unlike the Sirion, however, the New Century was made in two forms – first as a normal disc-playing mechanism, and a second variant which employed the shifting-disc technology. Q. David Bowers believes the New Century to have been manufactured by Mermod. Certainly Alfred Keller, co-patentee of the Sirion mechanism, subsequently appears to have moved his home from Leipzig (where he was designated as a resident at the time of the Sirion patent) to Ste-Croix by 1904. Subsequent Mermod disc machines employed Keller's patent mechanisms which all postdate 1902 in Swiss Patents and 1904 in US Patents.

What is certain, however, is that Mermod were recognised as manufacturers of musical movements only, these being shipped to main agents in other parts of Europe (including Great Britain) and America. *Musical Opinion* No. 260 of 1899 includes an item concerning Alfred Paillard, London agent for Mermod's musical boxes, which concludes: 'The mechanism is made by watchmakers in Switzerland, and the cases in England . . .'. Of the New Century machines which survive (I have personally seen only five), they fall neatly into two classes: those obviously cased in America, and those cased in Europe. An example of the latter is an instrument housed in a typically Central European style of cabinet not unlike a Polyphon upright model, and bearing a name on the case which reads 'Henri Vidoudez'. Vidoudez was in business at Rue du Jura 2, Ste-Croix in Switzerland for some while prior to 1898 (in which year he was awarded a medal at the Paris Exposition) but his business had ceased by 1909. An advertisement* states that he was a manufacturer of musical boxes, adding: 'Spécialité de pièces automatiques avec cylindres et plaques de rechange'. The probability here is that Vidoudez was one of probably a number of 'makers' who bought movements from Mermod Frères (who were also in Ste-Croix) and provided their own cases. The known Vidoudez example is a normal, single-play disc machine.

Significantly, the only shifting-disc New Century models of which I know exist in America in American-made cases. This is not to say that *all* American-cased models are disc-shifters. The connection between Aristides H. Jacot in America and Mermod might suggest that the assembly of disc-shifting New Centuries was something peculiar to America.

At least three types of disc, all of $18\frac{9}{16}$ in. (47·2 cm) diameter, have been seen, each operating in a different manner. The basic musical movement employs four combs each of 78 teeth arranged so that each a pair of unison combs is set on either side of the centre spindle.

* Reproduced in *Au Temps des Boîtes à Musique* by Daniel Bonhôte, p. 113, and *The Music Box*, Vol. 6, p. 135.

The discs, which have 'leg and foot' type projections, are held in position by two pressure bars hinged from either side of the diameter so that the right bar locks over the left, right being adjacent to the drive gear which engages in round-ended rectangular peripheral holes in the disc.

Discs in the 8000 series use *two* revolutions to play one tune, the disc shifting its centre after one turn to play the variation. Discs in the 4000 series have broader (wider) projections and play only one tune. The third type of disc, which I have not seen but which is recorded by Q. David Bowers* is apparently in the 6000 series and, like the 8000 series, plays two revolutions for one piece of music.

The New Century, in any form, is a very scarce instrument and is accorded a greater rarity than the Sirion (q.v.), itself a most uncommon piece.

OLYMPIA

After the legal controversy concerning patent infringement with the Criterion (q.v.), the New Jersey company of F. G. Otto & Sons introduced its third musical box, the Olympia, in 1898. It used the same type of zinc discs as the Criterion and was made in four sizes.

The last date so far seen for an advertisement concerning the Olympia is 1900 and one is tempted to suggest that, as with the Capital (q.v.) and the Criterion, Otto's attempts at entering the fast-booming American disc musical-box market were anything but successful. Regina (q.v.) with the company policy of big-spend advertising, undoubtedly took most of the trade while the upcoming Symphonion Manufacturing Co., with its line of Imperial Symphonion (q.v.) musical boxes, formed a formidable second line of defence. The company remained in business to produce an automatic piano (the Pianette) with punched metal tune-sheet patented in November 1906, but by 1909 only electrical goods were being made.

The Olympia appeared in the following sizes: $8\frac{1}{2}$ in. (21·6 cm) with discs in the 2000 series; $11\frac{5}{8}$ in. (29·5 cm); $15\frac{5}{8}$ in. (40 cm) with discs in the 4000 series; $20\frac{1}{2}$ in. (52 cm) with discs in the 6000 series. There was also a 27 in. (70 cm) model.

ORPHENION (Or-fee-nee-yon)

The Orphenion was devised by Bruno Ruckert, who began production in 1893 at Sedanstrasse 5–7, Leipzig. His mechanism contained a number of then unusual features, the most noticeable of which was certainly his method of rotating the comb-plucking starwheels from the disc. In place of formal projections, Ruckert merely formed scoop-shaped indentations in his disc which was made of zinc. He secured a British Patent for this – number 6941 – on 4 April 1893.

In the summer of 1898, the Adler (q.v.) factory was moved into Ruckert's premises and, although no direct reference can be found to suggest that this marked the closure of the Orphenion enterprise, it is significant that Ruckert did no more advertising after his 1897 catalogue (*see* Bowers, *Encyclopedia of Automatic Musical Instruments*, p. 132) and that in 1900 Ludwig Hupfeld, who had operated as a sales outlet for the Orphenion, advertised a large clearance sale of Orphenions 'just like new'. This was indeed the last reference to the Orphenion.

A range of models was produced starting with a 32-note, $5\frac{7}{32}$ in. (13·2 cm) disc handcranked manivelle which was not unlike the Lyraphon (q.v.) and including table instru-

* *Encyclopedia of Automatic Musical Instruments*, p. 127.

ments, wall-mounted models, and upright free-standing specimens, one of which was similar in appearance to the Symphonion Haydn and Eroica style. A feature of the table models was the exposed motor mounted after the fashion of the cylinder box, but most unusual was the air brake of the escapement or governor. This was in the form of two metal discs attached to a cross-staff so that it operated in a cut-out in the large, contoured bedplate.

It is my personal opinion that the Orphenion has one of the finest and most subtle sounds of all disc machines. The scarcity of these instruments is to be regretted and is due not just to their short-lived production but to the short life of the disc projections. These are subjected to three different types of wear. First is the gradual flattening-out of the projections which can, of course, be corrected with care and understanding. Then there is the wearing away of the leading edge of the scoop which has the effect of systematically altering the musical timing as the scoop wears back and so turns the starwheel later and later. The third type of wear is similar to the second and comes about through the scoops becoming slightly flattened. The starwheel points scrape along the underneath of the scoops until they are worn paper-thin whereupon they fracture and develop virtual slits, which destroys the music on the disc.

Six different disc sizes have been determined for the Orphenion: $5\frac{7}{32}$ in. (13·2 cm); $8\frac{1}{4}$ in. (21 cm); $10\frac{11}{16}$ in. (27 cm); $13\frac{1}{2}$ in. (34 cm); $16\frac{1}{8}$ in. (40·5 cm); 26 in. (66 cm). The smallest size exists as a manivelle and is referred to as Model 30.

ORPHEUS (Or-fay-us)
The Orpheus was made in Leipzig-Neuschönefeld by Ludwig & Wild and introduced on to the market in 1897 and factored through Breitkopf & Härtel the following year. Portability was not one aspect of which the manufacturers were proud and they stolidly proclaimed the sheer bulk and weight of the largest model which stood 86 inches high, 30 inches wide and 20 inches deep and played discs $22\frac{5}{8}$ in. in diameter on a comb of 220 teeth.* The table models typified the new style which was exemplified by Adler, Fortuna and Lochmann Original table instruments in that the motor was mounted to the right of the disc and covered by a glazed panel, in the Orpheus this being of elaborately etched glass.

An immediately noticeable characteristic of the Orpheus is that the disc drive holes are square-shaped as distinct, for example, from Polyphon's circular ones. Vertical models have richly decorated, etched-glass door panels. The table model rotates its disc anticlockwise.

Two sizes have so far been determined: $11\frac{3}{4}$–12 in. (about 25 cm), and $22\frac{5}{8}$ in. (58 cm).

PERFECTION
The Perfection disc-playing musical box appeared in two sizes – table models playing discs $10\frac{5}{8}$ in. (27 cm) and $15\frac{1}{2}$ in. (39·8 cm) in diameter. It was manufactured by the Perfection Music Box Company, Columbia Road and Lincoln Street, Jersey City, New Jersey. Production began during 1898 and continued until early in 1900, when it moved to Newark where it continued until about 1901 employing about thirty-two people.

The Perfection, described by Hughes Ryder who researched the instrument, was anything but perfect, being manufactured to include a design of damper which was extremely inferior. The invention of Julius Wellner of Jersey City and the subject of US Patent number 585246 dated 29 June 1897, the damping system was simplicity itself! No complicated wires or metal

* Arthur Ord-Hume, *Clockwork Music*, p. 109.

strips to set up and adjust – just a two-piece starwheel with a centre of soft felt which protruded sufficiently to damp the vibrating comb tooth before plucking. Of course, once the felt wore (as it very soon did), the Perfection became imperfect.

Instruments are today very scarce and exist only in the United States. The two models produced employed twin, unison combs (double the damper wear for a start!) and played zinc discs with rectangular drive holes. Subsequently, Wellner designed a self-changer disc musical-box (the subject of British Patent number 24378 dated 7 December 1899) but it is not thought that this was ever built.

POLYHYMNIA (Poly-him-nea)
Not to be confused with the Swiss Polymnia (q.v.), the Polyhymnia was marketed by the Metall-Industrie Schönebeck A.-G. which was founded about 1900 by Robert Treskow at Friedrichstrasse 27–28, Schönebeck. The business was still in existence in 1903 but had disappeared by the 1909 directories. The company advertised 'Duplex & Polyhymnia Musikwerke', and illustrated an upright instrument similar in overall appearance to a $19\frac{5}{8}$ in. (50 cm) Polyphon with a decorated glass panel in the door and the name written in large letters around the upper portion of the disc. Was this a stencil-brand from Leipzig in a custom case? One table model has been seen by Q. David Bowers, who says it bears a close resemblance to the Kalliope. This one plays a $7\frac{5}{8}$ in. (19·5 cm) disc.

POLYMNIA (Pol-lim-nea)
After the introduction of the Gloria (q.v.), the Geneva-based Société Anonyme Fabriques Réunies produced the Polymnia (not to be confused with the Polyhymnia, q.v.). This instrument was in some respects similar to the Gloria but it differed in one major respect. On 3 September 1902, Jean Billon-Haller of Geneva, one of the three partners in the SAFR, was granted Swiss Patent number 26589 for a method of operating starwheels from a musical-box tune disc using, instead of punched projections, a small dent or dimple. The instrument cannot have enjoyed good sales since today it is even scarcer than the Gloria – and there are very few of them to be found.

Two sizes have been determined. The first plays a disc $8\frac{1}{16}$ in. (20·5 cm) in diameter on a comb of 38 teeth and the direction of rotation is clockwise. The second is $11\frac{3}{4}$ in. (30 cm) in diameter on a comb of 54 teeth and the direction of rotation is anti-clockwise.

POLYPHON (Pol-e-fon)
When Gustave Brachhausen and Paul Riessner together left the Göhlis factory of Symphonion (q.v.) some time in 1899, they had but one thought in mind – to better the disc musical box and to build up from scratch what was to become Leipzig's biggest musical-box manufacturing company. Whereas Kuhno-Lochmann did not become the German equivalent of a corporation until 1900, Brachhausen and Riessner started out the way they intended to carry on and the Polyphon Musikwerke A.-G. (corporation) was established in 1890. The address was Bahnhofstrasse 61, Leipzig-Wahren, and the business was financed by the Leipzig bankers, Knauth, Nachod & Kühne, which also financed the establishment of Regina (q.v.) in America. As a public corporation, shares were available to the private investor as well.

In the years that followed, the Polyphon corporation grew into a giant and at the peak of its success – in 1899 – almost 1,000 were employed at the plant. Although it exceeded in size the company which sired it and its product – Symphonion – it chose to produce a clearly defined product line centred on only fourteen disc sizes or types. This was two-thirds of the complex product line selected by the former company. In spite of this, though, the styles of Polyphon musical box manufactured between 1890 and the immediate pre-1914 war years proliferated: no catalogue of models could ever hope to be complete. To add to the historian's problems today, a number of limited-run and apparently custom models were made. These included musical movements built into bureaux, china cabinets and bookcases. I myself possess two models which, while being quite original, are unlike anything catalogued in the many Polyphon lists of wares.

Stylistically, the Polyphon was in production long enough to encompass more than two decades of changing tastes. A clear example is the 15½ in. (39·8 cm) model which was first made in a richly styled, corniced and embellished case and went through a period of plain cabinets into a hinterland of German rococo.

Gustave Brachhausen left for America to establish the Regina company in September 1892, leaving Riessner on his own. Despite the success of the 1899–1901 period, Riessner decided to look further afield and ensure the future by product diversification. Initially cars were built, beginning with the Oldsmobile under licence. It differed from the American original in a number of details and between 1904 and 1906 was known as the Gazelle. Later it took the name which was applied to all Polyphon cars – Polymobil – and was built until 1908. Popular in its time, it was available with wheel instead of tiller steering. A four-seat version was also built with the engine under the front seat. In 1907, two of the company's own-design cars were introduced, the two-cylinder 8/10PS and the four-cylinder 16/20PS. After 1909, a new range of models appeared under the name of Dux. Meanwhile, in 1903, Paul Riessner patented a typewriter very similar to the Hammond even down to having two semicircular rows of square keys. This was the Polygraph. In 1905, a new model was launched with a straight three-row universal keyboard. A slightly different model came along in 1907, but production ceased in 1909. Then came the Polyphone pianos, pneumatically operated players, barrel orchestrions and phonographs. The years immediately preceding the war were difficult ones and the company off-loaded much of its inventory of musical boxes in order to concentrate on electric pianos, phonographs and cars. After the war, in 1919, Polyphon bought up the then almost bankrupt Deutsche-Grammophon record company.

Polyphon musical boxes were all well designed and well made with a high degree of craftsmanship. The smaller models, as with the Symphonion, were wound by the use of a lever which protruded through a slot in the front of the case. The 19⅝ in. (50 cm) model was fitted with a novel and practical sprung guard to the starwheels so that, when changing the discs, there was no risk of damage to either disc or starwheels caused by carelessly or accidentally striking the disc edge into the protruding starwheels. The moment the disc was correctly positioned, this guard was pushed back out of the way. Riessner also patented two significant improvements to the mechanism. The first was to incorporate a friction clutch into the winding-handle so that it was impossible to overwind the spring. He also patented a bursting link secured with a soft rivet so that in the event of an overwind or winding the wrong way, in spite of the clutch handle, the drive gear would break free with safety.

Musically, the Polyphon was well set up and most of the larger-sized discs showed subtle and sympathetic use of the chromatic resources available. If the Symphonion tone was more silvery, Polyphon gained a wider acceptance in the rental market because it produced a louder and less bass-reverberative sound which was more acceptable to public houses, beer gardens, funfairs and suchlike. In fact of all disc musical boxes it seems that the Polyphon was the only one to gain extensive popularity with rental outlets.

Of the fourteen sizes of disc made, six are significant in that they can be paired as for instruments without and with bells. The comb music arrangement on the $11\frac{1}{4}$ in. (28·1 cm) is identical to that of the $14\frac{1}{8}$ in. (36 cm) which has the addition of twelve bells. Others are the $15\frac{1}{2}$ in. (39·8 cm) and $17\frac{1}{2}$ in. (45 cm); and the $19\frac{5}{8}$ in. (50 cm) and $22\frac{1}{2}$ in. (56 cm). On each of these three pairs, if you could imagine cutting the extra diameter off the larger disc, then it would play perfectly on the smaller since the extra diameter concerns only the bells, which were always arranged on the outside part of the disc diameter.

The fourteen sizes were: $6\frac{1}{2}$ in. (16·5 cm) made as a manivelle or spring-driven, some with four bells playing the bass notes; $8\frac{1}{8}$ in. (20·7 cm) made as a manivelle or spring-driven; $9\frac{5}{8}$ in. (24·4 cm); $9\frac{3}{4}$ in. (24·7 cm) with six bells; $11\frac{1}{4}$ in. (28·1 cm); $14\frac{1}{8}$ in. (36 cm) with twelve bells; $15\frac{1}{2}$ in. (39·8 cm); $17\frac{1}{2}$ in. (45 cm) with twelve bells; $19\frac{5}{8}$ in. (50 cm); $22\frac{1}{2}$ in. (56 cm) with sixteen bells; $24\frac{1}{2}$ in. (62·5 cm); $25\frac{1}{4}$ in. (63 cm) projectionless discs for piano; 28 in. (71 cm) for piano; 32 in. (80 cm) for piano. The last three sizes are included for reference only since they did not play on musical combs. The largest size was the Polyphon Concerto, a piano with drums and cymbal.

Several models of the Polyphon were produced as phonopectines, which would play either flat gramophone records or play comb discs. Known in German as the Polygraphon and in English as the Gramo-Polyphon, sizes were the $11\frac{1}{4}$ in. (28·1 cm); $14\frac{1}{8}$ in. (36 cm); $15\frac{1}{2}$ in. (39·8 cm) and $24\frac{1}{2}$ in. (62·5 cm). The large Concerto piano was also made with a phonographic attachment.

REGINA (Re-jine-er or Re-jeen-er)

The Regina Music Box Co. was founded in Rahway, New Jersey, by Gustave Brachhausen, who established the Leipzig factory of Polyphon (q.v.), having originally worked for Symphonion (q.v.). The 35-year-old Brachhausen left for America in September 1892 and the first premises of the American company were in Jersey City and were set up with Paul Riessner and Johannas J. Korner, both Polyphon directors in Leipzig, as directors with Brachhausen. Finance was provided by the Leipzig bank which had backed the foundation of the Polyphon corporation – Knauth, Nachod & Kühne.

The company's first tasks centred on securing fresh patents and obtaining US Patents for those inventions already patented in Germany and England. Hitherto, since America had had no musical-box industry worth speaking of, the Polyphon company had not bothered to incur the cost of protecting itself against infringement of all its inventions in America. However, there had been some exceptions and these were the key patents, namely the arrangement whereby Lochmann's invention of the practical musical disc could be used, and the Brachhausen & Riessner invention of practical discs and machines for making them. That is why most Regina discs bear the legend 'Patented December 17, 1889 and June 27, 1893'. The first is the date of US Patent numbers 417649 and 417650 granted to Oskar Paul Lochmann covering discs and dampers. The second is of US Patent numbers 500369 to 500374 concerning Brachhausen & Riessner's tune sheets, dampers and other associated details.

During this period, the Regina company factored instruments imported from Leipzig, mostly, it seems, assembled in America from German-made components and contained in locally made cabinets. In 1894, the company moved to 54 West Cherry Street, Rahway, and here the production of wholly American-made Regina musical boxes began. The Leipzig styles were closely followed for some while, but, significantly, some sizes and styles were rapidly dropped and others exclusive to the Regina range introduced. For example, the smallest Regina was $8\frac{1}{2}$ in. (21·6 cm) in disc size, compared with Polyphon's $6\frac{1}{2}$ in. (16·5 cm). Whereas the largest size of conventional table model (this excludes the folding-top models wherein the disc was allowed to project considerably over the width of the case and deals only with those which contained the disc while playing) was $19\frac{5}{8}$ in. (50 cm), every model of the Regina was at some time made in a horizontal format, the largest being in console style.

From Polyphon's range of fourteen sizes, Regina retained only two – the $11\frac{1}{4}$ in. (28·1 cm) – this is universally and incorrectly termed '11 in.' – and the $15\frac{1}{2}$ in. (39·8 cm), and added five of its own to make a total of just seven sizes, nine if you include the 32 in. (80 cm) Regina Concerto which was identical in mechanics with the Polyphon Concerto and was not a comb-playing musical box at all, but a disc-operated piano orchestrion, and the $12\frac{1}{8}$ in. (30·8 cm) Regina Chime Clock which played only on bells. The $11\frac{1}{4}$ in. (28·1 cm) was a centre-drive disc and a peripherally driven version was made – the $12\frac{1}{4}$ in. (31·2 cm). Musically, the discs were identical, the only difference being the method of drive.

Within a few short years, Regina held something around 80 or 90 per cent of the American disc musical-box market and, during its musical-box era (from 1892 to 1921) the company produced 100,000 instruments, and at the peak around 1900, sales exceeded $2 million per year. Skilled workers were imported from Leipzig and Switzerland and the best production techniques made use of and a maximum of 325 workers employed. The first Regina musical box was despatched on 15 October 1894 and the last musical movements produced as late as 1919, despatch of the final box being in 1921.

Worsening market conditions which first appeared in 1901 resulted in the Leipzig backers (Knauth, Nachod & Kühne) putting in their own management team in 1903. A. Knauth now became president, P. Kühne vice-president and J. B. Furber general manager. Now restyled 'The Regina Company', a hand-pumped vacuum cleaner was introduced followed by an electric model in 1909. Between 1900 and 1922, the company manufactured many products ranging from player pianos to New Era printing-presses, from floor polishers to phonographs, but the company could not stave off bankruptcy and in 1922 filed its petition. In 1924, the company was reconstituted and remains in business today as a leading manufacturer of floor-care equipment. In 1957, the company moved to new premises close by and the old musical-box building now houses diverse industries.

The Regina stands today as one of the best musical boxes of the disc type the world has ever known. Analysed from every standpoint, the Regina shows in a favourable light. Casework was always of the highest order and represents the best of American craftsmanship at a time when other American musical-box makers were using cheap and poorly made locally made cases. Stylistically, the Regina was that most dangerous of all things – an eclectic anachronism, for it embodied the spirit of an American interpretation of European tastes. For this reason, Regina cases stand out as quite unlike contemporary American furniture styles. The student of the development of American furniture will find himself perplexed when he comes to trying to fit the Regina into his categories! Mechanically, the instrument was as near perfect as one could hope for. The self-changing models were better engineered than the Polyphon system upon which they were built. Some models used the coiled wire mainspring

231

style in place of the usual coiled flat spring, but the majority were otherwise conventionally powered.

Musically, the Regina benefited from the fact that its most popular and best-selling sizes were of sufficient tonal compass – the 27 in. (68·6 cm) was just over seven octaves! – to allow complex music to be performed with little or no need for abbreviation or adjusted key signature or modulation. Although the Stella (q.v) and Orphenion (q.v.), both in certain models, may have occasionally sounded better, the larger sizes of Regina remained outstanding on the dual points of scoring and capability. Larger models such as the Regina Corona style and the self-changers made use of piano-type soundboards in such a way that the case sang in a manner both spectacular and beautiful without the mechanical brashness of the largest of the Britannia (q.v.) and Imperial (q.v.) instruments which tried the same soundboard technique. As a final plaudit, the Regina has what is probably the most effective of the disc musical-box dampers – and the easiest to adjust!

The styles of Regina were very many and varied. Fortunately, all the Regina records and paperwork have been preserved and, unlike any other musical-box maker, serial numbers, styles, dates of dispatch and even the names of original buyers all survive* and the Regina Company history has been well researched and documented.†

The sizes of Regina musical-box discs are as follows: $8\frac{1}{2}$ in. (21·6 cm) manivelle or spring-powered; $11\frac{1}{4}$ in. (28·1 cm); $12\frac{1}{8}$ in. (30·8 cm) made only for the chime clock; $12\frac{1}{4}$ in. (31·2 cm); $15\frac{1}{2}$ in. (39·8 cm); $20\frac{3}{4}$ in. (52·4 cm); 27 in. (68·6 cm); 32 in. (81·3 cm) piano-orchestrion only. Some discs of the larger sizes were marked 'Continuous' and had no stop/start position. These were for dancing to and were intended to be repeated as often as required. This was also a feature of some Stella (q.v.) discs. The $15\frac{1}{2}$ in. Regina has been reintroduced in limited production by Dwight Porter as the 'Porter' (1977).

Four phonopectines were produced under the name Reginaphone. These were the $12\frac{1}{4}$ in. (31·2 cm); $15\frac{1}{2}$ in. (39·8 cm); $20\frac{3}{4}$ in. (52·4 cm); and 27 in. (68·6 cm). Not many were produced, however, and Hughes Ryder tells me the total was 356.

ROEPKE (Rope-ker)

Carl Albert Roepke came to England from Germany some time before 1890 and settled in Salford, a suburb of Manchester. Here he appears to have set about designing an unusual form of musical box, a book-playing lever-plucker. British Patent number 6077 dated 16 August 1890 covers the basis of his invention. His second patent, number 41 dated 1 January 1897, comprises a musical-box winding mechanism which incorporates a device to prevent overwind and attempted winding in the wrong direction as well as a clutch. A third patent, taken out in the name of Roepke & Company Limited, 33 Tib Street, Manchester, concerns the special metal hinge-fasteners and locks used to unite the sections of cardboard music.

The Roepke instruments bear a strong resemblance to the Richter-invented Libellion (q.v.) and one model seen bore a plate which stated 'Patentees Roepke & Co Ltd. Manufactured in Leipzig'. This could suggest that the skills of Leipzig were employed by Roepke to make the mechanisms perhaps for casing in Manchester, or that Roepke's patents are merely British versions of existing patented devices by others. There is additional evidence

---

* A most extensive résumé of Regina styles and serial numbers is contained in Q. David Bowers, *Encyclopedia of Automatic Musical Instruments*, pp. 170–212.

† Mary Kosiarski, 'The Regina Musical Box', *The Music Box*, vol. 7, pp. 2–4 and 54–6, and John E. Cann, 'Regina, the American Queen', *Bulletin* of the MBSI, June 1966.

that the Roepke products were made in Leipzig for we read in *Musical Opinion* for July 1897 with regard to the Music Trades Exhibition held at the Agricultural Hall: 'The Roepke Company (Lim.) intended to show various automatic instruments; but at the time of our visits the goods were not on show as they had been "delayed at the port" as a notice informs us.'

Only two instruments have so far come to light. One is a long-case-type vertical movement surmounted by a clock (significantly, a similar arrangement to that of the Libellion clock in the Nationaal Museum van Speelklok tot Pierement in Utrecht) which plays music 14 in. (35 cm) wide. The second survives close to its apparent place of manufacture: it is in the museum at Salford, Manchester, and has three bells. The case of this looks like a large, late cylinder box, and the music played is 5¾ in. (45 cm) wide.

SAXONIA (Sax-ohn-ear)

The Leipziger Musikwerke Phoenix Schmidt & Co. was established in 1886 at Georgestrasse 33 in Leipzig-Gohlis and maintained a permanent product display at the Konighaus, Markt 17. The business was concerned with the manufacture of free-reed organettes played by metal tune sheets and as such produced the Phönix, Ariosa, Intona, Diana and Lucia organettes. In 1909 the company introduced the Phönix Strassenorgel and the Schatullen.

The Saxonia was apparently the only disc musical box which the company offered and it appeared in an 1895 catalogue. Coin-operated and with '42 steel tongues', the instrument could be wall-mounted or free-standing and the advertising blurb concluded: 'the cheapest and nevertheless good toned automaton in existence'. Disc size might have been about 10 in. (25·4 cm).

SIRION (Sirree-on)

The Sirion is the best known of that nevertheless rare breed of disc machines which play two tunes from each disc by the simple expedient of shifting the disc a small amount in a direction parallel to the combs so that a fresh set of disc projections can engage the starwheels.

The undoubted invention of two men from Leipzig, there remains a great deal of mystery surrounding the manufacture and even the place of manufacture of the Sirion. The earliest advertisement I have so far traced for the instrument appeared in *Musical Opinion* for 1 January 1899.

The mechanism by which the Sirion performs its unusual functions is covered by a British Patent number 7443 dated 9 May 1896 and is in the name of Gustav Bortmann and Alfred Keller, who are described as 'Manufacturers both of Fichte-Strasse No. 30c, Leipzig'. Two further inventions were patented by Keller but these appear only in America and in the name of Alfred Keller alone – US Patent number 752683 dated 23 February 1904 and 788265 dated 25 April 1905. Both these stated that Keller was a German citizen then living in Ste-Croix and both patents are assigned to Mermod Frères. One concerns a speed governor comprising two spring-loaded metal quadrants pivotally mounted at their lower corners to a cross-staff on the endless. The other relates to a clutch-type winding system for mainsprings.

Both these features are on the Sirion although the machine appears to have entered production well before the patent dates quoted above. One further confusion is that the discs all proclaim 'Made in Dresden'. Does this refer just to the discs or to the instrument as well? Dresden was certainly full of metal-working factories and related musicwork craftsmen so either or both is possible. What seems certain, though, is that David Bowers's original assumption that the Sirion was made by Mermod Frères now seems likely, in part at any rate. The probability is that the mechanisms – the musical movements – were made by Mermod and cased elsewhere, just where and by whom remaining something of a mystery.

The Sirion was made in two sizes. The smaller, a table model, played discs $19\frac{1}{4}$ in. (48·9 cm) on four combs arranged in pairs either side of the radius. The bass was arranged as two short combs either side of the starwheels for alternative plucking while the main comb, catering for middle and treble notes, was duplicated for unison plucking.

The larger model used a disc $22\frac{1}{4}$ in. (56·5 cm) in diameter and played on six paired combs either side of the radius, basses alternately plucked as before, and the rest in unison. In 1898, this retailed at £23. See also under New Century.

SPIEGEL (Ssh-pee-gel)
Another defined case of a stencil-brand, the Spiegel was nothing more than the Lochmann Original (q.v.) suitably marked to be distributed by this well-known and old-established German trade house.

Musikwerke-Industrie L. Spiegel & Sohn was established in 1862 at Kaiser-Wilhelm-Str. 6 and 18 in Ludwigshafen and opened a branch in Mannheim at E2 Nr 1 in 1903, followed by a branch in Switzerland in 1908 at Freie Str. 103, Basle. The business operated as distributor of musical instruments *et al*. and among these the Spiegel-branded Lochmann disc boxes.

STELLA (Stell-ah)
The musical-box manufactory of Mermod Frères was founded in the year 1816 at Avenue des Alpes, Ste-Croix and is thus one of the earliest of the Swiss musical-box makers. Having for many years been engaged in making cylinder boxes, the business responded to the challenge of the German disc musical-box industry by a most ingenious and thorough redesign of the principles of the disc-playing mechanism. The result was the Stella which was manu-factured, according to information stamped on to the motor cover, under the following patents. All but the first is shown as being of Swiss origin. They read: 22 September 1885; 29 June 1897, number 13796; 31 March 1896, number 11848; 11 August 1896, number 16773; 2 February 1897, number 12748.

An analysis of this produces some interesting information, for it reveals that the first and unnumbered patent is, in fact, no less than the British Patent taken out on 22 September 1885 by Paul Lochmann of Symphonion (q.v.) fame. The number is 11261 and the patent is for a musical box having two combs on a vertical axis and rotated against a fixed tune sheet, or with stationary combs and a revolving tune sheet. The disc projections, according to the patent, are used directly for plucking the comb teeth. The existence of this patent informa-tion on the Stella implies that Mermod, possibly fearing litigation with the Germans over the use of the basic disc-comb principle, decided to seek permission and more than likely pay a royalty to Lochmann for the use of his 'invention'.

At any rate, aside from having combs and a spring-driven means of rotating a metal music disc, the Stella broke some refreshingly new ground and even today stands apart from other instruments of the genre as being something very special.

To begin with, the disc pressure bar with its inherent risk of damage when in the raised position (how many glass doors and lid insides have been damaged by being swung to against an open pressure bar, and how many pressure bars have been damaged in the process!) was completely redesigned by Aristides H. Jacot, resulting in the familiar full-diameter bar, axially pivoted at each end and carrying small steel disc pressure rollers suspended on a sub-axis. The act of applying pressure is achieved by rotating the bar by means of a small lever, the pressure wheels operating in a cam-like fashion.

Next was the method of plucking the comb teeth. André Junod devised a system of spring-loaded starwheels which were allowed to slide in a guide. The music disc itself had no projections at all, only slots into which the starwheel point could spring, be drawn forward and so pluck the comb tooth. Junod was granted British Patent number 4931 dated 4 March 1896 to cover this.

A further radical design feature of all but the smallest, single-comb Stella was the juxtaposition of the two combs. While the first was situated in the conventional position, the second one was mounted underneath the starwheels with the teeth pointing upwards (see Fig. 36). Silent winding, using a caged, weighted ratchet pawl, was another feature.

The Stella was introduced to the market somewhere about the end of 1896 and early months of 1897. The discrepancy between patent dates and first marketing is not unusual. The first London agent was Alfred Paillard who said in 1899* that the mechanism was made by watchmakers in Switzerland and the cases in England. Some models bore the name 'Grand'.

Unlike other disc manufacturers, it seems that Mermod did not themselves make cases for any of their Stella musical boxes, nor for the Mira (q.v.) which they also produced, but exported movements for casing elsewhere. American specimens were housed in American oak or mahogany cases.

London distributors for the Stella in later years, Imhof & Mukle, were still advertising the instrument in 1910 and it is therefore probable that the instrument continued in production until some while after that date. Mermod Frères was still in existence until at least 1913, by which time they were well established in the manufacture of other goods and the factoring, if not the making, of gramophones.

Musically speaking, the Stella discs were not well set up. Thin themes with arbitrary accompaniment feature on all but a few renditions. The limitations of the Stella comb, which excluded several important semitones, limited the keys in which music could be played and severely restricted modulation. Nevertheless, the instrument was generally able to counteract this by virtue of its distinctive sonorous tone. The Jacot Music Box Co. of New York published a catalogue of models prefaced with some plaudits for the mechanism. One read: 'In the Stella, as in all similar instruments, the length of a tune depends on the diameter of the tune sheet: but owing to our system of tune sheets WITHOUT PINS, we can set the notes closer together and therefore have tunes twenty to twenty-five per cent longer than on tune sheets of the same diameter containing pins. Our musical artists transpose all music to be reproduced by the Stella so as to obtain the very best results, musically, considering the compass of each style.' While tonally they are undeniably extremely fine, musically they were far and away exceeded by the best of Leipzig and New Jersey.

Early Stella discs were of a zinc-rich alloy, somewhat harder than that used by, say, Polyphon (q.v.), but later ones were produced of steel. Jacot in New York factored an electrically powered version of the largest Stella which he advertised on 1 September 1902 as 'the latest Electric Stella Orchestral Grand'.

---

* *Musical Opinion*, No. 260.

The Stella was produced in five sizes as follows: $9\frac{5}{8}$ in. (24·4 cm); 14 in. (35·5 cm); $15\frac{1}{2}$ in. (39·8 cm); $17\frac{1}{4}$ in. (43·8 cm); 26 in. (66 cm). In fact, this last size is under 26 in. measuring exactly $25\frac{11}{16}$ in. (65·2 cm). Some of the $17\frac{1}{4}$ in. (43·8 cm) discs had no stop or start to the music, being arranged for continuous playing for dancing. Because of the Stella's peculiar construction, which necessitated that all the starwheels had to be in the passive position before removing the disc, many specimens have broken treble teeth due to putting on a disc when the starwheels are partially turned. There was always, however, a slight break in the music at the point where the stop control finger entered the edge of the disc. The smallest size was also produced without a motor as a manivelle, while the Electric Stella, mentioned above, was the first truly electrically driven production disc musical box. None of these, however, has been seen.

SUN

In 1903, Paul de Wit's *Weltaddressbuch der Musik-Instrumenten Industrie* carried an illustrated advertisement by Schrämli & Tschudin of the 'Sun' Music Box Manufacturing Co., 2 rue des Pâquis, Geneva. Describing themselves as 'Fabrique de Pièces à Musique en tous genres', the advertisement listed all forms of musical boxes, both cylinder and disc, orchestrions, phonographs, singing birds and musical fancy goods of all types. The fact that no further reference can be found to this company suggests that they were only distributors of these instruments. The address was also that of several musical-box manufacturers, including F. Conchon & Cie.

The advertisement illustrates an upright musical box which bears a family likeness to Polyphon in proportions and pediment, but Symphonion as regards front door. Was the Sun another stencil-brand by a German maker? Nobody has so far found out.

SYMPHONION (Sim-foan-eon)

The first practical disc-playing musical box was the Symphonion invented in Leipzig by Paul Lochmann. Ellis Parr of London claimed some of the kudos for the invention but, whatever improvements he may have assumed responsibility for, it remains Lochmann who first made such an instrument.

The first Symphonion was produced in 1886 and serious manufacture began in the following year. The instrument was an immediate success and the company, Kuhno-Lochmann of Braustrasse 13–19, Leipzig-Gohlis, rapidly expanded its production facilities while at the same time perfecting the instrument. In the year 1889 a new company was formed, Symphonion Fabrik Lochmannscher Musikwerke A.-G. In 1900, the company underwent a major reorganisation when, according to Bowers,[*] Ludwig Hupfeld gained some financial interest. It was at this time that Paul Lochmann left his company to set up the Original Musikwerke Paul Lochmann GmbH (see under Lochmann Original) and the company name changed to Symphonion-Fabrik A.-G. with the address at Schkeuditzer Strasse 13–17b in Gohlis. Director was Franz Thumen.

The business remained in being until the outbreak of war in 1914 and, at the conclusion of hostilities, it continued in business as Symphonion Musikwerke under the direction of Paul Scheibe at Barengasse 14–40, Gera, Reuss.

As the progenitor of the type, Symphonion produced a wide variety of sizes, types and

* *Encyclopedia of Automatic Musical Instruments*, p. 214.

styles and, initially at any rate, was responsible for much of the developing technology of the disc musical box. In spite of the competition which the company faced from Polyphon (q.v.) the Symphonion remained an instrument of standing and quality. The Ehrlich Monopol (q.v.) bore a strong resemblance to certain sizes of the Symphonion and it seems likely that certain Monopol instruments were manufactured by Symphonion. In 1903, Symphonion reported that it was turning out between five and six thousand instruments a year and was making 100,000 discs annually.

Musically, the discs were well set up and the instruments, with their softer and more subtle tone than the Polyphon, are generally considered superior. The $19\frac{1}{8}$ in. (48·6 cm) model is, for instance, superior to the corresponding equivalent in the Polyphon range and the difference is even more noticeable in the quality of the $25\frac{1}{4}$ in. (64 cm) versus the slightly smaller $24\frac{1}{2}$ in. (62·5 cm) Polyphon.

Twenty-one different sizes have been determined; some of these differ so slightly one from the other that it is easy to mistake one size for another. Many variants were created by having virtually the same disc as a centre drive, then for another style using peripheral drive, so producing a slightly greater disc diameter. Discs were produced with the early Symphonion style of projection – a double punching – and with the later single-punch type.

All musical boxes were accorded style numbers and these are given following each disc size: $4\frac{1}{2}$ in. (11·5 cm) style 20, pinion-driven; $5\frac{3}{4}$ in. (14·5 cm) style 28, pinion-driven; $6\frac{1}{4}$ in. (16 cm) style 32; $7\frac{11}{16}$ in. (19·5 cm) style 10; $8\frac{1}{4}$ in. (21 cm) style 2/2N; $9\frac{1}{2}$ in. (24 cm) style 4/4N; 10 in. (25·5 cm) style 48; $10\frac{5}{8}$ in. (27 cm) style 6/6N; $11\frac{3}{4}$ in. (30 cm) style 25; $13\frac{1}{4}$ in. (33·5 cm) style 60/120; $13\frac{5}{8}$ in. (34·5 cm) style 30; 14 in. (35·5 cm) style 38; $14\frac{3}{4}$ in. (37·5 cm) style 121; $15\frac{3}{4}$ in. (40 cm) style 178/256; $18\frac{1}{4}$ in. (46 cm) style 193; $19\frac{1}{8}$ in. (48·6 cm) style 106; $21\frac{1}{4}$ in. (54 cm) style 130; $25\frac{1}{4}$ in. (64 cm) styles 192, 143/192, 292; $27\frac{1}{2}$ in. (70 cm) style 118; $29\frac{1}{2}$ in. (75 cm) style 162; 30 in. (76 cm) style 98.

The $10\frac{5}{8}$ in. (27 cm) disc is from an early period and some examples have been seen which feature an extremely simple single-tab projection. The $13\frac{1}{4}$ in. (33·5 cm), $27\frac{5}{8}$ in. (70 cm) and several other sizes use peripheral dimple drive for the discs. The smallest size was used widely for the musical movement in small clocks (see under 'Junghans') and while most of these were centre-driven, some are pinion-driven and therefore the discs may have serrated edges. A characteristic of the smaller spring-driven models is that they are wound by means of a horizontal lever moved across the front of the case.

See also 'Imperial Symphonion' for details of American-made instruments. The name Symphonion was also used in 1973 for the small Kalliope machine copied and introduced by Studio Oyen in Germany and, soon after the war, Lador made a toy gramophone-style musical box with this name which played from plastic discs having cast-in projections.

TANNHAUSER (Tan-how-zah)
Of the disc musical boxes which played two tunes per disc through a mechanism for shifting the centre of rotation of the disc, the best known are undoubtedly the Sirion (q.v.) and the New Century (q.v.), both of which entered production. The Tannhauser, on the other hand, is a great rarity. Although patented and thoroughly described mechanically, no example had been found until, in 1975, Q. David Bowers located one in Germany and, during a subsequent visit to my library of musical-box patents, was able to make a positive assertion that the mystery table disc-shifter he had seen was indeed the elusive Tannhauser. Since then, another specimen has been located in a Washington collection.

The invention of Traugott Alwin Plessing, described as an engineer of Constantinstrasse 18, Leipzig-Reudnitz, it forms the subject of British Patent number 5386 dated 16 April 1898. Part of the patent specification contains the following description:

This invention relates to a device for mechanical musical instruments by means of which it is possible to operate a music sheet or disc which is provided with the notes for two tunes in such manner so that either tune of the sheet can be repeated as often as desired without it being necessary to hear the second piece and without stopping the driving mechanism. The new arrangement hence differs essentially from arrangements of this kind hitherto used . . .

Models of at least three different sizes were made, the one located playing a disc 15 in. (38·25 cm) in diameter.

TROUBADOUR (Tru-bad-or)
Troubadour-Musikwerke B. Grosz & Co. was established sometime prior to 1895 at Brietkopfstrasse 9 in Leipzig-Reudnitz. By 1909 the business was at Gellerstrasse 8, Leipzig.

Once again there is some doubt that Grosz was actually responsible for the manufacture of the disc musical boxes which were sold under the name Troubadour. There are family resemblances between some of the Troubadour models and Polyphon (q.v.) but even more direct is the matter of the largest Troubadour model, the No. 79W Wall Automaton, which is described quite openly as 'Made in the same cabinet as used on Symphonion No 130 with the same top gallery as used on Symphonion No 101'.

Four sizes of Troubadour boxes have been determined: $7\frac{1}{16}$ in. (18 cm); $8\frac{7}{8}$ in. (22·5 cm) both normal and with four bells; $11\frac{3}{4}$ in. (30 cm); $20\frac{1}{2}$ in. (52 cm).

The smallest model made was wound through the centre spindle after the manner in which the small-size Kalliope (q.v.) is wound. The two middle-size models could be used for rotating Christmas trees by means of a device called the Triumph series of Christmas Tree Stands. One was entreated to purchase a drive unit for this purpose – an extension of the centre shaft which terminated in a pulley above the disc which could then be belt-coupled to a second pulley provided in the tree stand.

UNIKON (Oo-nik-on)
Not a disc musical box, the little Unikon was one of that small breed of disc-like boxes which in fact made their music from a folded tune sheet. Émile Cuendet and André Junod, according to Jaccard, were the inventors of the Unikon, whose music, unlike the Libellion and Roepke, was not of cardboard but of narrow strips of zinc joined together with hemp hinges. There were 41 playing teeth in the comb and the music was $4\frac{5}{16}$ in. (10·9 cm) wide. The sound, rather like that of a small Symphonion, was produced by spring-loaded keys which could pop up through a hole in the music and so control the movement of a plectrum to a comb tooth. Junod was granted a British Patent, number 4931, dated 4 March 1896, for a similar system. One surviving instrument is known and this is driven by clockwork spring motor and in addition to a number of bands it has one book of music over 12 ft (3·65 m) long. The highest serial number on any piece of music is 116, which might be taken as suggesting a limited production, both of instruments and music.

NOVELTY MAKERS

In conclusion, brief mention should be made of the many instruments fabricated by 'novelty makers' which used musicwork. Mention has already been made in this chapter of the Diorama: there was also the Oberon. This was actually made by Symphonion as a chocolate-dispensing machine ('After putting the coin into the slot the music plays, while the automaton spends a piece of chocolate &c. Can be filled up with every kind of ware of any dimension and weight'). This played 34 cm discs. Holzweissig made the 'Leipziger Chocoladenmühle', first shown at the Leipzig Exposition of 1897. In the form of a windmill, this dispensed bars of chocolate to the sound of a Kalliope $57\frac{1}{2}$ cm musicwork. 'Falstaff' and 'Gambrinus' were beer-barrel-seated automata playing 30 cm Symphonion musicwork. These, along with the 'Hercules' strength-testing machine (19·5 cm musicwork), were Symphonion products. Musical Christmas tree stands (which rotated) under the name 'Gloriosa' used Monopol 41-note disc movements as well as Kalliope and Symphonion.

'Gloriosa', with its working-power tested up to over 1 Cwt., forms a splendid Christmas-tree-stand, tending to enhance the festivities of the season by the slow revolutions of the tree; fine-toned good and suitable music also produces its effect. . . . Plays abt. $\frac{1}{2}$ an hour when fully wound up.

There were many of these 'mixed marriage' machines made and the same can be said of cylinder musical boxes (wherein the commonest are the Illusions-Automat and the Simonia). Except for novelties produced within the musicwork industry, it is a mistake to attribute the maker of the movement to the maker of the whole.

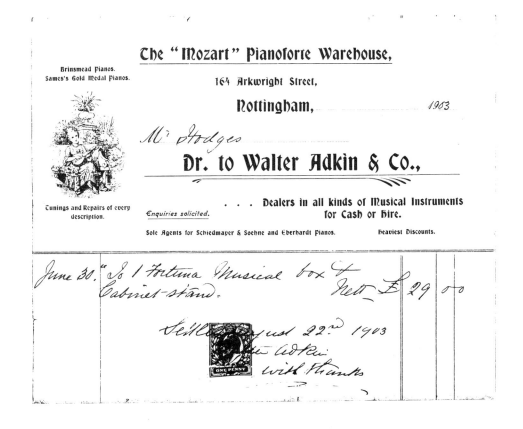

The "Mozart" Pianoforte Warehouse,

Brinsmead Pianos.
Sames's Gold Medal Pianos.

164 Arkwright Street,

Nottingham, _____ 1903

Mr Hodges

Dr. to Walter Adkin & Co.,

Tunings and Repairs of every description.

Enquiries solicited.

. . . Dealers in all kinds of Musical Instruments for Cash or Hire.

Sole Agents for Schiedmayer & Soehne and Eberhardt Pianos.   Heaviest Discounts.

June 30. " To 1 Fortuna Musical box & Cabinet-stand.   Nett £ 29 0 0

Settled August 22nd 1903
Walter Adkin
with Thanks

CHAPTER 8

The Musical-Box Nations – A Survey of the Industry

From this far-off point in time, we have the ability, one hopes, to do something which only now is possible – to look back at the once-great musical-box industry and assess its collective achievements and to determine the accomplishments of the different national centres which individually made up the whole.

Not unlike some species of vegetation, the kernel created many branches which subsequently grew to great proportions, greater even than their originator. Although Switzerland was, if not the actual birthplace of the tuned steel tooth, certainly the place where the miniature musical movement and, later, the musical box was born, Switzerland was not the only great centre. The Swiss industry began like all craft industries of the eighteenth century as a cottage craft and was not to be automated or organised until 1830. From then onwards, it seems almost that the Swiss considered that the musical box was their divine right and a right which no other country could challenge. Generations of workers must have lived through this age of self-perpetuated security and so, when the German industry sprung up first with low-cost mass-produced organettes in the 1870s and later with the disc machine, the Swiss were slow to recognise that their livelihood was not just threatened but in imminent danger of usurption.

As the better organised German industrialists swung into action and launched an aggressive sales campaign – itself something quite foreign to the Swiss temperament – it took Switzerland until the late 1890s to appreciate that the challenge of the Germans would not just quietly go away if they ignored it. And so the Vallée de Joux and Geneva lost their importance as virtually all the world looked first towards Leipzig, then Berlin also. From these two centres vast quantities of sophisticated musical boxes and other forms of mechanical music poured forth. It is a matter of conjecture whether or not the Germans produced more musical boxes between 1885 and 1914 than the Swiss from 1797 until 1914. It remains a probability.

In assessing the relative merits of the productions of the two countries, we are greatly aided by having access to virtually quarterly production figures published by the German musical instrument industry. Such trade figures are not so readily available for other centres. And after its foundation on 5 March 1901 the Leipzig-based Verband Deutscher Musikwerke- und Automaton- Industrie published information which, together with the Verein Deutscher Musikwerke-Fabrikanten set up in Leipzig on 15 November 1897, correlated employment figures, investment, production and development in the industry.

The clearly definable history of the musical box undoubtedly centred on Switzerland and began in the Jura Valley (La Vallée de Joux) close to the French border. At the north-east end there was La Chaux de Fonds and at the south-west end Ste-Croix. Chaux de Fonds was a well established centre of watchmaking, which craft had been introduced in 1679. This tiny industrious community 3,200 feet above sea level in the rugged valley, was virtually wiped out in 1794 when wind-fanned fire engulfed all its wooden buildings. Rebuilt and having to regain its former commercial importance, its workers turned to the manufacture of musical boxes. By about 1815* some craftsmen had moved to Geneva, where they were soon joined by others. Geneva in the far south-west now became a manufacturing centre. Concurrent with this, however, Ste-Croix, the principal village in the Jura and long reputed for the manufacture of repeater watches, began to assume an ever-increasing importance in the manufacture of musicwork. Jaccard relates how, from about 1860 onwards, the growth of the Ste-Croix industry was matched by a steady decline in the importance of Geneva as a centre of production until, around 1912, it had ceased musical-box manufacture altogether. The Vallée de Joux industry, which had seen the practical birth of the Swiss musical box, had already long since ceased to take any part in the scene. The foundation of the Ste-Croix industry is credited to Abraham Louis Cuendet before 1811 and the practitioners were Jeremie Recordon, Samuel Junod and his father Isaac, and Epars, who between them held a virtual monopoly for some while.

La Vallée mechanisms were called 'carillons à musique' and this may have some bearing on the choice of motif of several makers who chose a carillon-type clavier as their tune-sheet emblem. 'Tabatières' or musical snuff-boxes were made for a very long period of time and in 1883 George Grove† relates that the annual production of these was 30,000, half of which were priced below 50 francs while the whole range of musical boxes extended in price from 20/- to £50.

The large-sized musical box, called collectively the 'cartel' style (one meaning of 'cartel' is to challenge as in a fight), emanated from Geneva and became styled collectively as 'musique de Genève'. This term became synonymous with the cylinder musical-box and both German and Austro-Hungarian makers later used this to identify with the Swiss technology which made possible the practical musical box.

In the closing decades of the nineteenth century, Switzerland found her musical-box industry under considerable pressure from competition in Leipzig and Berlin. The unifying of the surviving leading manufacturers into the Société Anonyme was a positive step to meet the challenge head on. Other manufacturers such as Abrahams also entered competition to try to halt the erosion of the cylinder box market by the German disc musical-box by producing their own disc machines. And Mermod went one better by producing a disc

---

* Jaccard.
† *Dictionary of Music & Musicians*, 1st edn, 1883.

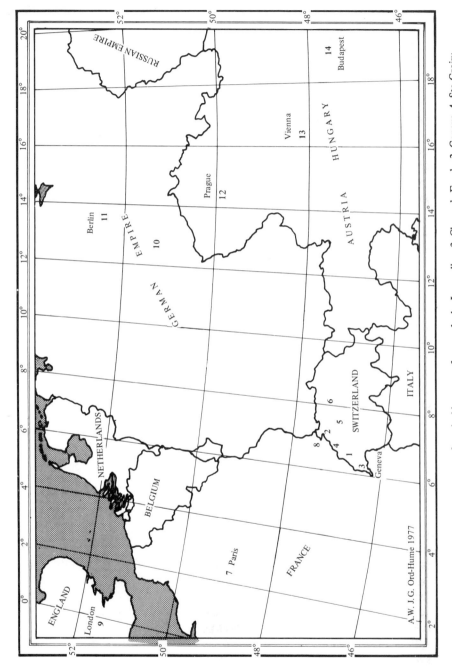

Figure 41 The European centres of musical box manufacture. 1. the Jura valley; 2. Chaux de Fonds; 3. Geneva, 4. Ste-Croix; 5. Berne; 6. Teufenthal; 7. Paris (several periods including that of Adre. Soualle); 8. Montbeliard (L'Épée); 9. London (early assemblers); 10. Leipzig; 11. Berlin; 12. Prague; 13. Vienna; 14. Budapest.

musical-box without projections. The story of the production musical-box was indeed that of Switzerland.

Two centres of musical-box manufacture are immediately identifiable in eastern central Europe. The first was Prague in Bohemia, now called Czechoslovakia. Next comes Vienna in Lower Austria. A probable third centre is worth considering as well – Budapest in Hungary.

Prague appears to have been a very early centre of musicwork and, as suggested in Chapter 1, it is possible that some of the very earliest musicwork emanated from Prague and also Vienna. Certainly by the early part of the nineteenth century, Prague was the home of a number of musical-box makers who produced the style of movement for fitting into clocks and automata which is so characteristic of the area – fundamentally with the comb reversed, i.e. treble teeth to the left of the cylinder.

Vienna also produced musical boxes of the same type, in fact the Prague and Vienna products are often virtually indistinguishable.

Budapest is included in this list as the result of careful surmise, for although so far no specific Budapest musical-box makers have been traced, musical automaton makers abounded and a number of musical-box agents practised. In consideration of Budapest's position in the Hungarian trade plus the fact that it later had a thriving gramophone industry, it would be difficult to consider the city as not having contributed to the musical-box scene although much of its output might never have reached Western eyes or ears.

One would expect the Budapest musicwork to follow the style of the Viennese/Prague movements and it would be interesting to try to trace examples of this presently hypothetical craft locale.

The musical-box industry in France is thought to have been of some considerable importance at two distinct stages in the history of musicwork. First there is the strong probability that French clockmakers were responsible for some of the very earliest uses of the tuned steel comb. This is discussed in Chapter 1. Certainly Breguet seems to have been making early cylinder musicwork around the end of the eighteenth century. Paris as a centre of clockmaking was nowhere near as important as London, yet here some early and as yet undefined contribution to the history of the musical box appears to have been made.

Paris produced its own handful of important makers such as Alibert, Bontems and Bordier, the last two being mainly makers of singing birds. Much of the main part of France's musical-box industry lay very close to Switzerland in the French Jura. Besançon, former capital of the Franche Compté and now chief town of the Doubs, bred fine clockmakers and makers of musicwork. The area is famous for at least one great family of musical-box makers, L'Épée. The founder of the industry was born just across the Swiss border in Neuchatel Canton and finally settled in Ste-Suzanne three kilometres south-west of Montbeliard where he set up a production which became known throughout the world. A large proportion of his output was sold under the name of Thibouville-Lamy of Paris.

Jaccard* tells us that in the 1860s there were two attempts to organise musical box factories in Paris but both had failed. One of these was most probably Adré Soualle who produced at St Denis, seven miles north of the city centre around that period.

The contribution of France, as regards volume, was fairly extensive and appears to have centred largely on L'Épée.

* 'The Origin & Development of the Musical Box', *Hobbies Magazine*, Chicago, 1932.

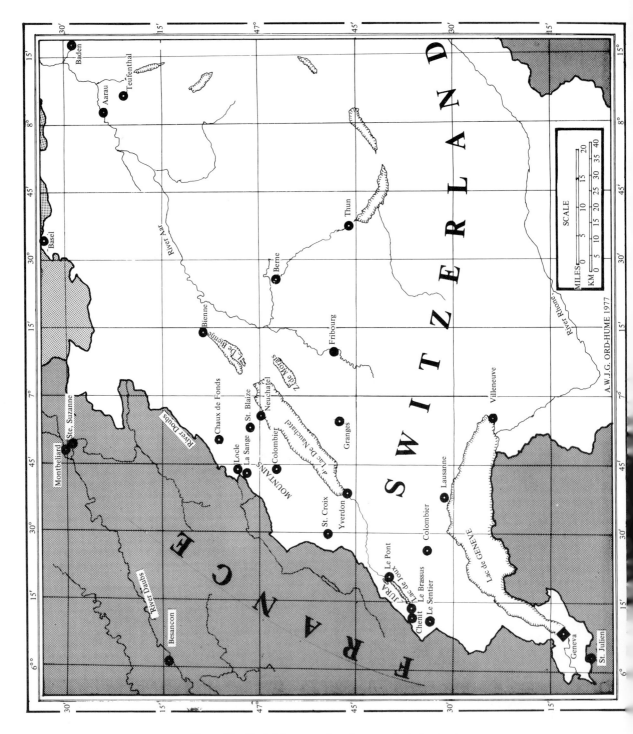

Figure 42   Musical box manufacturing areas in Switzerland.

244

Commenting on the importance of L'Épée, Chapuis relates how the Swiss musical-box makers underwent a financial crisis in the years 1882–5. This was severe enough to cause meetings among the Swiss manufacturers and mention was made of competition from Vienna, Prague and, especially, from L'Épée in France, whose products were preferred to those of the Swiss by many merchants. Indeed, the Swiss attributed their crisis primarily to L'Épée and this depression preceded that which was consolidated by the advent of the disc-playing musical box. In later years, L'Épée held an almost unique position in that the firm continued to make cylinder musical boxes right up to the outbreak of the First World War and long after other makers had ceased.

Germany was something of a late starter in the musical-box business. Several early makers were producing quality work in the middle of the nineteenth century, but no evidence of a concerted industry can be found prior to about 1870, when Ehrlich began making organ-ettes, followed soon afterwards by Lochmann.

It was the disc musical box, invented by Ellis Parr in London and Paul Lochmann in Leipzig and produced in the latter city, that really put Germany on to the path to becoming one of the world's major musical-box producers. Although not many cylinder machines were built, from 1886 onwards vast numbers of disc machines were turned out from factories in Leipzig, then also in Berlin and later other towns in Thuringia and Saxony. German technologists perfected the disc musical box and later took their knowledge, craft and experience to America and, in a veritable rip-tide of creativity, New Jersey and Leipzig became the most important centres of disc boxes in the world.

Statistics on the development of the German musical-box industry are copious and serve to mirror the immense growth and importance of mechanical musical instruments even in the face of the depression which blighted Germany and all Europe in the late 1880s.

The Leipzig correspondent of *Musical Opinion* wrote on 24 March 1884:

The manufacture of automatic musical instruments, such as orchestrions, musical boxes, orchestrionettes, etc., in the vicinity of Leipzig is assuming very respectable dimensions. The increase in the out-turn, during the month of February, over that of the same period last year, amounts to £1800.

Good though 1884 was, the musical instrument trade as a whole suffered a sharp decline as the year progressed. On 22 January 1885 the same correspondent wrote:

I cannot call to mind any year in which the trade look out, at the commencement, was apparently so hopelessly bad . . . For musical automata, such as orchestrions, etc., there seems however to be a constantly increasing demand, if we judge from the fact that in the £20 paid up shares of Ehrlich & Co, of Gohlis, purchasers at £80, including dividend, could not be accommodated; settlers holding out for £78, excluding dividend, which at 60 on the original shares amounts to £12, thus bringing the price up to £90.

The depression was to continue for several years to come and it was during this period that many manufacturers looked to the possibility of increasing trade with the United States and of opening up satellite companies within America. The 1886 report of the Leipzig Musical Automaton Factory showed a less satisfactory result than the preceding year but even so, after carrying over 7,915 marks to the reserve fund, a 10 per cent dividend was paid.

245

The year 1888 was distinguished in Germany by terrible floods brought about by continual summer rains which caused great havoc and can hardly have contributed to the economic recovery. A reporter wrote in August of that year: 'The trade with Russia and Austria is almost extinct; but for the better class instruments, some new markets are gradually opening up. As regards musical boxes and automata of all kinds, complaints are general that buyers insist upon lowness of price. A very large number of musical boxes are still imported from Switzerland into Germany.'

This was the start of the price-cutting war which threatened to devastate the German musical-box industry from then until the end of the century. The Swiss, quick to catch on now that they had been forcibly alerted to the size and power of the German industry, began flooding the market with low-cost mass-produced boxes. To avoid the effects of the price-cutting manufacturer, the makers of mechanical instruments in Germany formed themselves into an association in the late 1890s, carefully excluding those firms whose conduct was not of the highest commercial integrity. The exporters were also in a 'ring', giving a wide berth to non-members of the manufacturers' association.

Trade in Germany underwent a temporary return to normality and, with this change of fortunes, musical automata made the greatest advances and instruments were exported to all parts of the world. In November 1888, a Leipzig correspondent wrote:

It is not very long since the barrel organ and the Swiss musical box were the sole representatives of this class of instrument, whilst now it appears that about 82,500 of the different kinds of automata are constructed in the Fatherland, of which some 44,000 are exported. Fourteen manufacturers employ steam power, exhibiting a total of 280 h.p. and 1500 work people – exclusive of those who work in their own houses, on machines provided by the masters, and who number about the same – earn a good livelihood in the business, by turning out about three and a half million marks' worth of automata yearly. Messrs Ehrlich and Pietschmann are the two firms who must be credited with having done most to perfect instruments using perforated sheets of notes, and Kuhno Lochmann & Co. have proved formidable rivals to the Swiss, who at one time had the trade for instruments with cut metal reeds [tuned steel teeth] almost entirely in their own hands.

As 1888 came to a close, it was more than just the summer floods which receded and business expanded.

The manufacturers of musical automata have . . . no room to complain: the firm of Kuhno, Lochmann & Co., who make the symphonium [sic], tell me that they have as many orders as they can possibly execute before Christmas. This instrument is one of the best of its class, and is constructed on the principle of the Swiss musical box; this is to say, it has no reeds, but the sound is produced by a metal comb. On the other hand, however, its chief advantage lies in not being worked by a barrel, but by a circular perforated sheet, which, of course, can be exchanged at pleasure; and withal the price is lower than that of the Swiss goods.

Within that year, the value of all musical instruments exported from Germany to England was 14 million marks. By the end of the following year it had risen to 18 million marks and in 1890 it was close to 20 million marks – almost £1 million. Of this, a good proportion was given to musical automata and it was reported that the manufacturers were leaving no avenue unexplored in order to increase the available musical repertoire. Word came from Leipzig in 1890 that bagmen in India were told to keep their ears open, jotting down any native melody that might seem to be a favourite and then sending it back to Germany in order that it could be punched out as a steel disc. A subtle way round the question of copyright and royalties!

Whereas, in former times, Russia had been a major market for German goods and had taken almost as much as, if not more than, England in the way of musical automata, exports to that territory had been dwindling over the previous years under the regulating influence of continually rising protective imposts. The final blow came on 31 August 1890, when quite unexpectedly all import tariffs were increased by 20 per cent. This marked a doubly bad year for the German musical-box trade for the new American Republican president, William McKinley, had introduced a Bill to apply a similarly crippling import tariff.

Even so, the end of the year in Leipzig drew the comment:

The Christmas trade is as brisk this year as ever, and the musical automata, with perforated sheets of music, find a ready sale. The extent to which this trade is interfering with the sale of Swiss musical boxes, may be judged of from the fact that a single house in this neighbourhood has, within the last ten years, made and disposed of two hundred thousand automata, and has used up more than thirty thousand pounds' worth of boards for making the perforated sheets. [This refers to the manufacture of the Ehrlich Ariston cardboard disc-playing organette.]

The fortunes of the German musical instrument manufacturers took another turn for the worse in 1894 with the consolidation of a depression which had begun the previous year. Musical instruments were not selling, yet *Musical Opinion* was able to print a despatch from its Leipzig correspondent dated 23 June as follows:

The only firms which have reported that they are doing well are those who manufacture musical automata; and they are still unable to keep pace with the demands for their manufactures. The three large establishments of this class which exist in the vicinity of Leipzig, and employ amongst them over one thousand workpeople, have all, within the last twelve months, been compelled to enlarge their premises in order to enable them to satisfy, even in a measure, the requirements of the public. On the 6th instant the Fabrik Leipziger Musikwerke – formerly Paul Ehrlich & Co – in Gohlis, near Leipzig, celebrated the completion of their three hundred thousandth Ariston and the six millionth perforated note sheet; from which figures it may be conceived what dimensions this class of business has assumed, notwithstanding that the firm is not yet twenty years old.

Not quite two years later, at Easter 1896, the same correspondent wrote:

The Polyphon Music Works (Wahren-Leipzig) are so full up with orders running over a long period that they are compelled to refuse more. Lochmann's Music Works (Leipzig-Gohlis) have declared a dividend of twenty per cent, after writing off ample for wear and tear and depreciation. Neither this company nor the Fabrik Leipziger Musikwerke (formerly Paul Ehrlich & Co.), enterprising as both are, have time to bring out new forms of automaton works, being full up. A dozen other similar firms, some of them quite

247

recently founded, have about as much as they can get through. Another noteworthy feature is that there is a strong demand for the largest and most expensive instruments, so that automatons of over fifty up to two hundred tunes are being turned out. There is a strong demand for the products of the Leipziger Musikwerke ('Euphonika') which are too expensive for the pockets of the home trade. The large wholesale firms – some of whom take all the output of the sundry factories – are also full up with orders, while other makers kept away from [the Easter trade fair] owing to the impossibility of executing fresh orders.

Leipzig stands absolutely in the front with automatons. The amount of capital invested therein is enormous, and that it finds profitable employment is shown by the twenty per cent dividend declared by the Lochmann Co. . . . The demand for automatic music, and notably for the more expensive kinds thereof, is so great, the year 1896 promises to see a full recovery from the long period of depression from which the trading world in general has suffered.

This bright picture followed closely on the news that Lochmann's Music Works had issued mortgage bonds to the extent of 500,000 marks at $3\frac{1}{2}$ per cent interest. And in Berlin, the Berlin Musical Instrument Factory (formerly Ch. F. Pietschmann & Sons) proposed at an extraordinary general meeting to issue preference shares to the amount of one million marks at 6 per cent. Pietschmann had gone through a very lean time owing to the keenness of competition and price paring, but was obviously now well on the mend. And Leipziger Musikwerke Fabrik, formerly Paul Ehrlich, proposed enlarging their works. Indeed all looked very bright for the German musical-box industry.

The fortunes of the Polyphon-Musikwerke of Wahren, a Leipzig suburb, also expanded and, in 1898, after placing 70,000 marks to a second reserve fund account, it declared a dividend of 25 per cent.

In April 1899, in the year in which the first hurdle concerning the copyright of music performed on mechanical instruments was cleared, it was once more proclaimed that trade was still on the increase with prices remaining stationary. And, of the entire export of mechanical musical instruments, Great Britain took 42 per cent of the total in weight. 'As a matter of fact,' comments the correspondent, 'a very large percentage of the Saxon industries is entirely dependent on Great Britain's custom for existence . . .'.

As the twentieth century dawned, the German industry was undergoing certain major changes and within a few years, the up-coming pneumatic-action and barrel orchestrion had become the mainstay of the German mechanical musical instrument industry. Disc musical boxes were on the way out and, although Polyphon still sold discs as late as the 1920s, the industry effectively died with the outbreak of war in 1914. German technology had moved to America and sown the seeds of an industry which for technical and musical finesse was to form a worthy successor to the city of lime trees – Leipzig.

But as late as 1905 disc musical boxes were still responsible for much trade in Germany and the industry was valued at around £200,000 per year with employment being given to nearly 1,500 work people. Paul Ehrlich alone employed 300; Pietschmann of Berlin 240, and Kuhno of Leipzig 180. The majority of the remainder of the manufacturers employed fewer than a hundred and, in some cases, only eight or ten men.

The fracas which began in 1914 wrote finis to the chapter, and in the irony of things, in its attempt to dwarf the Swiss musical-box industry, it succeeded, only to be overthrown by events which it was not strong enough to resist. Switzerland, the neutral, quietly continued in the making of modern mechanisms.

In the early 1970s, the disc box was put back into production by Studio Oyen near Cologne, the instrument chosen being the Kalliope named, for commercial reasons, Symphonion.

It should not be forgotten that Augsburg was the centre of mechanical musical instruments as early as the start of the seventeenth century. Here clockwork spinets, mechanical organs and complex automata were being produced by a handful of craftsmen whose work remains without equal. This craftwork was almost completely extinct by the end of the eighteenth century. The same could be said of Dresden. Mechanical music also featured in clocks made in the small area of Schwarzwald, Baden, bounded by Freiburg, Waldkirch, Triberg, Furtwangen, Vöhrenbach, Villingen and Neustadt. This industry was set up about the middle of the eighteenth century and flourished into the great orchestrion era still supreme at the start of the present century.

The musical box was never the subject of a serious production business in the United Kingdom. While several Britons patented 'improvements', few if any of which contributed anything to the subject, and devious schemes for incorporating musical boxes into other articles (such as musical boxes in desks, pianos, closets, etc.), original musical-box construction did not exist. Admittedly the organette was produced successfully and in large quantities in the last two decades of the nineteenth century, but there was little else.

Exceptions centred on the importance accorded on a European scale to London as a centre of the watch- and clockmaking industry and as a centre of quality gold and silver craftsmanship. A large number of Swiss-produced musical movements were sent over to London for finishing and incorporating in London-made presentation precious metal cases – this explains the presence of a London hallmark on so many of the very early Swiss pieces. Later, movements for Swiss cylinder musical boxes were sent to London for mounting in locally-made cases. See caption to Plate 121.

Although no complete production was undertaken, cylinder pinning was carried on in London and several highly skilled repairers had the capability of producing one-off or custom-built pieces.

In the days of famed automaton makers such as Jaquet-Droz, Maillardet and Leschot, pieces incorporating musicwork were built in London. While this usually involved Swiss-made work, often considerable reconstruction was undertaken to suit the work being created.

Contemporary with this, these same workers (Swiss craftsmen who worked for a time in London) undertook the development of the mechanical singing bird, producing the definitive form seen today wherein a single, variable-pitch pipe is used.

All these works, admittedly of immense importance to the musical box, were undertaken by European craftsmen in London and as such it could hardly be described as an industry.

England can lay a measure of claim to having invented the disc-playing musical box, for it was Ellis Parr, a London musical instrument dealer and inventor, who claimed to have designed the first practical model and who subsequently united his talent with that of Paul Lochmann in Leipzig (who, one feels, was the real inventor) to produce the Symphonion – the world's first disc musical box.

Only one musical box appears to have ever been 'produced' in England and that was far from London in the Salford district of Manchester. Here, Carl Roepke, about whom little is known other than that he was a central European immigrant, built the strange book-playing box which bears his name.* Similar to Richter's Rudolstadt-built Libellion (one wonders if there was a connection), the Roepke was a most interesting and tonally satisfying product which suffered from the same problem as all the early cardboard-playing machines – the lack of durability of the music sheets where they were called upon to perform mechanical functions. How many of these boxes were made, several sizes and styles of which have been located, remains unknown. Unlike America's large musical-box industry, Britain probably contributed very little to the development of the musical box in her own territory.

It may seem strange that the British Isles should have engendered very little in the direction of a musical-box industry while America evolved its own thriving business in the making of musical boxes. The reasons are, though, not terribly hard to find. The United Kingdom was far too close to the European centres of mechanical music to make the establishment of an indigenous industry an economic proposition. With the United States, however, there existed two extremely valid reasons why a home-grown musical-box industry should have flourished. First was the obvious one – the geographical location relative to Europe which made ordering and delivery a lengthy process. Then there were the extremely high duties levied on imported musical boxes. A third reason was the recognition that the United States was potentially a thriving and lucrative market of considerable size impossible to develop from arm's length.

The American industry began first as an offshoot of the Swiss industry with the setting up of a Paillard agency in New York and the removal to America of some Swiss technicians, including Charles Henry Jacot, Louis Jaccard, Emile Cuendet, Joseph Bornand and others. Then the German industry also sent talent across the Atlantic, most notably Gustav Brachhausen from Polyphon, followed later by Octave Félicien Chaillet.

Although it was undoubtedly the influence of foreign knowledge and technology upon which the American musical-box industry was founded, it was American artisans and, largely, American cash which jointly funded one of the most surprisingly prolific eras of musical-box development.

In 1888, the Hon. Major Benjamin Butterworth's monumental compilation of American industry was published in Washington under the title *The Growth of Industrial Art*. In this he investigates the American musical-box industry and found that, in 1880, the amount of capital invested was $654,850 and the value of production stood at $853,746. Total employment in the industry was 573 and the wages paid came to $293,062 giving an annual average of just under $512 per hand. This must have involved the businesses of Paillard, Jacot and Cuendet, and probably Gautschi in Philadelphia.

A late starter in the musical-box industry, America was the setting for the production of some truly outstanding musical items. Apart from possessing a sufficiently wealthy market to encourage Swiss craftsmen to construct some of the very largest cylinder musical boxes ever made solely for America, it also produced what many collectors throughout the world believe to be one of the best if not the best disc musical box of all time – the Regina. Furthermore, America produced an unusual variant of the disc machine which demonstrated some sound engineering and creative thinking in the Capital, a musical box which played hollow tapered and truncated metal cones which earned it the nickname of the 'cuff' box.

* But, as related earlier, this may have been nothing more than a customised Leipzig import.

Initially, musical boxes made in America, both cylinder and disc, were almost indistinguishable from those made at European source – indeed it seems that components were being shipped across to America from Europe for some while (in the case of Mermod, Roger Vreeland, writing in the *MBSI Bulletin*, has found evidence of this practice as late as 1911) – little by little American ingenuity and local style took over. From earliest times, and certainly with disc boxes, cases were of American wood to American design. Then gradually came the development of American-bred designs and the most outstanding of these, aside from the

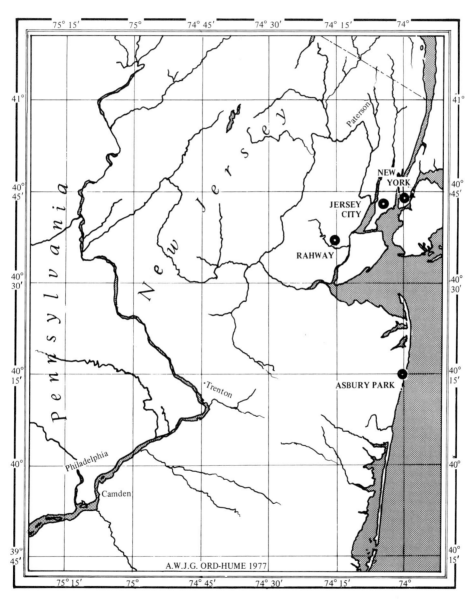

Figure 43a Musical box manufacturing areas in the United States.

251

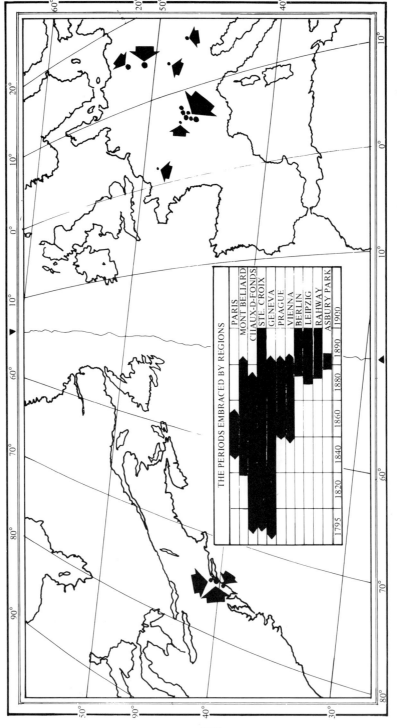

Figure 43b   American and European musical box industries and the periods in which various centres were operating. Arrow-ended period lines indicate uncertainty over start and finish dates.

Capital, were the later products of the Symphonion factory in New Jersey. Other disc boxes, such as the Criterion and Perfection, were solely American in origin.

For the wealthy American, Paillard in New York constructed some outstanding large interchangeable-cylinder machines which exhibited the highest-quality engineering and technology united within handsome cabinetwork. These were not production items, although the components may have been standardised, and each was probably a unique specimen.

Because of its timing, America's musical-box industry was something of a swan-song for the musical box as a whole. But if the musical box came in with uncertain origins, it went out with New Jersey assuredly ranking in equal importance with Berlin and Leipzig.

In 1889, Charles François Lecoultre went to Buenos Aires, Argentina, to set up a local musical-box industry. Although the enterprise failed and by 1910 he had returned to Geneva, we can assume that some pieces were made by him in South America but in no significant quantity (see Chapter 11).

From this survey, I have excluded reference to the present-day musical-box industry with the exception of the reference to the new Symphonion. A certain proportion of modern work also comes from Japan, but Japan's contribution to the classic musical box was, to the best of my knowledge, nil.

If one interprets the foregoing information, it emerges that the musical-box industry of the world extended (a) across Europe in two diagonal bands running from north-east to south-west from Leipzig to Geneva, and Leipzig through Dresden and Prague to Vienna and probably on to Budapest; and (b) in a narrow arc embracing New York City, Jersey City, Rahway and Asbury Park in the United States. By comparison, the transatlantic industry was very small and concentrated in a small, localised band, yet it was demonstrably an enterprising and prolific one.

CAVES A LIQUEURS

N⁰ˢ 5170, 5171, 5172   N⁰ˢ 5173, 5174

CHAPTER 9

Other Forms of Mechanical Musical Instrument

The purpose of this very short chapter is twofold: first, it provides a brief insight into the other corridors of the study of mechanical music and its instruments; and, secondly, it forms a natural break between the historical chapters and the concluding ones which offer advice to the collecteron how to go about his interests and provide biographical details of the many makers of musical boxes.

There are a number of instruments which are often loosely classed along with musical boxes. Now the musical box which forms the subject of this book (and its companion, *Restoring Musical Boxes*) is the mechanical instrument which makes its music by the plucking of a tuned steel tooth or reed and which has its musical programme in the form of a pinned cylinder, a punched disc, or a punched band or strip of material such as card or metal. However, other instruments share the same style of programme source, by far the largest family being that of the organette. This was a free-reed pneumatic instrument of which there were very many types and variations. Many of these are illustrated, along with their working principles, in my other book *Barrel Organ – The Story of the Mechanical Organ & How to Repair it*. I mention this because you may come across discs which you cannot at once identify: they many quite easily be for the organette. Another disc-operated instrument which plays projectioned metal tune-sheets just like, say, the Polyphon, is the Chordephon which is an instrument which plucks its strings and is thus a form of mechanical zither. The Guitarophone is another similar machine. A third stringed instrument, this one playing from punched card discs (exactly the same discs as the Ariston organette incidentally) is the Orpheus piano which, as its name implies, is a true percussion instrument with an iron frame and an up-striking piano action. Illustrations of many of these instruments can be found in another of my books, *Clockwork Music*.

Since the birth of mechanical music just about every single type of musical instrument has been mechanised. From the simple glockenspiel of tuned steel elements through to the harp, the banjo, the violin, concertina, saxophone, mouth organ, pipe organ, piano – all have their mechanical variants. Why, mechanised instruments even included the drum! The first traceable attempt to take the effort out of producing a drum roll is to be found in the notebooks of Leonardo da Vinci,* who sketched a mechanical kettledrum. Indeed, such an

* *Cod. Atl.* fol. 335r-C, in British Museum.

instrument was featured in Flight & Robson's great Apollonicon organ* but it did not reach utter plebeian banality until 1903 when a toy mechanical drum was manufactured in Germany which played itself from a perforated metal disc. This sold through the Utility Company in London's Oxford Street for the princely sum of 2s 9d. Another was made in Paris by fair-organ builders Limonaire Frères. This one was a portable mechanical kettle-drum or side drum for use by soldiers on the march. The drummer only needed to turn a handle on the side of the drum – and the twin drumsticks produced a perfect tattoo!

The most challenging instruments to automate were the ones with plucked and bowed strings such as the banjo, guitar and violin. Yet the inventors succeeded with such marvels as the Encore Banjo, the Wurlitzer Automatic Harp (a boon for lazy angels!), the Mills Violano-Virtuoso and the Hupfeld Phonoliszt-Violina. This last was made in many thousands, yet very, very few survive today. A full-scale piano with three violins, this was an outstanding musical interpreter. There was even a patent for a barrel-operated violin player – W. S. Reed was granted British Patent number 14005 for such an invention on 9 July 1901. Whether or not it was built is unknown.

It was the technological growth of the last decades of the nineteenth century that spurred mechanical music to greater heights as the show organ and dance organ took over as the faultless performers of music for the masses. In the half-century which ended with the close of the 1920s, mechanical orchestras blossomed, and then died. In 1909 at a Paris skating rink, a mechanical organ was built by J. Merklin & Cie – it had 13 stops and 793 pipes on the great and a similar number of solo stops with 375 pipes plus percussion effects. It was blown by an electric motor and played from perforated paper rolls like a player piano.

From the mechanical spinets of Bidermann in the early seventeenth century it had been a quarter of a millennium of splendorous progress which brought music into every walk of life.

The era began to revert to one of musical novelties. It probably began with the dawn of the new century. It was certainly showing signs of subsiding when, in October 1912, L. Serne and R. J. Hardy were granted British Patent number 23441 for a clothes brush incorporating a small comb-playing musical movement. The London firm of G. B. Kent & Sons sold the device for many years.

The range of mechanical instruments is a large one and much of it is set out in detail in my books *Clockwork Music, Player Piano* and *Barrel Organ*. Perhaps the ebullience of the period is best illustrated by the following quotation from *Musical Opinion* for April 1912 (p. 531):

It is said that a German – G. P. Hackenberg – anticipated electrical music as far back as the year 1863. His original announcement was as follows: 'I have determined, by means of electricity, to supply every house with music, just as it is with gas and water by means of pipes. About the middle of the town I will erect a central station – the music manufactory. It will include a piano as the machine and a first rate pianist to play it. Everyone who subscribes will be provided with a piano. Every such piano is connected by electric wires with the central piano, so that when my distinguished pianist plays the overture to "Don Giovanni", with the utmost virtuosity and the deepest feeling, all the pianos connected with the central one will perform the overture at the same time and in the same manner. If the demand is large, I shall have the playing go on day and night. It is only necessary to put on a metal stopper [*sic*] and the melodies will continue to flow in uninterrupted joyousness.'

* Fully described in *Barrel Organ* by the present author.

CHAPTER 10

Tips for Collectors

Whatever advice I may give, one thing must be obvious, and that is that it will be coloured by my own experiences and that of my friends through maybe forty years of avid collecting. Even if only just for this reason, any homily from me must be potentially dangerous (for men are not equal, only different) and of little consequence. This latter reason is because all the words of the so-called expert and philosopher alike cannot serve to sway the mind of the person who has decided, regardless of truth or consequence, that he wants something at all costs. Indeed, it would be debasing his standards to suggest that he could have his mind changed.

I suppose that the first thing to be learned is that, as in most fields involving humanity, ignorance often reigns supreme. Unwittingly, the vendor may completely mislead the potential buyer by his lay terminology or inexperience. Happily, though, the days of downright deception which once reigned are past. *Musical Opinion* for January 1909 relates a story with some sort of moral:

A common swindle, not unknown in England, is . . . shown up by a Munich paper: We have just received a letter from the victim of 'the musical box swindle', whose experience may be of value to intending purchasers of the cheap musical boxes advertised in some Swiss and German papers. The advertisement offers for sale 'musical boxes' warranted to play eight tunes and the price asked varies from one to three marks! Our correspondent sent for one of these instruments, enclosing the requisite funds, receiving by return a twopenny mouth organ with eight holes. This advertisement, our correspondent thinks, is a sharp Switzer-Jewish dodge.

The big problem which arises in trying to offer guidance when buying is that all the words and illustrations possible cannot make up for experience. Perhaps this is an admission of failure, but the quality of a box is not measured by any single factor: it is a cumulative appreciation of all that goes into its manufacture and all that emerges from it when it is played. And again let it not be forgotten that the finest box in the world will soon jangle the nerves and be left aside unplayed if it performs music unpopular with the listener or poor in arrangement.

The reverse of this is, of course, true. In this connection I will tell you about an event in my own collecting experiences. For one of those largely inexplicable and strictly personal reasons, I became very fond of a particular Irish melody which was popular at the beginning of the nineteenth century. I had heard this tune – 'Planxty Kelly' or 'Oh Fly Not Yet' – on a François Nicole box, a splendid example of perfection of about 1835, and resolved that if ever I found a box with this on I would buy it regardless of condition. Proving that all things come to those who are patient, some five years later my chance came. Another early Nicole with this tune on it appeared in a shop specialising in musical boxes in the Portobello Road, London. Here was a box which I could not honestly recommend to any collector who was not equipped for a massive rebuild, for the brass cylinder was a mass of bent pins like fish-hooks and the bass end was bald and deeply scored. The comb had several gaps in it, points were missing and the vestiges of the damper wires curled round the sides of the teeth. This, though, had to be my box; and now, in somewhat better condition, it forms a special, nostalgic item in my collection.

One thing at least is certain: that all collectors at some stage in their lives make mistakes and effect bad purchases, either through careless judgement or through being 'had' by an unscrupulous vendor. This is most frequently brought about not by any planned deception but by the sheer ignorance of the seller plus the inexperience of the buyer.

There is nothing very sinister about making mistakes and, in fact, they are so common as to engender a bond between collectors. We can analyse the underlying reasons for the 'bad buy' but before we do that we have to understand and recognise the three stages of acquisition. There is the first flush of excitement and enthusiasm at the moment of introduction to a likely candidate for the collection. That is stage one. Stage two is the 'shall I or shan't I' which *always* terminates in paying for it! The final stage is playing it in the confines of your own home and examining it in detail.

Stages one and two are usually reached with little trouble. The realisation, if realisation there has to be, comes with the third stage. Away from the previous owner, where you were at a disadvantage, trying so hard to sustain the upper hand and maintain an air of superiority in the face of your acquisitive instinct, you suddenly become aware of any faults in the instrument. The next ten minutes usually resolves the question as to whether or not you have made a mistake.

Admitting this and bearing in mind the dictum that mistakes are inevitable, we can now list a few general points as a guide when considering the acquisition of a musical box. This chapter, then, is something of a résumé of all that has gone before.

Generally speaking, the plainer the wooden case of a cylinder musical box, the earlier it is. Some later boxes were made with plain painted cases and Thibouville-Lamy made a plain series in the 1860s, but these were lever-wound. Boxes which are key-wound are usually prior to 1850, and should not be confused with the very late boxes (such as those produced by Paillard and Mermod in the 1890s) which were wound with a crank handle. Nicole and Bremond (and others) made some large overture boxes and some fine forte-piano boxes between 1850 and 1855 which were wound with a detachable ratchet handle from outside the case. These are uncommon and represent the transitional period from key to fixed ratchet.

The tune sheet forms an important part of a box and its absence does rather detract from the value. Not that the presence of this can make a bad box good or vice versa, but collectors prefer to have boxes with original tune sheets on them. Some vendors are known to write out their own tune sheets to replace missing originals. These should be viewed with suspicion. One member of the Musical Box Society of Great Britain, who is a stickler for detail, has

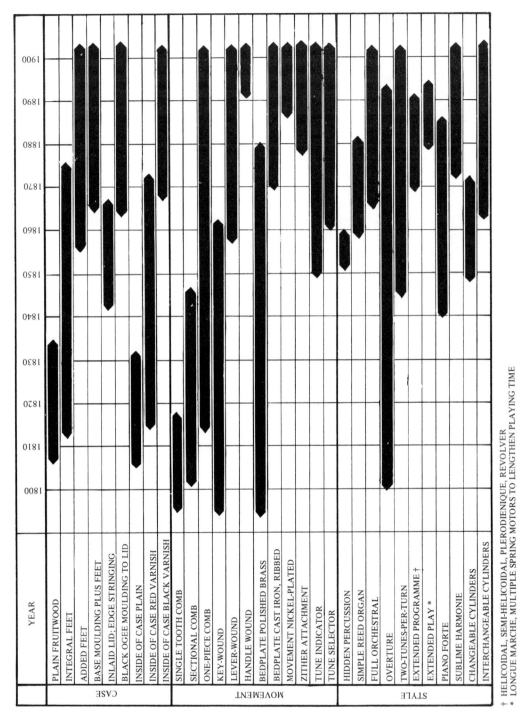

Figure 44 The dates of various styles in musical boxes.

† HELICOIDAL, SEMI-HELICOIDAL, PLERODIENIQUE, REVOLVER
* LONGUE MARCHE, MULTIPLE SPRING MOTORS TO LENGTHEN PLAYING TIME

258

spent many years acquiring boxes with perfect tune sheets; from these, he has prepared printing plates, and he can supply plain reproduction tune sheets to suit almost all the early styles of the better makers. Properly written up (not, please, with a ball-point pen), these can enhance the appearance of a box whose original sheet has been lost.

It has been known for boxes of an inferior make to be equipped with tune sheets bearing the name or style of a better box. This fakery and deception is generally not recent, but was effected by the dealer who originally sold the box new. Because many dealers kept a stock of tune sheets, some printed, legitimately, with their own names on the bottom, it was a fairly easy, though thoroughly dishonest, thing to do.

Different makers of boxes had their own styles of construction and it is these points which determine the parentage of a musical box in the absence of a tune sheet or when it is the subject of doubt. This is covered in previous chapters and in Appendix II.

Musical boxes of all types were usually sold through agents, music shops, piano dealers and so on. The dealer, as do modern radio and television retailers, probably handled many different makes of instrument, and it was common practice to affix to each one sold a waterslide transfer or sometimes a small ivory nameplate giving the dealer's name. An appreciation of this will avoid misunderstandings such as that conjured up in the mind of a Midlands lady who told me she had a Nicole Frères musical box made by G. Blenkinsopp of Reading! In their later years, Nicole Frères were also distributing agents for other makes of musical box, in particular Polyphon and Regina, and the Nicole Frères transfer with their name and London address frequently appears on these instruments. Other names which often turn up are Imhof & Mukle of Oxford Street, London, who were main agents for Stella disc machines and several cylinder boxes; A. E. Geater, who also imported the Stella; and, perhaps the most common of all, H. Peters & Co., who were the original Polyphon agents with addresses in Leipzig and London.

In the United States, possibly the most common label to turn up is that of the Jacot Music Box Co. of New York, although two others which occasionally come to light are those of Fred Sanders of Boston and Gautschi of Philadelphia.

The main distributing agents frequently had their own tune sheets, which were either placed on the boxes by their manufacturer at source or were affixed by the agent himself. Manufacturer-printed specimens include the Goldsmiths Alliance of London (Nicole Frères boxes only), and T. Cox Savory and B B & C. Agent/distributor labels include Wales & McCulloch in London and Jacot in New York. Some large music houses even operated a 'lending library' of musical boxes which could be hired out and these had special tune sheets. These, thought only to have been used in London, are rare indeed (see App. II, no. 88).

As described in Chapter 4, by the end of the musical-box era, tune sheets were highly colourful lithographs, often with the tune titles printed or typewritten on them. These boxes were made between the turn of the century and the outbreak of the First World War, when market pressure from the disc-playing musical box and the gramophone dictated that boxes should be as cheap as possible.

Small, cheap and simple movements, often with zither and tune indicator (these being the cheapest accessories to improve the looks of a mechanism aimed at the mass market), were made from about 1885–90 onwards. Clearly aimed at challenging the erosion of the market by the disc musical box, these were often fitted into unnecessarily large wooden boxes whose black-polished insides displayed large furniture. Imitation marquetry designs on the lids were applied by varnished transfers (decals) and this is often seen to be chipped. Apparently nicely-figured veneer on front, sides and back was nothing more than brush-graining using scumble on ochre-painted rough deal. Tone is characteristically loud and brash from a broad-toothed comb with only about fifty teeth, and where bells are fitted they are cheap and untuned, sounding an indeterminate high pitch bearing little or no relationship to the music being played.

I said earlier that the plainer the case, probably the earlier its date of manufacture. Another generalisation is that the larger the movement, relative to its case proportions, the earlier and the better quality it tends to be. As with all generalisations, this is a dangerous statement with exceptions to the rule but, when considered along with the other points enumerated, it will be found a safe premise to adopt.

With the miniature cylinder movements in snuff-boxes, the tortoiseshell-cased ones are of the early period and, of course, the gold and silver ones are of undoubted high quality since no maker would make a marriage of a valuable craftsman's metalwork with a poor movement. Many of the earlier small movements are found with sectional combs and, bearing in mind that the sectional comb was largely out of use by 1830–40, these can be dated as of the early genre if everything else fits. They were often made with soft leather or velvet purses to protect them.

The snuff-boxes in black composition cases are sometimes very fine and should not be looked down upon. These were in production for a very long time and examples may be found dating from the period between 1840 and 1880 – these forty years, as we have seen, having produced vast transformations in the development of the musical box.

One thing to remember is that whilst the tortoiseshell of the early snuff-boxes can be patched and made like new again the black composition of the later ones cannot easily be repaired and certainly not so effectively. These little boxes often seem to have had more than their fair share of being thrown around, and come down to us with chipped, cracked cases – sometimes with whole pieces missing from the box.

Silver and gold boxes present something of a problem. The majority of these were made in London – a recognition of the position which London held in this type of work – even for Swiss movements. The boxes can easily be dated from the hallmark and, since they were invariably made to fit around the movement, this effectively provides an accurate means of dating. However, the date of the box does not automatically date the movement and several instances have come to light where a much earlier movement has been put in a later-made box.* There could be two reasons for this: first, the movement may form part of an earlier stock of the manufacturer, and, second, the piece may be a re-casing of a movement previously contained in something else.

Buying a musical box today frequently involves an expensive transaction, so you are perfectly justified in taking your time. When offered a musical box, the prospective buyer should adopt a careful programme of systematic inspection. The sensible vendor will certainly not object to this as, presumably, he wants to make a sale and has no qualms about his merchandise. The fact that you may take an hour or more in making up your mind is thus of little consequence. In fact, since you are spending your money which, unless you are one of the few privileged, you have had to work for, you are entitled to know precisely what you are about to exchange it for.

The exterior case or box itself is an obvious starting-point. Loose, damaged or missing

* The reverse is also true!

260

veneer can be replaced if you have the time and skill, although large areas missing from an inlaid marquetry design may pose something of a problem and tax your skills as both artist and craftsman. Splits, cracks, warped lids, deep dents and cigarette burns all mar the appearance, and if the bottom of the box is split or loose you cannot expect the box to sound very resonant when played. Woodworm infestation is not in itself a serious drawback, provided that it is not extensive. Fortunately worm is virtually unknown in America and worms imported in a case from Europe do not live long enough to pose a greater threat. Where the wood of the case has crumbled or become spongy, little can be done without having a new box made. Extensive pulverising of the outer surface usually means that the case, or part of the case, has reached the end of its useful life and must be replaced. Worm often seems to affect only one part of a box, or just the bottom corner, so that if the damage is confined and not too serious you can restore it satisfactorily.

It goes without saying that you should check that the beautiful lid design is an inlay and not a clever transfer of the later period.

Now, open the box and look at the inside of the lid. Loose or broken hinges can be replaced, but check that the wood has not split beyond repair. Sometimes a box has had its lid broken off and new hinges badly fitted into fresh wood nearby, leaving a disfigured area where the original hinges once were. If the corners of the box are loose or open slightly, it is a fair indication that the box has either been stored in the damp or has been dropped. You have to decide if you can repair this.

Case locks are frequently found broken, but you may or may not worry about them. The keys were frequently lost and the lids of musical boxes never did take much forcing. So common was this that there is only a fifty-fifty chance of finding a box with a perfect lock. You stand even less chance of finding a box with its original key; but, as the locks were fairly simple, you might well be lucky enough to find one which will not only fit but is also in keeping with the period.

The inner glass lid, where fitted, may sometimes be broken. If just the glass is damaged, this is not too much of a problem. Usually, though, the frame of the lid will also be damaged and loose and may even have torn its hinges. This you can repair.

Now you must consider the movement. First of all, examine the comb carefully for (a) broken teeth, (b) broken tips, and (c) poorly executed repairs to teeth. If a tooth is broken off, this can be replaced and up to a dozen or so teeth can usually be repaired in a comb by the skilful worker without having a deleterious effect on its tuning. However, if these teeth are all together in one place, then it is a craftsman's job and your best advice is to leave the box alone unless you want to spend a lot on the comb. To have new teeth put into a comb by experts is not difficult; to put them in by yourself is not impossible: but it requires in the first instance more money, and in the second a fair amount of skill. Teeth at the base end of the comb, which are the most likely to be broken, are the hardest to replace as they involve both dampers and tuning leads.

A broken tooth cannot be picked out of the bottom of the case and stuck back in. How popular this fallacy is is shown by the number of people who keep broken teeth and offer them with the box. It sometimes happens that somebody who is endowed with neither great powers of reasoning nor skill has actually soldered the tooth back in. An appreciation of the dynamics of a vibrating steel tooth will show that this just cannot be done. Once broken, a new tooth must be fashioned and properly dovetailed in, so watch carefully for bad repairs. If in doubt, play the box and listen closely to any suspect teeth.

	1. **B A Bremond**—Stamped into top of cock			20. **Mermod Freres**—Printed design on discs for Stella
	2. **B A Bremond**—Stamped into top of cock			21. **J Cuendet**—Printed on tune-sheet
	3. **B A Bremond**—Stamped into top of cock			22. **Soc Junod**—Stamped on accessories with patent numbers
	4. *(Unidentified)*—Etched into comb			23. **Charles Paillard**—Stamped into top of cock
	5. **Ch & J Ullmann**—Stamped into comb, also top of cock			24. **G Baker-Troll**—Stamped into top of cock and tooled into inner lid strap
	6. **F Conchon**—Printed on tune-sheet (" Star Works ")			25. **Henri Metert**—Repair work stamped into bedplate
	7. **Richter & Co**—Attached medallion (stamped) and bedplate, cast			26. **Paillard**—Stamped into top of cock
	8. **F Conchon**—Printed on tune-sheet (" Star Works ")			27. **Barnett Samuel & Co**—Printed on tune-sheet
	9. **Mermod Freres**—Printed on tune-sheet			28. **Thorens**—Cast into bedplate (Edelweiss disc machine)
	10. **Bontems**—Stamped into brass plates, ⅜in x ⅜in			29. **Jean Billon-Haller**—Printed on tune-sheet
	11. **Woog, Samuel** — Stamped into top left of bedplate (early importer of L'Epee)			30. **Piguet et Meylan**—Stamped into music disc (different numbers)
	12. **Woog, Adolphe**—Stamped into top left of bedplate (early importer of L'Epee)			31. **Paillard, Vaucher, Fils**—Stamped into comb
	13. **F Conchon**—Stamped into top of cock, 5/16in wide			32. **Ami Rivenc**—Stamped into top of cock and reversed image printed on tune-sheet
	14. **Freres Rochat**—Stamped into brasswork, also sometimes in a circle or an oval			33. **Junod** *(?)*—Mark stamped into bedplate (variations)
	15. **Ch & J Ullmann**—Stamped into bedplate, 5/16in wide. Also found cast into underside of bedplate			34. **Berens, Blumberg & Co**—Stamp top left bedplate. Lecoultre agent
	16. **Berens, Blumberg**—Stamped into comb. Lecoultre importer			35. **Francois-Charles Lecoultre**—Very small mark stamped into bedplate in several places. About 5/16in long
	17. **Lecoultre Freres**—Stamped into comb			36. **Nicole Freres**—Very small mark stamped into bedplates of some early speciments. About 5/16in long
	18. **Mermod Freres**—Stamped onto accessories			37. **Langdorff**—Stamped into top of cock, also printed on tune-sheets
	19. **Mermod Freres**—Stamped onto accessories			38. **Ami Genoux**—Stamped on brass components

Figure 45   Trade-marks found on musical boxes and to whom they belong.

262

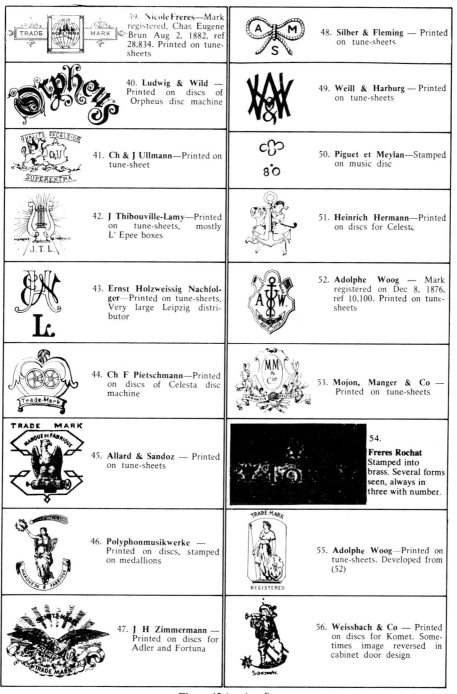

39. Nicole Freres—Mark registered, Chas Eugene Brun Aug 2, 1882, ref 28,834. Printed on tune-sheets

40. Ludwig & Wild — Printed on discs of Orpheus disc machine

41. Ch & J Ullmann—Printed on tune-sheet

42. J Thibouville-Lamy—Printed on tune-sheets, mostly L' Epee boxes

43. Ernst Holzweissig Nachfolger—Printed on tune-sheets. Very large Leipzig distributor

44. Ch F Pietschmann—Printed on discs of Celesta disc machine

45. Allard & Sandoz — Printed on tune-sheets

46. Polyphonmusikwerke — Printed on discs, stamped on medallions

47. J H Zimmermann — Printed on discs for Adler and Fortuna

48. Silber & Fleming — Printed on tune-sheets

49. Weill & Harburg — Printed on tune-sheets

50. Piguet et Meylan—Stamped on music disc

51. Heinrich Hermann—Printed on discs for Celesta

52. Adolphe Woog — Mark registered on Dec 8, 1876, ref 10,100. Printed on tune-sheets

53. Mojon, Manger & Co — Printed on tune-sheets

54. Freres Rochat Stamped into brass. Several forms seen, always in three with number.

55. Adolphe Woog—Printed on tune-sheets. Developed from (52)

56. Weissbach & Co — Printed on discs for Komet. Sometimes image reversed in cabinet door design

Figure 45 (continued).

263

The tips of the teeth are also liable to break off and these are difficult to see clearly. A quick glance may show all tips apparently *in situ* but, where the tip is missing, the damper wire usually remains underneath and may appear as the tip. Look closely at the comb tips.

If any are broken, so long as it is just the extreme tapered tip that is gone, then this can fairly easily be repaired without needing a new tooth. Teeth broken off behind the tip, where the full width of tooth has snapped, must be replaced *in toto* and cannot be joined without affecting the sound produced. If a zither attachment is fitted, look under it carefully, for it may conceal defective teeth.

If you should come across a box with all the comb teeth present and correct, but with every *other* tip missing, do not try to replace these. This characteristic was a feature of some boxes and, as stated earlier (p. 98) whereas this has erroneously been thought of as a means adopted by the maker to enable a twelve-air box to be fitted with a six-air comb thereby enabling him to use up surplus combs on hand, this is just not true. The real reason is that this is a sort of poor man's *sublime harmonie* box, the tipless teeth resonating to add timbre and sostenuto to the music being played on the teeth with tips.

Do remember that the box you are looking at may be from sixty to one hundred and thirty years old and it quite likely had a chequered career before you came to cast covetous eyes on it. It may have experienced mishaps in the past which have been put to rights again. The art of repairing musical boxes is probably only a tiny bit younger than the art of making them. Many of the early repairers were also makers and many were craftsmen whose work was of the highest order, so their repairs need not be scorned. In examining your find, you may detect where new teeth or points have been put into the comb. So long as they have been expertly replaced and they play satisfactorily, this is of no great consequence.

A generally reliable method of judging the quality of a musical box is by the number of teeth on the comb. The more teeth, the finer they must be, the greater the precision of the mechanism, and the better made the box. The first person to quantify this was H. A. V. Bulleid, who devised a useful formula which I quote with acknowledgement.

The common run-of-the-mill thirteen-inch Nicole Frères box has 97 comb teeth, notable solely because it is a prime number.

If the comb length is C inches, and the number of tunes is T, then the number of comb teeth is approximately 60 times C/T. Using the example of the thirteen-inch Nicole playing eight airs, the number of teeth is:

$$60 \times \frac{13}{8} = 97$$

A six-inch comb playing eight airs with three bells will have:

$$60 \times \frac{6}{8} - 3 = 42 \text{ music teeth}$$

A twelve-inch comb playing ten airs with eight-striker drum and six bells will have:

$$60 \times \frac{12}{10} - 14 = 58 \text{ music teeth}$$

A nine-inch comb playing eight airs two-per-turn is calculated the same way as a four-air box and will have:

$$60 \times \frac{9}{4} = 135 \text{ music teeth}$$

The formula can be altered to work with cylinders measured in centimetres by substituting c for the comb length and replacing 60 with 24 so that the number of teeth equals $24 \times c/T$.

Rust is an enemy of a comb. Deep, pitted teeth have lost some of their original metal and therefore will not sound as they were originally intended to. A dull tone usually results from a rusty comb. Surface rust or just a black stain, as is frequently found, need not jeopardise the comb. If it may be scraped off with the finger nail (do not press on the teeth!) then all will certainly be well. A badly rusted comb is useless.

The lead tuning-weights under the bass teeth of the comb sometimes suffer from oxidation and this is most likely to be found on boxes which have spent many years in an industrial or seaside atmosphere. Some makes of box are found to be much more prone than others to this problem, which turns the lead into a white powder. Table Polyphons seem very prone.

Leads thus affected are useless and must all be scrapped and replaced. Leads which have started to develop a greyish-white powder deposit on them may still be quite all right. A comb with extensively damaged tuning-weights will sound out of tune in the middle and lower registers, and usually be completely dead and without resonance. This is because the lead weights have swollen and have joined one another with their corrosion products. If the leads have dropped right off, the box will play bright and crisp, but completely out of tune and with no bass at all, for the bass notes, being free of their leads will sing out a much higher note.

Unless you want a lot of work, you are better off without a box such as this. A good check for corroded leads is to look in the bottom of the box. Shake it a few times; if you are confronted with a pile of grey powder, you know the leads have gone.

It sometimes happens that a comb with otherwise good leads plays dull or completely dead in the bass. Close examination may show that when one tooth is plucked, one or two adjacent teeth also move with it although they are not being plucked. The problem here is a simple one. The leads often curl with age and, although they retain their original mass and weight, wedge against adjoining leads, which ultimately curl. This is not serious and can be rectified. Again, many boxes are found which have had their combs and cylinders liberally oiled in an endeavour to remove the squeak caused by defective or broken dampers. Though the oil certainly will not make up for a missing damper, it will attract dust to the teeth and carry dirt between them. The result is a film of oil, probably mixed with dirt, which unites the leads. In the same way that oil is used in shock absorbers in industry, so here oil acts as an excellent, if undesirable, damper when on comb teeth and leads. All that has to be done here is to clean it off.

Now look at the cylinder. A dirty, dull and stained cylinder is of little consequence – in fact it probably means that the box has had very little use and is in its original condition and may therefore be a choice acquisition in unrestored condition. Quite often you will come across a box with a cylinder which has been liberally oiled. This is the legacy of the widely-practised Victorian layman's philosophy regarding mechanisms that 'moving parts must be oiled' and that if a part moved, then a regular purge with lubricant was vital to its well-being. Cylinders being 'moving parts', they had this treatment meted out to them, usually as a result of an incorrectly diagnosed damper squeak. Oiled cylinders attract dust and dirt and generally gunge up everything but, and it is a good but, the oil protects the surface. The bright, highly polished mechanism indicates a recent overhaul. If you buy from a reputable person or a good dealer who knows what he is about, he will have cleaned up the box to enhance its appearance, which is fair enough. However, watch carefully, because the cleaning may have been done as part of a repair which may or may not have been executed properly. The honest vendor will usually not mind telling you some of the history of the box and the good dealer can generally be trusted. Remember that you should buy a box on its overall merits and not solely on its appearance.

Examine next the cylinder pins. They should all be standing proud of the barrel; on some makes they are raked forward slightly but are all at the same angle to the cylinder. Bent pins will not play, and on early boxes they are too brittle to be straightened without breaking. In boxes made after about 1870, softer wire was used and this can usually be straightened, providing that not too many of the pins are damaged. Look for pins which are completely broken off flush with the surface. If the cylinder is dirty and hard to see clearly, feel with the finger tip for bald areas where many of the pins may have come off. If the box has had a run at any time in its life (caused by the spring power being released by damage to the endless screw and fan, thus flinging the cylinder round against the comb teeth), the heavier teeth at the bass end will probably have done the most damage to the cylinder pins. This will be evidenced usually by short, deep scores where pins have dragged on the points of the heavy teeth.

If more than a few pins are broken, the music will be noticeably affected and you must decide if you still find it attractive as it is. It is not possible to replace individual pins: the cylinder must be completely repinned and there may be up to seven or eight thousand pins in the cylinder to play the full programme of music.

By now you will probably have listened to the box playing. You must listen carefully to every tune on the box, not just the one the seller wishes you to hear. Check that each tune is perfect. Check that the number of tunes you hear matches the number of tunes on the tune sheet and also tallies with the number of shifts on the change snail. If the box has had a run at some time in its life, with the change repeat lever set to 'repeat', then only one tune will have been ruined. Rather than scrap a box or repin a cylinder because of this, a repairer would sometimes modify the cam on the change snail for that tune so that it played the previous tune twice although the snail was turned. Another trick was to solder a piece on to extend one point of the snail so that the change finger engaged with it for a greater arc of contact and turned it through two tune positions, effectively missing the dud tune.

Listen to see that each tune is played with a clear and definite melody and that it does not sound as if it is playing two tunes at once. Should the latter be the case, then the cylinder is not in register. This you can put right but it does mean that you cannot hear the box properly, so you must assess its potential visually. If the box has interchangeable cylinders, you should examine these carefully as well – one good cylinder and five ruined ones do not constitute a bargain.

Squeaking dampers (or the lack of them), can be put right by the careful amateur. Should the box repeatedly stick, stop, or slow down during the music, this may be the result of dirt in the wheels or, worse, damaged teeth in one of the gearwheels. Look closely for this as, usually, a new wheel is required if the teeth are worn or chipped.

The governor comes in next for scrutiny. The train comprises the block screwed to the bedplate, the cock supporting the endless screw, and the two brass wings which form the fan or butterfly. It should run smoothly and silently. There should be a red garnet stone in the end of the cock upon which the top of the endless screw pushes (early boxes have a plain steel top plate). If this is missing, a piece of hard metal may have been put in its place – a favourite dodge is to use a piece of razor blade and this is quite suitable, but watch in case a sharp edge sticks beyond the edge of the jewel plate on the cock. If the jewel or similar bearing is missing, then the box will not run properly. Press down on the top of the endless screw gently with the rounded end of a solid-type key and the mechanism should immediately run if there is power in the spring. New end-stones are easily obtained for a few pence.

If the fan turns slowly, it is probably due to dirt and maladjustment. Do not attempt to make any adjustment whatsoever at this point, otherwise you may be forced by an irate vendor to pay for a broken box.

The spring motor should now come in for inspection. At one point on the circumference you can see the head of the steel rivet which forms the hook holding the end of the spring to the inside of its barrel. This is a countersunk rivet which is always flush with the polished brass. If the barrel of the motor is badly dented or the smooth surface distorted at this point, or if the rivet has obviously been hammered, this is a clear indication that the spring was broken at some time and has been replaced, (the repairer having had also to repair the hook). The replacement spring may have been too weak or too short, and you can check this by letting the box play. If it only runs slowly and needs frequent winding, say after only one or two tunes, and if it can be wound with only a few turns of the key or ratchet, then the spring is the incorrect one for the box and must be replaced before the box can be much good. Most repairers used the correct springs in carrying out repairs, so do not be dismayed before checking carefully. Many later repairers did not bother to replace the stopwork when they repaired a spring. Look for this, but its absence is not serious.

The lid which closes the open end of the spring barrel and is usually the farthest away from the movement should be a tight fit. It provides the outer bearing for the spring barrel and if it is loose and has been for a long while it will have caused the gear teeth to become worn excessively.

Take hold of the motor barrel between thumb and forefinger and try to twist it from side to side. There should be no play; if there is, then the box has had a lot of use and the motor arbor bridge supports are badly worn, which means that you will have to bush their holes.

Look closely at the teeth on the great wheel forming the end of the spring barrel. These should be clean and not damaged. If they are chipped or any are missing, then you have more work to do. If the teeth appear slightly 'double' and there is a ridge half way down the side of each one, then the spring barrel is not meshing properly with the cylinder pinion due to excessive wear moving the spring barrel too far from the cylinder. This will be confirmed by wear in the motor bridges referred to above and requires a lot of painstaking work to put right. Also, depending on the amount of wear, the spring barrel might suddenly fly when wound, stripping off all the tops of the teeth on its great wheel.

The winding-lever or key comes next. You must now be careful, for if one of the ratchet clock springs is broken or missing you may let down the whole motor with your hand still in the way. (If this happens, make sure you know where the hospital is to reset your broken fingers.) Feel the spring carefully with the key or lever. You are safer with a lever because, if the pawl does not engage, the lever then will return under power against the bedplate of the mechanism. With a key, however, you will be left holding the spring and, in such circumstances, the only thing to do is to keep a firm hold on the key and jerk it out and let the spring fly. It will probably break the spring but will avoid damage to you. If you let go of the key, it will fly out and probably hit you in the face. It is seldom that you will be able to reach the pawl with your other hand and push it into mesh, so holding the tension.

When looking at a disc-playing musical box, many of the same points must be considered. One notable point is that it is usually harder to replace the teeth of the comb of a disc box; the teeth are much louder and therefore larger. The starwheels should be entirely free from rust and should turn evenly without sticking. The best way to check this is to play some discs on the box. If the disc sticks or makes a loud bang as its projections foul starwheels, then look first at the disc projections and see that they are in correct alignment and not bent or buckled. Next try all the starwheels. If any are jammed, it may be due to a broken disc projection getting wedged between two points or one point of the wheel may have become bent, so rendering it impossible to turn. All these can be rectified. Starwheels with worn, rounded points may need replacing.

If the discs are rusted, this detracts from their appearance but does not usually affect their playing unless the rusting is severe. However, discs with loose rust on them will soon clog up and damage a good musical movement. Make sure that the outer edges of the discs are not damaged, particularly with discs which are driven from a row of holes around the outer edge. With centre-drive discs, see that the drive holes are not torn, a frequent fault.

Dampers on disc machines, although larger and outwardly more durable, are more likely to get damaged than their cylinder-box counterparts for they work with projections that sometimes break off and jam in them and they are easily damaged by dirt, fluff and hairs fed into them from the backs of the discs, which have perhaps been rested on a carpet or dirty floor. Because of all this, many of the ex-public-house Polyphon and Symphonion models had their dampers removed altogether. Whilst this unquestionably avoided their becoming entangled with the starwheels due to dirt, their absence was for ever after betrayed by the inevitable chirpings, squeaking and clatter of a damperless performance. And the absence of the starwheel brakes which form part of the dampers will give rise to bangs and loud reports as the disc projections strike wrongly aligned points.

Dampers can be replaced but this is even more of a difficult task on the disc machine than on the cylinder box. Bad dampers must therefore constitute a major detraction from the desirability of owning a machine.

Examine the back of the discs and see that all the projections are there. A missing projection means a missing note. Replacement is a fiddling job and you do not want to have to replace more than a very few. Play a number of discs before reaching any conclusion on the machine and remember that the chances of obtaining any discs other than the common sizes of the better known makes of disc machine are remote, so this should be weighed carefully when considering an instrument with only a few discs.

Of course, it depends just why you are collecting. If you want a machine with a good repertoire of music, then it should have a good repertoire of discs. If on the other hand you are a collector of specimens and rarities, then it is up to you whether you wish to buy an unusual make or size of box with perhaps only one disc or perhaps even none at all.

All the foregoing words can act only as pointers. No single one of the defects listed should sway you against buying a box if it is a good one of its type. You need to be a wise man to turn down a scarce box as being unrepairable. Everything is capable of being repaired; it is simply a question of the time and skill you have available, or the money you can afford to pay to have someone else do it for you. To instance relative values, if you were to be offered one of Alfred Junod's Duplex cylinder boxes with a large number of teeth broken in both combs and the two cylinders needing repinning and a possible broken spring, you would be unwise to turn it down for it is a rare box worth having in almost any condition. But the offer of a late box with three tin bells and a 6 in. cylinder could happily be turned down (unless it was very cheap and you really wanted it), on the grounds of minor defects.

A sense of values has to be cultivated, but everything is qualified by what I said in the first paragraph of this chapter: if something takes your fancy and you go in with your eyes open, you will be pleased with it regardless of condition.

Many collectors have asked for advice on how to buy at an auction. I do not quite know what advice I am expected to give, for some of it must naturally concern how auction houses conduct their individual businesses. For example, it is not unknown among the smaller, provincial auctioneers to place 'runners' in the saleroom. These are men whose job it is to assess the pitch and enthusiasm of the genuine bidder, then gently to push the price up by counterbidding. The process is not illegal, in fact it is hard to prove or identify unless you are a regular visitor to a particular saleroom. Do not confuse this, though, with auctioneers' porters making a bid. They do this openly, bidding either for themselves (even they collect!) or for a client.

Buying at auctions does demand discipline, otherwise it is easy to get carried away and be involved in spending much more than you planned for. Some auction houses charge a buyer's premium, usually 10 per cent on the hammer price, so read the conditions of sale very carefully before you start bidding. Always attend the sale preview and examine the items you are interested in very carefully. Catalogue descriptions can be both misleading and inaccurate. At auction houses where you are known or which are of repute, it may not be a bad idea to have a word with the auctioneer before the sale to establish your interest and presence. This practice at the less responsible saleroom may, of course, serve only to identify you and your interests to the runners!

As a firm rule, establish your own maximum price firmly in mind and never bid over it. During the sale itself, bid by definite action and look straight at the auctioneer. Once he has picked up your first bid, he will automatically come back to you. For the benefit of the others in the room, and for your own information, avoid early bidding. Wait until the other bidding seems spent before you start, always assuming your maximum has not already been reached. A flurry of concurrent bids can give a runner the opportunity and his 'bid' will always be the first to be taken. Keep your wits about you and be sure you know who is bidding – and who made the last bid! A friend once found himself accredited with the bid of someone else, no doubt a runner, and only his sharp wits saved the situation.

Much of the foregoing appears to paint the picture of auctioneers as charlatans and salerooms as a racket. This is definitely not the universal case and I stress the warm and friendly relations which I personally enjoy with a large number of reputable houses. What I am doing is highlighting some of the practices which may be found at some of the jobbing hammer-houses. I can tell many strange and often funny stories about my saleroom experiences up and down the country, including one where I found myself in the thick of cross-bidding and backed out leaving both final bid *and underbid* in the hands of two runners! Then there was the sale in which a $19\frac{5}{8}$ in. Polyphon would not even start at the £5 call. In desperation the auctioneer looked at me, and after a long pause I called 'Fifty shillings!' – and got it! Mind you, that was a few years back!

Another problem which frequently comes up is how to transport musical boxes. If you are just shifting them in your car, only simple precautions are needed – make sure that the

269

movement has stopped at the end of a tune and, for added safety, carefully insert a long twist of tissue paper through the cock so that the air-brake cannot turn if the mechanism is accidentally jarred to the 'on' position. Disc machines do not require any special care other than to remove the disc. At all times, however, the box must travel flat, but this does not prevent, if necessary, your standing it down on its front or back or, at a pinch, even upside down, so long as the cylinder is horizontal. A couple of long, stout rubber bands will keep the lid closed.

Carrying a cylinder box by hand in the level position is often difficult, particularly if you are trying to manoeuvre a long box through a doorway. The box can be tipped, *but only in one direction*. Keep the spring-barrel end uppermost so that the cylinder change pin transmits the weight of the cylinder firmly against the snail. If you carry the box the other way up, the cylinder can bounce up and down on the arbor spring and this might damage dampers, tips and pins, as well as maybe hammering a dent in the snail if the cylinder bounces excessively.

Disc machines can be carried any way up but here is an important word of warning. Some boxes, particularly Stellas and Symphonions, have a silent winding-ratchet where the pawl falls clear by gravity. If the box is tipped up, there is the chance that if you move the winding-handle the pawl will fall out of the winding-ratchet and you will be left holding the power of the spring on the handle.

Sending a box by carrier, road, rail or sea requires careful preparation. I prefer to remove the comb and then the governor for this operation (on a cylinder box), and then screw both these pieces to a block of wood secured to the underside of the bedplate. Suitable stout packing pieces are then screwed round the comb to protect the leads. A thick piece of packing such as cork or stiff foam plastic is then forced between cylinder end and great wheel to prevent the cylinder hammering on the snail.

Crates used for packing must be amply strong and very large. I learned a lesson about this one the hard way! Years ago, an old organ builder in Truro said he had a small Symphonion for sale. I bought it and sent him a packing case which I thought would be big enough. When it came back, I prized off the lid only to find the entire inside packed tightly with a large Symphonion wall musical box. A note said how because the packing case was too small he had chipped off all the carved moulding to get it in but reckoned as how I wouldn't mind since that wasn't the musical bit!

For a standard-size cylinder musical box, you need a wooden crate three feet long and two feet square. First let the movement run down and then, by using the winding-key, just put enough tension on the spring to bring the movement to the end of a tune – ideally the first tune. I have said that I prefer to remove comb and governor but this is just a personal preference. The point to remember is that if the crate containing the musical box is dropped the most serious danger is the inertia load on the bottom teeth of the comb which carry the tuning leads. A sharp knock could fracture these teeth, although no other visible signs of damage may be apparent. If you remove the comb and screw it upside down into its own U-sectioned piece of wood and then tape it securely to the underside of the box, it will be safe. Fill the inside of the musical box with crumpled tissue paper to support the glass of the inner lid. If the key is separate, wrap this securely and pack it into its compartment in the musical box.

Firmly tie the lid of the musical box in the closed position. Do not use adhesive transparent or plastic tape as this may strip off the polish and even remove pieces of inlay when it is pulled off. Adhesive crêpe paper as used for masking in paint-spraying is ideal. Well tape the lid shut. Now wrap the entire musical box either in several layers of newspaper or in a piece of soft cloth and tie it not too tightly with string. Wrap three layers of corrugated paper round the box and protect the ends of the box well, either by turning over the corrugated or by taping in separate wads of corrugated. Foam plastic of the sort used in upholstery is the best final medium with which the encapsulated musical box is packed into the crate. It is easy, by the way, to forget that there must be the same amount of packing *under* the musical box as there is on top of it.

Incidentally, someone once sent me a musical box which was immersed in loose polystyrene chips. These look like doing a fine job but they behave like any other granular or even liquid material – and the heavy box just sinks through them to the bottom with vibration. Really it is worse than nothing, so if you are going to pack a box you just cannot be too careful.

Another point to watch is that all loose items such as keys must be packed separately – and then securely tied either into the packing case or to the musical-box package, otherwise the recipient may easily throw them out with the wrapping. I lost a Polyphon handle that way once.

Very large musical boxes are a different matter and I would seriously dissuade you from attempting to pack them yourself. Get a specialist firm of packers or shippers to take it on – it will be worth it in the long run. A certain friend of mine once received a huge crate containing three pianos which were all loose inside. The crate had been turned over and you can imagine what a terrible mess lay within waiting to be shovelled out.

Another question I keep getting asked is how to start collecting. To me this is a bit like asking how to fall off a ladder and the answer is really just the same – just let yourself go! What I suppose is meant is: How should the non-collector approach the subject?

When I started collecting, boxes were still classed as junk and were of little value. A spectacular one might make £10 or more (I remember a glorious and unusual interchangeable in a blonde wood and bird's-eye maple case making a staggering £17 in an Isle of Wight sale once), but the usual price was very much lower. I used to buy everything I was offered, both good and bad. In this way I acquired probably 500 items in the space of little more than a year. It was not uncommon to find four or five boxes lumped together in one saleroom lot which would fetch just a few pounds.

Today, with musical boxes commanding such high prices throughout the world, there is still something to be said for this philosophy of buying everything offered, if only on the grounds that so few boxes do come on the open market these days. But at the same time it has a serious shortcoming. You may find yourself offered several poor-quality boxes and then spend your money on them, leaving nothing with which to bite on that glorious box which you may be offered next week. I suppose it all depends on just how much money you have to spend. If you are short of cash (like the majority of us today), then the thing to do is to watch, wait and observe. Then, when the ideal box comes along, that is the time to jump in and pay out.

Other factors may govern just how you want to collect. Naturally your individual tastes will be reflected by your choice of boxes. You many want only miniature items, *objets d'art*, rare and early items, or you may only want interchangeable-cylinder boxes. Perhaps it's the disc-playing machine which you prefer, or maybe you choose to have an entirely thematic collection in that, for example, you will only collect Polyphons, Reginas or Criterions.

271

A thematic collection can be fine for the collector but perhaps a little dull for the viewer. A room full of key-winders may be the realisation of your dreams, but you must understand if, after being shown the first half-dozen, your visitors (assuming them not to be musical-box buffs) yawn and start jangling the small change in their pockets.

It is probably for this reason that most collectors aim not just to indulge their own wishes but also to have a few representative items of other types to add variety. The true mechanical musical instrument enthusiast is, of course, several aeons removed from this for he goes in for everything from orchestrion organs down to musical seals with a propensity for player pianos, violin-players and automata. As soon becomes obvious, he either formed his collection years ago when most of the stuff was at junk prices, or he is very wealthy. Perhaps I should say *was* very wealthy!

Even so, it is not a bad policy to formulate some general idea of which way you would like to see your collection develop – and then try to ensure that it progresses in the direction you consider best. Space should always be a prime consideration at the outset, although from personal experience I can say that it will have little limiting effect on your acquisitive nature. Nor will your bank manager.

Years of collecting experience have allowed me to define two criteria in acquiring possessions of this type. These I have established as follows:

Ord-Hume's First Law: Space will expand to accommodate an infinite number of possessions, regardless of their size.
Ord-Hume's Second Law: Shortage of finance will never prevent the purchase of a desired object, however improbable its cost.

I have seen a penniless collector with a room measuring ten feet by twelve which housed two grand pianos, an Aeolian Orchestrelle, a fair organ and half a dozen largish musical boxes which the owner was only able to demonstrate to onlookers who stood in the doorway by dint of physical dexterity and crawling around on the floor.

Do resist the temptation to modify a piece so that it will fit the available space. Allowing your home to become a sort of Procrustes' bed is the mark of a vandal, not a collector. However, it may be that you do find it necessary to remove, say, a winding handle or a detachable part for your convenience. If you do this, then securely fix the detached piece inside the case. If you get run over by a tram and your collection is dispersed, make sure that the next owner gets all the loose pieces – your executors may not be able to locate everything themselves. Plan for the future of your individual boxes.

Displaying a collection depends on the space you have available, the size of the collection and the individual size of the items. Nothing looks worse than having a valuable collection spread out all over the floor with the need to pick one's way carefully over them as if one were walking across a not too fresh farm meadow. Listening to and looking at boxes arranged in this fashion calls for a young back and, if you wear them, spectacles that don't keep slipping off. How much better to display them at table-top level where they can be looked at, caressed and listened to without risk of spinal injury.

Average size boxes really call for this type of display, but if you have a great number of them then obviously they are going to take up a great deal of space. Robust wall shelves are one answer but one of the most ingenious is that used by Murtogh Guinness in his New York City home. He uses stoutly framed benches which contain broad, deep shelves mounted on double-extending rollers rather like the slides on an office filing cabinet drawer. Although this means that boxes are hidden out of the immediate view, the shelves can be drawn out readily with little force to reveal two, three or even more items per shelf.

Of course, large, free-standing table musical boxes and disc machines do not present such a problem since they can be stood against a wall or used as a room centre island display.

Small items like snuff-boxes, *objets d'art* and uncased movements can be stored in a wall-hung showcase or a free-standing showcase so long as it is large and heavy enough not to risk being knocked over. A former president of the Musical Box Society of Great Britain had most of his snuff-boxes smashed when one end support of a shelf gave way, so make sure that all wall-attached cases or shelves are doubly well attached.

Display lighting is often not just desirable but highly necessary. Avoid hot lighting: give preference to warm-tinted fluorescent lighting tubes; but if spots must be used, sight them sufficiently far away so that their heat will be diffused. Make lighting installations adjustable as you may want to alter your display in time as you add to or otherwise change the collection.

Don't leave musical boxes open unless they are in a showcase – this will tarnish the mechanisms and allow dust to enter. If you must keep them open, ensure that the glass lid, if fitted, is closed. And do not place boxes in strong sunlight or anywhere near central-heating radiators or open fires. Heat in your music room should be at a low level – humidity control is much more important. Relative humidity should be maintained between 50 and 60 per cent. Standing pots of flowers on inlaid lids is only to be recommended if you wish to ruin the inlay and strip off the polish – it is the relative cold of the pot which does the damage, by causing condensation which finally lifts the finish.

How does a mechanical musical instrument collector move home? With great difficulty. . . .

There are many who, because musical boxes have become so expensive, aim to collect recordings and photographs of pieces in other collections. This is a fine branch of collecting and a properly indexed tape or record library and a well maintained picture library can fulfil a valuable adjunct to actual collecting. However, if you seek to photograph or to record, there are simple guidelines to follow.

First let's talk photography. I have in the past got into trouble for disapproving of Polaroid-type pictures so this time I won't mention them. Sufficient to say that you'll need a good camera, preferably what's known as an SLR (single-lens reflex) which lets you look at the subject actually through the camera lens during preparation. Always use a fine-grain (slow) film, always compose your picture carefully, avoiding unsightly or distracting backgrounds, highly-patterned carpets or drapes that will reflect in the polished surfaces of your musical box, and decide what features of the box you want to get in the picture – and see that you get them. Bedsheets make simple backgrounds to blot out aspidistras, televisions, gnawed woodwork or the dog: creased bedsheets photograph beautifully and look just like creased bedsheets. If sheets you must use, *stretch them*. Much better, use a thick plain blanket which will hang or drape better, which is a neutral, non-reflective colour and which won't show creases so badly. Make sure the backdrop, if used, covers the entire area of the picture – nothing looks worse than the edge of the backdrop revealing what you are trying to hide.

Photography is an art. You can be artistic with a 1920 Box Brownie if you just take pains. Wherever possible try to use a tripod, always use a cable-release to avoid jarring the camera when you click the shutter, and always try to use ordinary lighting, even if it means a time-exposure. Flash aimed directly at the subject (as when using, for example, flash cubes) burns out the detail from the centre of the picture and gives uneven illumination. Use a hand-held extension lamp (something like a desk-lamp with a 100-watt bulb in it) to pick out any badly illuminated detail. If you must use flash, use it to increase the level of background lighting by bouncing it off the ceiling or an adjacent wall. And if you don't have a thing called a polarising filter, move the camera around a little to avoid high-spot reflections. If they are quite unavoidable, the instant before you take the picture, breathe on the surface or spray it with aerosol polish to tone down the brilliance.

Lenses. A normal lens is about 50 or 55 mm focal length for a 24 × 36 mm negative camera and is ideal as a general purpose lens. For a few pounds extra you can buy add-on lens elements for most good cameras which will enable you to take extreme close-ups. A wide-angle lens (about 35 mm) will be useful in confined spaces, although don't forget that it does distort parallels and verticals rather. A medium telephoto (135 mm) is remarkably useful for picturing, say, an object on a shelf without having to get so close that the camera is looking up at it. Pictured from say ten or twelve feet away it will preserve its proportions perfectly. Also a telephoto is perfect for picturing tall objects (say a 27 in. upright Regina) with minimum parallax distortion by allowing you to stand well back from the subject.

Filters. Even for indoor black-and-white use, do not shun filters which can be used to heighten the colours and figuring of inlays, mahogany cabinets and so on. I use a light-blue filter wherever possible for indoor photography and always keep a UV (ultra-violet) filter on the camera.

If you are going to shoot colour, either negatives or slides, most of the foregoing rules still apply, except, of course, the bit about colour filters.

Many of the pictures in this book have been taken with equipment such as I have described. It takes a bit of time to get a good picture but it's worth it in the end. For all those holiday snaps I've seen showing somebody's thumb over the lens, I've seen dozens of half musical boxes with a left foot in the foreground.

On the subject of tape-recording I could prepare a separate book! It is difficult to know where to start but let me begin arbitrarily by saying that the better the equipment you use, the better the results. Ideally, you should use a reel-to-reel recorder rather than cassette or cartridge, preferably recording at $7\frac{1}{2}$ inches per second on no less than half track. And stereo recordings even of small musical boxes really do add a great deal to the performance, so this means that you should have two fairly good microphones.

Monitor recording levels carefully by playing through the tune you want to record. Avoid overloads on high frequencies which peak much more readily it seems than the bass or middle registers. Some recorders have automatic volume control – these are quite useless for recording musical boxes.

The box to be recorded should be rested on a thin tablecloth on a table or work-top and wound at least sufficiently to play the tune through without running down or without the clockwork letting loose with those all too familiar belches. Lay one microphone behind the box more or less centrally; make sure it is not actually touching the case. Place the second microphone (if you are recording stereo) at an angle of about 45° in front of and above the box so that it is from about four to six feet away. Play the box and adjust both recording levels to a similar intensity.

Switch on the recorder, hold the air-brake of the musical box, switch on the box, wait a couple of seconds, then release the fan. Do not switch the box to 'off' but, at the end of the tune gently and quietly stop the fan with your finger. Wait until the last resonance of the musical box has died away, then stop the recorder. You should have a perfect recording.

Don't try to record in a noisy room. If the electricity authority is tearing up the street outside, or you live on the flight path to Heathrow or O'Hare Airport, wait for a lull before even thinking about recording. Because you need to record at a fair level, you will also pick up the children kicking the dog, the hi-fi in the next room, Aunt Agatha shuffling around upstairs – and you own breathing. Ideally, tell everyone you are going to record and instruct them to keep quiet. Don't walk about the room yourself either as this can affect the tonal balance of reflected sound. And if you have squeaking floorboards the first you may hear of them will be on the tape! Silence really is needed for good recording. Stop ticking clocks, turn off the air-conditioning and cough *before* you switch on the tape.

Very small musical movements such as snuff-boxes and seals pose special problems. Any attempt to record them in the conventional way results in little music and a lot of mechanical noise. There is a simple dodge. Use a resonating surface such as a wooden tea tray, the lid of your grand piano or, at a pinch, the panel of thin wood in the centre of a door (don't take it *out* of the door – just hold the box against it!). I use a piece of $\frac{1}{4}$ in. plywood about three feet by two which I support by its extremities on, say, two piles of books about six inches above the table top. With one hand, press the musical movement in firm contact with the centre of the top surface. With the other, hold the microphone *under* the wood (the other side of your door panel) and, depending on the type and sensitivity of the microphone, either hold it about half an inch clear of the wood directly under the musical box or actually press one corner of the microphone against the wood. Unless you have more than two hands, have a friend operate the recorder while you play through one tune for him to adjust the proper sound level. Now proceed and make the actual recording. You'll be surprised just how good it will sound. If the box has a characteristic mechanical rumble, try recording it on a large sheet of glass using the same procedure. This will keep the treble sounds up while cutting out the unwanted bass resonance.

Incidentally, if you record a box with drum and bells, these percussion effects will drown the comb sound and overload the recording signal. Put a disc of blotting paper against the drum skin and place a small piece of masking tape on each bell just where it is struck. This will allow you to make a faithful recording.

You can make good recordings on a cassette machine, particularly a good stereo deck, but the drawback is that you cannot readily edit the tape. However, if you have a second cassette recorder or have a friend with one, you can effectively edit by re-recording the pieces you want by the technique know as 'line' recording, using a lead from the output of one recorder to the input of the other.

A heap of recording tapes is valueless unless you have a reliable retrieval system. Index your tapes as you make them – nothing is worse than inviting somebody to hear your tape of 'Mansaniello' on a key-wind Nicole and then spend an hour thrusting spools of tape on to the recorder trying to find the right track.

Records. There are now very many gramophone records of instruments available. Companies such as Saydisc and Saga in the UK and Bornand in America plus the Mekanisk Musik Museum in Copenhagen all issue recordings, while many private and public museums issue discs. You can now build up a library of commercial recordings of almost every type of mechanical instrument.

Whatever you collect and how you go about it is your own business for the whole operation is personal. As an exercise in social behaviour it is a never-ending source of pleasure. I wish I had a pound (or a dollar!) for every time I've been asked, usually by a twee, leather-headed female, if I ever 'switch' all my musical boxes on at once! Then again there is the time-honoured one about 'how much are they worth?' My answer is always the same now. 'Nothing,' I say, pausing for the look of incredulity. 'Who wants junk like this when you can have a nice polished record player, hi-fi or TV which can do everything these can do only better! They only have a collector's value and that depends on the collector.' If I am pushed further, I ask how much a man who doesn't want a Duo-Art reproducing grand piano, or a big Bremond on a stand, will give me for the thing. They usually get the point after that. And don't forget that it was Oscar Wilde who defined a cynic as a man who knows the price of everything and the value of nothing. . . .

Newspaper reporters are all the same. It's not your rare gold and enamel musical snuff-box they're interested in – it's a brash, nasty little organette with a croak in its reeds and leaky bellows. Again, to the lay person, value is equated with noise. The tinkly gold seal with miniature musicwork and five-tooth stacked comb may look pretty but it's not as spectacular as a late, tuneless, loud, mass-produced bell-box in a stained pine case.

On the question of values, let me tell you two quick short stories. The first happened to a friend of mine who sought out a Mills Violano-Virtuoso self-playing violin and piano. It was in poor condition and mostly junk, but the owner had carefully removed all the strings from the piano frame and hung them up in his shed. The machine he'd let go at rock-bottom price but those precious strings, now that was a different question! They were worth a thousand pounds. . . . The second tale is about a chap who went to see a man about a mid-period cylinder musical-box. The owner wanted a lot of money for it. The prospective buyer shook his head slowly. The owner pointed to the red end-stone in the escapement and said: 'Why that stone alone is worth more than my asking price!' 'Would you let me have the box if I gave you back the stone?' asked the chap. The misguided owner, to whom the box was valueless, agreed, whereupon the stone was carefully taken out (letting down the mainspring first, of course), and presented to the owner. The new owner happily took his box to the nearest clock shop, bought another endstone for a few pence and went merrily on his way.

Full details on the restoration of musical boxes and their repair can be found in the companion volume to this book, Restoring Musical Boxes, *also published by George Allen & Unwin. This sets out in simple language the processes of repair and is illustrated with 53 line drawings and 50 photographs. These two books together offer the most complete information to be found on the musical box anywhere in the world.*

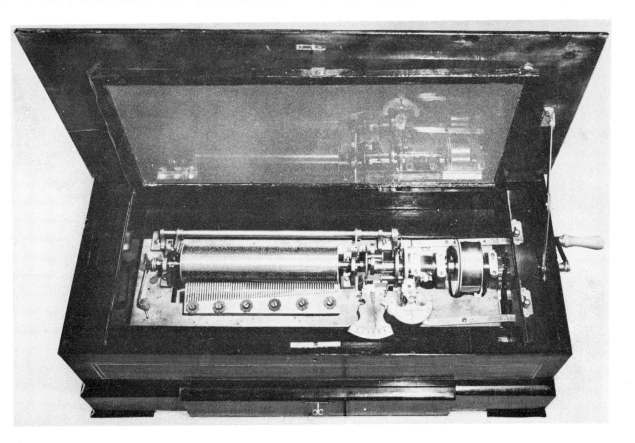

▲ PLATE 119
Junod's *Simplicitas*, a semi-helicoidal mechanism, could play long musical
selections without a pause, the cylinder pinning extending to continue during the
tune-change sequence. At the end of the programme, the cylinder backs away from
the comb to allow it to shift laterally: this is necessary since there is no 'end of
tune' clear space on the cylinder.

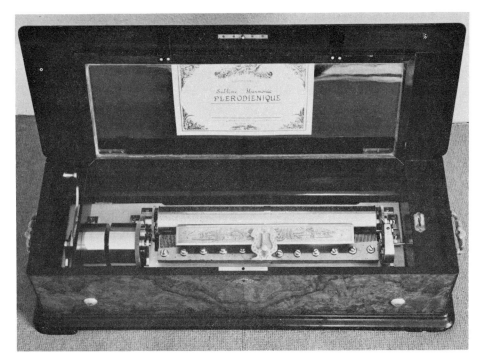

◄ PLATE 120
A more practical method of
playing long, uninterrupted
selections was the
plerodiénique which featured
two cylinders arranged end
to end, the small gap being
closed by a narrow brass
sleeve. The overall length
of the cylinder assembly
shortens during playing as
each individual cylinder
changes its tune position
while the other carries on
playing. This one was
made by Mermod &
Bornand.

◄ PLATE 121
This dramatic piece of musical furniture is a rare Paillard, Vaucher & Co. *Sublime Harmonie Plerodiénique* number 9735. It has nine cylinder assemblies, each measuring 42 cm in length. The invention of Albert Jeanrenaud of Ste-Croix, the patents were assigned to Paillard and the US patent was granted on 1 October 1882, to M. J. Paillard & Co. Aside from its outstanding musical capability, the case is a fine example of craft and decoration. The two lighter panels inside the lid are discolorations in the mirror silvering. Removal of the glass revealed both cause and an interesting discovery. London-published German newspapers dated between 1879 and 1881 had been used to pack the glass and the acid in the paper had tarnished the silvering. An identical box in the Guinness collection had London-published papers dated 1880–81 behind the mirror, and a similar case style PVF box now in a Californian collection revealed a copy of *The London Daily News* for 1885. This proves that at least some of Paillard's quality cabinets were manufactured in London.

PLATE 122 ►
View of the pleriodiénique showing the handsome lines of its case which is ebonised with brass and mother-of-pearl inlay. Gilt-metal mounts are used and both the lid edging and inner lid mirror edging are of gilded ormolu. However fine the box or how well-made it looks to be, it is often inadvisable to pick it up using the carrying handles provided as these may turn out only to be screwed with short woodscrews to the case. A dropped musical box is neither a pleasant sound nor a happy sight.

◄ PLATE 123
Truly spectacular proportions are offered by this enormous Paillard linear duplex model. Two cylinders are played at once and these are mounted end-to-end with the governor assembly between the two. The handle winds up the four huge drive springs in this coffin-sized cylinder box.

◄ PLATE 124
The very first Symphonion disc musical box was of this style. It featured a diagonal bedplate and was wound by a lever.

▲ PLATE 125
The popular table model Symphonion playing $11\frac{7}{8}$ in. diameter discs has *sublime harmonie* combs, handle winding and an inner glass lid.

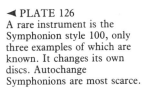

◄ PLATE 126
A rare instrument is the Symphonion style 100, only three examples of which are known. It changes its own discs. Autochange Symphonions are most scarce.

PLATE 127 ►
Another style is this $11\frac{7}{8}$ in. Rococo Symphonion with silk-lined lid. The apparent rich carving of the case is superbly simulated from thin wood veneer, sawdust and glue, presumably with the aid of a press.

◄ PLATE 128
Symphonion twin-disc models use two *sublime harmonie* units playing at once and the effect is very beautiful. This one is in an American oak case.

PLATE 129 ►
The three-disc Symphonion Eroica uses discs which are all slightly different to produce a very deep, rich and resonant sound. There are many styles of this machine which was very popular – and still is with collectors today.

PLATE 130 ►
This American-made Imperial Symphonion plays discs $17\frac{5}{8}$ in. diameter in an upright or piano-style cabinet. Again the discs come in sets marked A, B and C and the proper set produces a very fine sound indeed. A similar style of twin disc was also made by Imperial Symphonion.

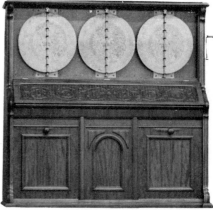

PLATE 132 ►
The very first Polyphon was in this style. Solid, one-piece iron bedplate and, like the early Symphonion, diagonal comb.

▲ PLATE 131
The Orphenion was a short-lived disc machine with not very durable zinc discs. The layout of its mechanism set a new style with its visible motor and governor.

△ PLATE 135
The mechanism seen in Plate 134 with the disc in place.

△ PLATE 133
The 15½ in. disc size was one of the most popular in Polyphons and this model, with beautifully styled cabinet containing a drawer underneath for discs is one of the more unusual of the many variants, both table and upright, which the company produced. Polyphon achieved an early pinnacle of perfection with machines such as this.

PLATE 134 ▶
The largest size Polyphon in regular production was the 24½ in. disc size model. This shows its mechanism and in particular the massive clockwork motor wound from the top plate. Early marques of this disc size had very deep cases with this inside-winding: later on much slimmer cases were used together with a smaller motor which was wound in the usual way via a handle protruding from the case side. Note the adjustable zither attachments to each comb.

◄ PLATE 136
This Polyphon plays 22 in. diameter discs with
an accompaniment on steel bar glockenspiels.
Musical arrangement is the same as with the
19⅝ in. disc with the addition of added diameter
to double the top melody line for the 16-note
accompaniment. Combs and motor are same as
in 19⅝ in. model. The glockenspiel may be
silenced at will using a small lever which holds
back the hammers.

PLATE 139 ►
This is a rear view of the box shown in Plate 138
For a while, Polyphon and Regina used coiled
wire springs in place of the usual flat spring in a
barrel. This spring, seen here running the full wi
of the bedplate, was tightened onto its spindle by
the act of winding and released its power in torsi
rather than tension.

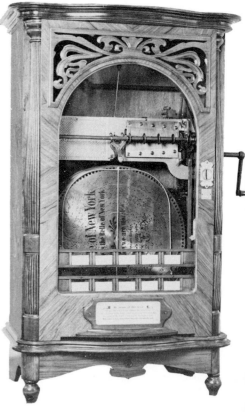

PLATE 138 ►
This 22 in. Polyphon changes its own discs from a stock of 12 contained in a
toast-rack storage in the lower case.

▼ PLATE 137
A rare model of the 22 in. Polyphon is the *Emerald*, a flat-cased
folding-top model playing 16 bells.

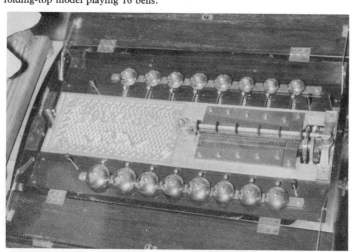

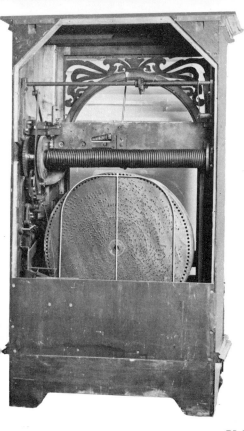

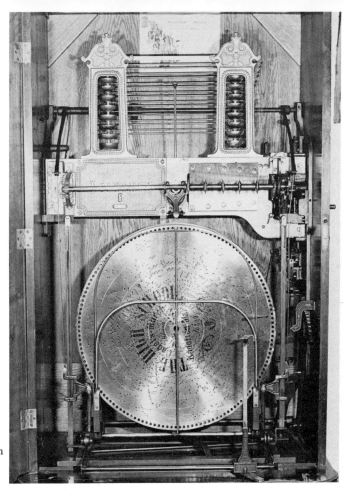

PLATE 140 ►
Another style of 22 in. bell-accompaniment Polyhon autochanger showing mechanism in detail.

◄ PLATE 141
Most common American self-changer, the 27 in. Regina highlighting its mechanism with the case opened.

PLATE 142 ►
The same machine in the case-closed state. A most handsome and very musical instrument.

▲ PLATE 144
Detail of Imperator mechanism showing the four combs.

▲ PLATE 143
F. A. Richter of Rudolstadt made the Imperator, above, between 1893 and 1900. Discs are 21 in. diameter and the comb arrangement is most complex, there being four musical ones arranged in pairs, plus 12 accompaniment bells played from the lower right comb. This means that the bells, although capable of disengagement, double up existing comb-playing notes as a true accompaniment.

PLATE 145 ►
Most popular of the BHA disc machine styles was the so-called 'smoker's cabinet' playing 9 in. discs. This was made with names such as Imperial, Alexandra (seen here) and Britannia, this last being the most common. For its size it produces a loud and not unpleasant sound.

▲ PLATE 146
Bearing BHA's Imperial label, this 17¼ in. model
features a resonating case with sound-board bottom.
Imagine the box turned up on its right end and you
will see how this developed from the acoustically more
successful upright style.

PLATE 147 ▲
Kalliope playing 9¼ in. discs with the addition of six-bell accompaniment,
optional by use of the lever in front of the comb. Note centre spindle
winding shaft.

▼ PLATE 148
Detail of the Kalliope mechanism showing motor, governor and bell strikers.

◄ PLATE 149
The large and overpowering proportions of the 25¼ in. disc size Komet made by Weissbach.

▼ PLATE 150
Komet mechanism. Compare with Plate 134. V at right is part of coin-chute with angle to slow down coin.

◄ PLATE 151
Kalliope playing discs 23 in. diameter. Note the unusual extension to the disc pressure bar. Case style is similar to Polyphon even to the disc bin beneath.

PLATE 152 ►
Comb and motor assembly of the Kalliope. Note there are four combs: two treble played by alternate starwheels, one bass with broad teeth played by spaced starwheels, and a second bass the other side of the centre spindle similarly arranged but playing in unison from a second row of starwheels – hence the pressure bar extension.

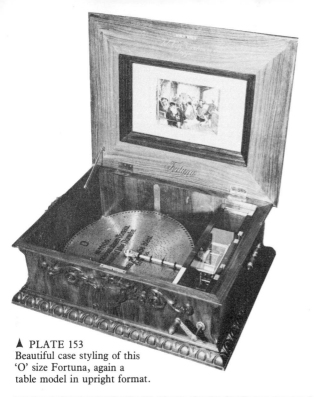

▲ PLATE 153
Beautiful case styling of this
'O' size Fortuna, again a
table model in upright format.

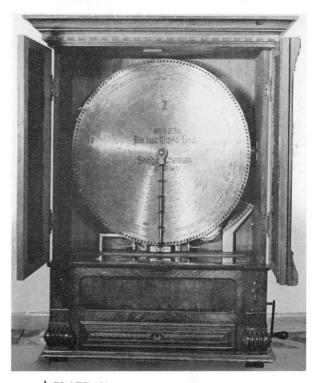

▲ PLATE 154
Large Fortuna playing 26 in. discs with reed organ,
drum and triangle.

◄ PLATE 155
F. G. Otto's Capital 'cuff box' used disc principles in a
new manner.

◄ PLATE 156
The Mira was a
Swiss attempt to
counter German
dominance in the
disc musical box.
Mermod's strong
American agency
succeeded very well
with this and its
stencil-brand, the
Empress. Unlike the
Stella, whose cabinet
styles it shared, the
Mira played discs
with projections.

▲ PLATE 157
This beautiful cabinet for the 18½ in. disc size Mira
hints at things to come in the way of later gramophone
and phonograph cabinets.

▲ PLATE 158   Mermod's other famous disc machine was the Stella which
had projectionless discs. Here is the 17¼ in. table model.

A rare variant of the disc musical box is the book-playing   PLATE 159 ►
lever-plucker among which the Libellion and the Roepke
(right) number. This instrument could perform long
musical selections non-stop.

▼ PLATE 160   Above is a table Stella, below is an upright version.
Because the disc pressure bar rotates and the disc has to
be slid under it, the case has a narrow door on the right to
improve access.

PLATE 161 ►
With discs 25¾ in.
diameter, this Orchestral
Stella is mounted in a
custom-made bombé front
Louis XV commode style
case of striking beauty.
Two combs each of 100
teeth are used.

CHAPTER 11

Musical-Box Makers, Patentees and Agents Identified

In compiling this list, there is ever present the realisation that it can never be complete. It is a physical impossibility to trace all those who, for example, were main agents for musical boxes in various parts of the world. It is only slightly less difficult to locate all who were active patentees or inventors – this task being limited quite often by either the assignment of patent rights or the establishment of a patent in the name of an individual which does not mention the manufacturer's name.

One could be forgiven for thinking that perhaps the listing of all manufacturers would be a comparatively easy task. Sadly, even this is not so, for, as with so many cottage industries, the individual makers have long since been forgotten. Indeed, even those well established makers about whom we thought we knew everything have now emerged as paradoxical as those about whom little was known. The Franco-Swiss habit of seldom recording first names and of uniting the surnames in marriage have created many problems of identification which are still to be solved.

Of course, one may justly ask what (or who) is a musical-box maker for, as with clockmaking, the name on the finished piece gives no indication of the many hands which contributed to the whole. There were, for example, men who only made springs, women who pinned cylinders, apprentices who filed brass, and tuners who created combs. For these, the 'unknown warriors' of the musical box, we can give no names, nor can we credit them with specific work.

Again, there are so many inventions grouped with the musical box, such as musical clocks, barrel organs, orchestrions, player-pianos and suchlike, that one experiences great difficulty in assessing a maker's justification for inclusion under the single classification 'musical-box maker'.

What I have done is to assess each name in the light of several parameters. These are: (a) Was this name responsible at one time or another for the making of a musical movement employing a tuned steel comb? (b) Is this name to be found on a musical movement? (c) Is this name, although not that of a manufacturer, likely to be mistaken for that of the true maker? (d) Is this name associated closely enough with musical movements to warrant inclusion?

289

Classification (c) includes principal dealers and main agents for the simple reason that their names usually appeared prominently and might be mistaken for that of the maker. How many times have we heard of a Polyphon by Nicole Frères (who handled the instrument as an agent in London), or *Musique de Genève* by Keith Prowse – the first part meaning simply a Swiss musical box, and the second being the name of a piano maker and musical-instrument handler.

There are anomalies, unavoidable in practice, but I have chosen carefully to try to avoid confusion. I have included makers of mechanical singing birds because they are accepted as being most akin to musical boxes. I have also included those repairers whose names appear most frequently and who usually have marked the work which has passed through their hands.

To complete this list even as far as this has taken many years of toil. The first to establish such a list was the late John E. T. Clark, upon whose foundations I worked to produce a revised listing for a subsequent edition of his book. His death prevented this coming to pass. My listing, with further expansions, appeared in my first book on musical boxes. The present listing which follows is once again considerably enlarged and the entries, where possible, have been expanded. Almost 520 names now appear against Clark's original 240. I am particularly indebted to those who have aided me in this work, namely Pierre Germain and Suzanne Maurer of Geneva, Hendrik Strengers in Holland, and the many members of the Musical Box Society of Great Britain and the Musical Box Society International who have sent me information, credited in the text.

A number of the names found on musical boxes are not those of the original manufacturer, but that of the importer or agent. And again, occasionally, a special customer would request his regular watch or clockmaker to acquire for him one of the latest musical boxes. This would be the subject of a special order, either direct to the manufacturer or his agent, and the final supplier would then most probably pen his own tune sheet or stamp his mark.

In the way of things, there are shortcomings in the listing. I would be delighted to hear of any amendments, corrections and additions that my readers may have to offer.

Trademarks, characteristic tune sheets, odd markings and so forth all form part and parcel of musical-box identification. I have already included some of these as illustrations and in Appendix II for the benefit of the collector who is trying to identify his musical box.

General references for this chapter make use of information from: Baillie, G. H.: *Watch-makers & Clockmakers of the World* (NAG Press); Britten, F. J.: *Old Clocks & Watches & Their Makers* (3rd and 6th editions, E. & F. Spon); Chapuis, A. and Jaquet, E.: *The History of the Self-Winding Watch* (Editions du Griffon); Chapuis, A. and Jaquet, E.: *Technique & History of the Swiss Watch* (Spring Books); Tardy: *La Pendule Française* (3 vols, published by the author, Paris); Loomes, B.: *Old Clocks & Watches & Their Makers*, vol. 2 (NAG Press).

ARF. These initials, of an unidentified maker, appear on many small musical movements of good quality.

A.S.V. See SOUALLE, ADRE.

ABRAHAMS, LES FILS DE BARNETT, H. Rue des Arts 3 & 7, Ste-Croix, Switzerland. Founded by an Englishman who went to Switzerland, Barnett Henry Abrahams, in 1857, and continued later by his sons. Manufacturers of musical boxes including the disc-playing Britannia and Imperial, and the cylinder-playing Victoria. Premises were opened in

London at 133–5, Houndsditch, which was the address of the STAR SILVER DEPÔT. The business was still in existence in 1900. See also BHA.

ACKLIN, ALOIS, Herznach, Aargau, Switzerland. Manufacturer of musical boxes, fl. 1900–9.

ADANK, JAQUES, Ste-Croix, Switzerland. c. 1820. Musical-box maker.

ALATERRE, J. Name appears with J. J. Barrière on small musical snuff-box in gold and white and blue enamel in the shape of a slipper. Paris, Louis XV, c. 1768–9.

ALIBERT, FRANCOIS, 10 rue J.-J. Rousseau, Paris. 1807–? Made good quality musical boxes up to about 1850 and issued a catalogue in 1845. Is famed as a maker of small snuff-box movements with sectional combs. In addition he produced larger movements up to 9 in. cylinder length with sectional combs. Made musical clocks under glass domes with detached movements also under glass domes which could be played at will by pulling a cord.

ALLARD & CIE, D., 2 Place des Alpes, Geneva, Switzerland. Founded in 1880. Manufacturers of musical boxes, singing birds, orchestrions and phonographs, fl. 1900. A semi-helicoidal cylinder box bearing this name is in the Guinness collection, New York.

ALLARD & SANDOZ, Geneva. Musical-box makers.

ALLEZ & BERGUER, Geneva. Makers of good quality boxes c. 1820–40. There is considerable confusion as to the spelling of the first name. Clark gives 'Alltez', yet Christopher Proudfoot examined a specimen at Christie's sale in 1977 and positively identified it as 'Allez'. Britten lists Alliez & Bachelard in 1829 as watchmakers, and Loomes lists Alliez & Berger c. 1850. Produced some large quality overture boxes. See also BERGUER.

AMERICAN MUSIC BOX CO., Hoboken, New Jersey, USA. Manufacturers of the Monarch and Triumph disc-playing musical boxes. See under CUENDET, ÉMILE.

AMEZ-DROZ, see RENOLD, HENRI. See also CARTIER.

ARNAUD Fˢ A very early musical movement survives in the Nationaal Museum van Speelklok tot Pierement, Utrecht, bearing this name stamped deeply into the brass bedplate. The movement has a V-type comb with bass at each end, treble in the middle. Baillie lists an Antoine Arnaud from Paris as a watchmaker c. 1780–1812. Tardy (vol. 1, p. 186) shows a Louis XV clock signed Arnaud à Paris with the note that he became a Master in 1780.

ARNO, O. H., 16 Green Street, Boston, Massachusetts. Devised endless-strip comb-plucking musical box with A. E. Paillard in 1887. Oliver Arno was also granted American Patent number 198866, dated 1 January 1878, for a percussion instrument comprising tuned steel bars struck by hammers from perforated paper strips. This was called the Melodette.

AUBERT, A., Clark relates that in 1907 two Swiss musical-box makers set up in business in Clerkenwell Road, London, chiefly as repairers. They were Messrs Jaccard & Aubert. Louis Jaccard had been with Paillard & Co. at Ste-Croix, and Aubert had worked for his father, Daniel Aubert, who was a musical-box maker. Jaccard had brought with him a cylinder-pricking machine and a large quantity of materials for repairs. Aubert was an expert at comb repairs and it seems that he stuck so close to his work in their Clerkenwell shop that, in due course, he developed consumption, from which he died in 1910. Louis Jaccard continued in business as a repairer and also dealer in gramophones, movements and springs until his death in 1934. He was 69 and was burned to death in his workshop.

AUBERT, DANIEL, Ste-Croix, c. 1879. A musical-box maker who patented a device for increasing the playing time of a musical box in 1881. He also made reference to its use in conjunction with a clock-case, needing winding only once in eight days.

AUBERT & FILS, Geneva. Makers of musical snuff-boxes whose name usually appears deeply etched in a rectangular depression on combs as 'AUBERT FILS'.

AUBERT & LINTON, London clock and watchmakers established *c*. 1863. Name seen on musical boxes. Thought to be importer rather than maker.

AUBERT, MOISE, Le Lieu, Vallée de Joux, Switzerland. Early nineteenth-century maker of musical boxes.

AUBERT & SONS, Ste-Croix, *c*. 1881. Good-quality musical boxes.

AUDEMARS, LOUIS, Le Brassus, Switzerland. Louis Audemars was born in 1782 and became an eminent clockmaker. He established a workshop and employed Louis-Elisée PIGUET and Jules-Louis PIGUET. His name is to be found on some quality musical boxes of the 1830–40 period. He died in 1840.

AUTOMATIC ZITHER CO., 29 E. 7th Street, New York. Agents for the Guitarophone clockwork zither playing discs $14\frac{1}{2}$ in. in diameter which rotated anticlockwise. This instrument was coin-freed and a label implored: 'Drop one cent.' See MENZENHAUER & SCHMIDT.

B.H.A., Ste-Croix, Switzerland. The factory of B. H. ABRAHAMS produced large numbers of cheaper quality cylinder boxes, usually with bells, as well as the Britannia and Imperial disc machines. Their London agent was the STAR SILVER DEPOT. In 1896 had its own London office at 128 Houndsditch, and later at numbers 133–5.

BACHELARD ET FILS, D., Geneva. Name on 'Forte piano expressif mandoline' musical box in the Bozer collection, New York. Governor fly is fitted with weights and the baseplate is stamped 'J.^{PH} Lecoultre-Duperrut à Genève' number 4522. This is a single-comb forte-piano.

BADEL, Geneva. Was making musical movements in 1826.

BAKER & CO., GEO. Geneva. Later known as Baker-Troll. George Baker, an Englishman, was a maker of very good quality musical boxes with an agent in London. Also made an improved revolver cylinder box playing three cylinders and having three interchangeable cylinders to fit into the hoops of the instrument. Was succeeded by CHEVOB (q.v.), who gave the date of establishment as 1873. Presumably this applies to Baker's foundation. *Musical Opinion* for November 1906 says that the business is 'now managed by M. Troll', which suggests that Chevob only took over *after* November 1906. See also TROLL, SAMUEL.

BAKER-TROLL & CO., GEO. Geneva. See BAKER & CO., GEO.; also TROLL, SAMUEL.

BALL BEAVON & CO., 31 Aldermanbury, London, E.C. Agents for various famous makes of musical box. Their initials, 'B.B. & C.' appear on tune sheets and it is apparent that they imported boxes with tune sheets specially printed with their mark. Later moved to 5 Pindar Street, Bishopsgate Without.

BARNETT H. ABRAHAMS. See BHA, also ABRAHAMS, also STAR SILVER DEPOT.

BARNETT SAMUEL & SONS, 32–36, Worship Street, London, E.C. Founded as early as 1832, Barnett Samuel was a musical instrument agent and wholesaler. Musical boxes were handled and these carried the distinctive agents' tune sheet of the firm which included its trade mark – a triangle and striker crossed, the initials B.S. within and the word 'Dulcet' below. This mark seems to have been used from about the turn of the century onwards. Barnett Samuel was an early agent for the Britannia disc machine. From early on, Barnett Samuel was closely involved in the gramophone and record business and ultimately became the Decca Gramophone Company.

BAROUX, E., London. Was a repairer of singing birds, etc., *c*. 1900.

BARRIÈRE, J. J. See ALATERRE, J.

BARTEL, A., Vienna, Austria. Maker of Viennese-style cylinder musical boxes.

BAUD, AUGUSTE, Auberson, Switzerland, c.1890. Musical-box maker.

BAUD FRÈRES, L'Auberson, Ste-Croix, Vaud, Switzerland. Modern repairer and restorer of musical movements.

BAUER & CO., Leipzig. Patented a disc-playing musical box in 1898 having 'twin' starwheels, one slightly smaller than the other. The large one was used to pluck the comb and the smaller wheel damped the tooth with its points. See also POLLNITZ, H. VON.

BAUTTE. Swiss maker of musical movements c.1820.

BEARE & SON, 32 Rathbone Place, London, W. In 1914, this musical instrument wholesaler was importer of Paillard musical boxes.

BÉCHET, Geneva. Maker of small musical movements, c.1820.

BEDOS DE CELLES, FRANÇOIS. Born 1709; died 1779. A Benedictine of St-Maur, Dom Bedos de Celles was both an organ builder and a writer on music and he published his monumental three-volume work L'Art du Facteur d'Orgues ('The Organ-builder's Art') between 1766 and 1778. Still a classic reference work, it contained an expansion of the teachings of ENGRAMELLE (q.v.) and devoted considerable space and many superb engravings to the craft of mechanical organ making and the arrangement of music for barrel-pinning. His work on barrel-pricking has been translated into English (The Mechanics of Mechanical Music, Arthur W. J. G. Ord-Hume, 1973).

BENDER & CO., K., 2a Dysart Street, Finsbury Square, London E.C. Also with offices and warehouses in Gilbert Street. In 1890 this firm was the first agent for Polyphon musical boxes. Later it handled various other makes of disc musical box. Subsequently opened another wareroom in Wilson Street, London, E.C.

BENDON & CO., GEORGE, 36–37 Ely Place, Holborn, London, and also at 1 Charterhouse Street. Claimed to be a manufacturer of clocks and good-quality musical boxes from its factory at Ste-Croix, Switzerland. Bendon boxes all feature a large white tune sheet with a prominent royal coat of arms. These tune sheets are all lithographed in Geneva. However, the possibility is that Bendon was but an agent and importer after the same manner as DAWKINS (q.v.). No maker of this name is recorded in the Ste-Croix directories.

BENOIT, GEBEL, Geneva. c 1805. Maker of singing birds. The premises, in a street subsequently named Rue Jean-Jacques Rousseau, and numbered 69, were indeed the birthplace, on 28 June 1712, of Rousseau. The text of a business card, published in The Gentleman's Magazine in 1831 and reproduced in The Music Box, Vol. 6, page 90, reads: 'Gebel Benoit et Comp au 2me étage de cette maison tiennent horlogerie et pièces à musique.' See also MARTINET & BENOIT.

BERENS BLUMBERG & CO., Geneva and London. Maker of musical boxes often mistakenly thought to be by Ball Beavon & Co. from their initials, which were stamped on bedplates and tune sheets. In 1861 their London address was 33 St Paul's Churchyard. By 1862, Berens, Blumberg & Co. had become Blumberg and Co. at 55 Cannon Street, Westminster, London, and 64 rue de Bondy, Paris, as wholesalers and exporters.

BERGUER & FILS. A key-wound cylinder musical-box was sold at a Sotheby's Belgravia sale on 23 March 1977, bearing the mark BERGUER & FILS and the serial number 11139. The engraved metal tune sheet bore the date '15 juillet 1863'. Britten lists four Berguers working in London prior to that date. May have been an importer. See under ALLEZ & BERGUER.

BERLIN MUSICAL INSTRUMENT FACTORY. Formerly C. F. PIETSCHMANN & SONS. Est. 1896.

BERNARD, FRANK J., New Jersey, USA. Invented improvements to musical boxes with the American Music Box Co.

BERNARD, JOSEPH AND FRANK, Geneva (1770–90). Makers of musical boxes, probably playing on bells.

BEUTNER, GEO. FREDERICK, Aldermanbury, London. Importers and distributors who, in 1880, handled musical boxes as agents. In 1893 was Beutner & Co. at 21 Addle Street, E.C. See BEUTNER, KÜHN & CO.

BEUTNER, G. F., & A. A. LATEULÈRE. Patented a changeable-cylinder musical box wherein the cylinders had a wide slot along the length corresponding to the end-of-tune position and enabling the cylinder to be dropped over a fixed arbor. (British Patent number 8196, 21 June 1886.)

BEUTNER, KÜHN & CO., $17\frac{1}{2}$, Addle Street, Aldermanbury, London. More than likely an amalgamated form of the Geo. Frederick Beutner Co., this company was Symphonion agent in 1889 and also handled other musical boxes and organettes. In 1885, was sole agent for Ehrlich's Orchestrionette and Ariston. By 1890, the business advertised as agent for Triumph, Symphonion and player-pianos.

BILLIET, V., St Ann's Lane, St Martin's le Grand, London, c. 1880–90. A repairer of musical boxes and singing birds.

BILLON-HALLER, JEAN. There were two Jean Billons; the father, Geneva-born in 1823, established a workshop for the making of blanks and combs for musical boxes. In October 1862 he formed an association with Louis Jules Isaac, a clockmaker born in 1830, as Société Billon et Isaac, for making blanks, combs and springs for musical boxes. Jean Billon junior, born in 1855, took over the business in later years and in 1880 married Émilie Lina Haller, from which time Jean Billon called himself Billon-Haller. In April 1887, according to the researches of Suzanne Maurer, the trademark of the SOCIÉTÉ ANONYME DE L'ANCIENNE MAISON BILLON ET ISAAC, now described as makers of musical boxes and their parts, was a butterfly with its wings spread and the letter 'J' in the left and 'B' on the right. Jean Billon-Haller took out several patents for improvements to musical boxes (in 1890 and 1891) concerning safety devices to prevent the damage caused by a run. In 1895, he invented a device for use in mechanical organs so that the work of the bellows could be varied to suit demand as dictated by the tune sheet. This was shown at the National Exhibition in Geneva in 1896 and earned its inventor a bronze medal. The same year, Billon patented improvements to the disc machine followed by dampers for same in 1897. These were as a prelude to the production of the Gloria and Polymnia disc musical boxes. The business was dissolved in September 1904. Jean Billon-Haller died in Geneva in March 1935.

BIRRER, F., Lucerne. Manufacturer of musical boxes, fl. 1900.

BLANCHARD, Geneva. c. 1880. Maker of mechanical singing birds.

BLUNDELL, HENRY, 7 Red Lion Street, London. Was making musical clocks in 1830 with cylinder movements. Also known as Walker & Blundell.

BOOM, MIGUEL, Port au Prince, Haiti. Inventor of the first attempt at making a changeable-disc musical box patented in America on 14 November 1882.

BONTEMS, CHARLES, 72 rue de Clery, Blaise, Paris. Maker of fine mechanical singing birds both in cages and in finely decorated porcelain pots of foliage. The firm was still in existence in 1960 and Charles Bontems was one of the last makers of singing birds.

BORDIER, A., Geneva. c. 1785. Maker of very fine musical snuff-boxes.

BORDIER FRÈRES, Geneva, Switzerland. Makers of small musical movements of the period 1815–30. May have been associated with Roman Bordier & Cie., the watchmakers.

BORDIER, M., Geneva, (1815–30). Small musical movements of the early sectional-comb pattern often found in bases for ormolu clocks by this maker.

BORNAND & CIE., EUGÈNE, Ste-Croix, Switzerland. Maker of good-quality musical boxes, c. 1850. The bedplate of a key-wound musical box which has been seen is stamped 'Eug.e Bornand & C.ie'

BORNAND, ADRIAN, Ste-Croix. c. 1860. A musical-box maker. His nephew, Joseph Bornand, was a comb tuner who went to America with other Swiss mechanics with Messrs Paillard when they opened a factory in New York in 1883. His son, Adrian (the second) remained in New York as a musical-box repairer up until the time of his death in 1954.

BORNAND FRÈRES, rue Centrale 17 and rue Neuve 6, Ste-Croix. Manufacturers of musical boxes, fl. 1900.

BORNAND-GALAZ, AUGUSTE. See SOCIÉTÉ ANONYME 'HARMONIA'.

BORNAND-PERRIER, ÉMILE, Auberson. Musical-box manufacturer, fl. 1900–9.

BORNAND, G. A., Swiss, who was the agent in London for THORENS, c. 1893.

BORNAND, JOSEPH, Ste-Croix, Switzerland. A maker of cylinder musical boxes of the 1880–90 period, who patented certain improvements to the design of changeable-cylinder boxes.

BORNAND, L., 4 ave. Victor-Emmanuel, Menton, Alpes-Maritimes, France. Name on singing-bird box in the C. de Vere Green collection.

BORNAND MUSIC BOX COMPANY, 139 Fourth Avenue, Pelham, New York, USA. Formed by ADRIAN BORNAND, the company is still in existence repairing musical boxes. Head of the company today is Mrs Ruth Bornand and there is a second branch of the company in California. Also markets gramophone records of musical boxes and musical-box literature.

BORTMANN, G., & MUNKWITZ, R., Leipzig. Patented disc machine improvements in 1897.

BOSSERT, F. W. (Otto Bossert's Wwe), Bernardstrasse 26, Offenbach am Main, Germany. Freidrich Wilhelm Bossert took out a British Patent No. 1919 dated 2 August 1864, for a musical photograph album having the musicwork mounted in the spine. Bossert's business was established in 1859 and was still in existence as late as 1909, presumably run by his son, as manufacturers of musical photograph albums.

BOUJOL, Geneva, Switzerland. A small worker who produced some musical movements c. 1826. He also made combs for other musical-box makers. A box bearing the name of DUCOMMUN GIROD (serial number 22184) in the Tillotson collection has this name stamped on the inside edge of the comb base.

BOURQUIN, ARRIGONE & CO., Paris. Musical-box makers.

BOURQUIN, GUSTAVE, L'Auberson, Switzerland. Patented in 1897 a comb musical box which played perforated rolls of paper via a system of starwheels.

BRACHHAUSEN, GUSTAVE ADOLPH, Leipzig, Germany. Was foreman for Paul Lochmann in Leipzig. When the Symphonion disc musical box was produced, Brachhausen left, taking with him PAUL RIESSNER. They set up in business as Brachhausen & Riessner Music Box Co. and began making the Polyphon musical box. Later established the Polyphonmusik-werke in Leipzig and, in 1889, he emigrated to America and founded the Regina Music Box Co. Brachhausen was never in an executive position with Regina and died on 2 October 1943. He was accorded many patents for improvements to disc musical boxes (under the aegis of both Polyphon and Regina), among them the self-changing machine.

The daughter of Octave F. Chaillet, the arranger and transposer of disc music, became his second wife.

BRADSHAW, JOHN A., Lowell, Massachusetts, USA. Invented improvements to the Paillard revolver mechanism in 1885.

BREITINGER & KUNZ, 39 9th St, North Philadelphia, United States. Musical-box agents and dealers operated by Louis Breitinger and Gustav Kunz, established 1877, *fl*. 1909.

BREITLER, Auberson, Switzerland. Established post-war as maker of small cheap musical movements for fitting into cigar and cigarette cases, etc. Now only a small business.

BREMOND, B. A., Geneva. Baptiste Antoine Bremond was born in Geneva in August, 1834. His father and grandfather were jewellers. The Bremond family originated from Uzès (about twelve miles to the west of Avignon) and settled in Geneva in 1698. Research by Pierre Germain shows that on 25 February 1858 B. A. Bremond entered into partnership with THEODORE GREINER at rue Sismondi, manufacturing musical boxes. However, while Greiner was described as a musical-box maker, Bremond was listed as a merchant. In 1859, Bremond married Anaïs Langdorff, the daughter of DAVID LANGDORFF. The partnership with Greiner was concluded five years later and by 1866 Bremond is listed at rue Pradier 7. In 1873, he was appointed manufacturer of musical boxes to HRH the Prince of Wales (the future King Edward VII of England). Bremond's life now entered its most prosperous period and from 1878 to 1886 he was a town councillor of Geneva. In 1880 his address was rue des Alpes 2 and in 1889 he was at la Lyre d'Or. Having had to report and advise on the Geneva musical-box industry, it was ironical that the competition from Germany, France and, aside from musical boxes, the gramophone, should single out his business for attack, but on 4 September 1902 he asked to be declared bankrupt. Even so, he remained as a musical-box maker until 1908 when his son, Philippe Albert Bremond (1863–1930) took over the business as Ph. Bremond until 1913. It was then known as Firm Bremond until 1916, when it closed. B. A. Bremond himself lived to the ripe old age of 91 and died in October 1925. Although recently Bremond's musical boxes have been accorded their just rewards, for a long while they were not rated highly as compared with those of his contemporaries. Always of faultless quality and united with quality examples of cabinetwork. Bremond probably drove himself into bankruptcy by striving too long to maintain quality in the face of cheapening competition. Significantly, the work of Greiner and of Bremond is extremely similar and their *voix célestes* boxes with deeply carved and incised frets behind the cylinder, often with a miniature oil painting let in, are obviously to a common design. Both craftsmen also manufactured boxes in cases with angled corners, and also made interchangeable-cylinder organ boxes in richly inlaid cases on desk-type matching tables.

BREWER, Camberwell, London, S.E. A main agent for Polyphons and other musical boxes from 1870 to about 1900.

BRIESE, THEODORE, Goethestrasse 34, Frankfurt, Germany. Briese advertised in 1909 that his business was founded in 1832 and that it was formerly known as J. Eckardt. If this is the ECKARDT of Stuttgart (q.v.) then it may refer to the continuation of a former business. Run by Auguste Briese Wwe, and Georg Briese, the business factored clocks, musical boxes and, later, gramophones. A Gustav Rebicek musical box (No. 3907 49461) has been seen with the comb clearly stamped 'Th Briese/vormals/J. Eckardt/Fabrik in Prag'. See also under REBICEK, GUSTAVE.

BRUGER & STRAUB, 79 High Holborn, London. Importers of musical boxes.

BRUGERCIA, C., 13 Richmond Buildings, Dean Street, Soho, London. A clockmaker who also made musical snuff-boxes, c. 1820.

BRUGIER, C. A musical box in the Bornand Collection bears the mark: 'C. Brugier, à Genève' and the serial number 792. The left-hand motor bridge is very thick and the comb has visible dowels. Possibly a mis-spelling of BRUGUIER?

BRUGUIER, Geneva, Switzerland. The Bruguier family was famed as makers of mechanical singing birds and musical boxes. Extensive research by Pierre Germain reveals that Charles Abraham Bruguier (1788–1862) was the son of Jacques Francois Bruguier, a watchmaker of Saint-Gervais, Geneva. A talented musical-box maker, he came to London in 1816 to live at 52, Great Marlborough Street; two years later he was living in Greek Street and it was here that his son, also Charles Abraham, was born in 1818 (he died in 1891). The father worked on musical boxes and automata in London, including a walking doll. About 1823 he returned to Geneva where he began making singing birds, improving on the mechanism brought to Geneva by Jaquet-Droz and Jean Frederick Leschot at the end of the eighteenth century. Germain deduces that between 1833 and 1837 Charles Abraham the father worked with PAUR at Sainte-Suzanne, one piece of evidence being a small musical movement in the Blyelle-Horngacher collection signed in two places 'Charles Bruguier à Mont Belliard'. By 1837, the Bruguiers were back in Geneva at rue du Cendrier 121 bis and the following year at rue de Coutance 75. Five years later, Charles Abraham junior married and in the 1843 census the two Charles Abrahams, father and son, are each listed as head of a workshop at two different addresses. Charles Abraham senior's daughter, Jacqueline, married in 1853 Jacques Bruguier (1801–73) who may have been a distant relative. The young Charles Abraham and his brother-in-law, Jacques, now continued the business. Jacques was a watchmaker and was also skilled in the making of mechanical birds. He and Jacqueline had a son in Geneva in 1855 – Jacques Alexandre Bruguier. Between 1870 and 1886 he, too, produced miniature singing birds at rue Bonivard 6, the premises of BAKER-TROLL (q.v.). In 1885, he and his uncle, Charles Abraham the son, were the last singing-bird makers in Geneva. Soon afterwards, the history peters out.

BRUN, CHARLES EUGÈNE. Born in Prussia of a Geneva family in 1855 or 1856, Charles Eugène Brun was the son of a pharmacist who joined the company of Nicole Frères as a partner with Pierre François Émile Nicole some time about 1880. He later assumed ownership of the business and moved it to London. The firm of Nicole Frères was officially entered in the Commercial Register of Geneva on 24 May 1883, when it was stated that the firm was established in London with a branch in Geneva. It is recorded that he became head of Nicole Frères in London in October 1881 (see The Music Box, vol. 6, pp. 186–7). For a few years, the Geneva factory was sustained but was finally disposed of, all work being concentrated in London. A representative named Jules Lany was maintained in Geneva. The business remained until 1906 when it was re-formed into the NEW POLYPHON SUPPLY CO.

BRUNN & KRUGER took over the remaining assets of Nicole Frères when the firm went out of business in 1903. Did not manufacture musical boxes but did have cases made for some Nicole Frères movements held in stock. Believed to be same as above.

BUHLER, Ste-Croix, Switzerland. A modern maker of small cheap musical boxes.

CPC, casting mark seen on some comb bases. Unidentified.

CADET, DAVID, Sainte-Suzanne, France. A clockmaker who went to Geneva c. 1820 and who made a four-comb musical box with sectional combs in groups of five teeth in 1840. Called 'Quatuor', this was probably the first four-comb box to be made. Said to have made musical boxes with the Viennese-style of movement. A rare example is a clock-base movement owned by Roger Vreeland of New Jersey and bears the serial no. 7960.

CALAME, JEAN, Ste-Croix, Switzerland. Founded post-war as maker of small musical movements. Discontinued *c*. 1960.

CALAME-JACCARD, P., Ste-Croix, Switzerland. Manufacturers of musical boxes *c*. 1890.

CAMPBELL, J. & CO., 116 Trongate, Glasgow, Scotland. Musical-instrument makers who acted as musical-box agents.

CAMPICHE, LOUIS, Ste-Croix, Switzerland. Invented method of obtaining isochronism (speed regulation independent of motor spring winding), in music-box springs in 1890. Earlier (1885–6), took out patents for the first proper mass-production methods for musical boxes by devising maximum interchangeability and standard components.

CAPT (or KAPT), HENRI DANIEL, Geneva. *c*. 1802–50. Very fine quality musical snuff-boxes and musical watches. Among the earliest manufacturers to adopt a single-piece comb. Also made some large overture boxes, *c*. 1840–50. Was associated with ISAAC PIGUET (q.v.) in 1802.

CAPT & JANIN. A small piece of musicwork with a seven-tooth stacked comb has been recorded with the imprint CAPT & JANIN. Horngacher-Blyelle dates this as 1802–12, Geneva.

CARTIER & AMEZ-DROZ. Name on 12-air 13 in. cylinder musical box with flutina in Bidden collection.

CATTELAIN, F., Geneva. A maker of singing birds, *fl*. 1850.

CAUS, SALOMON DE. *c*. 1600. A French engineer in the service of the Elector Palatin who described in his book, *Les Raisons des Forces Mouvantes*, the method of pinning music to a barrel illustrated by six bars of a madrigal by Alessandro Striggio.

CHAILLET, OCTAVE FÉLICIEN, Ste-Croix, Switzerland. A schoolteacher and musician who transposed and pricked the cylinders for musical boxes for several of the firms in Ste-Croix, including the makers of the large reed-organ accompanied musical boxes. He later went to Leipzig to set up discs for Paul Lochmann's Symphonion and, later still, he went to America to join the Regina Music Box Co. and set up discs for them. Many Regina discs carry his name as composer. His daughter married Gustave Brachhausen. Chaillet died on 18 December 1930.

CHAPUIS (or CHAPPUIS, or CHAPUIS ZOLLER). According to research by Suzanne Maurer, there were two musical box makers in Geneva named Chappuis. Abraham (sometimes spelled Abram) Francois Chappuis was born in 1777, the son of a watchmaker, Jean Pierre Chappuis. In 1803 he married Suzanne Françoise Zoller and in common with tradition from that time hence he was styled as Chappuis Zoller as well as under his own name. In June 1810, he formed an association with another watchmaker, Jean Paul Désiré, to manufacture and trade in musical boxes under the names Désiré & Chappuis. Intended to run for at least six years, this was dissolved on 30 June 1811 when Désiré left to arrange the liquidation: he died in 1851. Chappuis worked on his own now and by 1816 was at rue de Coutance 72, St Gervais, Geneva. In 1822 he moved to Plainpalais and by 1828 he was at rue du Molard 123, where he died in 1832. The second Chappuis was at rue Rousseau 55, between 1826 and 1831. This is thought to have been Jacob Chappuis. Several very beautifully made musical boxes are known with the name Abram Chappuis and Abram Chapuis Zoller. Undoubtedly a maker of quality.

CHEVOB ET CIE., Geneva. Est. 1873. 'Successors to Baker-Troll' is stated on a $15\frac{5}{8}$ in. diameter disc-playing musical box which has been found. A cylinder musical box has been seen bearing the inscription: 'Chevob & Cie. Late Baker-Troll & Co. By special appointment to HM the Khedive of Egypt, Sept. 7, 1907. 6, rue Bonivard, Geneva'. Nothing further is known about this company other than that they produced (or factored) at least one style of table model disc-playing musical box. See also BAKER, GEO.

CLEGG, BRIAN, Garetbry Manor, Shipdham, Thetford, Norfolk. Musical-box restorer who created in 1978 a replica twin-disc Lochmann musical box.

CLERK, Baulmes, Switzerland. Maker of musical boxes, *fl.* 1900–9.

CLUNE, WM. H., 727 Main Street, E. Los Angeles, USA. Dealer in musical boxes, *fl.* 1909.

CONCHON & CIE., F., place des Alpes 9, and rue des Paquis 2, Geneva. Germain traces François Michel Conchon back to France where he was born *c.* 1837. He married in Geneva in 1869 and was listed for the first time as a musical-box manufacturer in 1874. By about 1878 he claimed to employ annually fifty workers and to produce all the parts of his musical boxes in his workshops 'to reduce their cost'. The business ceased on 27 May 1898 and Conchon died in February 1913. Made good-class musical boxes and some excellent three- and four-comb pieces. His trademark, stamped on the endless cock, was two ovals arranged like a butterfly's wings, the left one carrying the letters 'F.C.L.' and the right a musical lyre with three dots between the ovals. Later he produced helicoidal movements under the style name 'A L'Étoile' and at this time his trademark was a five-pointed star interlaced with a lyre. A Conchon helicoidal, the cylinder making six revolutions before backing away from the comb, is in the Guinness collection, New York.

COX SAVORY & CO., T., 47 Cornhill, London. Well-known clockmakers and silversmiths in business from 1834 who were also Nicole agents. In 1851 they published a catalogue of musical boxes by 'Nicole Brothers'. The firm went out of business in 1864.

CUENDET, ABRAHAM LOUIS, Switzerland. Maker of musical boxes *c.* 1810.

CUENDET, ÉMILE L. Born in 1858 at Ste-Croix, Switzerland, he worked for C. H. JACOT and subsequently went with them to America where they held the Mermod Frères agency. He became foreman for the company in 1893 and began evolving new designs. By 1886 he was established at 21 John Street, New York, and ten years later became president of the American Musical Box Company of Hoboken. Here he produced the Monarch disc musical box, followed by the Triumph. He was advertising the Monarch from his John Street address in 1896: 'All styles from $8 to $400. Tunes 25 cents each.' He died in 1952 aged ninety-four. He was a master at making overture boxes.

CUENDET-DEVELAY, FILS, ET CIE., Switzerland. Makers of musical boxes *c.* 1891. In that year they devised a method of damping the teeth of a cylinder box comb by using a fork-shaped damper mounted upright below the tooth. They produced a musical box employing these patents and which played cylinders pinned to perform only one tune. The pins were like small nails and the idea was rugged durability, simplicity and cheapness of production. For the fortunate owner of the box, each new tune meant a new cylinder to buy, the only consolation being the wording of the label under the lid in place of a tune sheet which proclaimed 'Patent Undestroyable [*sic*] Dampers'. A later version of this box could play cylinders each having three tunes.

CUENDET FRÈRES, Ste-Croix, Switzerland. Manufacturers of large musical boxes who, in the first decade of the twentieth century, produced small movements to suit the changing market. The firm continued under the leadership of John Cuendet, aided by his brother

Edward, until 1964 when John died. In the closing years of business, Cuendet was outstanding amongst the modern cheap musical-box makers in that, even from a very small movement, superlative performance was achieved – often better than that from a movement with twice as many teeth. The later products used thirty-six- and fifty-note combs and, as well as popular music, Cuendet successfully pinned pieces by Haydn, Mozart and even Tchaikovsky's Piano Concerto No. 1. The writer has seen a 1964 fifty-note box which played the 'Harry Lime Theme' continuously on three turns.

CUENDET, JOHN E., Auberson, Switzerland. In 1870 was making musical boxes. Most likely the grandson of Abraham Louis and brother of Émile. The Cuendet factory still makes small musical movements.

CUENDET, JULES, Ste-Croix, Switzerland. According to a 1909 directory, Jules Cuendet was established as a musical-box manufacturer in Auberson in 1828 and was still flourishing in 1900. On the other hand, Jules Cuendet (which one is unknown!) was born in 1828 and died in 1926. He exhibited at the Éxposition Nationale de Genève in 1896, showing an interchangeable cylinder musical box with six cylinders, each playing three tunes. His trademark was an anchor entwined with a snake, and the initials 'JC' with the words 'Marque Deposée' above.

CURTET ET DUCOMMUN, Geneva. Were making musical movements c. 1826. This was most probably an early partnership by Frederick William Ducommun Girod.

CURTING, Switzerland. Was making musical movements c. 1820.

CUSTOT & DUCOMMUN. See under DUCOMMUN GIROD. Pierre Germain has identified this as probably being a partnership between Frédéric Guillaume Ducommun and François Gamaliel Custot (1792–1830), a mechanic who lived in rue Tour-de-Boél from 1823 to 1827. A musical movement in the Horngacher collection bears this name stamped in very small characters on the bedplate.

DAVID, Switzerland. A maker of musical movements, c. 1820. Another maker of the same name was working in Paris around the same time and he made musicwork, automata and singing birds.

DAWKINS, THOMAS, 17 Charterhouse Street, London, and, by 1914, 205–7 City Road, London, E.C. Much mystery has surrounded the Dawkins business and in particular, its involvement with musical boxes. Thomas Dawkins & Co. was established in 1870: an article on the company in *Musical Opinion* at the time of the death of Mrs Dawkins gives the date of foundation of the business as 1781, but Dawkins's own advertising states that the business was established in 1755. What is certain is that the business was originally that of music string maker and that it was founded in Frankfurt-am-Main under a name now lost. Thomas Dawkins married the daughter of the founder and, upon his death, Dawkins moved the business to London and added the importation of musical instruments. These were primarily military band instruments. Thomas Dawkins died in January 1879 and his wife, Rosetta Weisbart Dawkins, died on 21 April 1899, in her eightieth year. The business was by now carried out under the auspices of Thomas Dawkins junior, who became sole proprietor, and finally ceased about 1914. Musical boxes were a long-lived line with Dawkins and these bore the trademark of a sphinx-like animal looking to the left, stamped on the cock bracket. Tune sheets bore a representation of a similar animal, but this time it looked to the right. The comb screws almost always had very large diameter rosette-like washers punched in relief out of thin brass. The cylinders usually had raised bezels at each end which were knurled. Cylinder musical boxes came in a wide variety of shapes, sizes and styles, among these being a vertically mounted movement with a pair of hinged front doors – the cylinder remaining horizontal. This was known as the *buffet* style. Somewhat cheaper boxes were also factored but almost always the music was well set up and well presented both in appearance and arrangement. Although Dawkins claimed to have manufactured boxes, and in spite of previous investigations which have led some measure of support to the claim, it is now established that Dawkins was not a musical-box maker, but that he secured his wares from RIVENC, AMI (q.v.) and fitted these movements into London-made cases. Because Ami Rivenc boxes are scarce in Britain, it seems as though Dawkins may have secured the UK rights for Rivenc's boxes. The trademarks and features described are all found on Rivenc products elsewhere and Suzanne Maurer has traced the history of the trademark (MBSI *Bulletin*, vol. 22, p. 177). Rivenc seems also to have supplied his boxes either direct or through Dawkins to the National Fine Art Association of Farringdon Road, London. These bore a special oleograph tune sheet with the name National Music Box and a large display of coloured flowers. The National Fine Art Association was in the same building as John G. Murdoch and there may have been some connection. Rivenc-made Dawkins-attributed boxes remain good, well set up and generally possessed of a bright sound.

DELAY, L., Baulmes, Switzerland. Musical-box maker, *fl*. 1900–9.

DÉSIRÉ, JEAN PAUL. See under CHAPUIS.

DETMERING, J. CH., 21 Wexstrasse, Hamburg, Germany. Established in 1858, the business was wholesale distribution of musical instruments. A number of musical boxes and small movements have been seen stamped with Detmering's name. Larger instruments bore the company's shield trademark. Probably not manufacturers, only distributors.

DIETRICH, WILLIAM, Grimmaische Strasse, 13, 1, Leipzig. Agents for the Symphonion in 1903. By 1909 was at Klostergasse 3 and managed by Otto Dietrich. Established 1882. Probably related to Septimius Dietrich of Brühl 59, Leipzig, managed by Marie Elise, née Dietrich, and operated as agent for clocks and musical boxes. Business started in 1884.

DIMIER FRÈRES & CIE., Fleurier, Switzerland. The watchmaking family of Dimier began with Jean Antoine Dimier (1795–1863) from Geneva. His sons, Charles Louis (1822–96) and Auguste Antoine (1824–91) studied watchmaking in La Chaux-du-Fonds and set up their business in Fleurier about 1846. They traded extensively with China and adopted as 'trademark' the Chinese characters which represented their name. This was contained in a sixteen-pointed star. Two key-wound cylinder boxes have been seen by Tillotson in America who dates them at 1845–55.

DITTMAR, A. (Max and Hans Dittmar), Prinzessinnenstrasse 29–30, Berlin, S.42. Manufacturers of musical photograph albums, *fl*. 1909.

DOËS, Geneva, Switzerland. Good-class musical boxes *c*. 1850.

DRYSDALE, WILLIAM ATLEE, 6050 Overbrook Avenue, Philadelphia, USA. Described on his patents as an electrical engineer, Drysdale secured two patents for a singular self-changing musical box based on the $11\frac{7}{8}$ in. Symphonion mechanism. His instrument, re-discovered by Bill Edgerton of Darien, Connecticut, in 1978 and examined by the author in that year, bears a stamped patent number, 670771, 98. No record of this number appears in the U.S., British or German patent offices. However, British patent number 16883 of 19 August, 1899, relates in every respect to the surviving instrument. A subsequent American patent, 728449 of 19 May 1903, also refers to the machine. Drysdale's invention is for a most complex mechanism which will store a quantity of discs in a horizontal stack, drop these one at a time on to the playing mechanism, clamp it in position and play it a predetermined number of times before releasing it, lifting it up and pushing it to a rack at the rear of the machine. This musical box is remarkable for its complexity and one cannot imagine that Drysdale seriously considered it as a production machine. However, many of the novel features embodied in this unique instrument subsequently came to be employed in the record changer of almost half a century later.

DUCOMMUN-GIROD. Frédéric-Guillaume (William) Ducommun began making musical boxes in 1820 when he was about 25. Born about 1794 or 1795 in the canton of Neuchatel, he settled in Geneva around 1815. His father, David, and his brother, Henri, all worked for him. Research by Pierre Germain reveals that David Ducommun married his second wife in 1812. From an earlier marriage she had a daughter, Jeanne Catherine Girod of the same age as Frédéric Guillaume and he married her in July 1816. For a while Ducommun worked with Custot as CUSTOT & DUCOMMUN (q.v.) and in 1828 displayed several musical boxes at a Geneva industrial exhibition. At this time he was living at Tour-de-Boél 62 and had four children including sons Louis and Jean. The business was now styled Ducommun-Girod and in an 1835 directory he is described as making 'all kinds of musical boxes'. Brother Henri died in 1836 and their father, David, in 1837. The following year, Ducommun-Girod moved to quai des Bergues 29. By 1857 he was in association with his eldest son, Louis. Louis is accredited with the invention of the organ-box in 1861, although GROSCLAUDE (q.v.) attributes it to collaboration between Ducommun and Kimmerling. Frédéric Guillaume Ducommun died on 8 April 1862, his wife six years later. The two sons ran the business from April 1862 to May 1868 and, at the Paris Exposition of 1867, they won a bronze medal. In May of 1869, Louis Ducommun entered into partnership with MITTENDORF, LOUIS, a relationship which lasted five years as Ducommun & Cie. The address was at the corner of rue Kléburg and the rue du Mont Blanc, close to the Nicole Frères. Louis lived until about 1890. His younger brother, Jean, had opened a workshop in Geneva making parts for musical boxes until about 1885. He died in December 1899. Ducommun-Girod musical boxes were almost always very well set up and the music characterised by sustained trills in the upper register in a most attractive manner. A musical box has been seen bearing the legend on the tune sheet: 'Fabriqué à Genève pour F. Zogbaum & Fairchild' (Bornand collection, New York). L. Ducommun was granted a British Patent number 1766, dated 6 July 1871, for a method of lever-winding a cylinder musical box using a free roller instead of a ratchet.

DUCRAUX, L., Baules, Switzerland. Musical-box maker, *fl*. 1909.

DUNARD ET MEYER. Swiss musical-box makers *c*. 1820.

DUPAN ET MAIRE. Swiss musical-box makers *c*. 1820.

DUTERTE, AUGUSTE, Geneva. *c*. 1850. Musical-box maker.

ECKARDT, J. C., Cannstatt-Stuttgart, Pragstrasse 72–74. It was in 1873 that Eckardt established his business making musical novelties. He is best known for his musical Christmas-tree stands. His first patent for these was British Pat. No. 16638 of 12 December 1884, followed by 5428 of 29 March 1889 and finally 9013 of 12 May 1892, which also covered musical display stands for shop windows. By 1909, the business was run by Emil Eckardt and Ernst Teichmann. Also sometime at Tübingerstrasse 95, Stuttgart. See also under BRIESE, THEODORE.

EHRLICH & CO., A.-G., PAUL. The Fabrik Leipziger Musikwerke, formerly Paul Ehrlich & Co., A.-G. was established in 1877 at Möckernschestrasse 30d in Gohlis, Leipzig, and began with the manufacture of the Ariston organette. See EHRLICH, FREDERICK ERNST PAUL, also NEUE LEIPZIGER MUSIKWERKE A. BUFF-HEDINGER.

EHRLICH, FREDERICK ERNST PAUL, Gohlis, Leipzig. A prolific inventor in the field of musical boxes and organettes in conjunction with his brother, Paul Ehrlich. Patented many inventions, including methods of plucking a comb using sliding levers worked by a perforated tune sheet. Made the Monopol disc musical box, a disc-playing organette called the Ariston, the Orpheus disc-playing piano. The London agent was The Leipzig Music Works, Basinghall Street, which was run by a Mr J. Gilbert. See also under LOOG, HERMANN.

EHRLICH'S MUSIKWERKE EMIL EHRLICH. Established in 1903 at Magdeburger Strasse, 13, to produce the Orphobella player apparatus for pianos and other mechanical instruments.

EINSIDL, F., Vienna, Austria. Manufacturer of Viennese-style musical movements which are stamped: 'F. EINSIDL IN WIEN'.

ENGRAMELLE, MARIE DOMINIQUE JOSEPH. Born in 1727; died 1781. An Augustinian monk who became intrigued by the whole concept of setting music on a cylinder. He elevated the practice of the principle to the level of an art and in 1775 published a book in Paris entitled *La Tonotechnie, ou l'art de noter les cylindres* ('Tonotechnie, or the art of placing the notes on cylinders'). It was he who first set out the importance of the *silent* portion of a sound which established the whole character of a series of notes. Engramelle's work was subsequently expanded in the work of BÉDOS DE CELLES (q.v.).

EPARS, Ste-Croix, Switzerland. An early maker of small musical movements.

ESHLE. Modern German manufacturer of mechanical singing birds.

ETCHES, BRIAN, Arne House, Arne, Near Wareham, Dorset. A collaborator with HARDING (q.v.) in making new Polyphons, he designed and built a twin-disc musical box based on the $19\frac{5}{8}$ in. Polyphon comb/disc system and, with the Harding team, installed this in a unique table-style case. Completed and exhibited London, 1978. Manufacturer of combs.

FABRIK LEIPZIGER MUSIKWERKE. See EHRLICH & CO., A.-G., PAUL.

FACKLER, J., Clerkenwell, London. From 1890 he was in business as a repairer and musical-box agent. Clark relates that he also had a cylinder-pricking machine. In 1892, he was at 6 St. John Square, but later was at 112 Clerkenwell Road, London, E.C.

FALCONNET, PIERRE FRANÇOIS. Pierre Germain's research reveals that Falconnet was born in 1800 at Mont-Saxonnex in Savoy. He settled in Geneva around 1823, married in 1841 and died in 1861. Was a partner with François Charles LECOULTRE at some time. From January 1844 onwards he was associated with Lacroix first under the name Lacroix, Fils & Falconnet. The Lecoultre tie-up, deduces Germain, must have been between 1835 and 1844. Was also sometime in partnership as:

FALCONNET ET REYMOND, Ste-Croix. Makers of high-quality large musical boxes, *c.* 1830–40, usually playing operatic overtures. The name was always stamped on the comb or the bedplate.

FAVRE, ANTOINE, Geneva, Switzerland. Born in 1767; died 1828. Favre is accredited with the invention of the tuned steel tooth as used in musicwork in Switzerland. His invention, adequate evidence of which exists to show that it was reported and documented in 1796, appears to concern solely the replacement of the carillon in watches and small musical movements. He does not claim the invention of the tuned steel reed or tooth as his own, only a means of applying this to the watch. As such it remains unclear whether or not he was the first to make use of the tuned steel tooth in all forms of such musicwork, or whether he was just the first Swiss to apply an existing technology.

FELSING, CONRAD, Unter den Linden 20, Berlin W.64. A maker of large clocks for public buildings who also handled musical boxes and gramophones. In 1909 the business was operated by one Elizabeth Felsing, described as proprietor and also a police commissioner, and Willibald Felsing, described as an embassy officer.

FIELDER, EMIL, Klingenthal, Germany. Maker of small musical movements.

FORNACHON, EDMOND, La Mothe, Switzerland. Edmond Fornachon was one of the first to apply himself to redesigning the cylinder musical box to speed production. He was granted British Patent No. 6962, dated 24 May 1886, for methods of improving production and lowering costs. His patent shows cylinder arbors cast integrally with the bedplate and the cylinders arranged for easy exchange. Musical boxes to his design were produced by Mermod Frères. An eight-air cylinder movement has been seen with the name E. FORNACHON stamped on the rear end of the comb face. Around the middle of the last century, Messrs Fornachon were watch merchants in Neuchatel and were cousins of Breguet.

FOURNIER, Paris, France. In 1850, was in business as a maker of singing birds and automata.

FRANKFELD, ARNOLD, New York. Devised hollow boring jig for producing musical-box cylinders in quantity in 1873.

FREGOSSY. Name appears on cylinder spring of gold snuff-box with eleven sections each of three teeth and playing two tunes, c. 1815.

FRÈRES NICOLE. See NICOLE FRÈRES.

FRIDERICH, C., Geneva. Maker of fine-quality small musical movements c. 1800–30.

FRISARD, JACOB (also spelled FRIZARD and FRESARD). Born 5 April 1753 at Villeret in Switzerland, he settled at Bienne. He was a collaborator of JAQUET-DROZ and LESCHOT at Geneva, working along with MAILLARDET. He also worked in London for a time. Frisard specialised in the making of extremely small and delicate automata incorporating singing birds, but his incomparable skill lay in the making of the song cams for these pieces. In 1809, he organised an exhibition of his work at Zurich and later went to Constantinople but died in the Danubian provinces on the way home in 1812.

FURST CO., THE, 127, Newark Avenue, Jersey City, New Jersey, USA. Musical-box dealers.

GP & C. Initials seen on miniature musical snuff-box-type movement. Unidentified.

GAGNAUX, LOUIS, Ste-Croix, Switzerland. Was making musical boxes in 1895.

GAVIOLI, L., 26 Hunter Street, Brunswick Square, London. In 1891 advertised as makers and sellers of musical boxes. Gavioli was, however, mainly concerned with barrel-organs for street players, although it is probable that he also sold musical boxes.

GAUTSCHI, HENRY A. Born in Ste-Croix and involved with the Swiss musical-box industry, Gautschi went to America and settled in Philadelphia where he was for a long time agent for musical boxes. It is thought that he also made or assembled boxes from imported components. Trading under the title Henry Gautschi & Sons, Manufacturers & Importers, his saleroom was at 1030 Chestnut Street and his billheads advertised 'Factory at Ste-Croix, Switzerland.' Certainly an inventor, his first American patent was number 415034 dated 12 November, 1889, for a musical box. Next came 476458 of 7 June, 1892 for a musical box driven by a 'pneumatic motor'. Finally came patent number 743858 of 10 November, 1903, which was for a phonographic attachment to a musical box so allowing phonograph records to be played on demand. Musical boxes bearing tune sheets with Gautschi's label are not uncommon in the United States. One of these has printed upon it: 'Henry Gautschi & Sons, salesrooms 1030 Chesnut (sic) Street, Philadelphia. Superior

Quality. Manufactory at Sainte-Croix (Switzerland)'. A Paillard box of the full orchestral type belongs to Rita Ford in New York. This has an unusual, monochrome tune sheet bearing numerous small oval rubber stamps in blue giving Gautschi's particulars. However, a silver cartouche screwed into the inside of the case back says: 'C. Gautchi & Cie'. This name, along with its spelling, is unknown.

GAY & LUGUIN, Geneva. Makers of musical boxes who exhibited at the Great Exhibition, London, 1851. Their exhibition piece was an 'orchestral musical box' having a 19 in. cylinder 3·4 in. in diameter playing drum, silver bells, castanet, etc.

GEATER, G., 339 St John's Street, Clerkenwell, London. In 1900 were agents for several makes of musical boxes and supplied Imhof & Mukle and other firms. He imported Swiss and French movements and had inlaid boxes made for them in London.

GEATER, ALFRED, 105 St John Street Road, London, E.C. In 1899 was sole agent for the Stella musical box and described himself as 'Late A. Paillard'.

GENEUX, AMI. A key-wound musical box has been seen with every part stamped with a dagger and this name impressed on the bedplate. (See *The Music Box*, Vol. 3, page 599). This dagger mark is a characteristic of movements made by L'Épee.

GILBERT & CO., 57 Basinghall Street, London, E.C. In 1897, Gilbert advertised as sole agents for the Leipzig Music Works (formerly Paul Ehrlich & Co.), Gohlis, Leipzig, selling Helikon, Ariston and Aristonette organettes and Monopol musical boxes.

GOLAY, A. LERESCHE. Mandoline lever-wound cylinder musical-box in Burnett collection bearing the stamp and the tune sheet 'A. Golay-Leresche, Genève'. Winding-lever extremely unusual in that it is very long, double-jointed (i.e. hinged in its middle) and with an anchor-shaped end for a two-finger grip when pulling. Baillie lists as a watchmaker, *fl*. 1843.

GOLAY, HENRY DAVID, Geneva, Switzerland. Maker of musical boxes. In partnership with FRANÇOIS CHARLES LECOULTRE 1828 until about 1832. The Golay family came from the Vallée de Joux and were quality watchmakers.

GOLAY ET F. LECOULTRE. Early key-wound musical box numbered 5403 seen bearing this stamp. See GOLAY, HENRY DAVID.

GOLAY, LOUIS, Le Chenit, Switzerland. Good-quality maker of musical boxes and singing birds, *c*. 1800.

GOLDSMITH'S ALLIANCE LTD, 11–12, Cornhill, London. Musical-box agents who dealt largely with Nicole Frères and whose name appears on many Nicole tune sheets of the early period. They took over from A. B. Savory & Sons of the same address *c*. 1870.

GOUNOUILHOU, PIERRE SIMON. Born 1779, he came to Geneva at the age of 20 and rapidly assumed a position of respect amongst watchmakers. He produced a number of finely-crafted watches including a musical repeater watch in the Ilbert collection (British Museum). Usually signed watches: 'Sim Gounouilhou sur le quai neuf en l'Isle a Geneve'. Became associated with the Swiss school of watchmaking set up in the early 1830s and in 1836 published a report on the progress of students at the 'School of Movement Blanks' in Geneva. He died in 1847. One small snuff-box-type musical box has been seen (A. J. Colley) playing two airs with sectional comb in groups of three.

GRAF, HEINRICH. Described as Director of Telegraphs at Bielefeld, Germany, Graf devised a form of disc musical-box where the owner was provided with blank perforated metal discs, a box of special pins and a musical 'plan' of a tune from which he might make his own disc. Called Graf's Musik-Baukasten, it was produced in Berlin by LIEBERMANN & CO. Graf's

German patent was dated 13 May, 1910. His British patent was number 11617 of 13 May 1911.

GRANDJEAN, DAVID HENRY, Le Locle, Switzerland. Born in 1744, he became a famed maker of automaton watches, but his prowess at making mechanical singing birds elevated him into a class of his own. He made a magician watch which was presented to King Frederick William IV of Prussia in 1842. He died in 1845. His son Henri was born in 1803 and became a famous maker of precision timepieces. He was the founder of the Neuchatel Observatory, exhibited precision watches and chronometers at the Great Exhibition of 1851 in London, and won a prize. He died in 1879.

GRANGER. See under LECOULTRE & GRANGER.

GRANGES, Switzerland. An early nineteenth-century maker of musical-box movements.

GREINER, THÉODORE JEAN, Geneva, Switzerland. Born in 1820; died 1868. Musical-box maker in business in 1857. From 1858 until about 1863 he was in partnership with B. A. BREMOND and T. GREINER ET B. BREMOND. In 1867, however, Greiner was once more working on his own and secured a bronze medal in the Paris Exposition. After his death, his wife continued for a while, until AMI RIVENC took over Greiner's business about 1870, under the name of A. RIVENC ET CIE. Rivenc died in 1898. Made large and complicated boxes with full orchestral effects and reed organs.

GREINER, T., and BREMOND, B., rue Sismondi No. 2, Aux Paquis, Geneva, Switzerland. Name on an organocleide in the Guinness collection. Also made a number of large and complex musical boxes. See also GREINER, and BREMOND.

GRIESBAUM, KARL, Triberg, Germany. Makers of modern and cheaper mechanical singing birds, some of which are to be found fitted into silver and silver-gilt cases.

GROSCLAUDE, L. A., Geneva. Louis Auguste Grosclaude was born in 1841, probably at Le Locle. He was associated with Auguste Perrelet from 1871 to 1874 under the name A. Perrelet et Cie. and, from then to about 1880, he manufactured musical boxes on his own. After that, he spent nine years as a professor of algebra, geometry, astronomy and technical drawings at the École d'Horlogerie de Genève, founded in 1824. A maker of quality musical boxes who was awarded a silver medal at the International Exhibition in Paris, 1878. He also made tools for musical-box makers. Pierre Germain, who has researched Grosclaude, has traced four addresses: 5 rue du Mont Blanc; 16 rue Kléberg; 10 quai de la Poste; and 2 bis, rue Saint-Leger. See also LECOULTRE, C. and PERRELET, AUGUSTE.

GROT, Geneva. c. 1820. Musical-box maker.

GRUONER & BULLINGER, FABRIK FEINMECHAN. MUSIK-U. FEDERTRIEBWERKE, Winterbach-Schorndor, Germany. Founded 1904 by Xaver Bullinger for the manufacture of musical Christmas-tree stands and musical-box novelties.

GUBLET, Ste-Croix, Switzerland. Good-class musical boxes c. 1850.

GUEISSAZ, ANDRÉ, Ste-Croix, Switzerland. Musical-box maker c. 1890.

GUEISSAZ FILS & CO., L'Auberson, Switzerland. Made musical boxes c. 1870, including some large ones with dancing dolls, timpani, voix céleste and bells, one of which was for the Shah of Persia. fl. 1900. Still in business making small movements.

GUEISSAZ-FRÈRES, La Sagne, Chaux-de-Fonds, Switzerland. This name is sometimes found scratched on the bedplates of small musical movements made by other firms such as Paillard in the 1890 period. This might mean that they were repaired by them or that Gueissaz-Frères at one time sold them.

GUIGNARD, Geneva. *c*. 1820. A maker of musical movements.

GUNZ, OSCAR F., Rutherford Park, New Jersey, USA. Invented improvements to musical boxes in conjunction with Alfred Sueur in 1887.

HALL, WILLIAM, Newhall Street, Birmingham. In 1830, Hall was agent for musical snuff-boxes and also made tortoiseshell cases for such movements.

HARDING, KEITH, 93, Hornsey Road, London, N7. Clock and musical-box restorer. In 1977, his team of engineers built a replica $19\frac{5}{8}$ in. Polyphon which was called 'Jubilee' to commemorate that of Queen Elizabeth II. See also under ETCHES, BRIAN.

HARMONIA, A.-G., Auberson, Switzerland. The Société Anonyme 'Harmonia' was founded in 1896 and directed by Aug. Bornand-Golar. Manufactured the Harmonia disc-playing musical box. *fl.* 1909.

HARRIS, HEELEY & CO., 24 Union Street, Birmingham, and also 212 High Holborn, London (1810–40). Agents for musical boxes and also for the Bohemian Harmonicon orchestrion. This firm also made the cases for small musical boxes, the movements for which they imported. Some of their cases were extensively decorated with coral and lava cameos, bronzes, ormolu, alabaster, Boulle and tortoiseshell.

HARSTON & COY, A. E., Ruthven Street, Toowoomba, Queensland. Principal importers and dealers in musical boxes who were operating *c*. 1903–9. Established 1873.

HASSE, WILLIAM F., 107, East 14th Street, New York City. Described as 'successors to T. F. Kraemer & Co.'. Importers of Polyphon and Symphonion musical boxes and agents for the Regina *c*. 1894–5.

HELLER, J. H., Bundesgasse, Berne, Switzerland. Factory in Interlaken run by H. C. Heller. Makers of good-class musical boxes often with reed organ accompaniment variously called 'voix céleste' or 'flutina'. They also made orchestrions and exhibited one at the Vienna World Exhibition in 1873, which had 40 stops, 633 pipes and 12 barrels. Heller also made snuff-box movements and continued to make good-class musical boxes up until 1907.

HENRIOT, Geneva. Maker of quality musical boxes apparently *c*. 1850. Britten lists Henriot à Geneve as a watchmaker *c*. 1785. A six-air box playing one overture on two revolutions, and four other tunes, dating from about 1835 can be seen in Plate 59.

HENRY, D. W., San Francisco, USA. Opened business as musical-box dealer and importer *c*. 1870 at 3 O'Farrell Street, corner of Market Street. In 1880 was at 226 O'Farrell Street. Business closed soon after, according to Theobald (*MBSI Bulletin*, Vol. 22, page 192).

HETRO. See STUDIO OYEN.

HIRSCH, ÉMILE, & CO., Hatton Garden, Clerkenwell, London. Agents for Swiss musical boxes in 1880.

HOFFMANN, E. K. Was granted British Patent number 3241 of 7 August 1880, for a low-cost mass-production-type musical box incorporating the mainspring in the end of the cylinder and other simplifications of the mechanism (see *The Music Box*, Volume 8, page 125, 1977).

HOLZWEISSIG NACHF., ERNST, 91 Ritterstrasse, Berlin; Alterwall 64–66, Hamburg; and Leipzig. Main distributive agents for the Symphonion, 1903.

HÖSSLY, LOUIS, Ste-Croix, Switzerland. Patented rocking lever plucking disc machine for THORENS (q.v.).

HOWELL, JAMES, & CO., 5, 7, & 9 Regent Street, London. Were musical-box agents in 1870.

HUGHES, WILLIAM, London. A maker of musical automaton watches in 1766.

HUMBERT BROLLIET, Geneva. Partnerships which are recorded in horological circles include

Humbert & Perrelet, Humbert et Darier and Humbert-Droz, the latter, presumably the union of two family names by marriage, referred to by Chapuis & Jaquet (*The History of the Self-Winding Watch*) as 'a Swiss watchmaker . . . who had emigrated to Philadelphia after living in England several years'. A watch has been seen marked Humbert à Langres. As a maker of musical boxes, Humbert Brolliet made items of outstanding dexterity. One is recorded as playing twenty-four tunes, three per turn, each revolution taking three minutes. All Humbert boxes of all name combinations so far seen have circular or bun-type feet and a diamond-shaped stringing inlay on the case front and inside lid while lid tops have brass inlays.

HUMBERT FRÈRES. Joseph Humbert was working in Paris in 1789 and went to Geneva and then to Le Locle in 1795. By 1800, he was making mechanical singing birds. Aimé Humbert (brother? son?) lived in Neuchatel and became president of the Watchmakers' Union in 1860. Musical boxes have been seen stamped HUMBERT FRÈRES.

IMHOF & MUKLE. Founded in 1845 at Vöhrenbach, Baden, Germany, the firm opened an office and showroom at 46 Oxford Street, London, in 1870 and in 1883 at 110 New Oxford Street. Musical-instrument makers of repute, they were makers of barrel-playing orchestrions and exhibited at the 1862 exhibition in London. They later had an address at 547 Oxford Street, and were agents for various makes of musical boxes including Stella, Polyphon and Regina, these last two being supplied to them by Henry Klein & Co. of Wardour Street. Mukle was a descendant of a Black Forest flute-playing clockmaker. The firm is still in business today as Imhofs, a retailer of radio, television sets, tape-recorders, records and so on.

INGOLD, PIERRE FREDERICK, Paris and London. (1787–1878). A maker of singing birds.

IRION, JOH., Felsentra 57, St-Gallen, Switzerland. Maker of musical boxes and other mechanical musicwork. Established 1880.

JA. Initials stamped on comb are a feature of some Paillard boxes. Not identified.

JC. See CUENDET, JULES.

J.G.M. These three initials which appear on countless numbers of small musical movements commonly found in photograph albums were recently identified by Christopher Proudfoot. John Gloag Murdoch established his business in 1863 at 91–3 Farringdon Road in London. He did a prolific trade in musical novelties and photograph albums and imported many thousands of movements, many of which are also marked 'Made in France', which were stamped with his initials. Many albums have movements marked 'J.G.M. & Co., Paris' and it is known that Murdoch traded with Thibouville-Lamy (q.v.), which bought extensively from French musical-box makers such as L'Épée.

J.H.M. These initials have been seen stamped on the musical movements in photograph albums. They appear as 'JH' with the 'M' stamped centrally beneath, and stand for John Harrop of 55 Tib Street, Manchester, England. Christopher Proudfoot identified Harrop as publishers of musical albums and bibles lithographed in colour. One examined by the author was *The Victorian Album* published in 1897 to commemorate the Diamond Jubilee of Queen Victoria. These small movements appear to have been imported through John G. Murdoch (see J.G.M.) from Thibouville-Lamy (L'Épée products) or via Dawkins (Ami Rivenc products). By 1909, John Harrop Ltd was in business at 27 Dale Street, Manchester, as a furniture and piano dealer. The name does not appear in the 1914 directory.

JACCARD, ALEXIS, Ste-Croix, Switzerland. Was making small musical movements in 1872 and the firm is still in existence.

JACCARD & AUBERT, London. *c*. 1907. See AUBERT.

JACCARD, AUGUST, 120 Sutter Street, San Francisco, USA. Musical-box dealer and importer who came from Switzerland. *fl*. 1885.

JACCARD, EDOUARD, Ste-Croix, Switzerland. A maker of musical boxes.

JACCARD FRÈRES, Ste-Croix, Switzerland. Most probably brothers Alexis and Edouard, who produced good-quality musical boxes and who exhibited at the Great Exhibition, London, in 1851. They made some very large boxes which played four overtures.

JACCARD, JULES, Ste-Croix, Switzerland. A maker of musical boxes *c*. 1890.

JACCARD, LOUIS GUSTAVE. Went to America from Switzerland with Paillards when they opened a branch in New York. Worked with C. H. Jacot junior. He was born at L'Auberson on 25 June 1861 and moved to America, working with M. J. PAILLARD from 1883, and with JACOT from 1886.

JACCARD, WALTER, Ste-Croix, Switzerland. A maker of musical boxes.

JACCARD DU GRAND, CONSTANT, rue de Tyrol 13, Ste-Croix, Switzerland. Musical-box manufacturer, *fl*. 1900.

JACCARD, LOUIS JUSTIN, rue de la Sagne 3, Ste-Croix, Switzerland. Musical-box manufacturer, *fl*. 1900.

JACCARD & MARGOT SUCCESSEURS, L., Auberson, Switzerland. Musical-box manufacturers, *fl*. 1900.

JACCARD-ROD, ALFRED, Ste-Croix, Switzerland. Took out patents in connection with Hermann THORENS, maker of musical boxes.

JACCARD-THEVENAR, E., Auberson, Switzerland. Musical-box manufacturers, *fl*. 1900.

JACOT, CHARLES HENRY, & CO., Geneva, Switzerland. 1870. Subsequently went to America with EMILE CUENDET and, in 1886, invented Jacot's Safety Check to prevent accidental running down of a musical box should the escapement be damaged. Jacot produced a musical box fitted with this device and named it the 'Ideal Musical Box'. The safety check was actually devised by the son of the original C. H. Jacot when he worked in conjunction with Louis Jaccard, who went to America with Paillards when they opened a branch in New York. C. H. Jacot also patented many improvements in connection with musical-box dampers and, in 1883, published a booklet entitled *How to Repair Musical Boxes* which ran to three editions and was published in America. He was also agent for Mermod Frères musical boxes. The business was dissolved in 1911.

JACOT MUSIC BOX CO., 298 Broadway and, later, at 39 Union Street, New York City, as Jacot & Son. Established 1898. Musical-box importers, dealers and repairers. See also JACOT, CHARLES HENRY.

JACQUES, LOUIS, & SON, Le Brassus, Switzerland. Were makers of large musical boxes in 1850. Their name is sometimes misspelled 'Jaques'.

JAILLET, Geneva, Switzerland. Musical-movement maker *c*. 1820.

JANVIER FILS, SALOMAN, Ste-Croix, Switzerland. In 1830, were making large musical boxes having thin card tune-sheets written in ink. The word 'cartel' appeared at the top. Descended from the famous clockmaking family, they flourished from 1750 to 1835 in St-Claude, Besançon, Paris, Verdun and Ste-Croix.

JAQUET-DROZ, PIERRE. Born at Chaux-de-Fonds, Switzerland, 28 July 1721, married in 1752 and died at Bienne on 28 November 1790. World-famous maker of mechanical singing birds and outstanding automata. He also made complicated watches and musical clocks playing on bells, as well as organ-playing clocks. He made an unusual automaton clock for the king of Spain. His son, Henri Louis (born in 1752) was also a maker of automata as well as watches and clocks. In 1784, he moved the head office of his business from La Chaux-de-Fonds to Geneva and from that date forward it became mainly concerned with watchmaking.

JAQUET-DROZ, HENRI LOUIS, Geneva and Paris. Born in 1752, died in Naples, 15 November 1791, aged 39. Son of Pierre, he was a maker of singing birds and automata of remarkable complexity. Between 1760 and 1790, father Pierre and son contrived four automata which were acclaimed throughout the world: The Musician, The Writer, The Artist and The Grotto. The first three are preserved to this day at Neuchatel, Switzerland. Henri Louis is believed to have written the music played by The Musician and was originally trained as a musician. He also built The Shepherd automaton clock, now in the Madrid National Museum. He journeyed to England, France and Spain, was condemned to death in Madrid by the Inquisition as a necromancer and saved by the Bishop of Toledo.

JEANRENAUD, ALBERT, Ste-Croix. c. 1870. In 1882, he patented a long-playing musical box with two cylinders on the same axis which enabled long musical selections and complete overtures to be played on two independent sets of combs without a pause. This was known as the Plerodiénique. Jeanrenaud's patents were assigned to Paillard. In 1909, under the management of Paul Jeanrenaud, Ste-Croix, a business existed in Milan, Italy, under the name Società Italiana di Macchine Parlanti at Monte Napoleone 25, to sell gramophones and records made by Jeanrenaud in Ste-Croix.

JUILLERAT, ADOLPH E., 601, California Street, San Francisco, USA. Dealer and importer of Paillard musical boxes. Theobald (MBSI *Bulletin*, Vol 22, p. 196) records that he lived at 111 Sanchez Street, and later had premises at 23 Dupont Street. See also PAILLARD & CO., M.

JUNGHANS (Vereinigte Uhrenfabriken Gebr. Junghans & Thomas Haller A.-G.), Schramberg, Württemberg, Black Forest, Germany. Clockmaking business founded by Erhard Junghans in 1861. Produced two types of disc-playing musical clock, one having the disc played on the front of the works beneath the clockface; the other on top of the clock horizontally under a hinged lid. Junghans discs appear all to have been $4\frac{1}{2}$ in. (11·5 cm) in diameter and all bear the trademark of an eight-pointed star, the points of which touch an enclosing circle with the name Junghans and the letter 'J' inside the star. Symphonion also made clocks of this type, which used the same mechanism and the identical discs, but bearing the name and marks of Symphonion.

JUNOD, ALFRED, Ste-Croix, Switzerland. c. 1887. A clever musical-box maker of good quality who devised the Duplex musical box which played two cylinders at once on two combs mounted in parallel. Also made large boxes with spring motor and escapement mounted entirely beneath the bedplate.

JUNOD, ANDRÉ, Switzerland. Devised a disc-playing musical box which dispensed with the need for disc projections. Worked for Mermod Frères and was responsible for the designing of the Stella musical box which employed his principle.

JUNOD, FÉLIX, Ste-Croix, Switzerland. A maker of musical boxes c. 1860.

JUNOD FRÈRES, Auberson. Musical-box manufacturers, *fl.* 1900.

JUNOD, SOCIÉTÉ. This was the association formed by Alfred Junod, Jules Jaccard and Paul Calame-Jaccard for the design and manufacture of musical boxes. They patented a new style of cylinder box using a motor and endless assembly mounted under the bedplate. This was covered by US patent 445699 (3 February 1891), British patent number 12170 (2

August 1890) and French patent 207352. These boxes usually had a repoussé-type silver cartouche in the lid bearing the serial number of the box, and the mechanism was handle-wound from the right side.

KALLIOPE-MUSIKWERKE, A.-G., Dorotheenstrasse 20, Leipzig-Gohlis. This famous maker of disc musical boxes began around the start of 1895 when Emil Anton Wacker, Christian Heinrich Richard Bock and Gustav Max Espenhain founded the Kalliope Fabrik Mechanischer Musikwerke Espenhain, Wacker und Bock. The designers of the Kalliope were Wacker and Bock, presumably Espenhain providing funding for the enterprise. In 1898, the business was reorganised as the Kalliope-Musikwerke A.-G. at Bittersfelderstrasse 1, and within two years Espenhain had left to form his own Apollo Musikwerke. Kalliope remained in business until at least 1919, when it was merged with MENZENHAUER & SCHMIDT (q.v.).

KAPT. See CAPT.

KARRER, WWE. AD., Unter-Kulm, Aargau, Switzerland. Listed in the 1903 German music trades directory as a manufacturer of musical boxes. Adolf Karrer was granted British Patent No. 9024 dated 10 July 1896, for an extended-play design for musical boxes by the interposition of a pinion and great wheel between spring barrel and cylinder in the fashion of the *Longue Marche* style.

KARRER ET CIE., Teufenthal, Switzerland. A maker of good-quality musical boxes who also produced large orchestrion organs c. 1870 (see Buchner, *Mechanical Musical Instruments*). A very early changeable cylinder box in the Guinness collection, New York, bears the name HENRI CAPT À GENEVE on the brass tune sheet and the bedplate is stamped KARRER ET CE (*sic*) À GENEVE.

KARRER, RUDOLF, Teufenthal, Switzerland. Devised in 1881 a method of making less expensive and less complicated springs for musical-box motors.

KARRER, SAMUEL. A letter published on page 227 of *The Music Box*, vol. 5, from Dr Martin Karrer of Zurich, provides the following information: 'My great-grandfather was Samuel Karrer, born in Teufenthal. His father had an inn in Teufenthal and it seems that Samuel Karrer learned the business of merchant. I do not know how he learned the business of manufacturing mechanical musical instruments, but it seems that he did not take over an existing manufacturing plant, but that he formed one on his own in Teufenthal where he lived until he died in 1910. His business closed in about 1905, due to the fact that he had no heir or other successor to take it over; my grandfather had studied law and settled in Zurich. I do not know how big or important the Teufenthal plant was but it seems that he was quite successful in his business and exported a considerable portion of his production to places all over the world.'

KEITH, PROWSE & CO. This extremely old business still exists today, although it is no longer associated with musical instruments as such. It can be traced right back to the musical-instrument-making partnerships of Longman & Broderip, Clement and John Longman. Giles Longman took over the business of John Longman and in turn was absorbed into the business of R. W. Keith in about 1822. William Prowse joined about 1829, the firm now being named Keith, Prowse. Keith died in 1846 and Prowse, at the age of 81, in 1886. His (Prowse's) son-in-law, William Bryan Jones, continued the business as Keith, Prowse & Co. at 48 Cheapside, London until his death at 57 in May 1891. The company factored musical instruments, published music, and had a large piano factory in North London. A large number of clockwork public-house-type pianos were built and the company was also agent for German electric pianos and orchestrions. During the First World War, when music rolls for these instruments were impossible to obtain, Keith, Prowse developed a thriving business preparing new music rolls playing, in many cases, British patriotic songs. Keith, Prowse sold musical boxes at one time and boxes are found bearing their labels.

KELLY, LLOYD G., Windsong, Main Street, Barnstable, Montana. Acquired the remains of the Regina Music Box Company and continued to operate under this name for some years. Around 1975–6 made a small number of new $15\frac{1}{2}$ in. Regina disc musical boxes.

KIMMERLING. According to LOUIS-AUGUSTE GROSCLAUDE, the musical box with reed organ or flutina accompaniment was the result of collaboration between DUCOMMUN and Kimmerling. He does not say which Ducommun, nor is further information provided concerning Kimmerling, who may have been no more than an out-worker.

KLEIN, HENRY & CO., Oxford Street and Wardour Street, London. Agents for Polyphon musical boxes. Went out of business on retirement in 1903. See NEW POLYPHON SUPPLY CO.

KNAUS, LUDWIG SENIOR, Vienna. Made musical clocks and automata, including one called The Knights in 1750.

KNAUS, LUDWIG JUNIOR, Vienna. Made musical automaton clock called The Coronation during the latter half of the eighteenth century.

KRANZ. Swiss maker of cheap musical boxes c. 1870–90.

KULLRICH, FRANZ E., Berlin, Germany. Patented a musical picture case in 1869 which displayed pictures on a continuous strip which could be seen through a window in the lid as it played.

LADOR, ADRIEN, rue du Jura, Ste-Croix, Switzerland. Founded in 1890, musical-box manufacturers. Modern maker of cheap musical movements.

LAFLEUR & SON, London. c. 1880. Agent for French and Swiss musical boxes.

LAMI, Geneva, Switzerland. Little is known of this maker of miniature mechanical singing birds other than that he was born in 1810 and died at the advanced age of 92 in 1902. His singing birds were of a size and quality almost equal to that of the BRUGUIER family, but they are difficult to identify because he never marked his work.

LAMY. See THIBOUVILLE-LAMY.

LANGDORFF, DAVID. Born in 1804, Langdorff claimed that his musical-box manufacturing business had been founded in 1838. According to Pierre Germain, the business was located at 13 rue de Coutance in Saint Gervais, Geneva, in 1867. In 1844, David Langdorff was partner in the company known as METERT & LANGDORFF with Isaac-Henri Metert, the grandfather of Henri Metert who worked in London for Nicole Frères and who died there in 1933. Langdorff's relationship with Metert lasted from around 1838 until they dissolved the partnership in 1852. He died in 1873 and the business was carried on by his wife and his son, John Baptiste Langdorff, under the name Langdorff et Cie. In 1898, the name became John Langdorff until 1902, when the business was absorbed into the Société Anonyme des Fabriques Réunies des Boîtes à Musique, Anciennes Maisons RIVENC, LANGDORFF ET BILLON.

LANGE, HERMAN, London. c. 1880. A musical-box agent.

LANGFELDER, HENRY. Born in Germany, he went to the United States and worked with F. G. OTTO (q.v.) on the design and production of the Capital 'cuff' box. He also operated a company called the U.S. Guitar Zither Co. in Jersey City for factoring the MENZENHAUER &

SCHMIDT (q.v.) mechanical zither and, around the closing years of the century, returned to Berlin to take over that company. In 1919, his company took over KALLIOPE (q.v.).

LARK, GEORGE, May's Buildings, London. An organ builder who is described in Mortimer's Directory, dated 1763, as '. . . Also makes Musical Boxes for Minuet and Country Dances and Concerto and Bird Organs'.

LASSUEUR, AUGUSTE, rue de la Conversion, Ste-Croix, Switzerland. Established in 1895 as a musical-box manufacturer, *fl*. 1900.

LATEULÈRE, ANTOINE ALBERT, 75a Little Britain, London, E.C. A Frenchman who was working in London *c*. 1885–9 as a repairer of music boxes. He was also agent for French-made musical boxes and devised improvements in low-cost changeable-cylinder movements in 1886. In *Musical Opinion* for October 1899, a notice appeared reading 'Mr. A. A. Latellère [*sic*], musical box repairer, has moved to 21, Aylesbury Street, Clerkenwell.' See also BEUTNER.

LAWATER, L. A six-air cylinder-box passed through Christie's South Kensington auction rooms mid-1978. The case of this key-wound box featured an end flap and the whole case had a step rebated around its outer top edge over which the protruding beaded edge of the lid closed, securing the small, plain end flap and rendering the box dust-proof. The brass bedplate bore the minuscule number 7965 stamped top left, and the tune sheet of brass bore the number 2048 and the legend: 'L. Lawater à Geneve'. One of the six tunes was Bishop's 'Bid me Discourse' (1820). No record has been found elsewhere of Lawater.

LECOULTRE, C., Ste-Croix, Switzerland. A member of the famous musical-box and clock-making family who made some musical boxes. It is likely that C. Lecoultre amalgamated with one of the other Lecoultre brothers as Lecoultre Frères. Boxes marked with this name are rare.

LECOULTRE, DAVID, Le Brassus, Switzerland, *c*. 1810 onwards. Excellent-quality key-wound musical boxes up to about 1850. Also small movements. Said to have been the originator of the brass cylinder for musical boxes in place of the earlier platform movement.

LECOULTRE, D., & SON, Le Brassus, Switzerland. As David Lecoultre until about 1860 when the brothers Lecoultre amalgamated. Makers of musical boxes who exhibited at the Great Exhibition in London in 1851.

LECOULTRE, E., rue de l'Industrie, Ste-Croix, Switzerland. Manufacturers of musical boxes, *fl*. 1900.

LECOULTRE FRÈRES, Le Brassus, Switzerland. The Lecoultres were originally watchmakers, and this high standard of work is evidenced in all their early work. The Le Brassus company is thought to have been the first amalgamation of brothers David and François Lecoultre. All boxes seen are key-wound and it seems that none made after about 1869 now exists. They exhibited at the Great Exhibition in London in 1851. See also reference under REYMOND-NICOLE.

LECOULTRE FRÈRES, Geneva, *c*. 1860 onwards. These musical boxes represent the bulk of the Lecoultre production and were the first of the lever-wound style to be made. Boxes of all shapes and sizes were made, the earlier ones being of far better quality. In the late 1880 period, quality tailed off sharply and the traditional comment is that Lecoultre were 'weak in the base' on their musical set-up.

LECOULTRE ET FALCONNET, F. Makers of high-quality musical boxes, especially those playing overtures. One in burr-walnut case and with brass tune sheet listing three overtures (including Bellini's 'I Puritani' of 1834) was sold at Sotheby's Belgravia 29 June 1977.

LECOULTRE, FRANÇOIS CHARLES. Born in Le Chenit on 4 April 1801; died in Geneva, 8 January 1871. His father was a watchmaker named Louis Philippe Samuel Lecoultre and his mother was Charlotte Piguet, the sister of ISAAC DANIEL PIGUET. At the age of 20, he moved to Geneva and sought naturalisation as a Swiss. In 1827 he is listed as in charge of a musical-box manufactory and in 1828 joined the business of HENRY DAVID GOLAY. On the death of Golay he assumed control and finally, in the early 1840s, moved it to rue de Chantepoulet 39, where it remained for many years. François Charles Lecoultre did a great deal to foster the Geneva musical-box industry and, in his later years, he employed more than fifty workers. A frequent traveller to London, from where he established trading relations with India and China, he was a highly respected maker of quality musical boxes. In 1829, his brother Charles Philippe Lecoultre, joined him for a few years from Le Chenit and finally moved to Geneva with his family in 1833. He died in Geneva in 1850. François Charles Lecoultre married twice. By his second wife, a girl from Geneva, he had a son, Charles François Lecoultre.

LECOULTRE, CHARLES FRANÇOIS. Son of LECOULTRE, FRANÇOIS CHARLES, born 18 August 1834; died 7 January 1914. He took over his father's business in 1865 and moved it to rue des Alpes 12. He was responsible for a number of improvements in musical-box design and production, but about 1871 (according to Pierre Germain) he handed over the business to PERRELET, AUGUSTE, under whose name it remained until Perrelet's death in 1900. Meanwhile, Charles François Lecoultre had established contacts in South America and, having traded for some years with Hermanos Breyer of Calle Florida 49, Buenos Aires and its subsidiaries in Rosario and La Plata, he left the country in 1889 and tried to establish a musical-box industry in the Argentine Republic. He failed, but ran a repair shop until 1910, when he came back to Switzerland; he died four years later.

LECOULTRE, FRANÇOIS LOUIS. Born in 1782. In 1814, having made a large number of movements with a sectional comb having groups of five teeth to a section, he made the first one-piece comb. Production and manufacturing difficulties dictated that he did not adopt the one-piece comb generally until 1818. He was also said to be the first person, in 1814, to weight the bass teeth with lead. He died in 1829. He was the son of Abraham-Joseph Lecoultre, and his brother was HENRI JOSEPH LECOULTRE. Made mostly snuff-boxes.

LECOULTRE, HENRI JOSEPH, 60 rue Rousseau, Geneva and, in 1836, at 127 rue Montbrillant, Geneva. Born 23 May 1792, in Le Chenit, Vaud, son of Abraham-Joseph Lecoultre. Died October 1856. Settled in Geneva in 1822, where he was the first to make revolver boxes. Brother of François, he was principal builder of musical boxes in Geneva. He was also the first maker to produce a box with interchangeable cylinders and cylinders which could be fitted to other similar boxes. A movement bearing this name stamped on the comb and contained in a painted wooden case is in the Harding collection. Was in partnership with GRANGER (q.v.).

LECOULTRE-DUPERRUT, JOSEPH, 214 Saint Gervais Sq., Geneva. After death of his second wife, Henri Joseph Lecoultre married Aline Duperrut in 1841 and used the joint names. Aline died June 1851. See under BACHELARD.

LECOULTRE & GRANGER. The partnership between Henri Lecoultre (1792–1856) and Jean François Granger (1801–44) lasted between 1840 and the death of Granger in December 1844. The address was quai des Bergues 27, Geneva.

LECOULTRE-SUBLET. Name seen on two large quality cylinder musical boxes (one in Utrecht museum).

LEIPZIG MUSIC WORKS, 57 Basinghall Street, London, E.C. In 1898, this firm was agent for Monopol disc musical boxes made by Ehrlich. A Mr. Gilbert was the owner.

LEMAIRE, NICHOLAS CONSTANT. Born 25 October 1757 at Orchies, northern France, Lemaire was a pupil of Jaquet-Droz and made singing birds. In 1795, with Glaesner, started a watchmaking factory at Versailles, which lasted until 1801. Lemaire died in 1832.

L'ÉPÉE, AUGUSTE. Sainte-Suzanne, Doubs, France. In 1833, a native of Mont Béliard, named P. H. PAUR, came to Sainte-Suzanne from Geneva where he had established a factory for making musical-box combs and decided to set up a musical-box industry using Swiss workers. His workshop was established in a blacksmith's shop at the foot of the Mont-St-Michel. After six years of costly and fruitless trials he died almost a ruined man. For three months prior to his death, his partner had been Auguste L'Épée, born at Villiers, Neuchatel, on 8 September 1798, and living in Beaucourt. Before coming to Paur, L'Épée had been director of the Japy clock company in Beaucourt. He now bought Paur's business and set up his own factory with little capital and great perseverance. Research instituted by Mrs Mark Davis of Toledo reveals that he launched the fashion in France of musical movements in snuff-boxes, under dishes, in watches and so on, all of which had hitherto been a Swiss monopoly. In 1845 he had thirty workers and by 1850, by which time Auguste's sons Henry (1829–96) and Edouard were in the business, the factory was expanding. In 1857, Auguste L'Épée invented the manivelle or small hand-cranked musical box for children, and this one line necessitated new production facilities. In 1861, new workshops were built but, in the same year, Debain, the piano maker in Paris, instituted a law suit alleging infringement of copyright. The action, one of the many over the mechanical interpretation of music, dragged on several years until, in April 1863, the Court of Orléans found for Debain meaning, in effect, that the French manufacture of musical boxes playing other than national airs was no longer possible. The French government finally intervened to amend this invidious ruling and, on 4 July 1865, restored freedom. It had, though, cost L'Épée a considerable amount. New workshops again were built in 1869, but two years later Sainte-Suzanne was the centre of a big battle in the war with the Germans and the village was occupied by Prussian troops. L'Épée's factory became a field hospital until it was finally sacked by the soldiers who did great damage in particular to large numbers of finished musical boxes. Cruelty to Auguste L'Épée by the invaders hastened his death, which came on 7 February 1875 at the age of 77. The factory had, for some years, been run by the sons and the son-in-law and it was decided to keep the name as Auguste L'Épée. By 1878, 350 workers were employed. Large numbers of boxes were supplied to THIBOUVILLE-LAMY (q.v.) in Paris as well as to other outlets, but none appears to have been marked with the name. However, the crossed swords mark appears on several boxes attributed to L'Épée. In 1886, the company was co-patentee of an interchangeable-cylinder musical box with L. E. J. Thibouville-Lamy. Movements carry a number of distinctive features discussed in Chapter 4. Henry L'Épée and his son Frédéric (1868–1931) made the first gramophone mechanisms in France. Successor Henry L'Épée (1903–64) lost his life in a car crash. Musical boxes were produced until 1914; today the business is the manufacture of precision instruments. Historical details from Roger Vreeland and Mrs Mark Davis.

LE ROY, Paris. 1850. Made musical boxes and musical clocks and watches with automata over a long period. A famous clockmaking family first established in 1686. A flute-playing

315

clock bearing this name is in the Palace of Versailles. He also made clocks with singing birds and also the 'Marie Antoinette' organ clock.

LESCHOT, FREDERIC, Chaux-de-Fonds, Switzerland. 1733–84. Made mechanical singing birds. See also under ML.

LESCHOT, JEAN FREDERIC, Paris. 1746–1824. Made singing birds and also helped the Jaquet-Droz in making their automata. An outstanding maker.

LESCHOT, PIERRE, Geneva. c. 1750. A watchmaker who also made automata in connection with watches and clocks.

LEVIN MOSES, L., 16 Great Alie Street, London. In 1893 advertised as a maker and seller of musical boxes, although no work bearing his name has ever been seen.

LIEBERMANN & CO., Motzstrasse 90, Berlin W.13. Manufacturers of Graf's Musik Baukasten, a form of disc-playing musical box invented in 1910 by H. GRAF of Lutzowstrasse 85b, Berlin W.35. Featuring a series of perforated metal plates into which the owner could insert loose pins in accordance with a chart so as to produce a disc for playing on a comb-operated musical box, Graf was granted British Patent No. 11617 for this device in 1911. Only one specimen has been seen (Etches collection).

LIEPE, CL. AUG. Schonhauser Allee 146, Berlin N.58. Established in 1888 as a maker of musical photograph albums, fl. 1909.

LOCHMANN & CO., E. G., 3 Aldermanbury Buildings, London, E.C. Musical-box agents.

LOCHMANN, PAUL, Leipzig, Germany. Took out patents for the first musical box playing interchangeable tune sheets in 1885–6. Working in conjunction with Ellis Parr of London, he produced the first disc musical box (the Symphonion) in 1885. Took out many patents throughout the world for disc musical boxes. After the Symphonion factory at Gohlis, Leipzig, closed down, Lochmann produced a disc musical box called the Lochmann Original.

LOCHMANNSCHER MUSIKWERKE AKTIENGESELLSCHAFT, Gohlis, Leipzig. Paul Lochmann's factory in which the Symphonion disc musical box was produced. During its existence, the firm produced many other musical instruments besides the large Symphonion range. E. G. Lochmann and M. Lochmann, who were most probably Oscar Paul Lochmann's brothers, took out various patents for mechanical musical instruments, among these a keyboard-operated instrument playing a musical-box comb. Lochmann later produced a disc musical box under the name Lochmann Original. See also SYMPHONION.

LONGCHAMPS FRÈRES. Early makers of musical boxes, probably Swiss.

LOOG, HERMANN, LTD. Agents for the Ariston organette made by Ehrlich. Loog modified the instrument by providing a gaily decorated wooden lid and marketed it under the name 'The Hermann'.

LYON & HEALY, Chicago, USA. Importers of the Empress disc-playing musical box into America. This was the same as the Mira but was made especially for Lyon & Healy under this name by Mermod Frères.

ML. These initials, stamped on the comb, are characteristics of boxes made by MALIGNON & LESCHOT.

M.M.C. Initials stand for MOJON, MANGER & CO. (q.v.).

MACHEFER, L., 32, rue du Faubourg Poissonière, Paris. Agent and distributor of Swiss musical boxes made by GUISSAZ FILS & CIE. in Auberson.

MAGNIAC, FRANCIS, St John's Square, Clerkenwell. A manufacturer of complicated clocks and automata c. 1770–1814. He made for the Emperor of China two musical clocks with figures of soldiers, musicians, birds and beasts which were set in motion at the hours. He was Colonel in Command of the Clerkenwell Volunteers, organised in 1797 and disbanded in 1814.

MAILLARDET, HENRI, Fontaines and London. Born in 1745, he worked in London between 1784 and 1792 as a watchmaker and maker of mechanical singing birds and automata. He worked with JAQUET-DROZ, LESCHOT and FRISARD in the making of automata and was a highly respected worker. He became manager of the London branch of Jaquet-Droz.

MAILLARDET, JEAN DAVID & AUGUSTE. Fontaines. Two brothers of HENRI MAILLARDET who were formerly working with JAQUET-DROZ in the making of automata and later made singing birds and automata on their own account.

MAILLARDET, VICTOR. Fontaines and Calcutta, India. Son of JEAN DAVID MAILLARDET, he went to Calcutta, probably to represent his uncle HENRI MAILLARDET in his trade with the East.

MALIGNON, ALPHONSE. An early maker of outstanding quality cylinder musical boxes who excelled in the technique of the single-comb forte-piano format and employed extended play through the use of a slow-turning governor. Research by Olin Tillotson (MBSI *Bulletin*, vol. XXIV, p. 97) reveals that Alphonse Malignon was born in 1800 and from 1821 to 1833 he worked as a clerk. On 7 April 1827, he married Jeanne Judith Elizabeth Victor and from November 1833 to about 1835 he was in association with Leschot as Malignon & Leschot, jewellers and watchmakers. This Leschot, Tillotson concludes, was Georges-August Leschot (1800–84), son of Jean-Frederic Leschot who was partner of and successor to Henri-Louis Jaquet-Droz. Britten says that G-A Leschot joined the business of Vacheron and Constantin in 1839, remaining with it until 1882 during which time he is credited with the design of complex tooling for the mass production of watches. From about 1835 to 1868, it seems that Malignon worked on his own at 'Corraterie No. 11, first floor above the mezzanine' (according to an 1845 directory), and another shows: 'A. Malignon, 6 Rue de la Corraterie, 6'. Both Malignon and his wife died in 1875. There were no children. Very few Malignon boxes are known – Tillotson lists 14 including three single-comb forte-piano models. Combs are sometimes found stamped with the initials ML (q.v.).

MALY, ALOIS, 1 Tempelgasse 3n, Prague. Established in 1854 as a maker of musical boxes of the Viennese style. *fl.* 1909. Fine specimen in shagreen case in the Hughes Ryder collection.

MALKE, ERNST, Connewitz, Leipzig. Patented in 1889 a musical box played by a perforated paper roll as well as other musical-box improvements until 1895. See also MALKE & OBERLÄNDER.

MALKE & OBERLÄNDER, Leipzig, Gohlis, Germany. In 1896, Ernst Malke and F. H. Oberländer started production at Halle'sche Strasse 125–7 of what they termed their 'German-American musical box' – the Adler disc machine. This was protected by patents which appeared on the British register as follows: 7190 (8 April 1895) for coin-operated musical box and method of tune selection; 23232 (4 December 1895) for discs having slanted peripheral drive holes to provide more bearing for drive cog; 23233 (same date) for musical-box winding system operated by toothed wheel engaging in holes in the spring barrel; 23234 (same date) two or more musical boxes connected together so as to play at once; 5684 (13 March 1896) for a method of preventing overwinding; also a form of disc projection. The company produced a large number of varieties of instrument and the

317

penultimate patent related to an instrument shown in Leipzig in the autum of 1897 which was, apparently, extremely tall and played two discs 'which complement each other while playing'. Research by Hendrik Strengers shows that by early in 1898 the business, known as Schloback, Malke & Oberländer was relocated at Sedanstrasse 5–7, the former premises of BRUNO RUCKERT, maker of the Orphenion. Schloback entered the business in February of 1897 as financial backer. In the following year, JULES HEINRICH ZIMMERMANN, a wholesale dealer in Leipzig, became associated with the business. At the start of 1900, the first Fortuna-named boxes appeared, identical with the Adler and using the same eagle trademark. Within the next few months, Zimmermann acquired the business which now became Firma Jules Heinrich ZIMMERMANN and the name Adler was changed over to Fortuna.

MANGER, JOHN & CO., Geneva, Switzerland. 1860. Afterwards in partnership with Mojon, Montandon, and traded as MOJON, MANGER & CO. as makers of musical boxes.

MANNHEIMER MUSIKWERKE MARIA SCHMID, S.6, No. 3, Mannheim, Germany. Established in 1908 as a manufacturer of orchestrions and 'talking machines', the company was run by Emil Schmid and handled musical boxes and automata.

M.A.P. S.A., Switzerland. Initials which appear on modern Swiss small musical movements for use in sewing baskets, souvenirs and so on. Established post-war; no longer in business.

MARCHAND, A. Maker of good-quality miniature snuff-box musical movements.

MARGOT, AMI, Auberson. Musical-box manufacturers, fl. 1900. Today Frank and Paul Margot make small musical movements and novelties as Frank Margot & Son.

MARTIN-BORNAND, PAUL, Auberson. Musical-box manufacturers, founded 1870, fl. 1900.

MARGOT-CUENDET, A., Auberson, Switzerland. Musical boxes.

MARTIN, Ste-Croix. Name seen on quality cylinder musical box.

MARTIN, Switzerland. The Martin family was extensive and comprised watchmakers, musical-box makers and musical-box main agents or dealers. Augustin Martin is said to have made automaton watches at La Chaux-de-Fonds, where he was known to be working in 1779. Chapuis (*Histoire de la Boîte à Musique*) mentions that Henri Martin had been working at L'Auberson since 1874 and was a member of a committee of workers who tried as late as 1911 to attract more apprentices to make quality musical boxes. Martin Frères, established as musical-box makers in 1870 by brothers Paul and Louis Martin of L'Auberson, made a number of good-quality pieces until the early years of this century. One piece has been seen stamped MARTIN. The business was later styled as the next entry. As late as 1920 and possibly afterwards there was a musical-box distributor at L'Auberson called Francis Martin who handled the products of several makers including CUENDET and HELLER. It is most probable that he was related to Martin Frères and also to JACCARD JULES MARTIN (q.v.).

MARTIN & FILS, LOUIS, Auberson. Musical-box manufacturer, fl. 1900.

MARTIN, JACCARD JULES, Auberson. Manufacturer of small children's musical boxes and manivelles. fl. 1900.

MARTINET & BENOIT, Geneva, Switzerland. Were making fine-quality musical boxes and clocks c. 1850. Louis Benoît (1732–1825) decorated the automata of Jaquet-Droz and Maillardet. See also BENOIT, GEBEL.

MATTHEY S.A. Modern maker of small musical movements est. 1929 at Vuiteboeuf, Switzerland.

MAYER, LOUIS HENRI, High Street, Marylebone, London. Agent for musical boxes in 1887.

MAYSON, G.T., 1 Hazelwell, Brooklands Road, Sale, Cheshire. In 1977 completed a one-off new cylinder musical box, hand-made, playing Schubert's 'Trout Quintet' and variations.

MCTAMMANY, JOHN JUNIOR, Worcester, Massachusetts, USA. Patented in 1868 a number of ingenious applications of the perforated paper roll in connection with the organette. He produced a number of instruments but the venture was not a success and he had insufficient funds to renew his patents, which were then successfully exploited by others. He died penniless in 1915.

MECAL, Switzerland. Makers of modern musical movements in Geneva, who were in business during the 1930s.

MEEKINS, ALBERT, 121 Linden Avenue, Collingswood, New Jersey. Created a small number of reproduction Regina self-changing disc musical boxes c. 1976–7.

MEINEL & CO., OTTOMAR, Wittenberger Strasse 30, Leipzig-Eutritzsch. Established 1902. Makers of a toy drum operated by a perforated metal tune sheet.

MELODIES S.A., L'Auberson, Switzerland. Brand name of modern musical movements made by Jean Paul Thorens. See under THORENS.

MENZENHAUER & SCHMIDT, Spittelmarkt 2 and Rungestrasse 17, Berlin. Makers of the Menzenhauer mechanical zither patented in 1894 by Oscar Schmidt. This looked like a table disc musical box playing a $14\frac{1}{2}$ in. disc to play a stringed instrument. Called the Guitarophone, this struck its strings rather like the perforated paper tune sheets. The device was sold in America by the U.S. Guitar Zither Co. of 36–50 Ferry Street, Jersey City, New Jersey, the owner of which was HENRY LANGFELDER (q.v.) who also was associated with F. G. OTTO (q.v.) and the 'cuff' box. Langfelder subsequently returned to Germany to run the Berlin Company. In 1919, Menzenhauer & Schmidt took over KALLIOPE (q.v.).

MERMOD, FILS, 20 Chemin des Tramways, Geneva. Manufacturer of musical boxes, fl. 1900.

MERMOD FRÈRES, Avenue des Alpes, Ste-Croix. Not to be confused with Mermod Fils of Geneva (q.v.). Founded in 1816. Makers of musical boxes and of coin-operated cylinder boxes and, later, the Stella and Mira disc boxes. Described in the 1851 London Great Exhibition exhibitors' catalogue as high-class watchmakers. The firm comprised brothers Gustave Alfred, Louis Phillipe, and Léon Marcel. The firm was noted for remarkably ingeniously constructed musical boxes and the music on their cylinder machines was always set up in a most brilliant form. The introduction of a coin-operated cylinder musical box benefited from the complexity of their mechanism. They devised the so-called 'Parachute Safety Check' and, in the period 1890–1, made some good-quality 'Sublime Harmonie' boxes with interchangeable cylinders, silent handle-winding and horizontal, compensated endless escapement. The Stella disc machine, which played projectionless discs, was patented in 1885 and improved until 1897. The $9\frac{1}{2}$ in. model had two combs each of forty teeth and produced a sound equal in volume to many a larger machine. The Stella sold well but was not the success hoped for. The Mira disc machine had discs with normal projections and some models used the same cabinets. They made the Empress disc box for Lyon & Healy, Chicago, then the largest music house in Mid-West America. The Ideal was a cylinder box having interchangeable cylinders. As late as the closing months of 1911, musical-box business was still being transacted. Lee Munsick in the United States has correspondence from Marc K. Mermod, of 249 Audubon Avenue, New York City, to Ste-Croix, indicating that both the New York City Mermod depot (from which ordered stocks could be transferred to the Jacot warehouse), and the Lyon & Healy connections were still flourishing. John E. T. Clark maintained that the Stella had bankrupted the business of Mermod Frères. When the business closed is uncertain, but it was considerably later than might have been expected had the Stella been a failure – which it wasn't.

MERMOD-JACCARD, Ste-Croix, Switzerland. Modern maker of musical movements. The business today is run by the son-in-law of the founder.

MERMOD & MARGOT, Ste-Croix, Switzerland. Name seen on small snuff-box with sectional comb in groups of five.

METERT, HENRI. Suzanne Maurer identifies no fewer than *three* Henri Meterts. Isaac Henri was born illegitimately on 31 January 1801, son of Jeanne Antoinette Metert and a calico printer called Gottlieb Ast. At the age of 10 his mother died and when he was 22 he married Henriette Noyer. In 1844, directories list him as being in business with LANGDORFF, DAVID (born 1804, died 1873) at rue Coutance 140. They made quality musical boxes and exhibited at the Great Exhibition of 1851, obtaining an award. On 29 September 1852, their partnership was dissolved, Langdorff remaining in business at their former address. Isaac Henri Metert died on 3 June 1855, at Lancy, Geneva, aged 54. Jacques Antoine Henri Metert was born on 1 August 1854, at Carouge, Geneva. He was the grandson of Isaac Henri, his father, Marc Barthelemy Metert (who married Françoise Jeanne Chappuis) being the son of Isaac Henri. Said to have worked all his life as a mechanic for Nicole Frères, having started in their Geneva factory at the age of eleven. He later came to London and worked for Nicole Frères, first at Hatton Garden and then at Ely Place, until they ceased business in 1903. Metert then carried on the business at 28 Ely Place, London, E.C. until his death in 1933. In July 1906 advertised as trading in musical boxes, polyphons [*sic*] and phonographs. He produced mechanical singing birds and is said to have made a musical box which played all bells. He improved on Amédée Paillard's inventions regarding changeable-cylinder boxes in 1879, by devising a type of mechanism which would allow immediate changing of the complete cylinder by lifting a catch at each end. There is some mystery about the partnership of Metert, Petite & Co., of 14 rue Sismondi, Geneva, founded on 1 January 1878, for the manufacture of musical boxes. The partners were Henri Metert and Louis Petite, an accountant. The registered address was initially its workshop, rue J.-J. Rousseau, number 20. One year later, the partnership was joined by a merchant, Auguste Schmidely, and the name changed to Metert, Petite & Cie. and the objects increased to include electroplating. In 1882, Henri Metert left and the business changed its title to Société Genevoise de Nickelage. Some doubt exists as to whether this Henri Metert was the same one as that who came to London and who died in England in 1933 at the age of 80 years. One very large four-overture box is in the Utrecht museum. Marked Metert-Langdorff, it is a full mandoline with 10 teeth to each note. The 301-tooth comb is held down by 36 screws in two staggered rows.

METZLER & CO., 35–8 Great Marlborough Street, London, W., and 26–9, Marshall Street, Regent Street, London, W. Musical instrument dealers who advertised in 1880 'The American Orguinette'.

MEYLAN, PHILIPPE-SAMUEL. Born in Le Brassus in 1772, he was a member of a family of renowned watchmakers. He was to specialise in making very thin watches, some of which were characterised by being wound using a female spring arbor and a square-shanked key. Became an eminent maker of watches with automata, and early musicwork. In 1811, went to Geneva and formed partnership with Piguet (see PIGUET ET MEYLAN). He died in 1845.

MEYLAN ET LECOULTRE. Philippe Samuel Meylan (see above) manufactured musical boxes with a hitherto unidentified member of the Lecoultre family under this name, presumably after the termination of his partnership with Piguet in 1828.

MIKLAS, FRANZ, Vienna. Makers of small cheap musical movements c. 1912.

MILLIKIN & LAWLEY, 168 Strand, London. Surgical instrument makers who also sold musical boxes and, from evidence, those factored by WOOG for THIBOUVILLE-LAMY and made by L'ÉPÉE. The business was at this address between 1870 and 1879.

MILLINGTON, JOHN JAMES, Houndsditch, London. Musical-box agent in 1880.

MITTENDORF, LOUIS, Geneva, Switzerland. Maker of early musical movements. In May 1869, he entered into partnership with LOUIS DUCOMMUN, a relationship which lasted five years.

MOJON, MANGER & CO., 26–7, Bartletts Buildings, London E.C. c. 1880. Makers of large-size musical boxes, some with dancing dolls and with bells and drum. They also made coin-operated cylinder boxes and, later, mechanical harmoniums and pianos. According to their catalogue, they produced 'Table musical boxes playing 24, 36, 48, 60 and 100 airs'. They sold the Specialite musical box which had a double spring and played 20 to 150 minutes on one winding. The firm also made clocks and watches and had a factory at Chaux-de-Fonds, Geneva and a branch warehouse at Oxford Terrace, Coventry. Many of the larger musical boxes have the letters 'MMC' stamped on the cock.

MOJON, MONTADON & CO., Geneva, c. 1860. Made large musical boxes. Later became Mojon, Manger & Co., with offices and agency in London.

MONOPOL. See EHRLICH.

MOULINIÉ AINÉ, Geneva. Literally 'Moulinié The Elder'. A maker of high-class musical boxes playing overtures, who produced a number of large boxes c. 1850, including a most elaborate interchangeable-cylinder box. His key-wound boxes are notable in that sometimes the case end flap over the three control levers has its own lock. His name is often stamped in small serif capitals on the polished brass bedplate.

MULLER BROTHERS, Dean Street, Soho, London, also Geneva. Musical-box makers, and watch- and clockmakers.

MÜLLER, LEONHARD, Austrasse 7, Nurnberg, Germany. Manufacturer of musical boxes and their components. Established 1897, fl. 1909.

MURDOCH & CO., JOHN G. See under J.G.M., also RIVENC, Amlo.

MUSIKWERKE-INDUSTRIE L. SPIEGEL & SOHN, Kaiser-Wilhelmstr. 6 and 18, Ludwigshafen, Germany. Established in 1862 as agent for orchestrions. Later handled electric pianos and musical boxes some of which bore the name 'Spiegel' as a brand or stencil. In 1903, Franz Karl Schmidt opened a branch at E.2, Nr.1 Mannheim, and in 1908 at Bahnhofstr. 4, Pforzheim, and another at Freie Str. 103, Basel, Switzerland, this last being under the title Schweizer-Musikwerke-Centrale L. Spiegel & Sohn. Handled Lochmann Original products.

MUTREX FRÈRES, rue de la Charmille, Ste-Croix. Musical box manufacturers, fl. 1900.

MULLER, P.A., Pau, France. Built mechanical recorder c. 1907 and, in 1910, an electric piano-roll cutter.

NATIONAL MUSIC BOX. The National Fine Art Association, Farringdon Road, London, E.C. Advertised themselves as 'makers', but every 'National Musical Box' seen displays all the characteristics of RIVENC, AMI. See also DAWKINS, THOMAS.

NEUE LEIPZIGER MUSIKWERKE A. BUFF-HEDINGER. Established in 1904 at Herloss-sohnstrasse 1–4, Leipzig-Gohlis, from the former FABRIK LEIPZIGER MUSIKWERKE of Paul Ehrlich. As well as continuing to manufacture items such as the Ariston organette, Wwe. Buff-Hedinger made many other mechanical instruments including electric pianos. The connection with the old Ehrlich Company even extended to having the same telephone number – Leipzig 14!

NEW POLYPHON SUPPLY COMPANY, 1–3 Newman Street, Oxford Street, London. Established *c.* 1898 by Arthur Ficker (1879–1966) and Curt Herzog (1875–1956) who both came from Zschopau, outside Dresden in Saxony. Their company became the London agents for Polyphon musical boxes. In 1906, the business absorbed that of HENRY KLEIN, who had retired and, later in the same year, it took over the bankrupt business of NICOLE FRÈRES. During the First World War, Ficker and Herzog were interned as aliens and the company was restructured as the British Polyphon Company, headed by Robert Willis. In 1927, the name was changed to Dulcetto Polyphon and it became a public company. In 1935, it fell to the reigning slump conditions and went bankrupt.

NICOLE, DAVID-ELIE. Born at Lieu, Vallée de Joux, Vaud, on 8 November 1792, and died on 18 February 1871. Married Émilie Charlotte Plojoux in 1835 and produced two sons, Pierre François Émile and Julius François Eugène. The latter was born on 1 April 1848, and his death is unrecorded. He qualified as a student in medicine and subsequently travelled extensively. He is not thought to have been directly associated with the manufacture of musical boxes, but might possibly have undertaken some commercial work as an aspect of his travels. After the death of Pierre-Moïse in 1857, Pierre François Émile entered his father's business as partner.

NICOLE, FRANÇOIS. Born in Chenit, Vallée de Joux, Vaud, some time in 1764, 1767 or 1769, and came to Geneva, either in 1786 or 1792, where he lived and worked at rue Chevalu 60 (now rue Rousseau 9). The Geneva directory of 1835 refers to him as Watchmaker and Musical Box Manufacturer, rue Rousseau 60, but he is no longer shown as being in business in 1844. It is presumed that he gave up business between 1835 and 1844. He was probably about 69 in 1835. He had two sons, but neither continued in his business, one being a priest and the other working in Mexico (where he probably settled in 1847). He also had a daughter, Adrienne Césarine Louise Nicole, born on 27 February 1795, who married Henri François Raymond on 29 December 1827. François Nicole died on 24 November 1849, and his death certificate describes him as 'a gentleman of independent means' and gives his age as 83 years. Made small musical boxes in 1815, of first quality. He invented the steel spring damper for comb teeth in 1814, and was probably the first maker to improve tone and quality by filling the cylinder with cement.

NICOLE, PIERRE FRANÇOIS ÉMILE. Born the son of David-Élie Nicole on 31 November 1835 and died on 24 April 1910. Initially said to have taken up religious vows, but relinquished these to join his father's business in 1855, when the failing health of his father and the expansion of the business rendered it impossible for him to continue in business alone. His uncle, David Élie, was also in failing health and subsequently died. Following the death of his father, Pierre François Émile took as partner Charles Eugène BRUN, in or about 1880. It was around this time that ownership of the business was transferred to Brun.

NICOLE, PIERRE-MOÏSE. Born at Lieu, Vallée de Joux, on 24 May 1787, and died on 30 July 1857. He was the son of David Nicholas Nicole and Louise Charlotte Rochat. He did not marry. Pierre-Moïse was the senior partner of the Nicole Frères musical-box manufacturing business.

NICOLE FRÈRES. Established in 1815 at rue Kléberg 17, Geneva, Switzerland, as makers of musical boxes. Partners were PIERRE-MOÏSE NICOLE and DAVID-ÉLIE NICOLE. They were among the earliest makers to capitalise on the production of quality musical boxes by the association of their name with the product. Nicole musical boxes are generally of high quality and all are stamped with the name. They attained fame through excellent public relations at an early stage and their early work is often outstanding. Nicole Frères established its first London address in Hatton Garden, but subsequently moved to 21 Ely Place, London, E.C. In October of 1881, the business was effectively transferred to London with CHARLES EUGÈNE BRUN in charge and only a 'branch' maintained in Geneva. At this time the business became more diversified and handled, as agent, disc musical boxes made by Polyphon in Leipzig and Regina machines from America. Much uncertainty now surrounds the original classification of Nicole Frères musical boxes by their numerical listing. It was John E. T. Clark who first published a list of serial numbers and the dates of manufacture to which they apparently correspond. This list he acquired from HENRI METERT, but there are proven inaccuracies throughout the range and many boxes have now been seen with numbers below 17,000. There is also mounting evidence to suggest that after the closure of the manufacturing business in Geneva, Nicole Frères in London bought elsewhere and stamped their name on the acquired boxes. One manufacturer appears to have been Paillard. Nicole Frères appears to have changed over from key-winding to lever-winding about 1860–1, although a lever-wound box with a 37,000 series number has been seen, and a 39,000 series one with key-winding. John Clark's listing, with its accepted errors, is still a reasonable guide to dating and is repeated here:

Serial numbers from 17,000 up to 20,000 were made until 1839
Serial numbers from 20,000 up to 25,000 were made until 1843
Serial numbers from 25,000 up to 27,000 were made until 1845
Serial numbers from 27,000 up to 29,000 were made until 1847
Serial numbers from 29,000 up to 35,000 were made until 1860
Serial numbers from 35,000 up to 38,000 were made until 1861
Serial numbers from 38,000 up to 40,000 were made until 1864
Serial numbers from 40,000 up to 41,000 were made until 1870
Serial numbers from 41,000 up to 43,000 were made until 1872
Serial numbers from 43,000 up to 44,000 were made until 1880
Serial numbers from 44,000 up to 46,000 were made until 1882
Serial numbers from 46,000 up to 50,000 were made until 1888
Serial numbers from 50,000 up to 52,000 were made until 1903

After a particularly unsuccessful move into the production of gramophone records, Nicole Frères went bankrupt in 1906 and was taken over by the NEW POLYPHON SUPPLY COMPANY. HENRY METERT continued the repair side of the business until his death.

NICOLE FRÈRES LIMITED, 51 Long Street, Box 1383, Capetown, South Africa. Handlers of musical boxes. Also in Johannesburg. Headquarters in London.

NOWY, MICHAEL, VII/2, Lerchenfelderstrasse 33, Vienna, Austria. Musical-box dealer, established in 1881, *fl.* 1909.

OLBRICH, A., Vienna. Very good class musical boxes, the movements were mainly intended for automata, clocks and pictures, but some were also used in ordinary boxes. Distinguished by comb with bass teeth on right, treble on left. Usually made use of long cylinder pins on a small cylinder. Combs always finely tuned and deeply resonant.

OLBRICH, JOS., Vienna. Maker of very fine small musical movements. Probably brother of A. Olbrich, and work was the same.

OLYMPIA MUSICAL AUTOMATON CO., 70 Newark Avenue, Jersey City, USA. Musical-box manufacturers. Offshoot of F. G. OTTO (q.v.), set up in 1902.

ORIGINAL MUSIKWERKE, PAUL LOCHMANN GMBH, Querstr. 15–17, Leipzig. Operated by Paul Lochmann and Ernst Lüder. Established 1900. Factory in Zeulenroda (Thuringia). Makers of Lochmann's Original musical box, also disc-operated piano orchestrions.

OTTO, F. G., & SONS, 48–50 Sherman Avenue, Jersey City, New Jersey, USA. Established in 1875. Later as:

OTTO MFG. CO., 107 Franklin Street, Jersey City, New Jersey, USA. Musical-box makers. Patented, produced and sold the Capital Self Playing Music Box which operated on the disc principle, but which played metal cones rather in the manner of a cylinder phonograph. Earned the obvious nickname of 'cuff' box. First patents in America were 9 April 1889, and improvements patented up to 8 January 1895. Also made the Criterion disc musical box after the Capital. Also made the Olympia disc machine. (See under OLYMPIA MUSICAL AUTOMATON CO.)

OTTO HELBIG & POLKEIT, Gohlis, Leipzig. Makers of the Celeste disc-playing musical box.

PVF. Initials stand for PAILLARD, VAUCHER, FILS. See under PAILLARD.

PAILLARD. This firm began as a family watchmaking concern in Ste-Croix, Switzerland (probably the first being Pierre in 1722–35), becoming Paillard Frères from 1735 to 1770. In 1814, E. Paillard & Co. was to make the first musical boxes in Ste-Croix. At this time, the firm was run by Moses Paillard; and then, later, the firm was called Amédée Paillard & Co., a name which it held for many years. Later still, they became Paillard, Vaucher, Fils. The trademark was the initials P.V.F. The firm made good-class and also cheaper quality musical boxes over a long period, and certainly produced between 1814 and 1914. At one time, they had branches in Paris and New York. By 1898, the firm was also making the Echophone or Paillard Phonograph, metronomes and typewriters. Early in the 1930s, the firm began making, in addition to gramophones and typewriters, photographic apparatus and, in 1936, was reorganised as Paillard-Bolex, today one of the best-known names in cinematography. In the field of musical boxes, their improvements, developments and innovations were legion. The London agency was at 62 Holborn Viaduct, E.C.

PAILLARD, ALFRED E., Ste-Croix, and 680 Broadway, New York. c. 1887. Musical-box makers who were sales agents for the Capital and Criterion musical boxes made by F. G. Otto as well as Paillard and Mermod Frères. During the 1890s they were sued by the Regina Music Box Co. for infringement of patents, and the court case lasted nearly three years. Co-patentee with O. H. ARNO of the Arno musical box.

PAILLARD, AMÉDÉE, Ste-Croix, Switzerland. In 1860, he devised practical methods of making interchangeable-cylinder musical boxes, and also perfected the accuracy necessary to achieve interchangeability of cylinders between different boxes. He was a pioneer of mass production and interchangeability. In 1870 he patented his invention of a 'revolver' cylinder box in which two or more cylinders on a rotating axis could be brought to play on combs. In 1879, he took out patents for the first musical box designed to take changeable cylinders.

PAILLARD, ANTOINE, Paris. 1776. A clock- and watchmaker.

PAILLARD, CHARLES, Ste-Croix. 1875. Invented device to increase volume of sound produced by a musical box without dissonance by the use of multiple combs in 1875. Also contrived improvements to the 'Sublime Harmonie' type of combs in 1877, in conjunction with Louis Recordon-Sulliger of Ste-Croix.

PAILLARD & CIE., E., rue de l'Industrie 2–4, Ste-Croix, Switzerland. Under the directorship of Ernest Paillard, this company, which was formed in 1814, was producing musical boxes in 1900, models including the Columbia and Excelsior brand-names.

PAILLARD & CO., C., 62 Holborn Viaduct and, later, 28 Berners Street, Oxford Street, London, and 680 Broadway, New York. Patentee and manufacturers of the Amobean musical box with interchangeable cylinders. An advertisement dated October 1881 shows Paillard, Vaucher, Fils & Company at 62 Holborn Viaduct.

PAILLARD, ERNEST. Patented in 1881 a method of improving and simplifying tune changing on a musical box, also to enable ten and even twelve tunes to be pinned accurately on the same cylinder. At the same time, he devised a simpler method of making a musical box using stamped gears and sheet-metal stamped spring drum. He was manager of the Ste-Croix works for some time with his brother-in-law, Eugène Thorens.

PAILLARD, E. & A., BROTHERS, Ste-Croix, Switzerland. Brothers Ernest and Amédée exhibited under this name at the Great Exhibition held in London in 1851.

PAILLARD, JEAN JAQUES, Geneva. 1775–92. Watchmaker.

PAILLARD & CO., M. J. The American arm of the Paillard business was established sometime before 1866 when an advertisement said: 'M. J. Paillard & Co., Music Box Importers, 21, Maiden Lane (up-stairs), New York'. Soon afterwards, the business moved to 680 Broadway, New York, at which time it was said to have been founded in 1850. Initially operated as an agency for Swiss-made musical boxes and later was responsible for the partial manufacture of boxes for the US market. Alfred E. Paillard was head of the company during much of its existence. Premises in San Francisco were taken at 120 Sutter Street, a building used by other musical-box importers (see also JACCARD, AUGUST).

PARKINS & GOTTO, 24–5, Oxford Street, London. Agents for Nicole Frères musical boxes and other makes, *fl.* 1870.

PARR & CO., ELLIS, 16 Long Lane, London. Ellis Parr was a musical-instrument-seller who had the agency for several German pianos. He took out several patents for diverse inventions such as a music-leaf turner, and also one for a musical box. When LOCHMANN advertised the invention of his disc musical box, the Symphonion, Parr claimed infringement of his patent. Ultimately he became 'co-patentee' of the instrument and 'sole patentee' in England. Parr's business was established in 1809 (which probably means that he was the second or third generation) and other addresses recorded are 97 Wigmore Street and 17a Duke Street (1881), and 99 Oxford Street (1889). What happened to Ellis Parr himself is not known, but in *Musical Opinion* of 1 June 1891 is a brief item which reads: 'Mr Max Simon, who has carried on business since 1885, under the style of Ellis Parr & Co, will for the future trade under his own name.'

PAOLI, JOHN, Rahway, New Jersey, USA. Set up discs for Regina Company and patented disc machine improvements in conjunction with Regina.

PASCHE, LOUIS, Saubraz, Switzerland. Maker of musical boxes.

PATEK-PHILIPPE, Geneva. *c.* 1800. Small musical boxes and watches.

PAUR, PIERRE HENRI, Sainte-Suzanne, Doubs, France. From 1833 to 1839 he made musical boxes but lost heavily on his venture to establish a French industry. On his death, his partner, AUGUST L'ÉPÉE (q.v.) took over. See also BRUGUIER.

PERRELET, ABRAM-LOUIS, Le Locle, Switzerland. Perrelet was born in 1729 and died in 1826.

Nicknamed 'l'Ancien', he lived the whole of his long career in Le Locle and was renowned as a wise and creative watchmaker accredited with many inventions. Greatly respected by others, he was, as Chapuis says, in a sense the master of all the watchmakers in Le Locle. He appears to have been responsible for some work on early musical boxes and his successors were established as:

PERRELET & CO., AUGUSTE, 18 rue des Alpes, Geneva. Described as 'Manufactory of musical boxes'. By 1900, the business address was 11 rue Cornavin, Geneva.

PERRIN-CHOPARD. Tune sheets have been seen bearing the inscription PERRIN-CHOPARD à BERNE. This may be the tune sheet of an agent or distributor.

PERFECTION MUSIC BOX CO., Corner Columbia Avenue and Lincoln Avenue, Jersey City, USA. Founded in 1898; subsequently moved to 17 Mulberry Street, Newark, where they employed thirty-two people under the company president, Theodore Gerth. Produced the Perfection disc musical box.

PETERS & CO., H., Theaterplatz 1, Leipzig, Germany, and 84 Oxford Street, London. Founded in 1887 by Hans Clemens Peters to handle musical instruments. The business was the first agent for Polyphon musical boxes.

PHALIBOIS, HENRI, 22 rue Charlot, Paris, France. Manufacturer of automata, singing birds and musical novelties. The trade mark was the letters HP on a circular ground surrounded with a garland of flowers. Manufactured musical chairs, toilet-roll holders and other similar objects.

PIETSCHMANN & SOHN, CHARLES F., 28 Brunnen Strasse, Berlin, Germany. Pietschmann was at one time a major manufacturer of organettes and produced the Herophon and Herophonette. Later made the Celesta disc musical box. By 1892, the business was styled the Berlin Musical Instrument Manufacturing Company.

PIGUET, ISAAC-DANIEL. Born in Le Chenit, Switzerland, in 1775, Piguet was to become an early specialist in the making of costly and complicated watches, including those with carillons. He finally settled in Geneva where, in 1812, he formed a partnership with an equally talented maker, Philippe-Samuel Meylan (see under MEYLAN). After the dissolution of this arrangement in 1828 (see under PIGUET ET MEYLAN), Piguet worked under the name I-D PIGUET ET CIE. (q.v.), until his death in 1841.

PIGUET & SON, I-D (of I-D PIGUET ET CIE.) After the dissolution of PIGUET ET MEYLAN (q.v.) in 1828, Isaac-Daniel formed a partnership with his son Auguste who was born about 1800. Makers of high-quality musical novelties, watches and jewellery.

PIGUET ET MEYLAN, Geneva, Switzerland. Founded in 1811 by ISAAC-DANIEL PIGUET (q.v.) and PHILIPPE-SAMUEL MEYLAN (q.v.). Made musical items of superb quality based on the disc or 'sur plateau' format with fan teeth, a system believed to have originated with Meylan. Some of these movements were extraordinarily thin: a double-sided disc movement fitting in the base of a snuff-box in the author's collection is under 6 mm in thickness ($\frac{1}{4}$ in.). The majority of their pieces seems to have been marked with the characters 'P + M', which dates them as having been made between 1811 and 1828. The serial numbers on every piece provide the basis of an even more accurate means of dating.

PINCHBECK, CHRISTOPHER (the elder). A maker of musical clocks, automatic organs and mechanical singing birds who died in 1732. His son, Christopher the younger, also made musical clocks and watches and is better known for his invention of the so-called Pinchbeck alloy in 1732–66, and as maker of two fine clocks in Buckingham Palace.

POHL, A., Saxony. A clockmaker who is said to have built a lantern clock with carillon at

Olomouc in Moravia, between 1419 and 1422. This has claim to being the first carillon ever made.

POLLNITZ, H. VON, & BAUER, F. L., Leipzig. Patented a disc-playing musical-box in 1895. See also BAUER.

POLYPHON & REGINA CO., 21 Ely Place, London, E.C. Advertised Polyphons in December 1896. An offshoot of NICOLE FRÈRES (q.v.).

POLYPHON SUPPLY CO., 3 Bishopsgate Street Without, London, E.C. In 1898 were main agents for Polyphon musical boxes in London.

POLYPHON MUSIKWERKE A.-G., Bahnhofstrasse 61, Wahren, Leipzig. Established by two former SYMPHONION men, Gustave Brachhausen and Paul Riessner, to produce the Polyphon disc musical-box. The business, set up in 1890, was originally established in a large house and ultimately moved into very extensive premises where nearly 1,000 people were employed. When Brachhausen went to America to found REGINA, he retained his directorship in the company.

PREMILEX, Switzerland. Post-war maker of small musical movements run by man named Milleron. No longer operating.

PROBST-MULLER, WWE, Lucerne, Switzerland. Manufacturer and distributor of musical boxes, fl. 1900.

PORTER MUSIC BOX COMPANY, 5, Mound Street, Randolph, Vermont. Established by Dwight G. Porter, this company has successfully created extremely fine reproductions of the 15½ in. Regina disc musical box and, in 1978, introduced these on the market both in America and England.

PROWSE, KEITH. See under KEITH, PROWSE & CO.

RAFFORD ET MORNEY, Carouge, Geneva. A maker of musical movements in 1826.

RAVEL, JOSEPH, Geneva, Switzerland. Joseph Ravel was born in 1832 at Versoix. His father, Aimé, was of French descent and became naturalised Swiss. The family originated from Collonges-sous-Salève, a small village in the Haute-Savoie close to the Swiss frontier. Trained as an engineer, Joseph met and married Marie Delouart, a girl from the Basses-Pyrénées, and settled in Geneva manufacturing musical boxes. He appears to have been in business between the mid-1850s and 1860 and, in 1859, is said to have suggested the idea of providing an orchestral musical box with a reed organ having its own keyboard for the *ad libitum* use of the owner. The family finally left Geneva for St Jean de Luz near Biarritz in France where, in 1875, they had a son who was to carry the name of the family beyond musical boxes – Maurice Ravel, the composer. Joseph Ravel, his wife and their son, who died in 1937, lie buried at Levallois-Perret.

RAYMOND, DAVID MARC SAMUEL, 118 bis rue de Cendrier, Geneva. A maker of musical boxes, who worked in the same building as the headquarters of the firm of Nicole Frères. He married one Judith Nicole and had two sons, one of whom was named Henri François, was born in 1809 and subsequently moved to London c. 1835–40. It is not thought that this is the Raymond whose name is specifically linked with that of Nicole on signed musical boxes, but is probably the originator of those movements which are marked 'RAYMOND' alone.

RAYMOND (REYMOND), HENRI FRANÇOIS. See under RAYMOND NICOLE.

RAYMOND NICOLE (sometimes REYMOND NICOLE). Henri François Raymond was born in Chenit on 13 February 1796, and came to Geneva, where he lived at 85 rue de Coutance, at some time prior to 1822. He was working for François Nicole at this maker's address in rue

Chevalu. On 29 December 1827, Raymond married François Nicole's daughter, Adrienne Césarine Louise, whose birth is registered in the Geneva parish of Satigny. By 1828, it appears that Raymond, formerly the employee of François Nicole, was now his partner in business, whilst his wife was employed in pinning cylinders. Raymond assumed the name Raymond Nicole and by 1834, he is listed in the census as being proprietor of the business which had by then moved from the old address (at that time renamed and renumbered as No. 60 rue Rousseau). It is interesting to note that at this time the firm of Raymond Nicole was listed independently at this address, whilst that of his father-in-law, François Nicole, continued to be shown at No. 60. He employed at least two workmen who lived in his house, and became a citizen of Geneva on 6 May 1836, at this time stating that he had been in Geneva for eighteen years. He died on 7 January 1863, although he had retired some years earlier – the 1857 directory listing him as retired and living in the rue Cornavin.

REBICEK, GUSTAVE. The Westernised name adopted by GUSTAV RZEBITSCHEK (q.v.).

RECORDON, JEREMIE, Ste-Croix, Switzerland. Was making small musical movements in 1815.

REGINA MUSIC BOX CO., Rahway, New Jersey, USA. Founded by Gustave Brachhausen and Paul Riessner of the Polyphonmusikwerke in 1889. Made musical boxes initially almost identical with the Polyphon and later produced many styles of disc machine until finally ceasing business in 1919. During the period 1892–1919, some 100,000 Regina musical boxes were produced and sales topped $2 million a year for a time. About 325 persons were employed at the factory. When finally the decision was taken to cease production, much of the Regina musical-box production plant was dumped in the river, but Mr Lloyd Kelly of Hanover, Massachusetts, bought the remaining assets and sustains the company name to this day, making new discs on an improved original disc press. The former company, now known as the Regina Corporation, is still in existence, making electrical domestic appliances. Also at 259 Wabash Avenue, Chicago.

REINER, MAX, Balliz 20, Thun, Switzerland. Distributor of musical boxes, established 1896.

REIVEÜEL, Geneva. A maker of musical boxes c. 1885.

REMOND, LAMY & CO., Paris. Musical-box makers c. 1820. Later in association with Thibouville-Lamy.

RENOLD, HENRI (formerly AMEZ-DROZ), 28 rue de Berne, Geneva. Maker of accordions, fl. 1900. See also under CARTIER.

REUGE, ALBERT, rue Neuve 1, Ste-Croix, Switzerland. Musical-box manufacturer established in 1886 and now under the guidance of Guido Reuge, now over 70 years of age (1974). Present-day maker of small musical boxes and watches, also some good-quality modern Sublime Harmonie type.

REYMOND-NICOLE, Geneva. See RAYMOND-NICOLE.

RICHTER & CO., FRIEDERICH ADOLF, 65 Schwarzburgstrasse, Rudolstadt, Schwarzburg-Rudolstadt, Germany. Part of a large manufacturing combine known as Leipziger Lehrmittel-Anstalt of Leipzig which, at the end of the nineteenth century, was producing scientific apparatus, 'appliances for teaching', electric motors and an incredibly detailed building brick from which accurate scale models of famous buildings could be constructed. The firm also made a disc-playing musical-box called the Imperator, not unlike the $19\frac{5}{8}$ in. Polyphon, and also a continuous strip, 'book-playing' musical box called the Libellion which employed an ingenious system of sliding levers to pluck the comb teeth which Richter perfected between 1895 and 1901.

RIESSNER, PAUL, Leipzig, Germany. Co-partner with GUSTAVE BRACHHAUSEN in the Polyphonmusikwerke, he also was formerly employed with Paul Lochmann at the Symphonion works. Later went to America with Brachhausen and helped form the Regina Music Box Co.

RILEY, JOSEPH, & SONS, Birmingham. Henry and William Joseph Riley manufactured musical boxes and held a royal charter (Queen Victoria) c. 1890.

RIVENC, AMI. Research by Suzanne Maurer shows that Ami François Rivenc was born in Geneva on 15 May 1837. In May 1869, he took over the musical-box manufactory of Theodore Jean GREINER (q.v.) of Geneva who had died in the previous August. Rivenc thus became successor to Greiner, who had been associated with Bremond from 1858 to 1863. The new company was A. Rivenc & Cie., the 'Cie.' referring to Greiner's widow, who had managed the business during the interregnum. The factory was at 2 rue Sismondi. Later he listed his address at numbers 3 and 5. The business lasted from 1869 to 1874, after which Rivenc was working on his own. He died on 22 June 1898. During his career, he produced many thousands of musical boxes, ranging from small pieces for photograph albums through to large table cylinder machines. A large example containing a small pipe organ has been seen with the inscription: 'A. Rivenc & Co., Mfr, Geneva'. He also made double-comb/double-cylinder musical boxes – the Duplex style – but with coaxial cylinders, i.e. mounted in line. An unusual style of 'bird-chanting' box with an articulated bird whose sound came from musical-box combs – the Colibri – was also made. Ami Rivenc supplied boxes to Thibouville-Lamy in Paris, John G. Murdoch in London and also DAWKINS, THOMAS. Boxes previously thought to have been manufactured by Dawkins are undoubtedly of Rivenc's making, as are those sold under the label of the National Fine Arts Association, an offshoot of John G. Murdoch. Rivenc's connection with Bremond is demonstrated by one unusual box which survives today in the Walt Bellm collection, Sarasota. This particular piece, a rare *piece à oiseau*, is an eight-air mechanism with 17 whistle-type pipes played from flutina-type organ keys in the centre between the two comb sections. The tune sheet is the later Bremond style bearing a rubber stamp of a Dayton, Ohio, repairer named Schonacker. Screwed into the lid above the tune sheet is a silver plate reading: 'A. Rivenc & Co, Manufacturers, Geneva.' Within this particular box lies hand-written operating instructions on a piece of Rivenc letterhead paper. This also states: 'Repairer in New York, Charles Gonon, 66 Nassau Street'.

ROBIN, ROBERT, Paris. Born in 1742, he made mechanical singing birds, including a life-size singing canary for Marie-Antoinette. He died in 1799.

ROCHAT, Paris. Maker of musical clocks in 1825.

ROCHAT, AMI. See under ROCHAT, PIERRE. A singing bird in a cage bearing this mark is in the Howard Fitch collection.

ROCHAT & SON, DAVID, Le Brassus, Switzerland. Established about 1802 as a maker of miniature singing birds and was, at one time (from the end of 1804), involved with LESCHOT (q.v.). Also made complicated automata. In business until about 1813 but, for part of this period, was in business with LOUIS ROCHAT (q.v.) at LES FRÈRES ROCHAT (q.v.).

ROCHAT, LES FRÈRES, Geneva, Switzerland. 1810–25. Makers of mechanical singing birds signed 'F.R.' in a circle. Made musical boxes and singing-bird snuff-boxes, also pistols incorporating singing birds which popped up and sang when the trigger was pulled. Some pistols were 'double-barrelled' with two singing birds. These were finely made, embellished with precious metals and encrusted with jewels.

ROCHAT, H. A snuff-box has been seen playing two tunes on a one-piece comb, *c*. 1830, bearing this mark.

ROCHAT, LOUIS. See under ROCHAT, PIERRE. Maker of very small singing birds.

ROCHAT, PIERRE, Chez Maillan, Le Brassus, Switzerland. Born in 1780, he and his two sons AMI NAPOLÉON and LOUIS made musical boxes in the form of trinkets and various small items such as snuff-boxes, nécessaires and so forth. Apparently the family then lost considerably over a building speculation, whereupon the manufacture of cylinder musical boxes more or less ceased and the family moved to Geneva, where they excelled in the manufacture of quality miniature musical novelties and outstanding singing birds, which were all signed with the letters 'F.R.' contained in a circle. Also produced musical boxes and singing bird snuff-boxes. One unusual product was a jewel-encrusted pistol incorporating singing birds which appeared and sang when the trigger was pulled. Some of these exotic pistols were 'double-barrelled' with two singing birds. The Rochats were closely connected with Jaquet-Droz – Pierre being some time in his employ. Ami Napoléon made a speciality of the miniature singing bird and his work became renowned the world over. Louis, who was solely responsible for the pistol birds, also excelled in making most unusual automata, including a complex clock for which he was appointed, in 1829, Companion of the Watchmakers and Scientists of the City of Geneva. The smallest and most precise of the miniature singing birds made anywhere in the country came from the hands of Louis Rochat.

RODE, N. SP. This name appears on the movement of an egg-shaped watch clock $8\frac{1}{2}$ in. high and surmounted by a mechanical crowing cock, thought to have been made about 1894 in France.

ROENTGEN & KINTZING. Built automata for Marie-Antoinette.

ROEPKE, CARL ALBERT, Glasshouse Street, Regent Road, Salford, Manchester, Lancs. Formerly from Berlin, Roepke patented in 1890 a method of plucking a musical-box comb using a strip of moving cardboard or similar material. He manufactured The Orchestral Musical Box in England *c*. 1895. Carl Albert Roepke was described as 'watchmaker' in a directory of April 1890, giving his address as Claremont Road, Manchester.

ROEPKE & CO., LTD., 33 Tib Street, Manchester (from September 1897 to June 1898), and 31 Lees Street, Ancoats, Manchester, in January 1897. Manufacturers of the Roepke Orchestral book-playing, lever-plucking musical box.

ROUSSET. Early maker of mechanical musicwork.

RUCKERT, BRUNO, Sedanstrasse 5–7, Leipzig, Germany. Designer/patentee of the Orphenion disc-playing musical box first produced in 1893. By 1897, Ruckert appears to have gone out of business and RICHTER (q.v.) took over his factory for the production of the Adler and Fortuna. See under MALKE & OBERLÄNDER.

RZEBITSCHEK, FRANTISEK, Prague, Austria. Commenced work in 1813 as a watchmaker in Josephan, Bohemia, and produced Viennese-style musical boxes. In 1851, at the Great Exhibition held in London, he won first prize for musical boxes – four were shown playing two, three, four and six tunes. He made small movements for use in clocks, pictures, sewing baskets, goblets and other domestic articles.

RZEBITSCHEK, GUSTAV, Prague, Austria. Son of FRANTISEK RZEBITSCHEK (q.v.), he produced musical movements similar to those of his father. For the market outside Bohemia, he westernised the name to REBICEK (q.v.). Gustav took over running the workshops in Prague in 1870 and the business finally closed in 1897. See also under BRIESE, THEODORE.

SBI. These initials are often found cast into the bedplates and comb bases of Swiss musical boxes. They stand for Société Billon et Isaac or, to give the full name, SOCIÉTÉ ANONYME LIBRE DE L'ANCIENNE MAISON BILLON ET ISAAC, set up as such on 1 January 1867, in Geneva. See also BILLON-HALLER, JEAN.

SALLAZ & OBOUSSIER, Ste-Croix, Switzerland. A maker of good quality cylinder musical-boxes c. 1840–50. Characteristic of the period, these had polished brass bedplates and the inner glass lid was visibly hinged on its upper back edge instead of underneath as usual. Serial numbers were marked in small shaded numerals on the top left corner of the bedplate.

SANDOZ, LOUIS, Le Locle, Switzerland. Was making small musical boxes in 1818. His son, Henry Frédéric Sandoz (born 1815; died 1913) was responsible for many improvements in watchmaking, including the production of watchmaking tools and processes.

SANKYO, Japan. Makers of small, cheap musical movements for fancy goods, in business today.

SAVORY & SONS A.B., 11 & 12 Cornhill, London. Main importers of Nicole Frères c. 1860.

SCHAUB, F. Took out American patent on 8 January 1895, for the shape of the note projections for the Capital 'cuff' musical-box tunes.

SCHLINGLOFF, J. L., Hanau, Germany. Maker of modern, cheaper mechanical singing birds, some in silver cases, c. 1920.

SCHARPKE, ROB, Alexandrinenstrasse 49, Berlin, S. 14. Manufacturer of musical photograph albums, established 1888, fl. 1909.

SCHRÄMLI & TSCHUDIN, 'Sun' Music Box Manufacturing Co., 2 rue des Pâquis 2, Geneva. Makers of the 'Sun' disc-playing musical box, who were functioning in 1903.

SCHWARZ, HEINREICH & CO., Berlin. Makers of musical boxes.

SCHWEICHERT, N. Musician with military band connections who composed specially for Polyphon discs, and whose name appears on Polyphon disc No. 4974 ('Selection Maritana', arr. by —); 4190 ('Polyphon March' by —) and other arrangements.

SCHWEIZER-MUSIKWERKE-CENTRALE L. SPIEGEL & SOHN, see MUSIKWERKE-INDUSTRIE L. SPIEGEL & SOHN.

SCOTCHER, C. & SON, Bull Street, Birmingham, England. Importers and main agents for a number of musical boxes c. 1880.

SCOTT, Switzerland. Makers of small cheap modern musical movements.

SCRIBER. A key-wound cylinder box has been seen stamped on the bedplate 'SCRIBER À GENÈVE' and bearing the serial number 18604 in Nicole Frères style.

SEYTRE, CLAUDE FÉLIX, Lyons, France. In 1842 he patented a system of perforated cardboard strips for the automatic playing of mechanical musical instruments on the Jacquard principle. Built instrument called the Autophone.

SILBER & FLEMING, Wood Street, London. Early agent for Nicole Frères musical boxes and those of other makers.

SLAJOULOT, E., Paris, France. Maker of good-quality mechanical singing birds, c. 1900.

SLAWIK & PREISZLER, Prague, Czechoslovakia. Makers of very fine qualilty musical movements in the Viennese style. Usually fitted into clock bases, musical pictures, glass-domed automata.

SOCIÉTÉ ANONYME DE L'ANCIENNE MAISON BILLON ET ISAAC, See SOCIÉTÉ ANONYME FABRIQUES RÉUNIES DE BOÎTES A MUSIQUE, also BILLON-HALLER, also RIVENC, also LANGDORFF.

SOCIÉTÉ ANONYME FABRIQUES RÉUNIES DES BOÎTES A MUSIQUE. 18 quai de St Jean, Geneva.

Founded out of the 'ancient houses' of Rivenc, Langdorff and Billon, this musical-box manufacturer produced, among other boxes, the Polymnia. It claimed its foundations as 1838 and 1851 (the respective dates of the first two founders); *fl.* 1900.

SOCIÉTÉ ANONYME 'HARMONIA', Auberson. Founded in 1896 and directed by Aug. Bornand-Galaz, this musical-box manufacturer *fl.* 1900.

SOCIÉTÉ JUNOD. See under JUNOD, SOCIÉTÉ.

SOUALLE, ADRE. Alexandre Soualle established what was probably the first French musical-box factory at the Château Villetaneuse, St Denis, close to Paris. No exact dates are known, but it appears to have been around 1850–60. The venture is thought to have been short-lived and few Soualle boxes survive. The black-printed tune sheets bear the initials A.S:V in the top border and the legend: *Musiques de Paris, Fabriqué au Château de Villetaneuse près St. Denis (Seine).* The letters 'AS' are cast into the underside of the comb base but, although in the correct order, the letter 'S' is reversed. The boxes seen are all lever-wound and the name is stamped both on the comb and on the flat of the winding-handle.

SPERRY, N. A., 85 Pratt Street, Hartford, Connecticut, USA. Dealer in musical boxes, early twentieth century.

SPIEGEL & SOHN, see MUSIKWERKE-INDUSTRIE L. SPIEGEL & SOHN.

STAR SILVER DEPOT, London. Sole distributors of the Britannia disc musical-box made by BARNETT HENRY ABRAHAMS. The Britannia was the same as the Imperial, but was made exclusively for distribution in England by the Star company at 133 & 135 Houndsditch.

STARLACKER, L. Principal of the firm of Bender & Co., the first London firm to supply Polyphons via Messrs. Peters & Co. of Leipzig.

STAUFFER. Geneva. Maker (agent?) of good quality musical boxes *c*. 1878. Name usually stamped on flat of winding-lever.

STUDIO OYEN, Dabringhauser Strasse 10, PO Box 1164, 5678 Wermelskirchen, West Germany. Elmar Oyen and Hermann Himmelmann are commercial designers who, in 1973, decided to produce a new musical box based on the $9\frac{1}{4}$ in. disc Kalliope with bells. Although interchangeable with the Kalliope, for commercial reasons they called it Symphonion. Development and tooling costs totalled DM. 500,000 (£82,000, $196,000) and a new design of damper was patented which incorporated teflon fingers actually in the starwheels. Construction was undertaken by the Trossinger Metallstimmenfabrik Hans Eisen and a large number of instruments were produced in a variety of painted decorated cases. Apart from the plastic dampers (which are eminently practical) and a bedplate bearing the name Studio Oyen and the Eisen trademark 'Hetro', the boxes are mechanical and tonal replicas of the Kalliope. (See *The Music Box*, vol. 6 number 7, pp. 440–3 and 469 for a detailed description of the instrument.)

SUEUR, ALFRED, Ste-Croix, Switzerland. In 1886 was making musical boxes and invented many improvements. Later with M. J. Paillard & Co. in New York. Devised in 1892 the first coin-operated musical-box mechanism, later fitted to most large disc machines.

SUN MUSIC BOX MANUFACTURING CO., SCHRAEMLI & TSCHUDIN, 2 rue des Pâquis, Geneva. Founded in 1902, this company produced musical boxes and phonographs, including the Sun disc-playing musical box.

SYMPHONION, FABRIK LOCHMANNSCHER MUSIKWERKE, A.-G., Braustrasse 13–19, Leipzig-Gohlis, Germany. The Symphonion company started business on musical boxes in 1885 and produced the first disc musical box with that name. The business became an

'Aktiengesellschaft' in 1889. Following the establishment of the Original Musikwerke Paul Lochmann (q.v.) in 1900, the name of the business was eventually changed to Symphonion-Fabrik A.-G. Under this name it remained in business at Schkeuditzer Strasse 13–17b in Gohlis. The company pioneered the use of electric motors in disc musical-boxes, the first such product being advertised in 1900. The company moved into the piano-orchestrion business making both disc-operated and barrel-playing models, player pianos and phonographs. Although the latest catalogue seen by Bowers was c. 1912, it seems that the business continued into the late 1920s, by which time it was directed by Paul Scheibe and located at Barengasse 14/40, Gera (Reuss). See also LOCHMANNSCHER MUSIKWERKE.

SYMPHONION MUSIC BOX CO., Asbury Park, New Jersey, USA. Produced the Symphonion disc musical box in the United States c. 1893.

T.O.K., Tokyoseiki, Japan. Maker of small modern cheap musical movements.

TANNHAUSER MUSIKWERKE, Thuringerstrasse 1–3, Leipzig-Lindenau, Germany. The Tannhauser, a very rare marque of shifting-disc musical boxes, was patented in Germany on 21 May 1897 (German patent number 99899) and in Britain on 16 April 1898 (British patent number 5386) by Traugott Alwin Plessing, an engineer of Constantinstrasse 18, Leipzig-Reudnitz. Production seems to have begun late in 1899 and to have ceased during 1900.

TERROT & FAZY, Geneva. Makers of musical boxes and clocks c. 1810.

TESTE, JOSEPH ANTOINE, Nantes, France. Mid-nineteenth-century instrument maker who invented the Cartonium, which had forty-two free metal reeds and played perforated cards on the Jacquard principle. Patented in 1861, this also had a device which would cut cards to play on the instrument.

THIBOUVILLE-LAMY, JÉROME, 68, 68 bis and 70 rue Réaumur, Paris, and (after 1884) at 7, 9 and 10 Charterhouse Street, Holborn Circus, London. This very large musical instrument house was founded in 1790 and majored on brass wind instruments. It established factories in many parts of France and bought up most of the makers of instruments at Mirecourt (Vosges) where serinettes and larger barrel organs were produced under the company name. Very early on, Thibouville-Lamy entered into an arrangement with L'ÉPÉE of Sainte-Suzanne and for many years took virtually the whole of the European market for these French-made musical boxes which were sold under the Thibouville-Lamy name. The first London agent was WOOG. The company later became agents for other makes of musical box, and, by 1890, advertised a wide variety of types and styles. The Paris arm of the company closed about 1968 and the London business, its Charterhouse Street premises having been destroyed during the war, moved first to 34 Aldersgate and is now at 44 Clerkenwell Road.

THORENS, EUGÈNE, Ste-Croix, Switzerland. Was manager of the PAILLARD factory during the 1880s and was the brother-in-law of Ernest Paillard. Was a musical-box maker in his own right.

THORENS, HERMANN, Avenue des Alpes, Ste-Croix, Switzerland. Established in 1881 as a manufacturer of musical boxes, mainly small disc and cylinder movements, including the Edelweiss and Helvetia disc machines which appeared in a variety of sizes. Business finally taken over by PAILLARD after the 1939–45 war, and finally Paillard itself was taken over by the Austrian Eumig concern. Jean Paul Thorens now has a small factory in L'Auberson and produces musical movements under the trade name MÉLODIES S.A. See also HÖSSLY, LOUIS.

TRITSCHLER, JOHN & CO., Oxford Street, London. Was musical-box agent *c.* 1888.

TROLL, SAMUEL, 6 rue Bonivard, Geneva. Founded 1868, manufacturer of musical boxes. See also BAKER-TROLL.

TROLL FILS, SAMUEL, Geneva. Made small musical movements in plain wooden boxes *c.* 1880.

TROSSINGER METALLSTIMMENFABRIK HANS EISEN. See STUDIO OYEN.

TROUBADOUR-MUSIKWERKE, B. GROSZ & CO., Gellerstrasse 8, Leipzig III. Founder: Siegmund Schauer. Makers of Troubadour musical box. Later (1909) at Breitkopferstrasse 9 in Leipzig (Reudnitz).

TULLER, EUGÈNE, Ste-Croix, Switzerland. A maker of musical boxes.

ULLMANN, CHARLES, Auberson, Switzerland. A German-Swiss by birth who made good-class musical boxes of the cheaper variety between about 1870 and 1890. He had a London agent named Henry Gerhardt, and Messrs Imhof & Mukle also sold his musical boxes. Ullmann made possibly the best use of twelve-air combs and knew how to set his music so that the smallness belied the quality of the movement. At times he placed the control levers of his movements outside the cases. He also made the Excelsior and Superextra musical boxes, and quite often these have colourful lithographed tune sheets typewritten in blue. See below:

ULLMANN, CHARLES & JACQUES, 11 rue du Faubourg Poissonière, Paris. Established in 1881 as successors to Ch. Mathieu and Lecompte & Cie., musical instrument manufacturers and distributors. Became first Paris distributors for the Symphonion and produced musical boxes which it advertised as made at Ste-Croix, Switzerland. The Ste-Croix address was rue du Tyrol 9, and the business was still operating at least as late as 1909.

ULRICH, J. G. In the Jim Hirsch collection is a small cylinder musical movement bearing the inscription: 'J. G. ULRICH FECIT LONDON AD 1819 N? 4.' Baillie lists Johann Gottlieb Ulrich as an eminent chronometer maker who was born in 1795 and worked in London until his death in 1875. Loomes lists John Ulrich (the same?) as a clockmaker *c.* 1832. Britten says he had 'many addresses', but places him at 26 Nicholas Lane in 1835.

VC. See next entry.

VACHERON ET CONSTANTINE, Geneva. François Constantine and Jacques Barthelemy Vacheron were both born in Geneva in the same year – 1787. They formed a partnership in watchmaking which was famed for many years, producing high-quality watches, automata and musical movements. Constantine died in 1854. Vacheron retired in 1844 and died in 1864, but his son Charles César (born 1812; died 1868) took over the business. Today the business is known as Ancienne Fabrique Vacheron & Constantine, S.A. In 1817, several musical snuff-boxes were presented to the Duchess of Parma (the ex-Empress Marie-Louise) who 'found them to be admirable'. One of the finest examples was made in 1824 for the Prince Borghese, in very rich enamel, decorated with the arms of the family, and with all the orders held by this rather ostentatious brother-in-law of Napoleon. Vacheron et Constantine is thought to have supplied other musical-box makers with components, stamping them with the initials VC and a rose.

VALLE Y HERMANO, FELIPE, 11a de Tezontlale 6, Mexico. Musical-box maker, *fl.* 1909.

VALOGNE. Name on small quality cylinder musical box in the Guinness collection, New York, together with the serial number 1425 and a watch movement in the case front which discharges the music. Small 5-pointed stars are stamped into the bedplate round the name and serial number.

VAUCANSON, JACQUES DE. Born at Grenoble in 1709. In 1738, he exhibited three automata in

Paris. One was a man playing a flute, another a Provençal shepherd playing twenty airs on a galoubet and beating a drum, and the third was a quacking duck, which ate, digested and defecated. Certain evidence also links Vaucanson with the famous Silver Swan, once in Cox's Exhibition and now at the Bowes Museum, Barnard Castle. He died in 1782.

VAUCHER, F. T. A partner of the Ste-Croix firm of Paillard who was at one time a maker on his own account. See PAILLARD, VAUCHER FILS.

VERNAZ, ALEXIS, Ste-Croix, Switzerland. A maker of musical boxes c. 1880–97.

VIDOUDEZ, HENRI, rue du Jura 2, Ste-Croix. Musical-box manufacturer, fl. 1900.

VIDOUDEZ, PAUL. The name Paul Vidoudez & Fils remains to this day on the wall of a building in Ste-Croix plus the information that the business was the manufacture of musical boxes. No information is so far available on this maker, but it is interesting that the initials are the same as those of Paillard, Vaucher, Fils.

VIRGNEUR BROTHERS, Geneva. Makers of mechanical singing birds and musical boxes of fine quality c. 1820.

VOTEY, E. S., USA. Engineer who patented the pianola in 1897.

W. & H. See under WEILL & HARBURG.

WALES & MCCULLOCH, Musical Box Depot, 32 Ludgate Hill and 56 Cheapside, London. In the 1860s, they also had premises at 54 Cornhill, London. Principal agents for Nicole Frères and other makers of musical boxes. They were advertising prior to 1856.

WALLIS, JOSEPH, & SONS, Euston Road, London. Agents for French and Swiss musical boxes in 1890.

WEEDEN, WILLIAM N., New Bedford, Massachusetts, USA. Was granted US Patent No. 283307 on 24 August 1883, for a pocket-watch-size cylinder musical box of somewhat novel design. The case contained a large-diameter but very short cylinder pinned on the *inside*. This was allowed to rotate around a stationary comb having eight stacked teeth. It was stem-wound via an external toothed ring integral with the cylinder. A mass-production design, it sold for 50 cents in 1890. One example is known in the Howard Fitch collection, USA.

WEILL & HARBURG, Geneva. A maker of musical boxes who had a London office at 3 Holborn Circus and who ceased trading early in the 1880s. Their combs were always stamped 'Trade Mark/W. & H./Patent' and their initials also appeared on the tune sheets, which bore the legend 'Patent Indicator combined with Arrangement for Changing the Tunes at Will'. The characteristic referred to was patented in England in February 1869 (Brit. Pat. No. 593) by Henry Harburg, and consisted of a modified form of controls. The stop/start lever was fitted as an extension to the Y-lever of the gear train detent, and the change-repeat lever was integral with the change-wheel finger. On organ boxes, bellows feeder drive was by crank lever in place of the usual eccentric wheel in the gear train. A quality maker.

WENDLAND, MAX. Born in Dresden, worked at the Polyphonmusikwerke in Leipzig and was then sent to London in 1893 to repair Polyphons for the firm. He set up as a repairer on his own account in St John's Square, Clerkenwell, London, in 1903. His brother, Paul, invented the starwheel.

WILLENBACHER & RZEBITSCHEK, Prague. Makers of high-class musical movements for use in clocks, pictures, etc. See also under RZEBITSCHEK and REBICEK.

WILLIEUMIER ET AMEZ-DROZ, Geneva. Early-nineteenth-century makers of musical boxes.

WOLFF, ÉTIENNE AUGUSTE, Geneva. Musical movement maker c. 1775–91.

5191	**Plate,** large size, for dessert, 2 airs	...	...	...	...	each	1	3	0
5192	,, ,, .. .	...	...	...	...	,,	1	7	0

WOOG, SAMUEL, 4 Finsbury Circus, London, E.C. In 1860, Samuel Woog, importer of clocks and watches, became the first British distributor for the musical boxes of L'ÉPÉE of Sainte-Suzanne, France, which were factored through the Paris business of THIBOUVILLE-LAMY. In 1861, Samuel Woog moved to 32 Ely Place, Clerkenwell. Boxes which he factored were marked with the initials S.W. in an oval. Samuel died in 1865 and the business was taken over by his brother Jules Woog of 10 Bartlett's Buildings. In 1871, the business was taken over by Adolphe Woog, presumably a son of either Samuel or Jules. The business remained at 10 Bartlett's Buildings until 1879 when the firm and the musical-box agency was taken over by Charles Feis & Co. at the same address. While Adolphe was in charge, boxes were marked with the initials A.W. in an oval. The activities of Feis were superseded in 1884 when Thibouville-Lamy opened its London offices at 10 Charterhouse Street. When, in 1876, Adolphe Woog applied to register a trademark (see number 52 on Figure 45) he is described as a watch manufacturer of 12 rue du Quatre Septembre, Paris and 10 Bartlett's Buildings, Holborn.

WOOLLEY, LEONIDES G., Mendon, Michigan, USA. Inventor of an electrically operated musical box in 1881. He used the revolving armature not only for power but as a balance wheel to ensure smooth running.

WURTEL, FERDINAND, 38–42 Galerie Vivienne, Paris. Maker of musical automata. A musical picture in the Fortnum & Mason collection.

ZIMMERMANN, JULIUS (JULES) HEINRICH, Leipzig, Riga, St Petersburg, Moscow, London. There is some evidence to suggest that Zimmermann was originally a wholesale dealer in musical instruments who, rather like other companies before and after him, bought into industries which could further his aims. If one looks at the five centres in which he established companies, we find the first to have been in 1875, at Morskaja 34, St Petersburg; then 1882, at Schmiedebrücke, Haus Sacharin, Moscow; then 1886, at Querstrasse 26 and 28 (with factory at Sedanstrasse 17), Leipzig; then 1887, at Scheunenstrasse 15, Riga; and finally ten years later, in 1897, at 9 Great Newport Street, Charing Cross Road, London. He had branches in many other smaller places, including a number in Russia and, in 1903, he opened a saleroom at 4 Wells Street, off Oxford Street, in London. This was closed in 1905. Zimmermann is best remembered for his takeover of the business of MALKE & OBERLÄNDER, and the production of the Fortuna disc-playing musical box. Zimmermann also owned the Fiedler piano manufactory, established in Leipzig in 1871 by Gustav Fiedler.

ZOGBAUM & FAIRCHILD, F. Agent's name seen printed on top of Ducommun-Girod tune sheet as 'Fabriqué à Genève pour F. Zogbaum & Fairchild'.

ZUMSTEG, HEINRICH, Külm, Aargau, Switzerland. Musical-box maker who invented in 1885 a system of reduction gears to lengthen the normal playing-time of a musical box by four or five times on one winding.

British Patents Relating to Musical Boxes

The importance of Letters Patent in tracing the history of mechanical musical instruments cannot be over-stressed. Indeed, a whole reference work could be compiled on the subject of patents, patentees, their agents, and, of course, the devices covered by the patents.

Patents (from the Latin *pateo*, I lie open) were introduced as licences and authorities granted by the king and in the fourteenth century were a means of granting noble title. The protection of the rights of inventors in arts and manufactures were secured by an Act passed in 1623 allowing the protection by letters patent. Initially, letters patent – patent for short – were couched in the strict formal language of the time and told the enquirer well nigh nothing about the nature of the invention. However, eventually the patent had to be supported by a detailed description and illustrations and, usually although not always, by a model. The period of protection afforded by a patent was 16 years: very recently this has been extended but this has no bearing on our history.

The British Patent Office, the oldest in the world, established a system which was later adopted by all nations of the world. During the period of its operation which concerns us – namely the era of the musical box – it was considered to be the most important patent office in the world. Both Swiss and German inventors did not consider that they were adequately protected unless, in addition to their National patent office protection, they had their design made the subject of a British patent. For this reason, the patent office in London is a rich treasurehouse of information, much of it on schemes which never entered production, much demonstrating the state-of-the-art in technology.

To the student of patents, there are a few important guidelines to be observed. The first is that the granting of a British patent to a foreign applicant who had already secured a national patent (say, in Germany), could not become effective until a year after the foreign original. In other words, if we find a German inventor in Leipzig was granted a British patent in 1875, then its German counterpart would have been issued in 1874, usually in the comparable month and on the same date. The next point is that foreign applicants sought protection through registered patent agents in London who would accept their brief to undertake application procedures and see the job right the way through. Usually the name of the real applicant does not appear in the patent abridgments, only that of the agent. The patent itself, though, will usually say something to the effect that: 'I, John Smith of Glastonbury

Chambers in London, County of Middlesex, do hereby apply for the granting of a Patent covering Improvements in Musical Boxes. A communication from abroad by Messrs. Neuberger of Leipzig, Germany.'

The British Patent Office also operated a scheme which was quite different from that used in most other European and American patent offices. This concerned numbering. Whereas other offices began with number 1 and progressed onwards, thereby quickly clocking up some pretty impressive collections of digits, the British system was to re-start on the first day of January every year with number 1. This means that a British patent number tells you very little *unless the year is also given*. This is why on musical boxes and catalogues a UK patent is usually shown as '3456.89' which means that it was patent number 3456 of 1889.

At the time when interest in musical boxes was waning in the British Isles thanks to the infiltration of the gramophone and the organette, much of the interest in patenting novelties passed to the United States but even that marked only a short-lived reprieve and by the early part of this century the number of patents began to dwindle to almost nothing. I list patents up to 1928, but the important part of the listing lies in the years from 1870 to 1898.

I compiled this list of abridgments of patents on musical boxes only (this means there are no organettes, player pianos, organs or other devices included) over a period of three years working laboriously through the Class 88 1694–1930 abridgments at the Patent Office off London's Chancery Lane. I have been inspired to include this in the present work as a companion to the listing, albeit slightly inaccurate, which Roy Mosoriak included in his book *The Curious History of the Musical Box* showing American patents. I hasten to add that I believe my list to be complete and that the brief descriptions are my own summary of the abridgment itself. Where a patent covers an identifiable production product, I include this fact.

I acknowledge the help I have received from the staff at the Patent Office to whom, in this high-technological age, my interest in old patents for musical boxes must have seemed a trifle odd.

The system I have used in setting out this patent data follows the following scheme: column one = patent number; column two = date of patent; column three = name of applicant (with the name of the originator, where known, in parenthesis); column four = a brief description.

828	4 Apr 1861	John Walker Lee	Improved winding key for musical boxes
1365	1 Jun 1864	A. V. Newton (J. W. Jones)	Device for striking drum, triangle or tambourine, &c, on mechanical instrument
1919	2 Aug 1864	F. W. Bossert	Musical movement in spine of photo album
870	24 Mar 1866	Philip Stieffel	Improved wheelwork for musical snuff-box and an adjustable fly for same
269	28 Jan 1869	C. L. A. Hoelscher	Musical chair wound by sitting down
322	2 Feb 1869	Henry Bate	Musical box in spinning top
593	26 Feb 1869	Henry Harburg	Musical box tune indicator
932	27 Mar 1869	Jean & Abram Jaquillard	Combined musical box tune indicator and selector
1425	10 May 1869	R. F. Hoppe (C. H. Schwarz)	Musical box incorporating a travelling picture in lid
1941	26 Jun 1869	F. C. Lecoultre	Changeable-cylinder mechanism with cylinder slid out on carriage. Also tune indicator

1677	9 Jun 1870	J. H. L. T. Pörtner (Pollack, Schmidt & Co.)	Cabinets and stands for sewing machines incorporating musical movements
1766	6 Jul 1871	L. Ducommun	Lever-type winder for musical box using free roller instead of ratchet
1442	25 Apr 1874	J. W. Wignall	Musical box played by descending weight, rewound by galvanic battery
3697	26 Oct 1874	W. R. Lake (Charles Pailljrd)	Musical box having several combs of short teeth to give notes of short duration; combs tuned to slight dissonance
3851	7 Nov 1874	W. A. P. LaGrove	Musical movement inside toy
1282	25 Mar 1876	J. H. Johnson (G. A. Cassagnes)	The plating of musical-box combs with nickel
413	25 Jan 1878	J. Manger (A. Paillard)	Method of fitting changeable cylinders using helical spring to retain in bearings
3718	20 Sep 1878	E. T. Hughes (H. J. A. Metert & L. J. Petite)	Changeable-cylinder musical movement in which the cylinder is driven by a spigot from a false arbor
3711	16 Sep 1879	A. Browne (Aubert & Son)	Musical-box gearing for long-running when used in conjunction with clock
889	28 Feb 1880	E. Wright	Device to prevent musical box being overwound using special gears inside spring barrel
3241	7 Aug 1880	E. K. Hoffmann	Spring motor for musical box attached directly to barrel and wound from barrel
4872	24 Nov 1880	A. King	Musical box or organ fitted into furniture &c.
2626	16 Jun 1881	A. W. L. Reddie (H. J. Davies)	Improved musical clock with combwork
3423	8 Aug 1881	J. G. Dudley	Musical box played by electromotor
4154	31 Aug 1882	H. Robert & H. F. Gouvernon	Mechanism for playing tunes on bells or combwork for musical clocks
2136	27 Apr 1883	H. J. Haddan (W. Spaethe)	Musical-box barrels replaced by metal tune sheets
5748	15 Dec 1883	C. Pieper (P. Ehrlich)	Music sheet in disc form for musical box having projections cut into it or pinned on to it
2953	8 Feb 1884	C. Pieper (P. Ehrlich)	Organette or musical box played by swinging round like a rattle
4381	4 Mar 1884	W. R. Lake (E. Blay)	Dish warmer and plate stand with musical box
4968	15 Mar 1884	G. W. Nawrocki (H. Lorentz)	Automatic instrument playing from flat or corrugated tune sheets
15,459	24 Nov 1884	A. J. Dobson	Musical mechanism combined with top
16,320	11 Dec 1884	Ellis Parr	Pin barrels and tune sheets for automatic instruments
16,638	18 Dec 1884	J. C. Eckardt	Musical box incorporated in rotating stand for Christmas tree
6791	4 Jun 1885	G. Mermod	Safety check for musical box
7578	22 Jun 1885	F. E. P. Ehrlich	Machine for stamping out tune sheets

8591	15 Jul 1885	C. E. Juillerat	Manivelle displaying pictures through slots in case as handle is turned
10,944	15 Sep 1885	Ellis Parr	Musical spinning top using rotating spring-driven disc inside
11,261	22 Sep 1885	Paul Lochmann	Disc musical box with two combs on vertical axis and plucked directly by disc projections
428	11 Jan 1886	H. F. Hambruch	Musical box playing perforated tune sheet wrapped round barrel plucking comb by sliding or pivoting levers
2241	16 Feb 1886	John Manger	Means of holding cylinders in toy musical boxes to allow easy removal
4279	26 Mar 1886	C. E. Jacot, E. Bovy	Tapered spring in musical box motor to exert even pull on cylinder
4960	9 Apr 1886	V. & L. Weber	Stopwork for driving spring in musical box
5537	21 Apr 1886	Oscar Paul Lochmann	Comb playing musical box having a segmented barrel to which is fixed tune sheet. Hand cranked. Uses star wheels to pluck teeth
6391	12 May 1886	Friederich Ernst Paul Ehrlich	Comb-playing musical box with perforated tune sheet. Action for plucking teeth
6962	24 May 1886	Edmond Fornachon	Improved, cheaper design for cylinder musical boxes, arbor supports cast in bedplate; means of changing cylinders
7327	1 Jun 1886	A. Paillard (A. Paillard & Co.) (A. Sueur)	Zither attachment for musical boxes using roll of paper or other flexible material on cam-operated movable rail under comb
7969	15 Jun 1886	A. Paillard (as above)	A method of locking the drive barrel if part of mechanism is deranged, i.e. safety check
8196	21 Jun 1886	G. F. Beutner & A. A. Lateulère	Interchangeable cylinder musical box. Barrels are slotted to fit on spring-loaded frame in contact with change/repeat mechanism (used by Paillard)
9024	10 Jul 1886	A. Karrer	Extended-play musical box has extra pinion and great wheel in power train (first Longue Marche style)
9742	28 Jul 1886	F. E. R. Ehrlich & G. A. F. Müller	Musical box with vertically-mounted combs and direct-plucking disc projections (improvement on Lochmann 11,261 of 1885)
13,057	13 Oct 1886	A. Browne (A. Junod)	Interchangeable cylinder method
14,666	12 Nov 1886	J. Worthington	Toy musical box on wheels
16,087	8 Dec 1886	J. Y. Johnson (A. L'Épée and L. E. J. Thibouville)	Mechanism of interchangeable cylinder musical box
1745	3 Feb 1887	J. C. Heine	Musical box combined with table bell
2525	18 Feb 1887	John Manger	Improvements to 2241 of 1886
2720	22 Feb 1887	A. Eisen	Method of changing barrel in cylinder musical box
3801	12 Mar 1887	C. E. Hall	Coin-operated mechanism for dispensing small article in conjunction with musical box

4211	21 Mar 1887	J. Billon-Haller	Stop mechanism acting on main wheel of musical box as well as tune barrel combined with safety devices
5343	12 Apr 1887	H. H. Lake (O. H. Arno & A. E. Paillard)	Musical box operated by tune sheet playing on reeds as well as comb
8642	15 May 1887	Paul Lochmann	Musical box with tune sheet played by handle or spring motor
823	18 Jan 1888	A. Schmidt	Tune sheet-operated musical box played by sliding levers (lever plucker)
1086	24 Jan 1888	F. E. P. Ehrlich	Lever plucker similar to Schmidt above
4998	4 Apr 1888	W. T. Whiteman (U.S. Machine & Inventors Co.)	Coin-operated weighing machine with musical box to play tune each time used
6566	2 May 1888	J. Billon-Haller	Device for locking music barrels in changeable-cylinder musical box
9265	25 Jun 1888	A. J. Boulte (G. H. Kluge)	Device for actuating moving figures with a musical box
14,917	17 Oct 1888	Paul Lochmann	Spring-driven disc musical box with tune sheet passing between combs and directly plucking the teeth.
15,054	19 Oct 1888	J. Bedow	Cigar or liquor stand with musical movement in base
15,169	22 Oct 1888	J. Sauerteig & L. H. F. Lutz	Musical box combined with doll and driven by spring or handle
19,068	31 Dec 1888	J. G. Lorrain	Method of storing electricity to wind up musical box
19,069	31 Dec 1888	J. G. Lorrain	Variant of above combined with heated-air motor
2610	14 Feb 1889	G. C. Scheinert	Musical box with manually-played accompaniment
5428	29 Mar 1889	J. C. Eckardt	Musical device for Christmas trees and revolving shop window displays using four small musical movements
5442	29 Mar 1889	Paul Lochmann	Plucking and damping musical-box teeth using a starwheel
7471	4 May 1889	Paul Lochmann	Punch for making Symphonion-type disc projections
8510	22 May 1889	G. A. Keile	Lever plucking musical box using tune sheets in place of barrel
9142	3 Jun 1889	W. Brierley	Musical movement in hollow handle of skipping rope
14,306	10 Sep 1889	L. A. Barber	Musical-box cylinders replaced by electrotypes
15,358	30 Sep 1889	F. E. P. Ehrlich	Tune sheets made to fold up like a fan (only ever used on Ariston organette?)
15,359	30 Sep 1889	F. E. P. Ehrlich	Lever plucking mechanism using perforated tune sheet
16,314	16 Oct 1889	E. W. Hambleton & J. Carpenter	Watch built in case with musical movement which plays on opening
16,850	25 Oct 1889	F. H. Purchas	Sound generator for tuning musical-box combs

783	15 Jan 1890	J. Schünemann	Musical box with comb mounted vertically above tune sheet using plucking levers
6077	22 Apr 1890	C. A. Roepke	Musical box playing perforated tune sheet using plucking levers
7677	16 May 1890	J. L. Müller	Musical box playing perforated tune sheets using plucking levers
12,170	2 Aug 1890	H. H. Lake (Soc. A. Junod & Co.)	Means for facilitating changing of cylinders in musical boxes. Arbor bearings are open, cylinder arbor ends in knobs, and cylinder has full-length slot to allow it to drop saddle-fashion over fixed arbor
20,828	20 Dec 1890	Ellis Parr	Starwheels to play comb from musical-box cylinder, wooden barrel or other programme source
21,232	30 Dec 1890	A. R. Vaughan	Apparatus for withdrawing or replacing springs from/in musical box spring barrels
10,053	13 Jun 1891	Paul Lochmann	Musical box playing tune sheets either circular or rectangular
10,906	26 Jun 1891	J. Billon-Haller	Safety check for musical-box springs consisting of worm wheel engaging in spring barrel teeth and locked with knob
11,388	4 Jul 1891	H. H. Lake (Cuendet-Develay, Fils, et Cie)	Method of damping comb tooth using a fork placed below comb. Also style of interchangeable cylinder movement
13,732	14 Aug 1891	O. Thost & H. Richter	Musical box playing perforated tune sheets via plucking levers
13,903	18 Aug 1891	F. Pietschmann	Musical box playing perforated tune sheets via plucking levers
14,849	2 Sep 1891	J. F. Peasgood & P. Tracy	Coin-operated cylinder musical box allowing two tunes per coin
16,632	30 Sep 1891	F. T. Folland & A. H. Thomas	Musical box coupled to baby's cradle with rocking mechanism
19,523	11 Nov 1891	J. L. Müller	Lever plucking tune sheet musical box with provision for levers to damp
4451	7 Mar 1892	G. A. Brachhausen & Paul Riessner	Damping comb teeth in musical box using levers under starwheels. Starwheels engage in slots in disc without projections
8750	9 May 1892	Paul Lochmann	Albums for storing musical-box discs
9013	12 May 1892	J. C. Eckardt	Device for revolving Christmas trees or shop window displays with musical movement
12,055	28 Jun 1892	F. Pietschmann	Automatic instrument with plucking levers; method for damping comb teeth; centrifugal governor for musical-box motors
17,113	24 Sep 1892	E. & C. Stransky	Coin-operated disc musical box with disc changing facility
19,775	3 Nov 1892	Paul Lochmann	Disc-playing musical box driven by peripheral wheel; motor in box to reduce noise

23,150	16 Dec 1892	P. von Hertling	Musical box with projectionless tune sheets. Triangular plate above disc engages disc slot and so turns star-wheel beneath
23,945	28 Dec 1892	P. von Hertling	Musical box playing projectionless tune sheets which uses starwheels sprung against underside of disc
2887	9 Feb 1893	A. A. Lateulère	Gearing to wind up or drive musical-box spring and to disconnect when fully wound
5861	18 Mar 1893	E. G. Lochmann	Comb-plucking instrument played by keyboard
6075	22 Mar 1893	W. F. Needham	Musical box under bamboo table
6941	4 Apr 1893	J. Wetter (Bruno Rückert)	Tune sheets having scoop-like indentations in place of normal projections (this is the Orphenion)
8063	21 Mar 1893	P. von Hertling	Musical box playing projectionless tune sheet with means to rotate loosely-pivoted starwheels to pluck comb so reducing friction
10,515	29 May 1893	Paul Ehrlich	Design for tune sheet projection and machine for punching
11,546	13 Jun 1893	P. von Hertling	Development of 23,945 of 1892 and 8063 of 1893
11,672	14 June 1893	F. Pietschmann	Musical box with added percussion effects which can be hand-played
14,666	31 Jul 1893	W. A. Seifert	Musical box having projectionless tune sheet and trefoil cam starwheels
14,724	1 Aug 1893	O. P. Lochmann	Twin-disc musical box
17,125	12 Sep 1893	G. Brachhausen & Paul Riessner	Disc musical-box dampers using cam-shaped finger
18,145	27 Sep 1893	P. Riessner	Musical box incorporated with figure so that figure appears to be playing
18,356	30 Sep 1893	O. P Lochmann	Triple-disc musical box (this is the Eroica Symphonion)
18,858	9 Oct 1893	W. J. & H. Riley	Musical box with curved glass lid and vellum soundboard at back
20,867	3 Nov 1893	E. de Pass (E. Viollier)	Musical box combined with alarm clock. Alarm strikes a match, lights a lamp and plays a tune
2076	31 Jan 1894	S. A. Tilley	Velocipedes, rocking horses, roundabouts, switchback railways &c. with musical boxes
4005	24 Feb 1894	K. Behrens	Musical box combined with dynamometer
4556	3 Mar 1894	W. F. Smith & G. Harman	Combined musical box with magic lantern
9382	11 May 1894	A. Amthor	Several musical-box tune sheets fixed together to make long piece of music
9446	12 May 1894	F. A. Richter	Tune sheet fitted with holes for operating comb and slots for wind instrument valves
9539	15 May 1894	E. Paillard	Musical-box tune barrel tapered to allow more notes at treble than bass. Barrel is of

			thin metal with projections pushed out (this is Capital 'cuff-box')
11,234	9 Jun 1894	F. A. Richter	Starwheels for musical box operate wire dampers which engage recess in comb tooth
12,027	21 Jun 1894	F. Pietschmann	Double starwheels to pluck comb of disc machine, one to work damper
14,380	26 Jul 1894	F. A. Richter	Method of driving tune sheet using rubber-covered rollers
15,759	18 Aug 1894	T. E. Halford (H. Siefert & G. Jaeger)	Combined musical box with coin-freed weighing machine
17,041	7 Sep 1894	F. A. Richter	Plucking device for comb teeth using projectionless tune sheet
5951	21 Mar 1895	F. A. Richter	Driving long or endless bands of music from the middle using one driven and one idler sprocket (this is the Libellion)
7190	8 Apr 1895	E. Mahlke	Coin-operated musical box with means of selecting tunes
13,940	22 Jul 1895	H. von Pollnitz & F. L. Bauer	Comb/starwheel musical box playing projectionless disc; method of mounting starwheels
17,317	17 Sep 1895	F. A. Richter	Method of plucking comb using sliding levers (Libellion)
17,318	17 Sep 1895	F. A. Richter	Oval musical box using endless bands to exploit lever plucking system above
18,507	3 Oct 1895	C. A. Jensen (Otto Helbig & Polikeit)	Musical-box starwheel damping device. Points of wheel push vertical spring against side of tooth
23,232	4 Dec 1895	F. E. Malke & F. H. Oberländer	Tune discs with flanges to provide more bearing surface for drive
23,233	4 Dec 1895	F. E. Malke & F. H. Oberländer	Musical-box winding method with winding shaft engaging in rack-like teeth pushed out of motor barrel
23,234	4 Dec 1895	F. E. Malke & F. H. Oberländer	Two or more musical movements connected together by chains, sprocket wheels or perforated steel bands so as to play together
24,211	17 Dec 1895	A. J. Boult (E. J. Herrmann)	Musical-box cylinder shifted to change tune by spring, snail and quadrant
631	9 Jan 1896	P. Calame-Jaccard	Interchangeable cylinders for musical box
3941	21 Feb 1896	J. B. Howard (Otto Helbig & Polikeit)	Musical-box disc with projections formed by ending up two pieces
4931	4 Mar 1896	A. Junod	Disc musical box playing projectionless discs which use starwheels sliding in guides (this is the Stella)
5684	13 Mar 1896	F. E. Malke & F. H. Oberländer	Preventing overwinding disc musical box and new form of disc projection
7443	8 Apr 1896	G. Bortmann & A. Keller	Musical box with circular tune sheets playing two tunes per disc by shifting disc centre (this is the Sirion)
8624	24 Apr 1896	E. Schacht	Musical chair

11,469	26 May 1896	E. P. Riessner	Tune-changing device for coin-freed disc musical box
14,450	30 Jun 1896	F. A. Richter	Disc musical-box dampers from tune sheet with projections
14,916	6 Jul 1896	F. A. Herrmann	Strengthening drive holes in discs
15,505	13 Jul 1896	H. S. Grant	Musical box in toy
15,675	15 Jul 1896	A. Richter	Lever-plucking comb musical box
18,049	14 Aug 1896	A. Richter	Means of employing different sizes of discs on musical box
19,081	29 Aug 1896	A. Vernaz	Disc-playing musical box using starwheels and projectionless disc with comb vertically underneath
21,201	24 Sep 1896	J. Riedl	Dampers for starwheel-operated disc musical box
23,477	22 Oct 1896	C. Landenberger	Zither attachment for disc musical box
25,354	11 Nov 1896	F. A. Richter	Dampers for disc musical box
41	1 Jan 1897	C. A. Roepke (Roepke & Co.)	Musical-box winding mechanism incorporating overwind/wrong direction protection
5822	4 Mar 1897	J. Riedl	Tune sheet for musical box having semi-circular or chevron-shaped drive slots around periphery (Saxonia?)
6981	17 Mar 1897	P. Lochmann	Disc musical box with combs as separate assembly to facilitate setting up
10,599	28 Apr 1897	G. Bortmann & R. Munkwitz	Plucking and damping system for musical box with projections on disc-driving starwheels
13,115	27 May 1897	F. Gronau	Automatic instrument playing combs, reeds &c mounted on rotating shaft as set of wheels. Perforated tune sheet causes brakes to be applied on certain discs so producing sound
18,559	10 Aug 1897	G. Bourquin	Comb-playing musical box operated by perforated paper roll
19,653	26 Aug 1897	M. Claus & B. Püttman	Musical box with means of controlling the point at which any tooth may be damped so adding nuance and individuality to performance
20,713	9 Sep 1897	C. A. Roepke (Roepke & Co.)	Clip for joining sections of punched card together for use on comb-playing musical box
23,786	15 Oct 1897	E. F. Radicke	Clock in picture plays from musical box on the hour
26,806	16 Nov 1897	A. Junghans	Disc musical box in clock
4707	25 Feb 1898	V. F. Feeny (Bauer & Co.)	Disc musical box with double starwheels, one large and one smaller. Comb teeth are stepped. Small wheel acts as damper
5386	4 Mar 1898	T. A. Plessing	Disc musical box playing two tunes per disc by shifting centre. Device for selecting which tune to play (this is the Tannhauser)

6434	16 Mar 1898	M. Lochmann	Discs for musical box are cut through to the centre to facilitate changing without lifting pressure bar, also to facilitate joining together for long music
8891	16 Apr 1898	W. P. Thompson (Handische & Ladisch)	Musical box in mirror
9308	22 Apr 1898	E. Breslauer	Self-changing disc musical box
10,754	11 May 1898	T. P. Bache	Means of coupling musical-box springs for long running
13,143	11 Jun 1898	C. Raleigh	Musical box combined with kinetoscope
16,191	25 Jul 1898	W. H. Hoschke	Disc-playing musical box. Device for aligning starwheels before putting on disc, also stopping arrangement
17,197	9 Aug 1898	P. Simon (trading as E. Holzweissig Nachfolger)	Disc musical box mounted in piano
17,925	20 Aug 1898	C. Wilton	Disc musical box inside cabinet or sideboard
20,913	4 Oct 1898	E. Breslauer	Manually-changed disc musical box (see 9308 of 1898)
21,866	18 Oct 1898	L. A. H. Hupfeld	Musical box using motor other than clockwork
23,299	5 Nov 1898	M. Lochmann	Disc musical box with variable speed from special disc projections
5243	10 Mar 1899	R. Peter	Disc storage system
5569	14 Mar 1899	G. A. Brachhausen	Self-changing disc machine (Polyphon)
9398	4 May 1899	F. W. Golby (E. E. Rühle)	Musical box automatically wound by electric current
10,681	20 May 1899	E. Fiedler	Terrestrial globe with musical box
13,360	27 Jun 1899	W. L. Wise (L. W. Baldwin)	Weighing machine with musical box
16,883	19 Aug 1899	W. A. Drysdale	Disc musical box with self-changer plus device to govern how many times disc will play (this instrument survives in incomplete, prototype form in the Bill Edgerton, Darien, collection: it is based on $11\frac{7}{8}$ in. Symphonion)
20,814	17 Oct 1899	H. H. Lake (B. H. Abrahams)	Disc musical box with device for adjusting driving spindle to tune sheet and starwheels
23,200	21 Nov 1899	E. P. Riessner	Disc musical box having long slot in tune sheets; also projectionless version using organ-type keyframe and sticker linkages. Self-changer
24,378	7 Dec 1899	J. Wellner	Self-changing disc musical box
24,877	14 Dec 1899	W. P. Thompson (Fabrik Lochmann'scher Musikwerke)	Self-changing disc musical box (Symphonion)
25,522	23 Dec 1899	F. A. Richter	Means of holding tune sheets on to starwheels or pluckers of musical box

2469	7 Feb 1900	E. P. Riessner	Resonant plates struck by hammers as starwheels pluck musical-box comb from disc with projections
4469	8 Mar 1900	A. Staffelstein & F. Kluge	Helicoidal tune sheets for long pieces of music on musical box. Discs are split and joined together
9427	22 May 1900	F. A. Richter	Disc musical box combined with moving pictures
9913	29 May 1900	G. Varrelman	Self-changing disc musical box
11,816	29 June 1900	F. A. Richter	Lever-plucking comb musical box
13,196	21 Jul 1900	A. C. F. Staffelstein & H. F. F. Kluge	Machine for stamping out special helical tune sheets as in 4469 of 1900
16,794	20 Sep 1900	G. A. Brachhausen	Self-changing disc musical box
21,215	23 Nov 1900	H. H. Lake (B. H. Abrahams)	Self-changing disc musical box
14,243	12 Jul 1901	G. C. Dymond (Fabrik Lochmann'scher Musikwerke)	Coin-operated self-changing disc musical box
1864	23 Jan 1902	C. W. Edwards	Musical box combined with skipping rope
2583	31 Jan 1902	W. P. Thompson (Fabrik Lochmann'scher Musikwerke)	Self-changing disc musical box operating horizontally (this is the table Symphonion self-changer)
8782	15 Apr 1902	J. McTammany	Comb-playing musical box combined with strings. Teeth plucked and strings plucked from a perforated tune sheet
11,617	13 May 1910	H. Graf	Tune sheet for disc musical box having many plain holes into which owner can insert pins to make music (this is Graf's Musikbaukasten)
808	11 Jan 1911	I. Goldberg	Alarm clock with musical box
23,441	14 Oct 1912	R. J. Hardy & L. Serné (H. Oltmans)	Musical movement incorporated in clothes brush
26,553	19 Nov 1912	R. J. Hardy & L. Serné (H. Oltmans)	Musical movement incorporated in toilet or wrapping paper holder
319,912	11 Sep 1928	O. Rechnitz	Rotary rattle-type floor-wax dispenser with musical movement

HOW TO CHECK UP ON A PATENT

British patents for mechanical musical instruments can be viewed at the British Library, Patents Division, 25 Southampton Buildings, Chancery Lane, London, WC2. This is close to Chancery Lane Underground station. The illustrated Abridgments, which contain a brief description of the particular patent together with, usually, one salient drawing taken from the patent, are divided up into many classes, that concerning us being Class 88 (ii) Musical Instruments, Automatic. At the time of writing, abridgments from 1909 onwards are on open access and the three earlier volumes (the earliest of which is not illustrated) are available on application to the enquiry desk. Each volume of abridgments contains several sections of abridgments for the period of the volume, each section having its own index first of the names of the patentees and then by type of instrument. To examine a patent, application has to be

347

made for the bound volume containing that particular patent to be brought up from the vaults. If you know the number *and the date* of the patent you want, you can make written application or telephone your request (01-405 8721) for the volume to be available to you at a specific time – a boon if you have a long way to travel. Photocopies of patents normally have to be applied for in writing, prepaid, and despatched from the patent archives in Kent but if you can show good reason that you need the patent in a hurry, copy facilities are available in the library.

American, German, Swiss, French and other countries' patents are available for inspection either in abridgment or on microfilm, in the foreign section which is just across the road from the library.

There is a most useful list of names of patentees grouped into years in the form of a total index, so if you know the name of the applicant (or his agent), this multi-volume index, on open access, is invaluable.

In the United States, the classification system is somewhat more complex, but copies are easier, usually, to obtain. The main US Patent Office is in Washington, but copies are held in the New York Public Library, Patent Division, 521 West 43rd Street which is close to the Port Authority bus terminal and about 10 minutes walk from Grand Central station. Telephone enquires can be dealt with on (212) 790 6524.

United States patents for automatic or self-playing musical instruments come under the main heading of Class 84 and its sub-divisions. Using these, it is quite easy to locate all the patents for one type of mechanical musical instrument. For example, all automatic instruments are found under 84.2; those employing a pinned cylinder are 84.106; those with a comb are 84.94R; those with bells 84.103, and so on. There is a useful guide to all these sections available at the enquiry desk and once again illustrated abridgments of all patents are open to examination by application. All patents or abridgments can be photocopied immediately; there is a copy service in the library or, if the patents are on microfilm, there is a viewer machine which will make thermo-copies instantly.

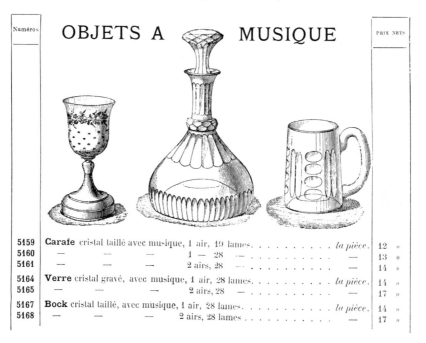

Numéros	OBJETS A MUSIQUE	PRIX NETS
5159	**Carafe** cristal taillé avec musique, 1 air, 19 lames . . . . *la pièce.*	12 »
5160	— — — 1 — 28 — . . . . —	13 »
5161	— — — 2 airs, 28 — . . . . —	14 »
5164	**Verre** cristal gravé, avec musique, 1 air, 28 lames . . . . *la pièce.*	14 »
5165	— — — 2 airs, 28 — . . . . —	17 »
5167	**Bock** cristal taillé, avec musique, 1 air, 28 lames . . . . *la pièce.*	14 »
5168	— — — 2 airs, 28 lames . . . . —	17 »

Musical Box Tune Sheets – A Guide to Identification

The importance of the tune sheet in identifying the maker and date of a musical box has already been emphasised (see page 32). Here are some ninety different styles.

1 Barnett Henry Abrahams (BHA). Large and multi-coloured lithographed sheet clearly showing the trademark at the top and the words: 'BHA Ste. Croix, Switzerland & London' in the left and right of the lower margin. This is sometimes cut off. Programme is all from *The Geisha*, dating it as 1896–8.

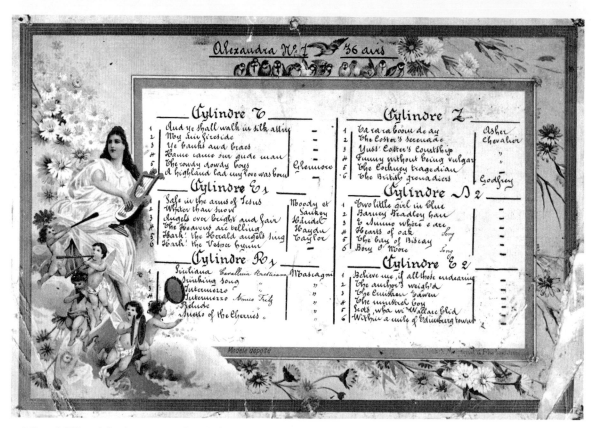

2 Junod. This style has been seen used on the Alexandra interchangeable-cylinder box as well as other Junod boxes. A second style is shown on page 361. Each cylinder has a separate identity and its tunes are all listed.

3 Allard & Sandoz. This sheet is from an organocleide having two cylinders each of six tunes. Note the trademark at the top.

4 F. Alibert. Few miniature musical movements were provided with tune sheets unless the movements were sold uncased to a finishing house. This one is from a nécessaire.

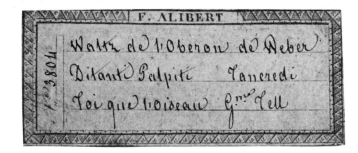

5 Allez & Berguer. Plain-style label identified by initials AB on bottom edge. Bedplates were also stamped in most cases with the name in full.

N?.	MUSIQUE de GENÈVE à AIRS		ÉTOUFFOIRS en ACIER.
		A	B.

6 George Bendon. Characterised by the royal coat of arms, this sheet is always lithographed in black on white or off-white. No colours were used.

7 Ball Beavon & Co. This is the tune sheet of Lecoultre (see also page 365) as shown by the initials L.B. in the top right-hand border. The style also appears with L.F. in place of L.B., and also with Lecoultre printed where the initials B.B.& C. appear on this one. All are Lecoultre.

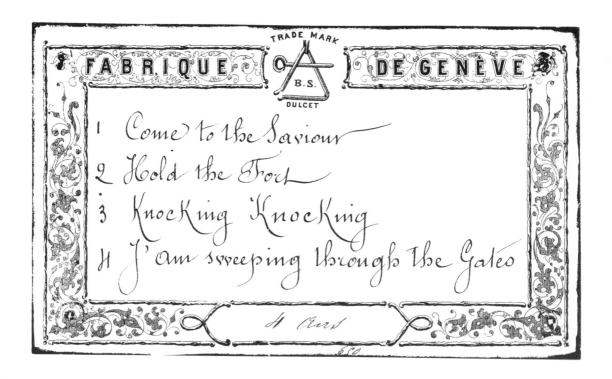

8 Barnett Samuel & Sons. With the trademark of triangle, striker, initials B.S. and the word 'Dulcet', Barnett Samuel were leading importers. The style is very similar to one of those used by Bremond (q.v.) and Ami Rivenc (q.v.). Hymn tunes.

9 Billon-Haller. The butterfly trademark with the initials JB identifies Jean Billon-Haller's work. Many also had 'Swiss Made' stamped on the cock.

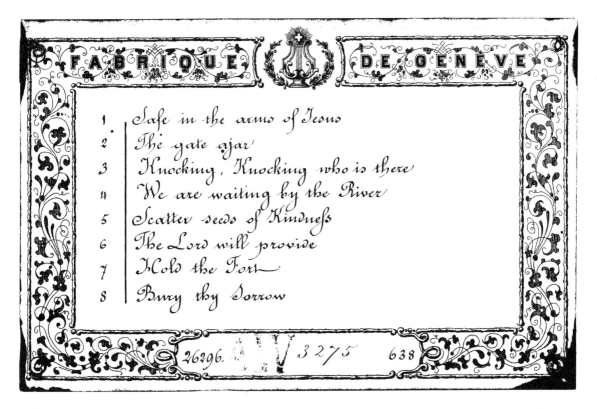

10 Bremond. The characteristic of this period of Bremond tune sheets is the lyre at the top surmounted with a Swiss cross. Compare this feature with the lyre and mask used by Ducommun Girod (q.v.). Compare tune-sheet style with that of Barnett Samuel & Sons (q.v.) and Rivenc (q.v.). All-hymn programme.

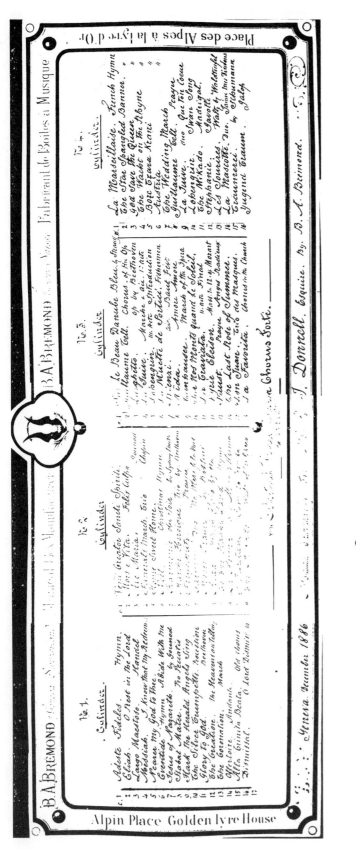

11 Bremond. This custom-built four-cylinder interchangeable is important and unusual in that the date of manufacture is given. Obviously a special for an important customer.

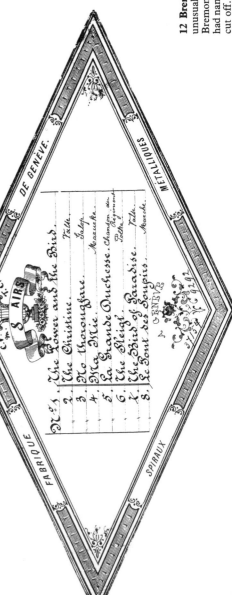

12 Bremond. Diamond-shaped tune sheets are unusual and were used by both Lecoultre (q.v.) and Bremond. Designs were identical. Bremond usually had name engraved in lower margins, usually (as here) cut off.

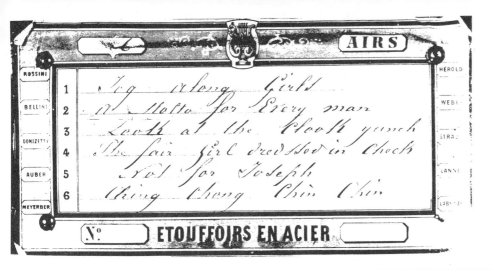

AIRS

ROSSINI
BELLINI
DONIZETTI
AUBER
MEYERBER

HÉROLD
WEBER
STRAU
LANN
LISZ T

1. Jog along Girls
2. A Motto for Every man
3. Look at the Plook punch
4. The fair Girl dressed in Check
5. Not for Joseph
6. Ching Chong Chin Chin

Nº ETOUFFOIRS EN ACIER

13 Bremond. An early style which appears in several variants.

14 Bremond. Usually printed in red and black, this style dates from the early 1870s.

BRUNSWICK PLACE   GOLDEN LYRE   A LA LYRE D'OR   PLACE DES

Musical Box Manufacturer   B. A. BREMOND GENEVA

Six Airs
Flutes Voix Célestes.

Nº 1.	Boze Tzara Krani	Hymne Imperial de Russie	Beyer
2.	Ballade		Weber
3.	Freyschütz	Prière d'Agathe	Weber
4.	Don Giovanni	Il Mio Tesoro intanto	Mozart
5.	Marche des Noces		Mendelsohn
6.	Don Giovanni	Minueto del ofs.	Mozart

N. 8761.

Musical Box Manufacturer   B. A. BRÉMOND – GENEVA

8 Airs

Nº 1.	H. M. S. Pinafore	. . . . .	We sail the Ocean blue
„ 2.	id	. . . . .	He is an Englishman
„ 3.	Les Cloches de Corneville	.	Waltz
„ 4.	id	. . .	Chorus of the Servants
„ 5.	Sweethearts	. . . .	Waltz by d'albert
„ 6.	Le Petit Duc	. . .	Chanson du petit bossu
„ 7.	Fatinitza	. . .	March
„ 8.	Nancy Lee		

18516

LITH. DUC GENÈVE

15 Bremond. A variation on the style above, this one dates from 1879–81 period.

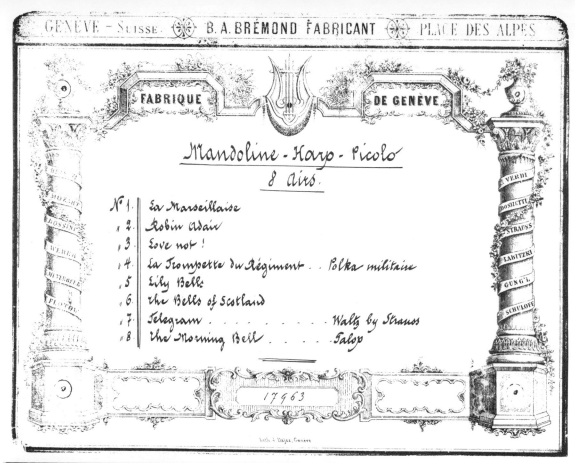

16 Bremond. Slightly earlier than that shown overleaf – about 1877 – this is typical of many contemporary similar styles with wreathed architectural columns bearing composers' names.

17 Bremond. Dating from 1860–5, this is a scarce fragment of an unusual style of tune sheet.

18 Perrin-Chopard. Reproduced here for its identical appearance to the Bremond sheet above, this one may have been used as a stock design by other makers.

19 Bruguier. Printed in blue on thin paper, this style is thought to have been used by other makers as well, possibly Lecoultre. This particular one is from a box marked on the bedplate with the maker's name and has, as tune eight, a waltz composed by Bruguier.

20 Bruguier. Almost identical to the one above, this one is attributed to the same maker. Both date from 1838–45 period.

21 Conchon. Similar in style to one of Bremond's early sheets (q.v.), this is from a box bearing both Conchon's name and trademark. 'Traviata' (1853) and 'Les deux Aveugles' (1855) suggest around 1858.

23 Conchon (attrib). The monogram at the top is the same as that used in Conchon's trademark.

24 Ducommun Girod. Printed in black on white paper. Note the trademark of a lyre surmounted by a mask.

25 L'Épée. A highly colourful sheet in blue, red, green and brown printed on a buff or off-white card. One of the very few French musical-box manufacturers.

26 Heller. Apparently intended for the German-speaking market, this product of the famous Heller company bears reproductions of medallions at the top, one of which is dated 1873. See overleaf for an earlier style.

27 Heller. Somewhat earlier than the style on the previous page, this appears to date from the mid-1860s. Compare with the style below.

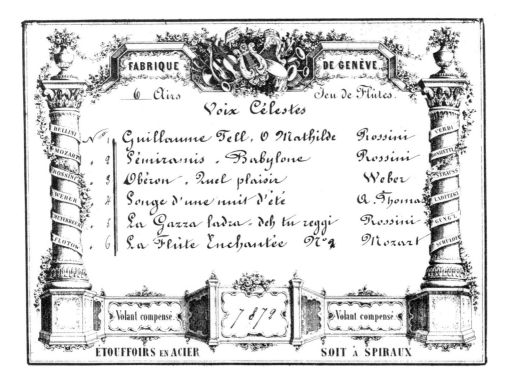

28 Heller. All three of these Heller cards are printed in black ink on white card. This style was also used by other makers including, particularly, Bremond and Greiner.

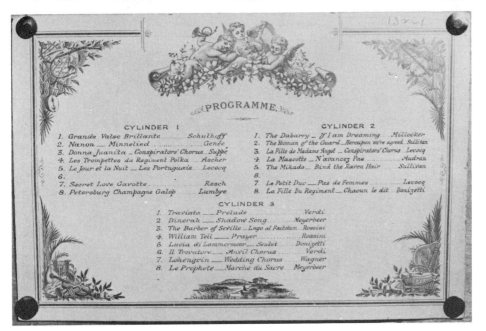

29 Jacot (attrib.). This somewhat formal style, printed in blue on white card, appears on some American-marketed boxes and thus might be found on Paillard, Mermod or Jacot items. Tune six on cylinders one and two appear to be the second halves of the previous melodies.

30 Jacot (attrib.). Full colour lithographed tune sheet seen on some American-factored boxes. Note the shield trademark in the top left-hand corner.

31 Junod. Style used also on Alexandra (q.v.). Seen in several variations featuring the lyre surmounted by six-pointed star.

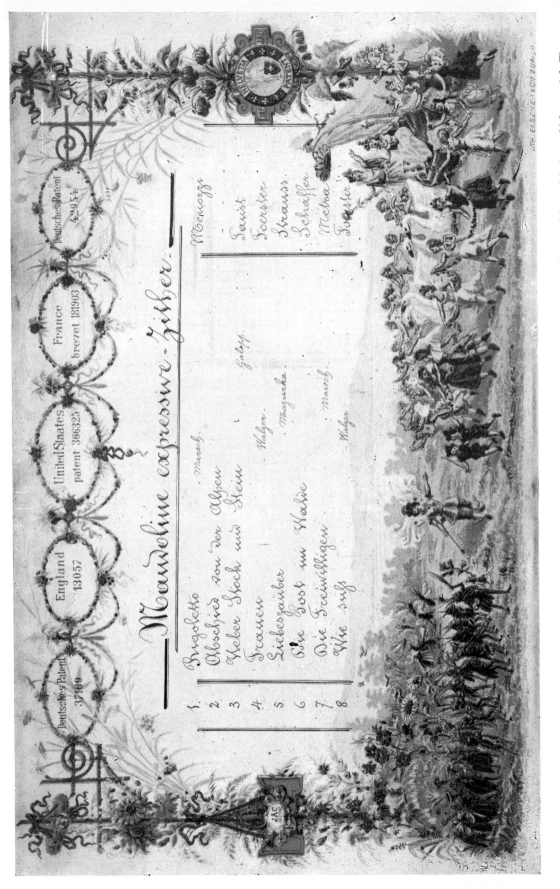

32 Junod. This style appears in several sizes – the one here is very large, measuring 310 mm by 203 mm – all bearing the Swiss patent insignia centre right, and the letters JAC centre left. The patents referred to are in the name of Arthur Junod and are assigned to Jacot & Son of New York. The English patent is of 1886. Printed in full colour, it is lithographed in Zurich.

33 Langdorff. The dates of the first two tunes suggest a date of early 1850s.

34 Langdorff. Note trademark (Geneva coat of arms) at top. From the late 1860s.

35 Langdorff. Interesting reversal of flanking figures in this style which dates from the early 1880s – Lecocq's 'Le Petit Duc' was 1878, and Suppé's 'Boccaccio' was 1879.

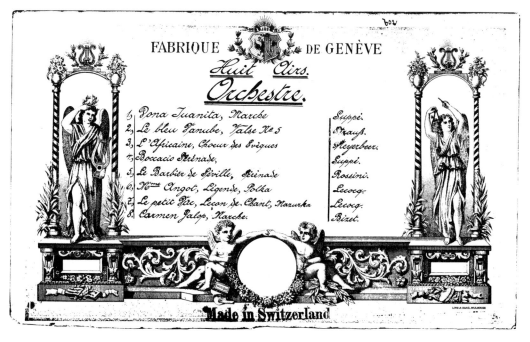

FABRIQUE DE GENÈVE

Six Airs. Mandoline Basse Piccola

Faust March, Soldier's Chorus Gounod
Come where my love lies dreaming.
Home sweet home. Bishop
Il Trovatore, mira di acerbe. Verdi
Mandolinata Paladilhe
Au Crépuscule, Valse. Faust

LANGDORFF & FILS FABRICANTS

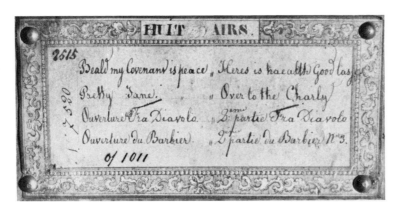

36 Langdorff. Similar to style overleaf, this one would seem to date from the early 1860s. Note that this one has the name printed on the bottom.

37 F. Lecoultre. White paper printed with blue border, movement number written up side. Dating from the 1830s. Note that the eight titles are written side by side with the last two being two turns each.

38 D. Lecoultre. White paper printed black, name printed faintly in hatched lines, top right corner. Several similar styles varying in detail of garland and centre.

39 Lecoultre Frères. A popular and fairly common style, but more usually found with BB&C in the lower centre cartouche (q.v.).

40 F. Lecoultre. A very early style is this one. Note the script initials FL in the top right-hand corner of the centre reserve, and also BB&C in the centre of the bottom border.

41 Lecoultre. From the late 1850s comes this style, a variation on the later one at the top of this page. Again BB&C is at the bottom.

42 C. Lecoultre. From the 1840s comes this early design with the name engraved in the bottom right-hand border. An early movement number – 772 – is interesting.

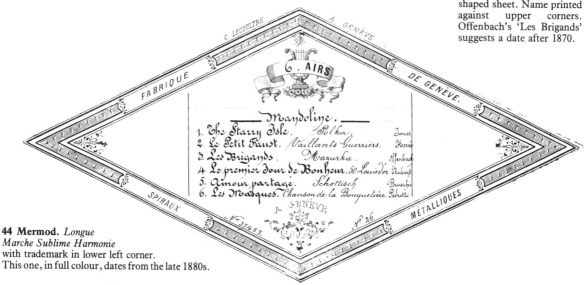

43 C. Lecoultre. Besides Bremond (who at one time used exactly the same style), Lecoultre was the only other maker to use a diamond-shaped sheet. Name printed against upper corners. Offenbach's 'Les Brigands' suggests a date after 1870.

44 Mermod. *Longue Marche Sublime Harmonie* with trademark in lower left corner. This one, in full colour, dates from the late 1880s.

45 Mermod (attrib.). Both Mermod and Junod had 'noiseless winder' patents, so this might just be Junod. Dates from around 1880.

46 Mermod. The Peerless was one of Mermod's brand of interchangeable-cylinder instruments. Note the legend 'Any number of cylinders can be obtained for this box' and the Mermod trademark, lower left corner.

47 Metert. Henri Metert used the stylised square piano motif at the top of his sheets, not to be confused with the upright piano of Langdorff (see item 33). This one, from a forte-piano box, probably dates from the 1850 period.

48 Mojon Manger. Late full-colour tune sheet. The last tune, a dance from Sidney Jones's operetta *The Geisha*, dates from 1896.

49, 50 Nicole Frères. Dating from 1882 the sheet above is usually lithographed in brown or grey and is not particularly inspiring in design. The one below, however, comes from a six-cylinder revolver-type model and is printed in black and gold. The legend '16p 24l' means 16 pouces 24 lignes – the size of the cylinders.

51 Nicole Frères. Made in 1870, this instrument played 18 tunes at two per turn – there being nine changes on the snail.

52 Nicole Frères. A style common in the mid-1840s, this appeared in a large variety of forms, some with agents' or importers' names printed along the bottom. A few of the variations follow.

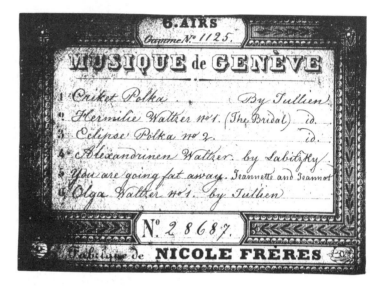

53 Nicole Frères. Boxes made for importers T. Cox Savory of London often appear with this style of sheet.

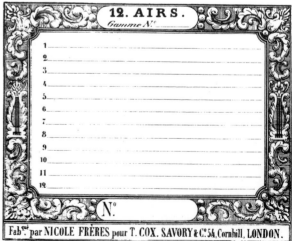

54 Nicole Frères. This style was used from the early 1840s through to the 1860s and later. Some are printed on blue card, others on green, the majority on white. Reason for colour change in uncertain.

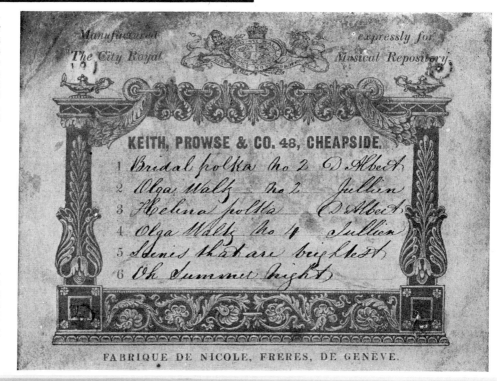

6. AIRS

Gamme N.°

MUSIQUE de GENÈVE

1 _____
2 _____
3 _____
4 _____
5 _____
6 _____

N° _____

Fab.^qué par NICOLE FRÈRES pour T. COX. SAVORY & C°. 54 Cornhill. ~ LONDON

55 Nicole Frères. Another of T. Cox Savory's branded tune sheets. The variations shown here are but a sample of the many styles which Nicole Frères used over the years. Much later, after the company had become London-owned and based, it used tune sheets bearing the terrestial globe trademark (see p. 263).

56 Nicole Frères. Special agents' tune sheet for Keith, Prowse on box made in 1846. This was one year after the premiere of Wallace's *Maritana* and the year in which company founder R. W. Keith died. Printed blue on white paper.

57 Paillard, Vaucher, Fils. This is a very large tune sheet and comes from the box illustrated in Plate 121. Also found fully hand-written on slightly earlier PVF Plerodiénique pieces. Date around 1882.

Manufactured *expressly for*
The City Royal *Musical Repository*

KEITH, PROWSE & CO. 48, CHEAPSIDE.

1 Bridal polka no 2 D. Albert
2 Olga Waltz no 2 Jullien
3 Helena polka D. Albert
4 Olga Waltz no 4 Jullien
5 Scenes that are brightest
6 Oh Summer night

FABRIQUE DE NICOLE, FRERES, DE GENÈVE.

RECHANGE   RECHANGE

SUBLIME HARMONIE PLERODIENIQUE

Nouveau Système *Nouveau Système*

1er CYLINDRE	4e CYLINDRE	7e CYLINDRE	8e CYLINDRE
1 Diamants de la Couronne	1 Fra Diavolo	1 La Norma	1 La Gazza
2e CYLINDRE	5e CYLINDRE	2 Il Trovatore	2 Les Contes
1 Le Barbier de Séville	1 Invitation à la Valse	3 Le Pardon	3 Orphée aux Enfers
3e CYLINDRE	6e CYLINDRE		9e CYLINDRE
1 Semiramis	1 Guillaume Tell		1 Valse brillante
			2 Johns

P.V.F.   Ste CROIX (Suisse)   P.V.F.

58 Paillard. Numbered 21832, this colourful tune sheet with its juvenile theme dates from the early 1880s – the latest work is Sullivan's *Pirates of Penzance*, premiered in 1880.

59 Paillard. Similar in every respect to that shown above, this one bears the number 23212 and must come from but a marginally later period than the other.

60 Paillard. Imported by M. J. Paillard of New York and numbered 23116, it would suggest a date in the early 1880s. Note an example of the frequent mis-attribution of tunes – 'L'Africaine' (1864) was by Meyerbeer.

61a, 61b Paillard, Vaucher, Fils. These two tune sheets come from a set of six accompanying an inter-changeable-cylinder box Style 711. All are coeval and were in use for some years.

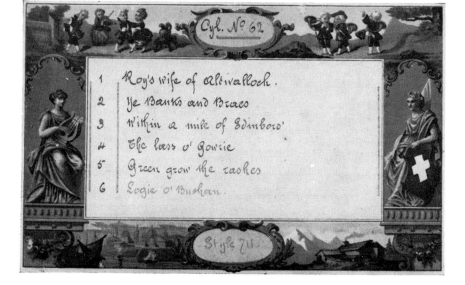

62 Paillard. Among the very many types of interchangeable-cylinder musical box made by Paillard was the Columbia. This sheet comes from an example obviously made for the German market.

63 Ami Rivenc. Similar in style to Bremond (q.v.) and Barnett Samuel (q.v.), Rivenc's boxes were all marked with the representation of the Brunswick Monument at the top which was also stamped on the cock. This one dates from after 1881.

64 Ami Rivenc. Bottom of this page is the somewhat fanciful sheet from the Colibri bird-chant box. It represents a style used for more tuneful music as well.

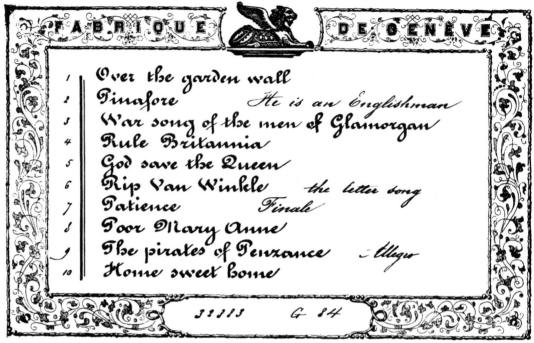

FABRIQUE DE GENÈVE

1 | Over the garden wall
2 | Pinafore   He is an Englishman
3 | War song of the men of Glamorgan
4 | Rule Britannia
5 | God save the Queen
6 | Rip Van Winkle   the letter song
7 | Patience   Finale
8 | Poor Mary Anne
9 | The pirates of Penzance   Allegro
10 | Home sweet home

32313   G 84

Colibri.

Chant N° 1.
2.
3.
4.
5.

MARQUE DE FABRIQUE

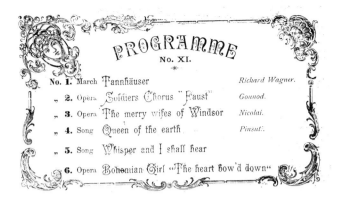

65 Roepke. The unusual lever-plucking, book-playing Roepke musical box plays cardboard music bearing this type of label which is printed in two colours.

66 Roepke. Also from the Roepke, this time the table-top instruments, is this inside-lid label which provides operating instructions.

67 Adre Soualle. Alexandre Soualle was one of the few French musical-box makers and he appears to have been in business for a very short while. This is the only style of tune sheet seen. Note the legend 'Musique de Paris'.

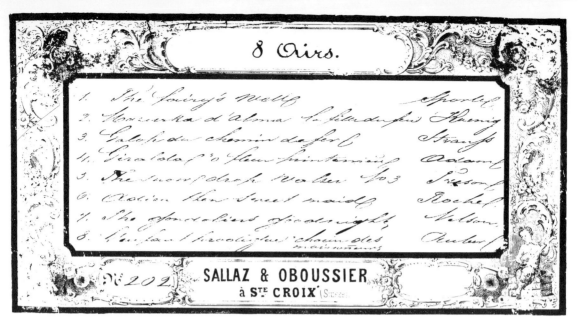

68 Sallaz & Oboussier. Probably this is an agent's label since no maker of this name appears in records. A badly written, badly printed sheet coloured blue.

69 Thibouville-Lamy. In spite of the wording on the sheet above, Thibouville-Lamy did not make boxes: all seem to have been supplied by L'Épée and fitted with Paris tune sheets.

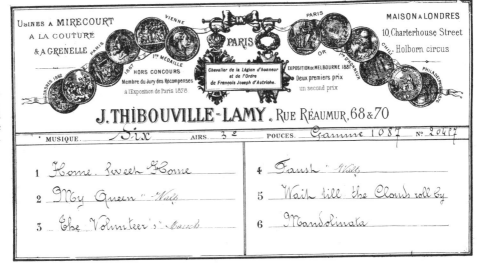

73 Samuel Troll. A glorious gallimaufry this, with just about all the features ever likely to be found in a tune sheet – architecture, theatre, heraldry, the muses, fairies, allegory, musical instruments, swags, garlands, tassels and the names of composers. About 1885.

74 Hermann Thorens. Plain-style printed label rubber-stamped 'Made in Switzerland'.

75 Charles Ullmann. Rubber stamped at the bottom 'Manufactured in Switzerland', Ullmann tune sheets are most readily identified by the heraldic emblem and style names. Titles were frequently, as here, duplicated from typewritten masters on a jelly duplicator.

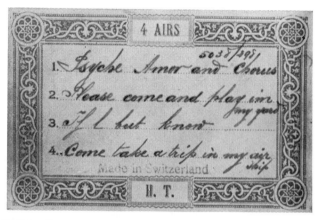

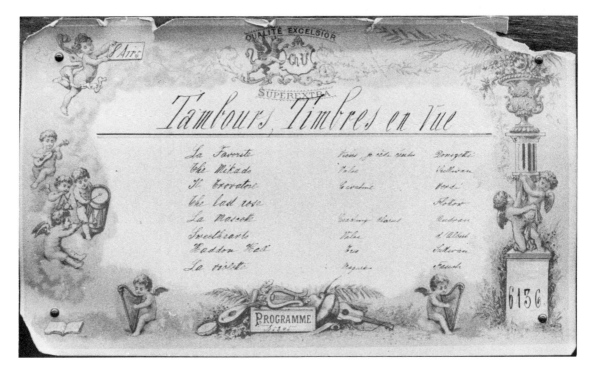

76 Charles Ullmann. This is a less common style of Ullmann sheet and probably predates the previous example on the facing page. Although Ullmann made the best possible use of small comb mechanisms, the tune sheets often seemed the best part of the box.

77 Weill & Harburg. With the trademark and monogram at the top, this is an unusual style of tune sheet with its open-bottom layout.

78, 79 A. Woog. Woog imported L'Épée movements, apparently bypassing Thibouville-Lamy. His trademark is seen at the top. The torn label at the bottom reads 'Millikin & Lawley' who were retailers. Below is a so far unidentified tune sheet.

80, 81 Two unidentified tune sheets, that above dating from after 1880 and attributing 'Le Carnaval de Venise' to Paganini! The sheet below, from a box sold in America, is lithographed in Lausanne and lists 45 airs. Compare with item 2 on p. 350 which might lead one to suppose it to come from Junod.

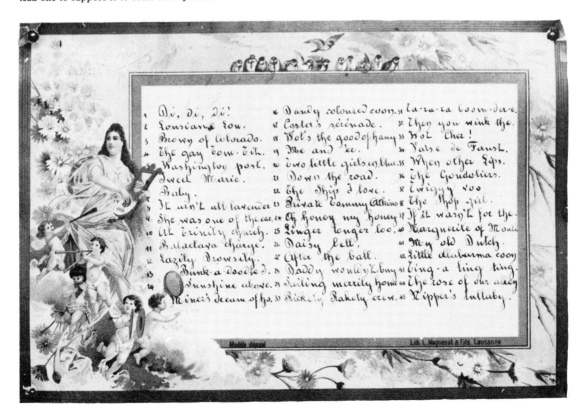

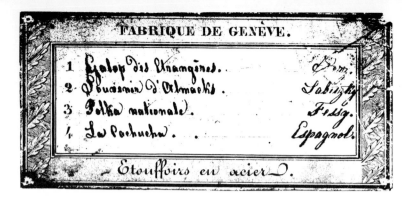

82 An early black-printed paper tune sheet by an unidentified maker. About 1850.

83 Appearing to date from the mid-1880s, this unidentified tune sheet bears the style 'Diva-Harmonic'.

84 With the same top trademark as Langdorff, this unidentified tune sheet bears the monogram C&A but makes us no wiser.

85, 86 Paillard, Vaucher, Fils. Sullivan's *HMS Pinafore* was first produced in 1878. An almost identical version of this tune sheet bears 'P.V.F. St. Croix (Suisse)' in the cartouche at the bottom. The tune sheet below is a mystery. There are two embossed medallions at the top and the lettering suggests a German market. About 1860–70.

87 Probably by the same maker as that overleaf – it has the same medallions embossed at the top plus two more printed in – this has an Amsterdam agent's label on the bottom. Second tune, Lecocq's 'Geroflé-Girofla', dates from 1874.

88 No uncertainty about this one – it is from Nicole Frères number 39275 of 1862 – but the interest lies in that it is an example of a rental company label. Surely very rare. The obliterated words read 'All damage must be paid for by the hirer'!

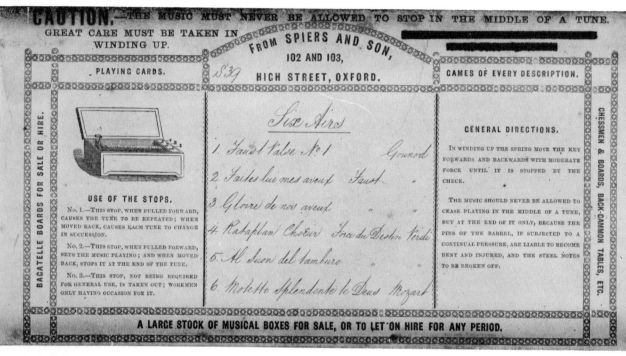

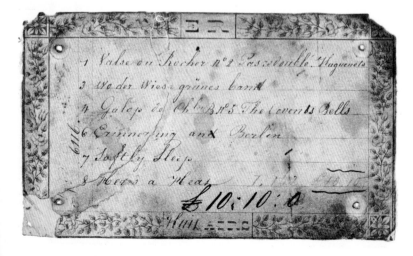

89 Another mystery to end with. Initials ER at the top, printed in blue on thin wove paper and the first tune dating from 1836. No other clues – except an intriguing price from another age.

Bibliography

(a) MUSICAL BOXES

Buchner, Dr Alexandr, *Mechanical Musical Instruments*, Batchworth Press, London, *c*.1954.
British Patent Office, *Musical Instruments 1694–1908, Abridgments Class 88*, London.
Bulletin, journal of the Musical Box Society International, USA, 1965–77.
Chapuis, A. *Histoire de la Boîte à Musique*, Éditions Scriptar, Lausanne, 1955.
Chapuis, A. & Droz, E. *Automata*, trans. Reid, Éditions du Griffon, Neuchatel, 1958.
Chapuis, A. & Gelis, E. *Le Monde des Automates*, Société Anonyme des Impressions Blondel la Rougery, Paris, 1928 (2 vols).
Clark, John E. T., *Musical Boxes – A History and Appreciation*, Allen & Unwin (3rd edn), London 1961.
Clark, John E. T., *Musical Boxes*, Cornish Brothers, Birmingham, 1948.
Devaux, P., *Automates et Automatisme*, Presses Universitaires, Paris, 1941.
Jacot, J. H., *The Jacot Repair Manual*, New York, 1890.
Maingot, E., *Les Automates*, Librairie Hachette, Paris, 1959.
Mosoriak, R., *The Curious History of the Music Box*, Lightner Publishing Co., Chicago, 1943.
The Music Box, journal of The Musical Box Society of Great Britain, London, 1962–78.
Ord-Hume, A. W. J. G., *Collecting Musical Boxes and How to Repair Them*, Allen & Unwin, London, 1967.
Ord-Hume, A. W. J. G., *Clockwork Music, An Illustrated History of Mechanical Musical Instruments*, Allen & Unwin, London, 1973.
Ord-Hume, A. W. J. G., *Restoring Musical Boxes*, Allen & Unwin, London, 1979.
Tallis, D., *Musical Boxes*, Muller, London, 1971.
US Patent Office, Washington, USA.
Webb, G., *The Cylinder Musical Box Handbook*, Faber & Faber, London, 1968.
Webb, G., *The Disc Musical Box Handbook*, Faber & Faber, London, 1971.

(b) MECHANICAL MUSICAL INSTRUMENTS IN GENERAL

Bonhôte, D., & Baud, F., *Au Temps des Boîtes à Musique*, Éditions Mondo, Lausanne, 1975.
Bowers, Q. David, *Put Another Nickel In*, Vestal Press, New York, 1966.
Bowers, Q. David, *Encyclopaedia of Automatic Musical Instruments*, Vestal Press, 1972.
Conservatoire Nationale des Arts et Métiers, *Automates et Mechanismes*, Paris, 1960.
Conservatoire Nationale des Arts et Métiers, *Les Boîtes à Musique de Prague* (catalogue), Paris, 1966.
Crowley, T. E., *Discovering Mechanical Music*, Shire Publications, Buckingham, Buckinghamshire, 1975.
Haspels, Dr J.-J. L., *Muziek op Rolletjes*, Utrecht, 1975.
Marini, Marino, *Museo di Strumenti Musicali Meccanici*, published by the author, Ravenna, Italy, 1973.
Ord-Hume, A. W. J. G., *Clockwork Music*, Allen & Unwin, London, 1973.
Roehl, H., *Player Piano Treasury*, (1st edn), Vestal Press, New York, 1961.
Roehl, H., *Player Piano Treasury*, (2nd edn), Vestal Press, New York, 1974.
Simmen, Rene, *Mens & Machine*, Van Lindonk, Amsterdam, 1968.

Waard, Rompke de, *Van Speeldoos tot Pierement*, Toorts, Haarlem, 1962.
Weiss, Eugene H., *Phonographes et Musique Mécanique*, Librairie Hachette, Paris, 1930.
Weiss-Stauffacher, H. & Bruhin, R., *Mechanische Musikinstrumente und Musikautomaton*, published by the author, Seewen (Switzerland), 1973.

(c) CARILLONS

Lehr, André, *Leerboek der Campanologie*, Nationaal Beiaardmuseum, Asten, Netherlands, 1976.
Lehr, André, *Van Paardebel tot Speelklok*, Europese Bibliotheek, Zaltbommel, Netherlands, 1971.
Price, Frank Percival, *The Carillon*, Oxford University Press, London, 1933.
Verheyden, Prosper: *Beiaarden in Frankrijk*, Beiaardschool te Mechelen, Antwerp, Belgium, 1926.

(d) MECHANICAL ORGAN

Cockayne, Eric V., *The Fairground Organ*, David & Charles, Newton Abbot, 1974.
The Keyframe, journal of the Fair Organ Preservation Society, Stalybridge, Cheshire, 1965–78.
Ord-Hume, A. W. J. G., *Barrel Organ*, Allen & Unwin, London, 1978.
Protz, Albert, *Mechanische Musikinstrumente*, Bahrenreiter, Kassel, 1939.

(e) MUSICAL CLOCK

Bassermann-Jordan, *Uhren*, Klinkhardt & Biermann, Braunschweig, Germany, 1976.
Bender, Gerd, *Die Uhrenmacher des hohen Schwarzwaldes und ihre Werke*, Muller, Villingen, Germany, 1975.
Holzhey, Gunther, *Flötenuhren aus dem Schwarzwald*, Berliner Union, Stuttgart, *c.*1971.
Jüttemann, Herbert, *Die Schwarzwalduhr*, Klinkhardt & Biermann, Braunschweig, Germany, 1972.
Ord-Hume, A. W. J. G., *Musical Clocks & Watches*, published by the author, London, 1973.

(f) PLAYER PIANO

Ord-Hume, A. W. J. G., *Player Piano*, Allen & Unwin, London, 1970.
Player Piano Group *Bulletin*, London, 1965–78.

(g) THEORY OF MECHANICAL MUSIC

Bedos, François de Celles, *L'Art du Facteur d'Orgues*, Paris, 1778.
Engramelle, Marie Dominique Joseph, *La Tonotechnie ou l'Art de Noter les Cylindres*, Paris, 1775 (facsimile reprint, Minkoff, Geneva, 1971).
Ord-Hume, A. W. J. G., *The Mechanics of Mechanical Music*, published by the author, London, 1973.
Schmitz, H. P., *Die Tontechnik des Père Engramelle*, Bärenreiter, Kassel, 1953.

Associations for Collectors of Musical Boxes

THE MUSICAL BOX SOCIETY OF GREAT BRITAIN, 40 Station Approach, Hayes, Bromley, Kent BR2 7EF, England (journal *The Music Box*, quarterly).

THE MUSICAL BOX SOCIETY INTERNATIONAL, 495 Springfield Avenue, Summit, New Jersey 07901, United States of America (journal *The Bulletin*, thrice yearly).

Both the above-mentioned societies have world-wide membership and both cater for collectors of all types of mechanical music machines.

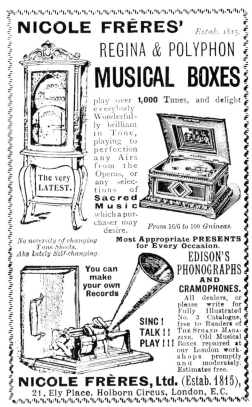

Picture Credits

The instruments pictured in this book represent items in many collections. These are itemised below. Notable musical-box dealers and restorers have also contributed pictures. These also are listed but their names do not necessarily mean that the items depicted remain in their possession. The Fortnum & Mason collection was dispersed in 1975, most of it passing into the Victoria & Albert Museum in London where only some of its items are currently on show. The Cyril de Vere Green collection has also changed hands with the major part now the property of the Nationaal Museum van Speelklok tot Pierement in Utrecht, the world's only State-sponsored museum of mechanical music. However, the smaller items still form the surviving nucleus of the de Vere Green collection. Plates not referenced here are either at the express request of the owner of the item, or are author's own collection. The artists behind many of these pictures, mostly listed under 'Acknowledgements', deserve special thanks.

  Dan Adams (via Q. David Bowers): 143, 144
  Richard E. Baker: 56
  Walt Bellm's Museum: 102, 123, 128, 130
  C. W. Bruce (the late): 9
  Dr Robert Burnett: 19, 20
* Christie's South Kensington: 64, 70, 74, 87, 88, 89, 94, 95, 101, 111, 112, 145, 161
  Alan K. Clark: 57
  Brian Clegg: 151, 152
* John Cowderoy: 68, 69
  Catherine Dike: 13
  Brian Etches: 90, 91
  Howard Fitch: 79
  Fortnum & Mason: 59, 72, 82, 92, 97, 134, 135, 137, 139, 140
  George Foster: 137
  Cyril de Vere Green: 7, 8, 21, 23, 34, 37, 38, 39, 48, 49, 53, 54, 55, 132
* Keith Harding: 29, 50, 51, 65, 71, 73, 83, 84, 86, 96, 98, 133, 147, 148, 159
  Arthur Heap: 156, 157
  J. A. Holland: 149, 150
  Fondation Horngacher-Blyelle: 14, 52

Symphonion Armoire décorative No. 42,

à 41 lames.

Grösse,
dimensions, size:

82×72×24 cm
32¹/₂×28¹/₄×9¹/₂ inches.

Gewicht,
poids, weight:

netto   13 kg
brutto   26 „
net   abt 29 ℔
gross   „ 57 „

Avec glace, panneau en bois décoré, console, et galeries pour mettre des verres. bouteilles, cigares &c.; en retirant ces objets, l'instrument commence à jouer.

Feuille à musique No. 10.

Index

This index embraces the text of the first eleven chapters (except for the names of makers etc. listed alphabetically in Chapter 11) and the captions to the Plates and Figures throughout the book. The two Appendices and the trademarks listed in Figure 45 have not been indexed. References to photographic illustrations are given in bold.

The companion volume to this book is RESTORING MUSICAL BOXES. Within more than 190 pages it describes the whole process of the restoration, repair and conservation of musical boxes of all types including the familiar cylinder and disc type as well as the smaller snuff-box type and the sub-miniature pieces found in watches and objets d'art. A valuable addition to this fully-illustrated guide is a glossary of musical box terms which is translated into French and German for the benefit of European readers.

The chapter titles are as follows:
Chapter 1 Tools for the job
Chapter 2 Overhauling the cylinder musical box
Chapter 3 Restoring the disc-playing musical box
Chapter 4 Restoring miniature musical movements
Chapter 5 Restoring musical-box cases
Glossary of terms
List of French and German terms
Bibliography

In addition there are 50 photographic illustrations, 53 fine line drawings and a number of additional text figures. Together these two works provide the serious collector, museum and repairer with the most comprehensive library of reference material ever compiled on the subject.

Other titles available on mechanical musical instruments by the same author include CLOCKWORK MUSIC, a 334-page illustrated history of mechanical musical instruments from the musical box to the pianola and from automaton lady virginal player to the orchestrion, and BARREL ORGAN, 567 pages devoted to the history and restoration of the mechanical organ. For player and reproducing piano enthusiasts, a new work is in the course of preparation.